D1393667

REFLECTIONS ON

CHARACTER AND

LEADERSHIP

On the Couch with Manfred Kets de Vries

On the Couch with Manfred Kets de Vries offers an overview of the author's work spanning four decades, a period in which Manfred F. R. Kets de Vries has established himself as the leading figure in the clinical study of organizational leadership.

The three books in this series contain a representative selection of Kets de Vries' writings about leadership from a wide variety of published sources. They cover three major themes: character and leadership in a global context; career development; and leadership in organizations. The original essays were all written or published between 1976 and 2008. Updated where appropriate and revised by the author, they present a digest of the work of one of today's most influential management thinkers.

Published Titles
Reflections on Character and Leadership

Forthcoming Titles
Reflections on Leadership and Career Development
Reflections on Organizations

REFLECTIONS ON
CHARACTER AND
LEADERSHIP

Manfred F. R. Kets de Vries

JOSSEY-BASS
A Wiley Imprint
www.josseybass.com

Other Wiley Editorial Offices

John Wiley & Sons Inc., 111 River Street, Hoboken, NJ 07030, USA

Jossey-Bass, 989 Market Street, San Francisco, CA 94103-1741, USA

Wiley-VCH Verlag GmbH, Boschstr. 12, D-69469 Weinheim, Germany

John Wiley & Sons Australia Ltd, 42 McDougall Street, Milton, Queensland 4064, Australia

John Wiley & Sons (Asia) Pte Ltd, 2 Clementi Loop #02-01, Jin Xing Distripark, Singapore 129809

John Wiley & Sons Canada Ltd, 6045 Freemont Blvd, Mississauga, ONT, L5R 4J3, Canada

Wiley also publishes its books in a variety of electronic formats. Some content that appears in print may not be available in electronic books.

Library of Congress Cataloging-in-Publication Data
Kets de Vries, Manfred F. R.
  Reflections on character and leadership / Manfred Kets de Vries.
    p. cm.
  Includes bibliographical references and index.
  ISBN 978-0-470-74242-6 (cloth)
  1. Leadership–Psychological aspects. I. Title.
  HD57.7.K483 2009
  658.4'092—dc22

                             2009004180

British Library Cataloguing in Publication Data
A catalogue record for this book is available from the British Library

ISBN 978-0-470-74242-6

Typeset in 10.5/12 pt Bembo by SNP Best-set Typesetter Ltd., Hong Kong
Printed and bound in Great Britain by TJ International Ltd, Padstow, Cornwall
This book is printed on acid-free paper responsibly manufactured from sustainable forestry in which at least two trees are planted for each one used for paper production.

To my brother Florian—
the intimacy of our many shared memories
has been a source of great solace.

CONTENTS

ACKNOWLEDGMENTS   xiii

PREFACE   xv

Psychoanalysis and organizational life   xv
First case: an entrepreneur   xix
The clinical paradigm   xxi
About this book   xxii

PART I: LEADERS, FOOLS, AND IMPOSTORS   1

INTRODUCTION   2

Playing the organizational fool   4

1 THE ENTREPRENEURIAL PERSONALITY   6

Introduction   6
Entrepreneurship: views from other disciplines   8
Common psychological themes in the entrepreneurial
     personality   10
The effects of family dynamics   17
Case study: The entrepreneur's story   18
Falling into extremes   22

The Medusa women   24
The meaning of work   26
Competition and self-defeating behavior   28
The symbolic nature of the enterprise   29
The process of change   31
The entrepreneurial life cycle   33
Working effectively with entrepreneurs   39
Endnotes   42

2 THE HYPOMANIC PERSONALITY   43

Introduction   43
The Dionysian quality of charismatic leadership   44
Case study: Hypomania in action   46
Elation and its vicissitudes   50
Managing a hypomanic   53
Hypomania in the workplace   55
Possible interventions   56
Self-help measures   58
The plus side for organizations   60
Endnotes   61

3 THE ALEXITHYMIC PERSONALITY   62

Introduction   62
The 'dead fish' syndrome   62
Identifying alexithymia   63
Alexithymia as a communication disorder   64
Where do the origins of alexithymia lie?   66
Degrees of alexithymia   68
Alexithymics in the workplace   69
The Alexithymic CEO   70
Working with an alexithymic manager   72
Managing an alexithymic   73
Searching for solutions   75
Endnote   78

4 THE IMPOSTOR SYNDROME   79

Introduction   79
What makes an impostor?   82
The creative artist as impostor   85

The impostor as national leader   86
The impostor: a character sketch   89
Case study: The impostor as entrepreneur   92
Endnote   97

**5 NEUROTIC IMPOSTORS: FEELING LIKE
    A FAKE**   98

Introduction   98
What creates imposturous feelings?   99
The neurotic impostor in the workplace   103
How the fear can become a reality   105
How neurotic impostors can impact on businesses   108
Finding solutions   109
Endnotes   111

**6 THE ORGANIZATIONAL FOOL: BALANCING
    A LEADER'S HUBRIS**   112

Introduction   112
The role of the fool   112
The fool as cultural hero   114
The benefits of humor   115
What makes a fool?   117
The organizational fool   117
The value of the fool   123
Endnote   123

PART II: THE PATHOLOGY OF LEADERSHIP   125

INTRODUCTION   126

7 PRISONERS OF LEADERSHIP   130

Introduction   130
Case study: The case of Robert Clark   131
Case study: The case of Frederick the Great   132
Externalizing inner conflicts   135
The search for authority   136
Regressive group processes   139
Case study: The case of Ted Howell   141
Distance and aggression in leaders   142
Managing leaders' behavior in organizations   143
Endnotes   145

8   THE SPIRIT OF DESPOTISM: UNDERSTANDING
    THE TYRANT WITHIN   146

    Introduction   146
    Setting the scene for tyranny   149
    What motivates tyrants?   150
    How tyrannies operate   150
    How despotic regimes are maintained   152
    The despot's toolbox   153
    The economic costs of tyranny   158
    The need for democracy   159
    The dangers of power   160
    Why despotism must be fought   161
    Unjust deserts   163
    Judicial remedy   163
    The International Criminal Court   165
    Endnote   166

9   LEADERSHIP BY TERROR: FINDING SHAKA
    ZULU IN THE ATTIC   167

    Introduction   167
    The life and death of an absolute despot   168
    Deconstructing the despot's inner theater   171
    The colluding mind   179
    A tyranny of self-deception   183
    Leaders and followers   186
    Shaka's legacy   190
    Endnote   191

PART III: TRANSFORMING LEADERSHIP   193

INTRODUCTION   194

10 'DOING AN ALEXANDER': LESSONS
    ON LEADERSHIP BY A MASTER
    CONQUEROR   198

    Introduction   198
    The life of Alexander   199
    Alexander's legacy   205
    Lessons in leadership à la Alexander   206
    Conclusions   210
    Endnote   210

11   LEADERS WHO MAKE A DIFFERENCE   211

Introduction   211
The effects of leaders on their organizations   212
Different leaders, same results   213
The architectural aspect of leadership   214
The charismatic role of leaders   223
Conclusions   226
Endnote   226

12   REAPING THE WHIRLWIND: MANAGING
         CREATIVE PEOPLE   227

Introduction   227
Characteristics of creative people   228
Stimulating creativity   230
Playing in a transitional world   231
Two roads to creativity   233
Creative management   236
Watching for the danger signs   240
Endnote   241

PART IV: LEADERSHIP IN A GLOBAL CONTEXT   243

INTRODUCTION   244

13   THE DEVELOPMENT OF THE LEADER WITHIN
         THE GLOBAL CORPORATION   247

Introduction   247
A case study in internationalization   248
Forms of global organizations   249
Qualities needed in global leaders   253
Training, transfer, teamwork, and travel   260
A framework for analyzing the development of the
   global leader   262
Conclusions   263
Endnote   264

14   IN SEARCH OF THE NEW EUROPEAN
         BUSINESS LEADER   265

Introduction   265
The challenge of diversity   267
Internal and external competition   270

Is a single model possible?   271
A middle path   272
Dealing with change   273
The making of the European leader   275
Leadership in Europe and beyond   277
Endnote   278

**15 LESSONS FROM THE 'WILD EAST': RUSSIAN
    CHARACTER AND LEADERSHIP**   279

The Russian character   279
Contextual factors in the formation of the Russian
    character   282
Russia's transition: from cooperatives to capitalism   295
New leaders and new followers   296
Eight leadership lessons   300
Challenges for global Russian business leaders   302
The end of the beginning   305
Endnotes   305

**CONCLUSION: CREATING HIGH-COMMITMENT
ORGANIZATIONS**   307

The future of organizations   307
Meta-values for great companies   308
Motivational need systems   309
Leaders and meta-value creation   313
Concluding comments   314
Endnote   315

REFERENCES   317

INDEX   333

ACKNOWLEDGMENTS

This book is the first in a three-part series, *On the Couch with Manfred Kets de Vries*. It grew out of an idea from my long-term editor, Sally Simmons, who suggested three years ago that it was time for me to think about putting together a sort of 'collected works.' The first incarnation of the book was dauntingly long but after many months and revisions, the material, following a logic of its own, has fallen more or less naturally into the collection of essays here. While most of the chapters in this book are based on previously published material (the original sources are given in each chapter), it has all been substantially revised and updated, although I have retained the period feel of some articles where appropriate.

Although it is ostensibly me on the couch, there are others clustered round waiting their turn—collaborators in some of the original articles—to whom I owe thanks. They are Elizabeth Florent-Treacy, Konstantin Korotov, Christine Mead, Stanislav Shekshnia, and Abraham Zaleznik.

As always, I am pleased to have the opportunity to acknowledge the invaluable help and support of Sheila Loxham, my assistant, whose cheerfulness, good humor and good sense never fail—despite being sorely tested in a year when serious injury and subsequent lengthy recovery have made me occasionally less than sunny to be around.

In the 20 years that I have known and worked with her, Sally Simmons has become more than herself and is now a company, Cambridge Editorial Partnership. I would like to thank the members of her team who have worked on this book: Carol Schaessens, whose efforts at conflating a huge amount of material were so successful that not even I can see the join, and Mary Conochie, who patiently retyped chapters that could be sourced only from hard copy. As for Sally herself, I have previously described her as 'an editor's editor,' 'an unusual editor,' and on one occasion as 'the last woman standing.' She has supplied many of the drum rolls and fanfares in this book but perhaps her most valuable contribution has been to help me see material with which I had been over-familiar through fresh eyes.

PREFACE

PSYCHOANALYSIS AND ORGANIZATIONAL LIFE

I am often asked why I have done so much work on entrepreneurs, when the world of work has always been under-studied in psychoanalytic literature, and the answer is very simple. I come from a family of entrepreneurs: my father is an entrepreneur and my brothers are entrepreneurs, all in different businesses. But I was never drawn that way myself, largely because, for mysterious reasons, my father thought that I was unsuited to the business world, which of course turned somewhat into a self-fulfilling prophecy. I decided to go in another direction. I began by studying chemical and mechanical engineering, both of which lasted an exceptionally short time. Then, making a rather negative choice, I decided to study economics, as a way of keeping my options open. I always felt, to quote the great economist John Maynard Keynes, that it really was a dismal science. The concept of the *homo economicus* always bothered me, the reason being that the assumptions made by economists about people were so far from the reality embodied by the entrepreneurs in my family. The way they made decisions was anything but rational. They were very talented, however, at rationalizing their decisions after the fact.

When I was 16, my father had sent me to the Harvard Summer School, which was a fantastic experience—the diversity of people was very exciting, much more so than university life turned out to be in Holland. While studying, I told myself that I would go back to the States one day, and I did. I returned to the USA after I'd finished my doctoral examination in economics in Holland, by which time I had realized that I had the potential to be some kind of an academic. I decided to take time out traveling and booked a place on a Norwegian freighter. It was a very cheap way to cross the Atlantic—my father was a good client of the freight company—but also an extremely boring crossing of which the only highlight was a storm. When the boat docked in Boston I couldn't get off it quickly enough. Out of pure nostalgia I visited Harvard again, this time including the Business School. I was curious about the programs and courses they were offering. I discovered the school was running a sort of 'missionary' program—the International Teachers Program—intended to spread the Harvard case-method all round the world. I was still thinking vaguely about joining the corporate world—banking would be an option—at this stage but I saw this program as a chance to spend a year at Harvard. During the interview process, the program director of the International Teachers Program mentioned an unusual course being given by Abraham Zaleznik, who had a chair in what was then called Social Psychology of Management, something of a misnomer, given the strong psychoanalytic focus of the course. The seminar he suggested I should take was 'Psychoanalytic psychology and organizational theory.' I decided to enroll—and it changed my life.

I still remember that our first assignment was to read Ernest Jones's biography of Sigmund Freud, which consisted of two pretty impressive tomes. In spite of my relatively poor English, I read all the material over one weekend and I was probably the only person on the seminar who bothered to do so. The course was quite exciting for a budding business economist as it included case studies such as 'The Wolfman,' 'The Ratman,' and 'The Psychotic Dr Schreber,' quite different from the material you get in an economics course. With hindsight, I would now question the validity of some of Freud's case interpretations, but at the time they brought me into a completely different world and stimulated my fantasy life. Suddenly I saw a lot of new connections in literature, film, and art: it was like having an additional lens, moving from a two-dimensional to a three-dimensional world. In addition, I was living in a foreign country, with all the mental turmoil that accompanies that sort of temporary life, which deepened the experience. Certainly, it affected my dream life. Because my life experiences were so different, I paid a lot of attention to my inner world. I did a lot of dream analysis to get a better understanding of myself.

It was during this time that I began to play with the idea of integrating the worlds of clinical psychology (i.e. psychoanalysis) and management. When Zaleznik offered me a position as his assistant, the direction I was heading in was confirmed. In addition, I was accepted into the doctoral program at the Harvard Business School, although I was also advised to do an MBA. The thinking was that if I didn't make it through the doctorate, I'd at least have the MBA to fall back on. It turned out that the International Teachers Program covered the second year of the MBA so, ironically, I did the first year's course of the MBA in my second year. Looking back, Harvard was an extremely important learning experience. Being in one class section with a hundred extremely competitive individuals helped me understand and learn to speak the language of executives.

My doctoral dissertation under Zaleznik was on entrepreneurship; I finished it extremely fast and almost immediately my writing career started. Roland Christensen, a delightful man, and one of my thesis advisers, asked me to write a short excerpt on entrepreneurship from my thesis as a student note to use in his classes, and various articles followed. In addition, I was involved with Zaleznik in a very large research project on individual and organizational stress. At the same time, I became interested in starting some form of psychoanalytic training. As I became more familiar with psychoanalysis as a method of investigation, I experienced a need to deepen my clinical expertise. Without such exposure, I felt that the application of theoretical ideas to organizations would be a rather barren exercise. I decided I wanted to become a psychoanalyst. But with my background in economics and business administration I would be a very atypical candidate for a psychoanalytic training institute, particularly as the psychoanalytic world in the USA at the time was very medically oriented. And I had to deal with another problem: to be accepted at an institute was one thing, but I would also have to pay for the training. To do that, I needed a job. It wasn't so easy to get an interesting job in the Boston area. I knew that for a number of political reasons—Zaleznik not belonging to a specific area—there would be no offer forthcoming from the Harvard Business School. Joining Zaleznik was great as a learning experience but had not been a very smart political move.

I decided to go to France where the *Institut européen d'administration des affaires* (INSEAD) was getting off the ground. A dean had been hired to build a faculty. I also felt that France would give me the chance to pursue my wish to become a psychoanalyst, as they were more relaxed about accepting people with more unorthodox backgrounds. At the same time, I started psychoanalysis with Joyce McDougall, one of the most famous, and original, psychoanalysts in the world. My stay at INSEAD lasted for two years. To put it bluntly, I was fired. The reasons were never made very clear to me, but the school's financial problems were one of them. It probably didn't help that I was not very subtle presenting my ideas about how the functioning of the school could be improved, suggestions that were not wholly appreciated. When I worked out that I was being fired—the dean was quite evasive about it—I protested about the reasons given for my dismissal and the way it was handled, which led to a protest by other faculty members (fearful who would be next in line, as there was no system of due process) and ultimately to the establishment of a faculty evaluation committee that ensured that hiring and firing would no longer be a flavor-of-the-week process. Ironically, INSEAD made me an offer a year after they sacked me, but I turned it down. Looking back, getting fired turned out to be a lucky experience for me, as it contributed to interesting learning opportunities.

I returned to the Harvard Business School as a research fellow for one year, joining the Production and Operations Management area. I worked for a man called Wickham Skinner who wanted my help writing case studies with a human touch. I hoped, now that I was back at HBS, that I would be offered a longer-term appointment. But for a number of reasons it was not to be. Having received the highest teaching rating at the school may have been a black mark against me. Obviously, I could not be a researcher. But the most telling lesson was that the Organizational Behavior area was blocking Zaleznik from making tenure track appointments. In addition, the opinion of one of the power holders in the Organizational Behavior department was that I would never write anything. That particular person must have had a very good understanding of human behavior. One of the small pleasures in life is doing something people say you'll never do. I believe this is my twenty-ninth book. I have always thought that academics are masters in character assassination.

Luckily, Henry Minzberg was more visionary than Jay Lorsch and had another view on the matter. At the time he was looking for faculty members who didn't fit the standard OB mold. I was certainly part of that group of misfits. He offered me a position at McGill in Canada. The Faculty of Management was relatively new and offered many growth possibilities. What also attracted me to Montreal was that it had a very open-minded psychoanalytic training institute. I was particularly attracted to Maurice Dongier, at the time the head of psychiatry and the director of the Allen Memorial Institute, a psychiatric think tank. He was adventurous enough to accept me as a candidate for training despite my unorthodox background. He turned out to be the right person for me, at the right time. Not only did he give me many insights but he also became a very good friend.

Anyone who goes through this sort of training faces a real dilemma about what direction to go to afterwards. I thought clinical work was interesting—but there were an awful lot of psychoanalysts about. Very few psychoanalysts, however, really understood organizational life.

That's where I thought I could make a real contribution with my clinical training.

FIRST CASE: AN ENTREPRENEUR

I started my psychoanalytical training in the 1970s and by the end of that decade I was ready to take on my first patients. Lo and behold, my first patient was an entrepreneur: this was an extremely rare opportunity as entrepreneurs rarely go on the couch; they are far too busy running around. But this man was in bad shape, in the grip of a real-life soap opera—his wife had deserted him, he felt his company was falling apart, and he was estranged from his children. In addition, he had a number of psychosomatic symptoms: teary eyes that blurred his vision and permanent mouth ulcers—classic stress symptoms. I don't think the psychiatrist who referred him to me meant to do me a favor. I'm fairly sure he thought the patient was too much of a challenge. But I interviewed him and saw him as an interesting patient (particularly given my interest in entrepreneurs), so I thought why not? One of the things I noted when I first met him was that he seemed to be subject to an 'anniversary reaction,' that is, the anxiety that some people feel when they reach the age at which one of their parents died. My patient was approaching the age his father had been when he died in a mental hospital. His father's illness had been kept very secret by the family. My patient thought that something similar would soon happen to him. This delusionary idea contributed to the process of unconscious self-destruction in which he appeared to be engaged.

The psychoanalytic process got off to a flying start. My patient improved by the week. He thought he had been given a miracle cure, because he felt so much better after only six weeks. In addition, the company was doing so much better. His relationship with his wife and children had also improved. And his psychosomatic symptoms had disappeared. Given the impatience of entrepreneurs, it came as no surprise that he wanted to quit. This is what is sometimes called a 'flight into health.' It was not easy to persuade him that more work needed to be done. But I managed to convince him to continue. In fact, I saw that patient five times a week for four years, admittedly quite a long time for an entrepreneurial type.

This story has a nice epilogue. My patient was always very grateful for the way I helped him. He kept in touch with me, writing to me to let me know how he was doing. A few years ago, he called me. He told me that his wife had died, and he had decided to write his autobiography.

As he'd needed help with the writing, he had taken on a ghost writer. What began as a professional relationship turned into something more. He had married her, and they were living happily ever after in Florida. He was still working on his autobiography, and he wanted me to write a little part about him, which I did. As a matter of interest, he is still in contact with me.

Seeing someone five times a week for four years puts things in a very different perspective from having only one interview with someone, which is usually the situation when you are writing a case study. Listening to someone every day, you can follow closely the way certain decisions unfold. The interplay of this entrepreneur's fantasies, daydreams and dreams in the decision-making process was fascinating. Why he took certain actions, and how he rationalized those actions afterwards, was an intriguing process to follow. Although he was far from an easy case, I could not have been luckier with my first patient. I was also fortunate that my first supervisor was Clifford Scott, a leading figure in psychiatric and psychoanalytic history, and one of the editors of the *International Journal of Psychoanalysis*. He was one of the pioneering few who started to analyze schizophrenic and bipolar (manic-depressive) patients on a regular basis. My interactions with him convinced me of the difficulties and dangers of basing theories on simplistic survey research or sporadic interviews. It also taught me how far off the mark rational planners are when discussing the way people make decisions. Having had an entrepreneur on the couch helped me truly understand the relationship between the world of the mind and the world of work.

I've always been irritated by the fact that the world of work has been largely ignored by psychoanalysts, and still is, which is remarkable considering how much time we all spend at work. Psychoanalysts have studied artists and writers, the boundary between creativity and madness, and so on, but the world of organizations has been neglected. The first serious attempt by a psychoanalyst to study work was at the Tavistock Institute in London in the early part of the twentieth century; then in the 1960s the work of my old mentor Abraham Zaleznik at Harvard and Harry Levinson, who was working at the Menninger Clinic in Topeka, Kansas, began to emerge.

I was intrigued about the way they were working at the boundary of psychoanalysis and organizational life. It was a clarion call to me, given my own studies in the twilight zone of economics, management, and psychoanalysis. Now I view myself as belonging to a second generation of people with a clinical orientation to organizational analysis. Forty years on I have probably become one of the better-known practitioners in this field.

THE CLINICAL PARADIGM

I see my contribution as a very modest one. Hasn't it been said that we all stand on the shoulders of giants? I see myself as a bridge builder, closing the gap between various disciplines. When I was studying organizational behavior, I thought that too much attention was being given to structures and systems and not enough to the person—the Harvard Business School was certainly oriented toward that trend. I wanted to bring the person back into the organization. It's my experience that by using the clinical paradigm people have an extra level of magnification through which to look at organizational phenomena. It's not that other approaches are wrong; but I maintain that people who have a modicum of clinical understanding are generally more astute at interpreting what, at times, can be extremely puzzling phenomena. Out-of-awareness behavior plays an important role in human encounters. Thus using yourself as an instrument can be highly effective. In addition, understanding what drives people helps us understand personality problems better, realize what certain symptoms signify, make sense of interpersonal difficulties, and see through group phenomena and social defenses. A holistic approach to the study of people is needed if we really want to understand people phenomena better.

While stating the importance of the clinical paradigm in organizational work, I like to emphasize that, despite my psychoanalytic training, in my interventions I'm very far from being a classical psychoanalyst. I do whatever works. I want to help people—probably part of the influence of my maternal grandfather, who went out of his way to help people during World War II. And probably as a result of being born during that war, I have always been extremely wary of ideological movements in general, and in the social sciences in particular. In my work, I also draw on cognitive theory, family systems theory, group dynamics, motivational interviewing, neuropsychiatry, and developmental psychology.

An increasing number of people realize that a purely rational model of looking at organizations is unrealistic. While I am myself most comfortable using the clinical paradigm as a springboard, I don't argue for its pre-eminence compared with other forms of intervention. But I do recommend that all agents of change supplement behavioral or humanistic models of the mind with clinical conceptualizations about intrapsychic and interpersonal issues, like people's underlying motivational needs, their unconscious processes, defense mechanisms, social defenses, resistance, transferential processes, and the role of character.

ABOUT THIS BOOK

Reflections on Character and Leadership examines some of the major issues about leadership. What makes a leader? What is good leadership? And what is bad? What happens to organizations if a leader derails? What are the impacts of successful and failed leadership on followers and organizations?

Part 1: Leaders, Fools, and Impostors presents some character types that are thrown into sharp focus against an organizational background. I look closely at the organizational impact—positive and negative— of entrepreneurs, hypomaniacs, alexithymics (those people who seem dead from the neck up), impostors and fools. I examine their behavioral symptoms and the effects of their behavior on other people and the places in which they work. I suggest ways in which various personality types can be managed—and how to cope if you are managed by them.

Part II: The Pathology of Leadership is a collection of observations about what happens when a leader derails and organizations are paralyzed by a culture of fear, mistrust and insecurity. Lessons about toxic organizational leadership are drawn from an extended study of the tyrannical reign of the African king, Shaka Zulu, in the nineteenth century.

Part III: Transforming Leadership turns back once more to the side of the angels. One of the biggest challenges to leaders is how to nurture and contain a climate of creativity within an organization. The chapters in Part III look at the ways in which truly inspirational leaders—from Alexander of Macedon to Branson of Virgin—construct organizations that are great places to work.

Part IV: Leadership in a Global Context addresses what qualities and leadership skills are needed to take organizations to success across cross-cultural boundaries. This part not only discusses salient issues faced by global organizations, but also specific attention is given to Russia. The opening up of Russia to Western business—and the growth of the West as a fruitful market for Russia—has brought a growing number of Russian entrepreneurs onto the global business stage. There is increased awareness of the culture of this fascinating country and the nature of the Russian 'soul.'

In the Conclusion, I end with some thoughts on how to create and sustain high-performance organizations.

Manfred Kets de Vries
Paris 2009

PART I

LEADERS, FOOLS, AND IMPOSTERS

INTRODUCTION

In using the characterological approach, the therapist, coach, consultant or other change agent tries to identify a set of interrelated themes—the focus is on patterns that tend to fall together. Certain themes—like certain organizational types—occur frequently in combination. Some people might consider this a negative form of labeling but you can also look at it as a way of being helpful, of defining the treatment of choice for a person. A less stereotypical way of simplifying a complex world is to engage in a thematic analysis, looking at the central themes that permeate a person's inner theater. Thematic analysis is less constricted—no attempt is made to identify a finite number of character types.

Of course, the identification of character is rarely a clear-cut task. When I enter an organization, I try to keep an open mind. I always have to fight against premature closure. In order to deal with the flow of information that floods me when I enter an organizational system, I have to create a certain amount of transitional space so that I can 'play' with the data I am given. I make a great effort to use myself as an instrument.

Many of the stories I heard from executives seemed to me, to borrow Churchill's famous phrase, like puzzles inside a riddle wrapped in an enigma. I found many confusing, and my confusion made me curious. I wanted to delve deeper to make some sense of the material being presented to me. And it made me realize the extent of my ignorance and the difficulty of understanding certain situations. I had to learn to live with my ignorance, to tolerate ambiguity, and to turn a deaf ear to the sirens of premature closure. This is part and parcel of the clinical process:

the client will, in various ways, contribute the kind of material that provides insight into the discontinuities that make for his or her specific behavior. My encounters with leaders brought home to me the infinite ways in which human beings deal with stressful situations, the unique nature of our adaptive capacities, and the danger of getting stuck in vicious circles. Mental health comes down to the ability to choose, to avoid being caught in a repetitive cycle. Mental health means helping the person having more choices.

Let's face it, in the developed world we could describe about 20% of the population as perfectly all right—nice family, age-appropriate frustration while they were growing up, parents who are kind and supportive, etc.—fantastic. And there are 20% who are unlucky, growing up with violence, abuse, alcoholism, and worse. Some manage to get out of it, because they have a relative, teacher, neighbor, family member—someone who cares about the child, a lucky break that builds up resilience. And then there are the 'neurotic' rest of us, somewhere in the middle.

I am fortunate, in that my observations are based on firsthand encounters I have had over the years with numerous individuals, as part of my psychoanalytic practice and clinical organizational interventions. For example, I met a number of executives whose behavior struck me as mechanical. I became intrigued by the robotic way they dealt with their environment and the inappropriateness of their reactions to stressful situations. When did this behavior begin? What led up to it? Do certain types of organizations contribute to it? My investigations were furthered by research into a clinical phenomenon sometimes called alexithymia—people who seemed to be emotionally illiterate. Then there were the people who appeared to create havoc in their organizations, with their off-the-wall approaches to problem solving and disregard for conventions and other people. How should they be managed so that all that energy would be recognized for what it was, a potentially invaluable resource for creating original solutions and innovation rather than chaos?

I once had a difficult encounter when I could make neither head nor tail of an individual's behavior and actions. Eventually I realized that this person had the personality make-up of an impostor. During the period I was in contact with him, I was almost seduced myself by his fantasies and impositions—I was aware of a strong wish to collude with them, to loosen my grip on reality, and to believe his stories, in spite of all the evidence that he was an impostor. This encounter led me to reflect on his manipulative behavior and in turn to investigate more general questions of what makes impostors who they are, and what makes people feel imposturous, a very prevalent condition among the best and the brightest.

At a certain stage in the 'Challenge of Leadership' program that I run at INSEAD for top executives, each participant is obliged to take the 'hot seat' and present themselves to the others, telling their own story in their own words. It is a challenge to present your life in a structured way, identifying some of the signifying moments that made you the person you are. It is a fantastically cathartic thing to tell your own story with up to 22 people listening to you, but it's risky and it needs a very skilled facilitator to manage it. Because everyone wants to do this, the end result is a group of people who all have a stake in each other's personal development; they have in a way touched each other and created a very rich kind of information network. Vicarious listening can be very powerful. And what everyone realizes as a result of this process is, 'My God, I'm not alone.' I hear this over and over again, the calling card of the neurotic impostor—which is quite different from the real impostor. All those successful, senior people have a mass of insecurities welling up inside them. They are so hard on themselves, putting themselves down, lowering their self-esteem and beating themselves up all the time—must do better, must get better results. I say that everyone is normal until you know them better—but we all have some issues we have to deal with. And it comes out in the end; it's there for everyone to see.

PLAYING THE ORGANIZATIONAL FOOL

On many occasions I have been asked to present certain painful issues, which have dragged on for years, to the power holders in an organization. These issues have often been put on the back burner for far too long, where they are conveniently forgotten by executives afraid to bear unwelcome news. This is where it's useful to know how to play the wise fool (the morosophe) and extend people's capacity for reality-testing.

The fool I'm talking about is the age-old figure who acts as a foil for the leader—and every leader needs one. Down through the ages, fools played a traditional role, stabilizing the perspective of kings, emperors, and other rulers. For example, there is the wise Fool in Shakespeare's *King Lear*, the guardian of reality for Lear and audience. The fool customarily shows the leader his reflection and reminds him of the transience of power. He uses antics and humor to prevent foolish action and groupthink. Humor humbles. It creates insights. That makes it a very powerful instrument for change. Let me illustrate this with a story: a couple goes to a fair where there's a large fortune-telling machine. The husband puts in a coin and receives a card telling him his age and what kind of person he is. He reads it out to his wife, smiling smugly: 'You're brilliant and charming. Women fall all over you.' His wife grabs the card from him and turns it over. 'Oh dear,' she says, 'They got your age wrong, too.'

Leaders in all organizations need someone like this who is willing to speak out and tell the leader how it is. That's precisely the role of the fool. To be effective, organizations need people with a healthy disrespect for the boss, people who feel free to express emotions and opinions openly, who can engage in give and take. If a leader wants honest feedback, he should ask himself whether he's created an organization that has room for a fool. Very often, it is a wife or husband who plays this role. Some companies have tried to institutionalize the role, with limited success. Nevertheless, I sometimes see a wise fool operating within an organization.

Typically, it is an older executive, someone who is out of the succession race and no competition for anyone, asking questions that take people by surprise. For example, I was recently in an investment bank and met one particular man who was clearly protected by the chairman, yet for whom I could see no real role. What was so important about him? I realized later that he was the organizational fool. He asked unusual, sometimes disturbing questions, and the chairman tolerated this and encouraged him because it was useful. This man could get away with asking awkward questions because he was no threat to anybody. Nevertheless, he had a very useful function. Once in every seven meetings perhaps he would make an observation that really struck home.

The organizational fool is very much the role I play with my clients. I can say silly or provocative things, try to get people to look at things from different angles, because it's easier for someone from the outside to do it. Happiness is looking in a mirror and feeling comfortable and at ease in what you see. I am the man with the mirror.

CHAPTER 1
·······················

THE ENTREPRENEURIAL
PERSONALITY

Entrepreneurship is the last refuge of the trouble-making individual.
—Natalie Clifford Barney

INTRODUCTION

Attitudes toward entrepreneurship have undergone major changes since
the Industrial Revolution. Social awareness has replaced individualism
as a virtue, and this has had an impact upon the development of entrepreneurship. The coveted individualism of the entrepreneur lost some
of its glamor when it started to include exploitation and irresponsibility.
Although the era of the Carnegies, the Krupps, and the Rockefellers has
passed into history, this doesn't mean that entrepreneurs are a thing of
the past, as just a cursory look at the developments in Russia, India, or
China shows. But whatever the era, entrepreneurship is a fascinating
phenomenon. People have always been curious about the personality
make-up and motivations of the entrepreneur.

So what distinguishes entrepreneurs from other business people?
Although it would be difficult to define entrepreneurs as a group,
they do have some characteristics in common. Entrepreneurs are
achievement-oriented; they like to take responsibility for decisions, and
dislike repetitive, routine work. Creative entrepreneurs possess high
levels of energy and a great degree of perseverance and imagination,
which, combined with a willingness to take moderate, calculated risks,
enables them to transform what often begins as a very simple, ill-defined

idea into something concrete. Entrepreneurs also have the ability to instill highly contagious enthusiasm in an organization. They convey a strong sense of purpose and, by doing so, convince others that they are where the action is. Whatever it is—seductiveness, gamesmanship, or charisma—entrepreneurs somehow know how to create an organization and give it momentum.

Why Study Entrepreneurs?

Studies of work behavior from a psychotherapeutic or psychoanalytical perspective have been relatively scarce. Most of the existing literature concerns itself with cases of work inhibition or compulsion. Occasionally, one finds a discussion of people in the creative professions. No attention has been paid, however, to entrepreneurs, even though they are major contributors to economic development.

The paucity of clinical material about entrepreneurship in psychoanalytic and psychotherapeutic literature suggests that entrepreneurs are unlikely to turn to psychoanalysts or psychotherapists when they encounter personal difficulties. They are not usually given to the kind of self-reflection and inner orientation called for by the clinical profession. And only in extreme situations (given the amount of time that needs to be invested in it) will they choose psychoanalysis as a form of therapy. Although most of my research on entrepreneurship has been of the more traditional management type (Kets de Vries, 1970, 1977, 1985), I was in fact fortunate enough to have an entrepreneur come to me for psychoanalytic treatment. This gave me the opportunity to study the inner world of one particular entrepreneur in great depth.

In presenting a clinical case study of an executive, I follow a tradition started by a number of other researchers interested in the nature of managerial work. In their search for rich description, these students of executive behavior realized (for pragmatic considerations) that they had to limit their sample size if they really wanted to understand managerial behavior (Carlson, 1951; Stewart, 1967; Mintzberg, 1973; Kotter, 1982; Noel, 1984, 1991). What differentiates my observations from the work of others is that the subject of analysis in others' studies has been the general manager, not the entrepreneur.

Some of my observations are also based on extensive studies of entrepreneurs operating in a wide range of industries all over the world, including Russia and Asia. My usual entry into their companies was as an expert in strategic human resource management with a special interest in entrepreneurship and family business. Sometimes senior executives asked for my help because they saw my clinical background as useful in untangling complex family and business situations. In a few cases, I played more of a coaching role to the entrepreneur. In many instances I dealt with 'dramatic' cases; this needs to be mentioned, as my sample may be biased.

From a clinical point of view, entrepreneurs are interesting people to study. Many have personality quirks that make them difficult to work with. For example, their bias toward action, which makes them act thoughtlessly at times, can sometimes have dire consequences for their organization. It begs the question: What should you look out for if you are considering taking an entrepreneur on board, working for one, or encouraging these people to start new ventures? What are the problems going to be? Where are the pitfalls? How are you going to avoid them? What provisions can you make to accommodate the typical entrepreneur? Do entrepreneurs have more personal problems than other people? In short, what is the anatomy of the entrepreneur? These are all questions that I explore in this chapter.

ENTREPRENEURSHIP: VIEWS FROM OTHER DISCIPLINES

An entrepreneur is usually defined as an individual who is instrumental in the conception and implementation of an enterprise. (The term is derived from the French verb *entreprendre*—to undertake.) In this process the entrepreneur fulfills a number of functions, which can be summarized as managing/coordinating, innovation, and risk-taking. The latter two in particular characterize the behavior of entrepreneurs. Innovation implies doing things that are out of the ordinary by finding new opportunities. Risk-taking concerns the entrepreneur's ability to deal with uncertainty and ambiguity—his or her willingness to take economic and psychological risks. Because of the nature of their activities, entrepreneurs are major creators of employment and catalysts of change.

The absence of case material on entrepreneurship in clinical literature stands in stark contrast to the contributions on this subject from other disciplines such as economics, sociology, anthropology, psychology, and organizational theory. Research on entrepreneurship seems to be truly interdisciplinary. This is not surprising: all these different perspectives contribute to a considerable amount of confusion as to what entrepreneurship is all about—and may explain the wide diversity of factors supposedly influencing entrepreneurship.

Sociological and Anthropological Approaches

According to these disciplines a factor such as societal upheaval is considered to have considerable impact in the making of new entrepreneurs. Societal disruptions, which create structural changes in society, contribute to status incongruities, and have repercussions on family life, appear to affect the choice of non-traditional career paths (Hagen, 1962). Other studies indicate that entrepreneurs are more likely to come from ethnic, religious, or other minority groups (Weber, 1958; Sayigh, 1962; Hirschmeier, 1964; Kets de Vries, 1970). The experience of feeling 'different' seems to have an important influence on entrepreneurs. If the family of the entrepreneur does not seem to fit into the established order of things, their offspring may have little choice but to create a new niche for themselves in society.

Several writers have described the origins of entrepreneurs in ethnic and religious minority groups. The sociologist Max Weber's thesis of the Protestant ethic is a familiar example. It is evident that the belief in a value system different from that of society at large can lead to frictions between the family and the outside world. Members of a minority group can be subjected to discrimination, which has repercussions within the family, causing tension and stress, but also makes for new challenges. These minorities will feel less hampered by the complicated social structure of the society they live in, and be more prepared to challenge established patterns. The combination of feeling different from mainstream society, plus not having the same opportunities as the predominant group, may encourage these people to strike out on their own.

There is another prominent feature in the backgrounds of such individuals: in many cases, their fathers were self-employed, perhaps by necessity—they may have had no alternative. Occupations were closed to them because of their 'difference,' which put them under strain. Self-employment, with its uncertainties and socio-psychological risks, will be more familiar to them. Given this familiarity, they may be more prepared (and inclined) to give it a go themselves.

The Economic Perspective

Economists tend to discuss entrepreneurship in terms of a receptive economic climate (Schumpeter, 1931; Knight, 1940; Redlich, 1949; Baumol, 1968). They refer to such factors as favorable tax legislation, the availability of risk capital, a well-functioning banking system, and the existence of 'incubator' organizations like those found in

Silicon Valley, Route 128 in Boston, or Sophia Antipolis in the south of France.

The Psychological Perspective

Here the emphasis has been on the assessment of specific entrepreneurial traits using a variety of psychological tests (Brockhaus and Horovitz, 1986; Gartner, 1989, Shaver and Scott, 1991). Unfortunately, because of a lack of consistency among instruments used and methodological problems, a very confusing and not always consistent psychological picture emerges.

Among some of the qualities regularly attributed to the entrepreneurial personality we can list high achievement motivation, need for autonomy, power, and independence (McClelland, 1961, 1975, 1987). In addition, some of these studies define entrepreneurs as moderate risk-takers, anxious individuals who are 'inner directed,' meaning that they possess an 'internal locus of control' (Lefcourt, 1976; Phares, 1976; Shapero, 1975; Brockhaus, 1980; Miller, Kets de Vries, and Toulouse, 1982).[1]

COMMON PSYCHOLOGICAL THEMES IN THE ENTREPRENEURIAL PERSONALITY

It is not difficult to recognize an element of mythology and legend in articles about entrepreneurship that appear in journals like *Fortune* magazine, which devote part of each issue to preaching the gospel of enterprise and business leadership. Not surprisingly, the themes of individual success and failure are highly popular; they catch the readers' imagination and are empathy-provoking since they awaken the rebellious spirit in each of us. Mythological heroes like Prometheus and Odysseus have now been replaced by that folk hero of the global world, the entrepreneur. He has become the last lone ranger, a bold individualist fighting the environmental odds. He is that individual who after enduring and overcoming many hardships, trials, and business adventures finally seems to have 'made it.' However, as the stories of many entrepreneurs show us, success is very fragile, and easily followed by failure.

Most of the stories about the rise and fall of entrepreneurs contain a number of common themes. We are usually introduced to a person with an unhappy family background, an individual who feels displaced and seems a misfit in his particular environment—a loner, isolated and rather remote from even his closest relatives. This type of person gives the impression of being a reject, a marginal person, often with conflicting relationships with family members. We observe an individual who utilizes innovative rebelliousness as an adaptive mode with occasional lapses toward what appears to be delinquent behavior—demonstrating his or her ability to break away, to show independence of mind. Due to these reactive ways of dealing with feelings of anger, fear and anxiety, tension remains within the individual since he fears that punishment, in the form of failure, may follow. Failure is expected and success is often perceived only as a prelude to failure. Interrelated with this strange pattern of elation and despair, of successes and failures, we also observe a kind of person who, nonetheless, demonstrates a remarkable resilience in the face of setbacks, with the ability to start all over again when disappointments and hardships come his or her way.

The person we are describing, the entrepreneur, or the 'creative destructor' to use Schumpeter's (1931) terminology, is a highly complex individual—often inconsistent and confused about his motives, desires and wishes, a person who appears to operate under a lot of stress who often upsets others by his seemingly irrational and impulsive activities.

Taking a more in-depth look at this person's personality, six main themes stand out in entrepreneurial behavior: a need for control, a sense of distrust, a desire for applause, a tendency to 'split,' scapegoating, and the flight into action.

Need for Control

The need for control is a significant theme for many entrepreneurs I have known. Occasionally, their preoccupation with control affects their ability to take direction or give it appropriately and has serious implications for how they get along with others. Some entrepreneurs are strikingly ambivalent when an issue of control surfaces—they are filled with fantasies of influence, power, and authority, yet also feel helpless. They seem to live with the fear that their worst fantasies will come true and ultimately place them at the mercy of others.

Consequently, some entrepreneurs I have studied have serious difficulty addressing issues of dominance and submission and are highly suspicious about authority. This attitude contrasts greatly with that of managers. While managers seem able to identify in a positive and constructive way with authority figures, using them as role models, many of the entrepreneurs I have observed lack the manager's fluidity in moving from a superior to a subordinate role. Instead, they often experience structure as stifling. They find it very difficult to work with others in structured situations unless, of course, they create the structure and the work is done on their terms.

To use a disguised illustration, Larry Malcolm,[2] a successful US entrepreneur in the sporting goods industry, is a typical example. In my discussions with him, he talked about his inability to work for others. After he dropped out of college, Malcolm started work as a sporting goods salesperson for a department store. He liked the experience (sports had always been his great passion), but a fight with the department head over the right way to display merchandise prematurely ended his stay. He then found a clerical position in a clothing company that manufactured active wear. Although he managed to stay on longer at this job, he disliked the working environment, felt stifled, and finally quit.

In his third job, he didn't fare much better. By this time, Malcolm had begun to realize that working for others was not his forte. Not knowing what to do and wanting time to think about the future, he took his savings and made an extensive trip to Europe. At a sporting goods fair in Germany, he met a designer whose work he liked, and on the basis of the man's designs, managed to get a few orders from a department store and a number of small retail operations when he returned to the States. All of a sudden, Malcolm found himself running his own business.

Larry Malcolm's story is not unusual. Many entrepreneurs seem to be driven by a magnificent obsession—some idea, concept, or theme that haunts them and that eventually determines the kind of business they choose to be in. Malcolm's great passion was sport, and everything related to it. This partly explains his talent for finding more functional as well as attractive designs. But focused interest is not the only factor. Listening to entrepreneurs' case histories, I have found many situations where, as with Malcolm, it was their inability to submit to authority and accept organizational rules that drove them to become entrepreneurs.

Those overly concerned with being in control also have little tolerance for subordinates who challenge their authority. In organizations, at times, this desire for control can lead to extreme behavior. For example, every morning one entrepreneur responsible for a $60 million consumer product operation habitually opened not only his own personal mail but also all mail (including e-mail) directed to the company. In addition, it was his habit to approve all requisitions, no matter how small. He said it gave him a feel for the overall functioning of the organization. Excessive concern with detail may have been appropriate in the start-up phase of a company but will increasingly become a burden to the organization, as it stifles information flow, hampers decision-making, and inhibits the attraction and retention of capable managers. In this entrepreneur's situation, although his subordinates admired many of his qualities, they deeply resented not being given any authority. The good, creative performers left; the downtrodden and mediocre stayed.

The lack of true accountability in this situation meant that information needed for decision-making did not circulate. As a result, sales and profits stagnated and the future growth of the enterprise was endangered. Buyers of entrepreneurial companies started by such people should be prepared to inherit a passive and somewhat ineffectual management group.

Sense of Distrust

The need for control is closely linked to suspicion of others. Some of the entrepreneurs I have known stand out as extreme examples because of the strength of their distrust in the world around them. They have a strong fear of being victimized or taken advantage of. They are always prepared for the worst. Paradoxically, many of them feel at their best when their fortunes are at their lowest. When they are riding the success wave, they imagine themselves incurring the envy of others. So as not to tempt the wrath of the gods, when people ask them how things are, they respond by saying that business is only 'so-so' or 'not too bad.' But if their fortunes turn and they are close to bankruptcy, they seem to feel as if they have paid some necessary price, done their penance for having been successful. Because it produces a sense of relief, ironically, their predicament can have a positive effect. With the alleviation of anxiety, they have the energy to start anew, which they do with enthusiasm and a sense of purpose.

People who possess these kinds of personality characteristics are continually scanning the environment for something to confirm their suspicions. This behavior pattern does, of course, have its constructive side: it makes the entrepreneur alert to competitors', suppliers', customers', or government moves that affect the business. Anticipating the actions of others protects them from being taken unaware. But such vigilance can also lead them to lose any sense of proportion. Focusing on certain trouble spots and ignoring others, entrepreneurs like this may blow up trivial things and lose sight of the reality of the situation.

When a strong sense of distrust assisted by a need for control takes over, the consequences for the organization will be serious: sycophants will set the tone, people will stop acting independently, and political gamesmanship will be rampant. Such entrepreneurs will interpret harmless acts as threats to their control and launch destructive counteractions against them. Understandably, this kind of thinking may contribute to a toxic work environment.

In one case, headquarters sent a consultant to help the chief executive of a newly acquired company to assess profitability by product line and develop and implement a strategic plan. When the consultant arrived, the ex-owner would not let him look at the financial statements on the grounds (he explained to headquarters) that the consultant might use the information to help the competition. On another occasion, when his machines were idle and he had to lay off employees, the same person refused to sell goods-in-process to a non-competing business. He argued that he had once been burned when a competitor used his goods-in-process to manufacture a line of products that competed with his own, and he was not going to let it happen again.

In another instance, the vice-president of human resources of a conglomerate was surprised to discover that the former owner of a subsidiary had television cameras monitoring the front and back entrances of both his plant and his office building. To allay his fears that employees were stealing from him, the manager kept on his desk two split-screen consoles that he watched constantly.

The problem with countering such distorted forms of reasoning and action is that there is always a degree of reality behind the fear and suspicion. If one looks hard enough, one will always find some confirmation of the entrepreneur's suspicions—someone stealing something, or acting against the company's interests. Unfortunately, the person who manages this way forgets the price the company pays in deteriorating morale, low employee satisfaction, and declining productivity.

Desire for Applause

The common heroic myth begins with the hero's humble birth, his rapid rise to prominence and power, his conquest of the forces of evil, his vulnerability to the sin of pride, and, finally, his fall through betrayal or heroic sacrifice. The basic symbolic themes—birth, conquest, pride, betrayal, and death—are relevant to all of us. And some entrepreneurs act out the same myth. They feel they're living on the edge, that their success will not last, but they also have an overriding concern to be heard, recognized, and regarded as heroes.

A very gifted entrepreneur, who was experiencing great stress while working out how quickly to expand his business, described to me a recurring dream he had. In the dream, he would be standing on a balcony, looking down, and see a group of women smiling admiringly up at him. This scene would soon fade and the admirers would turn into harpies. Feeling suffocated, he would wake up screaming. He also recalled dreams of himself as a swaggering cowboy climbing an ever-narrowing trail leading to the top of a mountain. But below the top, a gate blocked the road. To move past it, the man would have to risk sliding down.

If one looks at these dreams as symbolic, albeit in a simplified way, one sees certain wishes and fears standing out. One of the more noticeable characteristics of both dreams is their grandiosity; they involve high positions—balconies and mountains—and the way to reach both is fraught with many dangers.

One way of looking at the need for applause is to see it as a reaction against feelings of insignificance. Some entrepreneurs I have met hear an inner voice that tells them they will never amount to anything (Larry Ellison of Oracle is a good example of this: in his case he apparently hears the voice of his stepfather). But regardless of who put this idea into their minds, these people are not retiring types who take such rebukes passively; they are defiant, and try to deal with them creatively through action. They will ride to the top in spite of all the dangers; they will get the applause; they will find a way to master their fears.

A manifestation of this need is the interest some entrepreneurs show in building monuments as symbols of their achievements. They suffer from the 'edifice complex,' as some people have humorously named it. Sometimes this takes the form of an imposing office building or production facility; sometimes it is a product that assumes symbolic significance. For example, one entrepreneur wanted to show people in the section of town where he grew up that he had amounted to something, and built an imposing head office and new factory. The contrast between his building and the decrepit surroundings in which it stood was striking. That this action jeopardized the company's financial position—it was done during a period of economic decline when all advisers advocated off-shore production—made the decision even more bizarre.

The Tendency to 'Split'

An individual's personality consists of enduring, pervasive behavior patterns created by complex, deeply embedded, psychological characteristics. Although each of us may behave differently, we all have defenses that help us deal with the stresses and strains of daily life. The relationships we develop with others are colored by the kinds of defenses we use.

People who are in trouble psychologically (who have difficulty balancing their internal and external lives) often resort to the defense of 'splitting' as a way of coping. Splitting is a tendency to see everything as being either ideal (all good) or persecutory (all bad). The way these people see themselves and others becomes so dramatically oversimplified that they fail to appreciate the complexity and ambiguity inherent in human relationships. They tend to see things in extremes, idealizing some people and vilifying others. The attitudinal pendulum shifts all too easily.

One entrepreneur I studied made a point of hiring young MBAs just out of school. He would marvel at their mastery of the latest management techniques and hold the new executives up as examples to his other employees. He would tell them that these were the kinds of managers he needed. Inevitably, his lavish praise would stir up enormous resentment among the rest of the staff (with predictably spiteful consequences). But also, just as inevitably, the president's infatuation with his latest recruits would soon exhaust itself and disappointment would set in. No recruits could live up to his exaggerated expectations, and eventually, like the other MBAs who preceded them, they would leave.

When this same man sold his company, he was at first quite enamored of the acquiring company's CEO, praising his new boss's accomplishments to all. It gave him great pleasure to dwell on certain incidents illustrating the CEO's achievements. But as with all the others, this infatuation did not last long. A request for more information about a new advertising campaign from the private equity firm that had acquired his company was the turning point. The ex-owner interpreted the request as a vote of no confidence, an attempt to find fault with his actions, and even as part of a plan to get rid of him. He had had similar reactions to other requests from headquarters. Almost overnight, the CEO changed in his eyes from hero to chief villain. Eventually, because the entrepreneur withheld information, the CEO had no choice but to make his fears come true, and let him go.

Scapegoating

We all have a tendency to externalize internal problems: we project our own discomforts and fears onto others. When we attribute a threat we feel to someone else or to an event, it becomes more manageable. But if this tendency becomes exaggerated and if it turns into the predominant reaction to stressful circumstances, it can become problematic. Scapegoating is a method people commonly adopt to maintain their view of themselves as blameless. People who act this way experience little sense of personal responsibility. They distance themselves from the problem and deny and rationalize away whatever responsibility they may have had. They refuse to see what they don't like and blame others.

One entrepreneur who had sold his company, but remained in charge, refused to accept reports that sales were dropping rapidly or to acknowledge that a number of creditors were ready to pull the plug on the company. Instead of recognizing that the downturn resulted from mismanagement on his own factory floor and in his design department, he denied his own responsibility and blamed any adverse indications on the government or on customers' malice. He argued that the new product line had miraculous potential, and nobody in the company was bold enough to contradict his statements. Instead, his subordinates continually reassured each other that the president's opinion must be correct. Despite a hands-off policy, head office eventually had to intervene and end the entrepreneur's employment contract prematurely. It took many years of effort to get the company back into the black.

Flight into Action

Finally, several entrepreneurs I have worked with defend against feelings of anxiety (evidenced by their restlessness and irritability) by turning to action as an antidote. The anxiety of dealing with events in a reflective manner is too much for them. They prefer to flee into action, even if it is impulsive and thoughtless, without considering all the facts. This is not because waiting out events has no attraction for them. Rather, they have such a strong fear of passivity (because it could make them overdependent and thus controlled by others) that they have to act counter-dependently.

These common themes in entrepreneurs' personalities do not spring out of nowhere. They develop from causes lying in their early childhood experiences.

THE EFFECTS OF FAMILY DYNAMICS

For a number of male entrepreneurs that I interviewed, childhood was a disturbing experience. (Many female entrepreneurs have similar experiences but, so far, my sample is too small to arrive at valid conclusions.) In many of their memories, the father appeared to be the main villain.

He would frequently be blamed for deserting, manipulating, or neglecting the family. Death can be interpreted by a child as the ultimate form of desertion or rejection—and a remote or absent father makes a poor role model. It can leave the developing child, and later the adult, troubled by a burdensome psychological inheritance centered on problems of self-esteem, insecurity and lack of confidence.

The absence, or remoteness, of the father image in the family is often complemented by the mother assuming part of the father's role. In conversations with entrepreneurs, their mothers usually come across as strong, decisive, controlling women who give the family some sense of direction and cohesiveness.

Henry Deterding, the main figure behind Royal Dutch Shell, was six years old when his father died. The father of Karl Benz, the entrepreneur who laid the foundation of the Mercedes-Benz Corporation, died when his son was one. John Johnson, who started the Johnson Publishing Company (which publishes magazines like *Ebony* and *Jet*, aimed at African-Americans), experienced the death of his father when he was 13. Deterding, Benz, and Johnson experienced poverty or near-poverty in their youth. And so we can go on.

These are only a few examples from an eclectic group. Themes of poverty, death and loneliness recur, indicating how many entrepreneurs had disrupted childhoods, and emphasizing the influence of psychological deprivation, although these factors do not explain everything in a complex picture. Many of the stories told by entrepreneurs skim the surface. Thus to get an even better understanding of the inner world of the entrepreneur a clinical case study may be illustrative.

CASE STUDY: THE ENTREPRENEUR'S STORY

The case study that follows looks in considerable detail at one particular entrepreneur. First, however, in order to appreciate the context in which it was made, I will make a few comments about the psychoanalytic process.

The Psychoanalytic Process

Although the sample size in the other studies of managerial work has been small, in no instance has it been limited to a sample of one, as in the case I present here. The individual under investigation was not studied for a few hours, a day, a week, or a month, however. He is somebody whom I saw for five 50-minute sessions a week over a period of four years. Some people find it helpful to devote a part of their day to reflection. Such an intense process is rare outside the helping professions: this kind of continuity, however, gives the psychoanalyst an opportunity to observe microscopic changes in mood states and behavior. The rich description that this sort of experience allows should compensate for sample size.

Length of treatment is very much a consequence of the process of working through insights acquired during the psychoanalytic process— the time it takes to deal with resistances. Insight by the client into the origins of many patterns of behavior can be acquired relatively quickly. However, in psychoanalytic treatment, the bulk of the time is spent on reporting, experimentation, and the exploration of new ways of dealing with present life experiences. The Chinese have a saying, 'The eye cannot see its own lashes,' which sums up the process. Changing established behavior patterns can take quite some time, as many people have a tendency (particularly in situations of crisis) to fall back on their old ways of functioning. In human behavior, the wish to recover is strongly matched by the desire to cover.

When listening to a person's story, it is essential to bear in mind the distinction between narrative and historical truth (Spence, 1982; Edelson, 1993). The most critical part of a person's story is how he or she remembers it. That version of the truth will create the psychological impact that shapes personality. Whether or not the remembered version is true to the facts is much less important. Our sense of identity is very much the heir of the personal myth by which we live, a myth that connects the past with the present (Hartocollis and Graham, 1991). The psychoanalyst pieces these stories together from different fragments into an integrated whole.

The insights provided by this exploratory study have been enhanced by knowledge derived from a considerable number of structured and unstructured interviews with entrepreneurs, plus a large questionnaire-driven research database (Kets de Vries et al., 1989). Although these other studies have helped me to understand better the dynamics of entrepreneurship, none, however, has provided me with the kind of insight that I derived from the intense, clinical dialogues I had with this client.

Most importantly, this case history permits a rare look at the inner world of an entrepreneur, a look that goes beyond the party line that is so often found at the heart of traditional interviews. This case history provides a rich store of information in which the interplay of personality and environment, and the process of personal change, can be observed in great depth. It tests some of the conjectures made about the entrepreneurial personality and gives the reader a modicum of understanding of the complex psychological interrelationships behind the behavioral observations. It also gives us a better comprehension of the person–organization interface, helping us appreciate that many of the management theories of how people make decisions in organizations are oversimplified. This case history makes clear that in many instances the explanations of why certain decisions are made turn out to be *ex post* rationalizations.

It is clearly impossible to summarize in writing all that happened during the large number of sessions that made up this psychoanalytic intervention. For the sake of brevity, I have limited myself to a number of salient themes that, in my opinion, particularly affected this individual's relationship to work and his organization. It will be seen that the themes that characterize the entrepreneurial personality, which I described earlier, come to the fore.

The Presenting Picture

Mr. X, a 44-year-old entrepreneur and father of four children, sought psychoanalytic treatment following separation from his wife after 21 years of marriage. In the initial interview, he described how he had thrown his wife out of the house. Apparently, her increasing need for more independence had become a bone of contention. Her newly found assertiveness also became noticeable at work (she was employed in his business). He complained about her lack of caring and suspected that she was emotionally involved with a younger man working at the office. In addition, he expressed strong annoyance that his children had taken the side of his wife.

Mr. X's other complaints were rather vague at first, but after further prompting seemed to be of a depressive nature. He acknowledged that he had suffered from depression before, but that to the best of his knowledge it had never been so serious. As things were now, he felt completely worthless. Life had no prospects. He feared that he was losing his mind. His sorry state reminded him of the fact that his father had died in a mental hospital, a memory that still haunted him.

According to Mr. X, his wife's departure also had serious repercussions at work, as her role in the company had been quite important. In fact, her leaving had meant the loss of two valuable employees as the young man had also left. Mr. X was now extremely worried about the future of the company and wondered whether it would survive all this upheaval. He had been an active person but now felt paralyzed at work.

He would sit for hours behind his desk staring into space. He could no longer make effective decisions. He was ashamed to admit that he had taken to reading horoscopes, using the information as a major input in strategic decision-making. He feared bankruptcy.

Going to work had become increasingly painful. At the office he had only negative thoughts; how he would be humiliated by his bankers, creditors, and customers; how they would gloat about his failure; and how his mother and other family members would react. Many times he had been completely unable to go in to work. Instead, he would spend the day in bed. Even taking care of the everyday household chores had become more difficult. At work, he felt disoriented, unable to give directions or make decisions. This really troubled him as he had always felt proud of his activity and decisiveness.

Mr. X also listed a number of somatic complaints. Although he had been an excellent sleeper in the past, he was now troubled by nightmares and suffered from insomnia. Sores in his mouth and throat also caused him great discomfort. He suffered from severe headaches that affected his eyesight. On some occasions he had actually temporarily lost the vision in one of his eyes. He also complained of diarrhea and nausea. After the separation from his wife he had had relationships with other women but had been troubled by impotence. Physical check-ups had shown nothing wrong with him. The doctors he had consulted suggested that his problems might be of a psychological nature. He knew he needed help, and so, despite his initial reluctance, he decided to try psychoanalytic treatment.

Background

Mr. X was the youngest in a family of six children. He had two brothers and three sisters. His father was a salesman who also dabbled in a few entrepreneurial ventures. Because of his work schedule, his father was often away from home. Mr. X remembered him as a boisterous man who laughed a lot and brought him presents from his frequent business trips. He had always felt that he was his father's favorite.

When he was seven years old, his father became bedridden. Having his father in the house gave the boy the opportunity to spend more time with him. He began to feel close to his father. Eventually, his mother and older sister had his father transferred to a mental hospital where he soon died. Mr. X was only eight years old at the time. Later, he wondered whether the hospitalization had really been necessary. The true nature of his father's illness, however, had been shrouded in secrecy. He had tried a number of times to find out what had really happened, but had not been able to uncover the truth. The whole incident seemed to have been suppressed as a dangerous family secret. Mr. X suspected that his father had committed suicide which, given his family's religious orientation, would explain the secrecy around the incident.

He described his mother as a very controlling, overprecise, critical woman who constantly worried about money and the future. After the death of his father she had to bring up the children alone, not an easy task since his father's death had resulted in a considerable drop in family income and standard of living. According to Mr. X, this affected his mother's entire outlook on life. He felt that she saw everything in a negative light. She never made a positive comment. Nothing he did was ever good enough. He also described her as a perfectionist. He had never been able to live up to her standards. Apart from the death of his father, his childhood was described as uneventful and quite happy. He felt proud of the fact that he had been something of a rebel as an adolescent.

Major Issues

The themes that emerged during the course of analysis centered on Mr. X's relationships with women and his attitude to work. The tone of a large number of sessions in the first phase of the analysis was pessimistic; life was seen as a sacrifice. He also had a terrible fear of being alone. With his wife gone, he felt completely deserted. According to Mr. X, he once used to have everything. Now things were different; his health had been ruined; his life was in a shambles. He felt worthless. He wondered what had kept him so busy at work in the past.

Mr. X's inner world seemed to be one of fragmentation and it took very little to set off some form of disequilibrium. In an effort to arrive at some kind of inner cohesion, it was extremely important to him to be in control. He revealed that throughout his childhood he had been scared of losing control. He was reluctant, for example, to fight with other children for fear that he would lose control and kill someone. Denial of inner reality and flight into external reality through work had become a way of life. His defensive structure, however, of escaping into action—'the manic defense' (Klein, 1948)—no longer seemed to work.

FALLING INTO EXTREMES

Initially, in analysis, Mr. X resorted to the defense of splitting described earlier (Freud, 1966; Kernberg, 1975, 1985). As symptomized by his dramatic mood swings, an all-or-nothing attitude prevailed. Very little was needed to push him in one direction or the other. After having had an extremely intense, positive relationship with his company, during which he would tell everyone his wonderful vision of the future, the opposite was now the case. He detested the company and everything associated with it. Running a company was much too complicated; there were too many things to think about. It was just too much trouble. He often felt like giving the company away. Similar feelings were expressed about his car and his house. Possessions came with too much baggage. His relationships with others were seen in a similar light. Obviously, this behavior pattern colored his relationships and affected the way he ran the business, as well as influencing his relationships with customers and suppliers. And at times it led to disastrous action.

La vie en rose

It soon became obvious that denial of feelings of depression through unrealistic optimism, laughter, humor, frantic activity, and excessive control had always been an important element in maintaining Mr. X's psychic equilibrium. In this context, it is interesting to note his attempts to fight his depressive state by eliminating negative thoughts. He had read a number of self-help books in an attempt to improve his ability to do this. For many years this had been one of his strategies of dealing with life—even though this appeared to be ineffective, since he was not completely clear about the reasons why he needed help.

As analysis progressed Mr. X began to see his early relations with others in a different light. He was willing to admit to himself that his childhood had not been as happy as he had made out. He realized that he had always preferred recalling only happy memories. In reality, it had been quite difficult to be the youngest in the family. The other members of the family treated him like a baby. They never paid attention to his needs. They thought he was spoiled and incapable, although he never experienced it that way himself. Looking back he felt he had had a rough deal. Moreover, he now realized that growing up under these circumstances did not help provide him with a sense of inner security.

Mr. X recalled how he would panic when his father and mother went out in the evening. He would scream not to be left alone. He was afraid of being tormented by his brothers and sisters who, according to him, were envious of him as his father's favorite. Mr. X's anger was specifically directed toward his oldest brother, whom he detested. A major reason for his resentment was that this brother had tried to take the place of their father after his death. He also felt that this brother never treated him fairly, and made fun of him.

Mr. X remembered how, apart from screaming, he used to complain about physical symptoms to get attention and sympathy, to no avail. Only one of his sisters seemed to be willing to lend a friendly ear. Many times during therapy he would mention that the saddest thing he could imagine was to see a young child cry, an ill-disguised reference to himself.

Mr. X had conflicting memories of his father, a powerful, flamboyant man who brought him presents, but who also had a darker side. Another image emerged of a father who beat his children. He recalled that his father would stifle his behavior, forbidding him to speak at the dinner table: 'Children should be like flies on the wall; they should not be heard.' He also had an Oedipal memory of himself sitting in the car between his father and mother pulling at the gearshift to bring the car to a halt. But when that happened, his father had not been angry; instead he had shown understanding of his son's budding assertiveness.

A more realistic picture of his father began to form. There was the kind, powerful man who catered to his needs. But then Mr. X would ask himself whether, in fact, his father had not been a very shallow person, a fake, and all posturing masked by laughter. These reflections made him realize how much he was like his father. He acknowledged that he behaved in a very similar manner; he would cover up his real feelings by making lots of noise.

Now, when he thought about his father, he felt like crying. What became clear during the sessions was that it could be seen as a form of belated grieving. Apparently, because of the secrecy around his father's death, true mourning had not really been permitted at the time. Now, while he was mourning his father, a stark image appeared of an abandoned child crying into his handkerchief.

THE MEDUSA WOMEN

During childhood, Mr. X's anger toward his mother was reflected in his fear of becoming an orphan. He used to pray every night that his mother would not die. But he was also afraid he would sleepwalk and kill his mother in his sleep. At the same time he had the irrational thought of hanging himself. Obviously, anxiety and guilt about his aggressive desires were regular companions. It took some time, however, before he recognized the origin and meaning of these feelings.

Gradually, in the course of analysis, he began to admit his anger toward his mother. He remembered how his mother would say that she should not have had six children, a statement that still troubled him. As the last child, it had made him feel unwanted. His arrival must have been an accident. His mother had always seemed busy, never available. Because of her seeming indifference, it had become a major theme in his life to prove to her that he was worth having. He wanted her to be proud of him, to admire him. But whatever he had achieved in the business world, it never seemed good enough. She never gave him any praise. He blamed his mother for driving his father crazy (as he felt she was driving *him* crazy). He actually questioned whether his father had been crazy at all, and wondered whether his mother had just wanted to get rid of him when he became bedridden and found that putting him in a mental hospital was the handiest solution.

Given the kind of relationship Mr. X had with his mother, it came as no surprise that he perceived women as dangerous, overcontrolling, not really to be trusted. Here the splitting defense mechanism was also evident as Mr. X would divide women into two categories, the easy and the proper. He had always been fascinated by prostitutes (and still was), but the fascination was accompanied by fear. Prostitutes were tempting but they could also be infected with diseases. He recalled an incident when he visited a prostitute. He felt that he had not treated her like other men. He had not taken advantage of her; he had gained her admiration. Paradoxically, he also remembered that as a young adult he had had many short relationships with women, treating them rather callously, usually dropping them when they became too clingy. He disliked feeling 'choked.'

It was clear that Mr. X felt threatened by women. His dreams illustrated the role women played in his inner life. In many of his dreams, phallic women, portrayed as women with guns, would appear and lie on top of him, having intercourse while putting him in a passive position. He would wake up, frightened, feeling smothered. In other dreams, however, women would admire him from a distance. He described one dream in which he was persecuted by a number of large bees who kept striking at him. They were almost impossible to brush off. He associated this imagery with all the women he had dealt with in this life. Women could cling and sting, but also give honey. They could repel but also give pleasure. Gradually, however, dreams emerged in which he became more assertive with women, not taking such a passive role. Most importantly, in these dreams the degree of anxiety he had previously experienced was missing.

THE MEANING OF WORK

Being in Control

Starting and managing an enterprise had multiple meanings to Mr. X. It signified much more than a means of making a living. He had found out early in life, while employed by a German company, that working for others was too stifling. Being controlled by Germans was more than he could handle, particularly in the light of his vivid childhood memories of World War II. Indeed, at times when he let his fantasies run wild he would associate Germans with baby killers. They wanted everything done by the book; they were perfectionists like his mother; they did not permit any individual initiative. While he was associating in this way, the irrational thought came to him that the Germans may have had some responsibility for taking his father away from him. Obviously in Mr. X's inner world, there was some kind of connection between his mother and Germans. He had previously compared his mother to a Prussian general. She exerted totalitarian control. To be independent, to be in control, meant to be free from mother. His inability to work for other people (who would tell him what to do) made him decide to start on his own as his father had done before him. That was the only way to get some power, and no longer be subjected to the whims of others.

The importance of control became very clear in the transference process during analysis. During the session Mr. X's perception of the analyst would oscillate. At times I was perceived as the benevolent father figure. At other times, however, analysis meant domination. I would turn from an idealized, benign, all-powerful father into a nagging, controlling, never-satisfied mother. Lying on the couch, Mr. X even experienced physical sensations of choking. At times, he wanted to be considered the favorite patient, at other times he wanted to quit. He would ask how much longer it would take before he was 'cured,' when he would be able to function on his own again. Obviously, 'cured' in this context meant liberation from the 'controlling' analyst.

Mr. X recalled how, as a child after his father's death, he had been troubled by their poverty, by his mother's financial preoccupations, by his inability to obtain certain things, and by his envy of wealthier schoolmates. To these frustrations was added his insecurity about his position in the family. Home had never seemed a safe environment. He always had to be on his guard. He recalled vividly an incident where his oldest brother cheated him of the little money he had. As a child he had vowed to change all that. He was going to have money. He was going to be a smarter businessman than everybody else. However, even as an adult, when someone took advantage of him, it filled him with intense rage. This was an indication of the extent of his narcissistic vulnerability.

Setting up his own enterprise seemed to be overdetermined. But it also presented a paradox. It was a compromise solution for dealing with an injured self. By starting his own business, Mr. X combined a life of insecurity with the prospect of security. The excitement of dealing with an unpredictable environment became a way of warding off painful underlying feelings of depression. Owning a company also meant defying his mother, who had always emphasized security. But it was also a way to be in control and escape her clutches. Moreover, starting a business could lead to great success. He could become financially independent. He might even do better than his father or siblings, and force his mother to admire him. But, in addition to what the business meant to him intrapsychically, there was the thought that he had given his bedridden father a promise to amount to something. To be successful in business would be his way of fulfilling that covenant.

The Need for Admiration

A central theme for Mr. X was that success in business would provide him with the admiration he sought. Deep down it also meant pleasing both parents. Success would make him special in their eyes; it would get their attention.

Thus it was not surprising that he threw his wife out of the business when she started to compete and no longer admired him. In addition, her interest in his younger employee had revived Oedipal concerns[3] and sibling rivalry. It had also created a paranoid fear that they were going to steal his money. And money symbolized success, power, and prestige. Without money he was not going to amount to much. After his wife left him, however, owning the company had suddenly become completely meaningless. Instead, it had turned into a symbol of defeat. Obviously, Mr. X found it difficult to go on without having a cheerleader around.

The breakdown of his marriage occurred at a time when he started to become concerned about ageing, remembering that he had now reached the age at which his father had become bedridden and was sent by his mother to a mental hospital to die. For some time Mr. X suffered from a 'nemesis feeling,' the sense that he was repeating someone else's life script. He wondered whether he would share his father's fate.

Symptomatic of this anniversary reaction was his hypochondriacal concern that he had cancer and was going to die.

Grandiosity and Depression

As I noted earlier, success in business, and the consequent admiration received were very important for Mr. X's self-esteem. During the course of the analysis, it became increasingly clear that, as a child, Mr. X's emerging narcissistic needs had never been dealt with in an age-appropriate manner. Affection had always been a precious and rare quality during his infancy. With so many siblings, a negative, overcontrolling mother, and an absent (later deceased) father, there was not much love to go around. His mother had never been able to give him the narcissistic supplies he needed.

Fortunately, his father's interest in him had helped alleviate this somewhat, but his father's death when Mr. X was still very young had created a vacuum, leaving him even more vulnerable. This event had also revived Oedipal guilt (as reflected in fantasies of being victorious over his father, but also feeling responsible for his death), further hampering age-appropriate growth and development. The kind of situation to which he was subjected resulted in the acquisition of many of the qualities listed by Miller (1979) in her description of depression and grandiosity. A 'false' self, fragile self-esteem, perfectionism, fear of loss of love, envy, un-neutralized aggression, oversensitivity, a readiness to feel shame and doubt, and restlessness were all evident.

Mr. X's mother, seemingly depressed herself and with strong obsessional traits, had fostered the development in Mr. X of extremely high standards—a very severe superego. As a lifestyle, Mr. X pursued ways to be grandiose as a cover for the ever-lingering threat of depression, which originated in his inability to fulfill the internalized expectations of his mother. To this was added the loss of the father whom he had never properly mourned. This needed self-image of specialness could be viewed as a compensatory reaction refuge against never having felt loved (Kets de Vries and Miller, 1985).

COMPETITION AND SELF-DEFEATING BEHAVIOR

Mr. X was caught in a bind. On the one hand being subjected to domination and terror of older siblings and mother was a way (painful though it might be) of getting some sort of attention. But, understandably, this form of relating was unsatisfactory. He hated it, and it led to his strong desire as an adult to avoid becoming stuck in a similar situation. He needed to be in control. If pain was involved, he would be the one to inflict it. He was never going to be a helpless victim again.

It is interesting to note that when in a triangular situation (an Oedipal reactivation of the childhood situation), Mr. X experienced an even greater need to compete for attention. The women he desired most, those whose admiration he needed most, were the ones attached to powerful, successful business colleagues. At times, in order to impress these women, he would take impulsive business decisions that he would later regret. He also recalled that when his wife admired another man, his jealousy was so intense that he would fly into a rage. He would start a personal campaign to defile that person. Nothing would stop him. This state of mind had often led to inappropriate actions that endangered his business.

Furthermore, Mr. X's work habits had strong sadomasochistic overtones. His intensive work behavior, his need to keep himself busy, his desire to be involved in everything, were driven by a great need for perfection. Nobody in the company could do things as well as he could. He would always find something wrong with the work of others. Acting in this manner represented his despair and rage about his inability to fulfill the archaic internalized expectations of his mother. Moreover, he would externalize his mother's incessant demands and the ever-present criticism of his older siblings, and play a similar role toward his subordinates in his business. Predictably, as a boss he was very difficult to deal with.

But, as we have seen, playing the controlling, powerful businessman was only one of Mr. X's leadership styles. There had been times when he was no longer able to handle the constant stress he had imposed on himself. In fact, he had rarely found work pleasurable. Intrapsychically, it symbolized submission to authority—and this was viewed as an obligation. Somehow he felt assigned to the role of martyr in the larger scheme of things. Success, power, and money were elusive entities. They could be taken away at any time.

THE SYMBOLIC NATURE OF THE ENTERPRISE

The enterprise became an extension of Mr. X, vulnerable to attack, and prone to failure. It was much more than merely a business, representing in many ways his enfeebled self. In that respect, it was like a house of cards, ready to collapse. Of course the unpredictable way he ran his business, with its negative effects on the behavior of his employees and company performance, added a dose of reality to this concern.

In one dream, his business looked like a bombed-out church; in another, his business transformed into a sinking platform. Moreover, many dreams also contained an Icarus motif. In them, he would fly, trying to soar higher and higher. But this pleasurable interlude would soon be broken by feelings of anxiety. His wings were falling off and he might crash.

A considerable amount of the material brought up in analysis concerned machinery, which fascinated Mr. X. Many of his dreams centered on machines, reviving pre-Oedipal and Oedipal memories of preoccupation with his body image, physical functions, and sexual curiosity. In one dream he was hiding behind a machine and looking through the cracks, afraid to be caught; in another he was busy with a mud-throwing machine. His excitement about machinery and preoccupation with primal scene imagery seemed to be closely interwoven.

The enterprise also symbolized his ability to rebel. Setting up an enterprise somehow became a personalized statement of separation. It would make him a person in his own right. Unfortunately, however, he had only been partially successful in doing this. It seemed as if the separation-individuation phase that each infant faces had never been fully resolved (Mahler, Pine, and Bergman, 1975). The precariousness of his individuation was indicated by the ease with which developmental conflicts became reactivated.

In addition, the business also took on the quality of a transitional object (Winnicott, 1975), a plaything evoking the illusion of unity with the mother and creating an intermediate area of experience. It resembled a space between inner and external reality, a place where he could re-enact his fantasies; through play he could master his anxieties. It is interesting to note that many of the products made by his various companies could be retraced to these playful fantasies of childhood. The kind of imaginary companions he had had, the way he would magically transform his toys during play, all fulfilled a role in the eventual choice of industry, and the kind of products he was making. This lingering imagery very much colored some of his strategic decisions in the company and determined the selection of his portfolio of companies.

As a symbolic extension of his self, the business became his way of reparation: he would keep his 'promise' to his dead father and care for the needs of the simultaneously repulsive and desired mother. Business success also provided Mr. X with the means to acquire confirming and admiring responses, to fight his inner sense of worthlessness and low self-esteem. The business became the means to acquire money, prestige, and power, thus warding off feelings of weakness, passivity, and helplessness.

The enterprise also enabled Mr. X to recreate a family situation according to his wishes. His temporary wish to reorganize the company, move towards centralization, and put all his businesses under one roof (a very poorly conceived business idea) could be traced back to this. As the owner of a business he could set up situations where he could take charge and make the rules. Through hiring and firing he could create an environment that would correspond to his alternating states of pessimism and grandiosity.

THE PROCESS OF CHANGE

Redressing the Balance

In the course of the analysis, Mr. X's attitude toward the people in his life began to change. His relationship with his wife gradually became more balanced. Feeling more secure (having had the opportunity to explore his reactions toward her during our sessions), he asked her out for a date. For the first time in many years they had a really significant conversation. More of these meetings followed. The sadomasochistic quality of their previous interaction disappeared. In their relationship, it became less important to question who was controlling whom. He began to accept that his wife could be both assertive and affectionate. After a number of these trial encounters, his wife moved back into the house.

Another major change was apparent in his attitude toward his mother. He made a strong effort to empathize with her. He tried to understand what it had meant for her suddenly to find herself a widow with only limited means and a large family to raise. To his great surprise he discovered that by behaving differently toward her, their relationship started to improve. This changed relationship gave him increased peace of mind.

Changes in his behavior were also noticeable at work. He made an effort to create a more relaxed atmosphere. He no longer needed to be so competitive. He became better at neutralizing his aggression. He no longer had regular outbursts of anger. He began to perceive the world as less threatening. He was less worried about competition. He was more at ease with the suppliers and customers. He had discovered that unrestrained aggression was not the only way to succeed in business.

Ironically, as a first step toward creating a more pleasant atmosphere at work, he fired an older woman whom he had hired soon after his wife had left him. This woman reminded him of his mother, with a similar pessimistic outlook on life. She had created a very negative atmosphere at the head office. Now, seeing things more clearly, he wondered what had ever made him hire her. Was it because he needed to have a criticizing woman around, for lack of an admiring one?

Mr. X no longer wanted to sell his business. At times, however, he fantasized about the money he could get for the company. It made him wonder how his mother would react if he showed her how much his company was worth. Maybe that would make her admire him. But he realized that he did not really want to let go of the company. Although it had become less of an emotionally overinvested entity, having his own business was still very important for his psychic equilibrium.

Increased insight about the reasons for his behavior made working more pleasurable. Understanding why he behaved as he did widened his area of choice. He felt less like a prisoner of his past. Previously, he had had a need to create work, to be constantly busy. Without it, he felt lost. Now, however, he was making an effort to take life more easily, to find more effective ways of managing the business. He tried to redress the balance between action and reflection. He spent more time thinking about what he was trying to achieve.

Mr. X also tried to be less of a perfectionist and realized the importance of giving his subordinates space. They would learn by their mistakes, and should be allowed to make them. He realized that some of his best people had left the company because of the way he had treated them. He now tried to change this by hiring stronger people, individuals who were willing to stand up to him. He developed the ability to delegate. He became better at controlling his tendencies to micromanage and became interested in developing his people, taking on the role of mentor and coach.

The scope of the human resource function (previously restricted to salary and wage administration) was broadened. It became more strategically and developmentally oriented. He started to invest in leadership training and development. He also began to make plans for management succession after having discussed the matter with his sons, who were interested in coming into the business. Together they decided that each son would run a part of the business. To prevent future conflict, each would eventually have the chance to become majority shareholder of his share of the business.

Mr. X's new way of running the company was reflected in the very positive results on the balance sheet. As the corporate climate changed, and employees felt increasingly empowered, product innovation took off. The launch of new product lines was accelerated. Employees started to experiment with better ways of satisfying their customers. Both product and process innovation were on the rise but so was customer satisfaction. Good corporate citizenship behavior became the norm, with people going out of their way to help each other be more effective in the organization. Market share increased, and so did profitability.

Mr. X struggled a long time with his need for power and prestige. There was constant temptation to speed up the growth of the company. He recognized that this was driven by his need to feel more powerful and realized the danger of too rapid growth and overexpansion. For a long period in the analysis he would oscillate between the grandiose fantasy of building a conglomerate and his fears of it becoming too big. At times, he felt like the mythological King Midas; everything he touched seemed to turn to gold. But then he became anxious that growth might endanger his relationship with his wife and ruin his health. Being too conspicuous might also invite disaster. Others might grow envious and spoil his success, as often happened while he was growing up. His depression and his symptoms of physical illness might return.

Gradually, however, he began to see the relationship between his need to expand the company and certain key themes in his inner world. This gave him an increased sense of freedom, of no longer being a prisoner of the past. His actions became more balanced. It also made for more thoughtful decision-making. He stopped reading horoscopes when deciding strategic moves. He became less impulsive when making decisions in the company.

THE ENTREPRENEURIAL LIFE CYCLE

Turning the Tables

This case study helps us to understand better the process entrepreneurs go through to become the kinds of people they are. We have seen how the entrepreneur emerges from childhood as a psychological risk-taker subjected to a high degree of psychosocial risk. Through intrapsychic transformation, original feelings of helplessness, dependency, and rejection are replaced by a proactive style in which power, control, and autonomy become predominant issues. What used to be an inclination toward submission and passivity becomes an active, more impulsive mode of behavior. The role of the passive, helpless victim is replaced by acting the role of the person in control. For male entrepreneurs, the psychological absence (real or imagined) of the father may make the child experience an Oedipal victory, creating a highly ambivalent attitude towards people in positions of power and authority.

His inability to function in structured situations makes it necessary for the entrepreneur to design his own organization where he is in control and at the centre of action. His achievements in setting up enterprises become important tangible symbols of prestige and power. But his achievements are not sufficient to ward off a persisting sense of anxiety and other stress indicators. Rejection, dissatisfaction, and a fear of failure follow many entrepreneurs like inseparable shadows.

The Reactive Mode

Before society at large recognizes their capabilities, potential entrepreneurs enter a period of disorientation, without apparent goals, during which they are testing their abilities. These future entrepreneurs drift from job to job, encountering difficulties in the acceptance of their ideas, in conceptualizing and structuring possible 'new combinations.' Other people perceive them as a deviant, someone out of place, provocative and irritating because of their seemingly irrational, non-conformist actions and ideas. Non-conformist rebelliousness become entrepreneurs' mode of behavior, their way of exerting power and control over an environment perceived as dangerous and uncontrollable. The entrepreneur's actions do not derive from the inner strength and self-assurance that a secure, consistent family upbringing would have provided. Instead, the driving ambition can be seen as a means of trying to contradict strong feelings of inferiority and helplessness. Hyperactivity is a reaction against anxiety.

This special kind of 'reactive model' makes for a sense of impulsivity: the entrepreneur's actions are determined by speediness, abruptness and short-term, operational planning. These people are characterized by a low tolerance for frustration and tension and a low attention span, constantly in pursuit of immediate gains and satisfactions. For the entrepreneur the initial impression, the hunch, is often taken as the final conclusion with no further serious search and deliberation process. There seems to be an absence of concentration, logical objectivity, judgment, and reflectiveness, as if the process of cognition is impaired and does not fulfill its integrative function. This apparent lack of analytical thinking, and the absence of active search procedures and self-critical reflections become the predominant mode. Paradoxically, however, in spite of their tendency toward impulsive behavior, these entrepreneurial types make a deep, emotional investment in the companies they create.

The Significance of the Organization

The preparatory period of entrepreneurship, as we have seen, is accompanied by authority conflicts, failures in organization, socialization, difficulties in adapting to organizational structure, and predictable job-hopping behavior, which sets the stage for the unique relationship of the entrepreneur with his enterprise. As we have seen in our case example, the enterprise becomes the new setting where the entrepreneur's problems in adaptation and conforming to structure are accentuated and dramatized. Naturally, the business becomes the tangible symbol of the entrepreneur's success in overcoming odds and assumes a much greater emotional significance than the reality of the situation may warrant.

Unlike a manager's relationship with other people's organizations, the level at which an entrepreneur deals with his own organization is far more intense and conflict-ridden; this pattern cannot be explained merely by the higher financial risks at stake. While previously, they coped with life by avoiding structure and organization, their own organization becomes the end of the road. There is no other place to go, a development that contributes to the emotional significance of the enterprise.

A Growing Dysfunctionality

But the very fact of the entrepreneur's complete psychological immersion with the enterprise—a factor that may have been a key ingredient in its initial success—can lead to serious dysfunctional developments if the business continues to grow. Entrepreneurial organizations frequently reveal an organizational structure and work environment completely dependent on and dominated by the entrepreneur, around whom the entire decision-making processes center. They are headed by individuals who frequently refuse to delegate, have no interest in analytical forms of planning, and regularly engage in bold, seemingly unpredictable, proactive moves. These might account for the initial and continued success of the enterprise, but the lack of a conscious planning effort carries a high risk. The entrepreneur has no sense of priorities and may spend as much time on trivia as on major strategic decisions. Within the organization, power depends on proximity to the entrepreneur, is constantly changing, and creates a highly uncertain organizational environment. This state of affairs contributes to a highly politically charged atmosphere where changing coalitions and collusions are the order of the day. The formal organization chart is either nonexistent or outdated by the time it is drawn up. It would be represented most accurately by a spider's web with the entrepreneur in the centre. The organization usually has a poorly designed or poorly used control and information system (with no information sharing); there is an absence of standard procedures and rules and a lack of formalization. Instead, subjective, personal criteria are used for the purpose of measurement and control. Job descriptions and job responsibilities are poorly delineated or non-existent. The number of people reporting to the entrepreneur will be large, adding to a general sense of confusion.

Although entrepreneurs, in the initial stages of developing the business, might have had the ability to inspire their subordinates, the mere fact of growth has complicated this process. Their aversion to structure, their preference for personalized relationships, and their reluctance to accept constructive criticism makes growth, with its implicit need for a more sophisticated infrastructure and suprastructure and greater decentralization, increasingly difficult to handle. And if this pattern prevails, few capable subordinates will remain in the organization; the ones left will usually be poor caliber and spend a great part of their effort on political infighting.

Decline in the Enterprise

I am describing here the potential danger of the entrepreneurial mode; that given the nature of the entrepreneurs' personal conflicts and their peculiar leadership style—useful as these qualities might be initially— growth may lead to the eventual destruction of the enterprise if the entrepreneur's attitudes remain rigid and he or she refuses to formalize the organization or change decision-making patterns.

If the enterprise continues to grow, the effectiveness of the organizational structure and the means of decision-making will be increasingly inadequate to cope with the complexities of the external environment. The degree of environmental dynamism (changes in technology, market behavior, and competitors' reactions), heterogeneity (differences in the needs and behavior of organizational constituents), and hostility (cut-throat competition, resource shortages, etc.) determine how long these entrepreneurs will be successful while they continue to follow their old style.

Obviously in a very static industry segment the strain on the organization will not be noticed immediately. But eventually the organizational strains become intolerable and utter disorganization and financial losses are often the outcomes of the entrepreneur's leadership style.

Issues around Succession

Given the entrepreneur's rigid attitudes and frequent inability to modify behavior, abdication and succession are often the only alternatives if the enterprise wants to continue to grow. Although from a rational point of view it may be better for both enterprise and entrepreneur if the entrepreneur distances him- or herself and starts something new, from an emotional point of view this is not such an easy transition. The entrepreneur will find many rationalizations to avoid taking this step, starting with the argument that there is no one good enough to take over, a statement with the implicit message that there is no alternative but for the entrepreneur to stay on. The paradox of the situation is that the entrepreneur has created a high-dependency work environment. Because he or she has always regarded any encroachment upon positions of power and control with suspicion, it is highly unlikely that a capable administrator will have managed to rise through the ranks, making the founder's statements about the impossibility of stepping down a self-fulfilling prophecy.

Many entrepreneurial organizations have difficulties shifting to a more formally organized enterprise. The ambivalent, paternalistic aptitudes of the entrepreneur become a burden to the company as soon as the organization's structure demands sophistication. The need for greater systematization places new demands on the entrepreneur, demands he or she may be unable to meet. At this point, the situation is ripe for the professional manager and a more formalized style of leadership, and turns paradoxical: the successful entrepreneur, who has guided the enterprise through the formative period of growth and maturity, moves unconsciously on a collision course that may contribute to his or her own elimination.

Family members also fall into the category of possible intruders threatening the entrepreneur's position of control. Since family dynamics are often acted out in organizations, the presence of family members in the business intensifies the eruption of conflicts (Levinson, 1971).

There is a confusion of roles between the social system of the family and the business system (Kets de Vries, Carlock and Florent-Treacy, 2007). At the root of these conflicts are feelings of rivalry, where the conflict-ridden relationship that the entrepreneur had with his parents is now transferred towards his son. There is frequently a re-enactment of the old family romance, when the son or daughter of the entrepreneur is exposed to the same treatment the entrepreneur felt he or she once endured. But now it is the entrepreneur who is in the position of authority and control.

This unholy repetition of family dynamics occurs, particularly with the sons of male entrepreneurs. In their turn, they are now dependent on the entrepreneur's whims, vulnerable to his erratic and unpredictable behavior and kept in an infantile position. The idea of abdication, of stepping down, is obviously resented by the entrepreneur; the fact that he will be succeeded by his son gives rise to more complicated feelings. The resentment will be increased incrementally with the trauma of reawakening old feelings of rivalry, with all their connotations of frustration and despair.

Edsel Ford's relationship to his father, Henry Ford, the founder of the automobile company, is a good illustration of the abrasive dimensions these conflicts can reach and the destructiveness of this type of rivalry to the enterprise (Jardim, 1970). Henry Ford's refusal to change strategy, or to make alterations to the Model T, and his unwillingness to encourage Edsel Ford in his efforts to build an infrastructure and suprastructure brought the company to the edge of bankruptcy. Under extraordinary pressure, changes were eventually made but at an extremely high cost in material resources and manpower. Sometimes, extreme old age or death are the only circumstances under which control can be taken away from the entrepreneur. Unfortunately, by that stage it might be too late to save the enterprise.

Successful entrepreneurs who manage to guide their enterprises through the formative period of development into a stage of growth and maturity may follow a path that eventually leads to their own functional self-elimination. They are people at the crossroads, enigmas, on the one hand highly creative and imaginative but, on the other, rigid, unwilling to change, incapable of confronting the issue of succession. Succession becomes identified with loss—death being the most dramatic form of loss—and therefore becomes taboo. But the issue of succession is inevitable not only for reasons of age but also because of increasing maturation and growth of the company. The entrepreneur is no longer alone; other interest groups such as employees, family members, bankers, customers, suppliers and the government have become involved. Depending on the strength of the entrepreneur's position, they can have some influence on the policies of the enterprise. But change achieved by this type of pressure is usually only modest. A more drastic type of change is needed for continued growth and success and for this, a sense of psychological maturity on the part of the entrepreneur is required—a willingness to confront his conflict-ridden behavior and overcome and surpass the problems of the past. But adaptation to present-day reality (and foregoing the legacies of his personal history) requires a considerable basis of self-awareness and insight.

The entrepreneurial personality is a study in contradictions; imaginativeness and rigidity, the urge to take risks, and the stubborn resistance to change. People often speculate about the possibility of changing the personality characteristics of creative people to eliminate the destructive qualities while preserving, if not enhancing, the constructive tendencies. These speculations are often based on wishful thinking—to have the best of both worlds of innovation and maturation. Greater self-awareness and discipline would undoubtedly serve these people well in making the transition from starting up an organization to taking on a meaningful leadership position during later stages of growth. But it is a rare individual who can develop this kind of awareness. Perhaps the more intelligent plan for entrepreneurs is to move away from their old ventures while moving towards other areas of innovation. Instead of trying to change themselves, they can continue to be pioneers, but on new frontiers.

WORKING EFFECTIVELY WITH ENTREPRENEURS

Anyone who deals with an entrepreneur—private equity firms, investment bankers, consultants, or individuals who work for one—would do well to be aware of the possibility of a complex drama playing out in the entrepreneur's inner world. Doing so will help them understand what otherwise could be brushed aside as irrational behavior and actions. Unfortunately, the complex mosaic of contributing factors that leads to some entrepreneurs' peculiar actions is often neither recognized nor understood.

Obviously, the individuals who should be the most concerned with this inner world are the entrepreneurs themselves. Entrepreneurs who resort to a manic defense—who never ask themselves why they are running, or where to—are in for an eventual shock. Too many entrepreneurial businesses self-destruct because of these behavior patterns. It is difficult to break the vicious circle, however, without some form of professional help. The recognition of this need is a step in the right direction.

However, many entrepreneurs only realize that they are in trouble when it is far too late. They are not able to balance action with reflection. They have no sense of the continuity between past, present, and future. Unfortunately, the old adage that those who do not understand the past are forced to repeat it is true. If more entrepreneurs were aware of the fact that they are the keepers of the keys to their own prison, if they accepted the craziness inside them and did not run away from it, they could make more of an effort to do something about their situation.

In this discussion I have focused on the dark side of entrepreneurship. The cases I've outlined here are extreme; many of the relationships between entrepreneurs and others do not deteriorate so dramatically. Entrepreneurs do not necessarily have more personal problems than other people, nor do they inevitably have personality disorders. What one can extract from the previous comments, however, is that entrepreneurs have their own unique ways of dealing with the stresses and strains of daily life. In saying this, I want to emphasize that the boundaries between very creative and aberrant behavior can be blurred; normal and irrational behavior are not discrete categories on an established scale. The mix of creative and irrational is what makes entrepreneurs tick and accounts for their many positive contributions. Entrepreneurs create new industries and jobs and stimulate the economy. Their visionary qualities and leadership abilities enable those around them to transcend petty concerns and attain great achievements.

In one case I know, the president of a conglomerate worked hard to build a relationship based on mutual trust with the entrepreneur running a company he was considering acquiring. The two talked about the working arrangements and operational procedures each would accept. While the entrepreneur expressed his concern about preserving his independence, the president described the information he would need from any subsidiary to make him feel comfortable. They also agreed that the entrepreneur could call on the president at any time for assistance. After the acquisition, the president kept his promise to let the entrepreneur run his own show; he kept interference from headquarters at a minimum. The arrangement about assistance turned out to be critical. The president soon found out that the entrepreneur was using him regularly as a sounding board, which he did not mind since it enabled him, in an atmosphere of mutual trust, to bring a healthy dose of reality to the entrepreneur's occasionally high-flying schemes. This loose-knit arrangement turned out to be very successful. The new acquisition became one of the most profitable in the conglomerate's portfolio of companies.

Collaboration with the kind of entrepreneurs I have described in this chapter can be very trying. The last case provides a clue, however, to how executives and venture capitalists can work with these imaginative, but sometimes difficult, people. The challenge is to develop a relationship based on mutual trust that will allow the executive and the entrepreneur to talk openly and regularly, and that will enable the latter to test ideas against reality.

To facilitate this process, venture capitalists and chief executives should respect the entrepreneur's need for independence and design control and information systems accordingly. Living with such an arrangement is not easy and executives at the head office will need to maintain an appropriate balance between monitoring performance and letting go of control. One way to ensure the autonomy of acquired companies is to minimize headquarters staff in order to prevent excessive interference.

Top executives should take additional precautions before taking an entrepreneur on board. Before buying an entrepreneurial company, look carefully at the quality of management that will come with the deal. Can the talent pool of the company you're about to acquire be trained and developed? Or are you facing such mediocre management that will make it very difficult to build a team that will fit the acquiring company's culture? Is there a degree of trained incapacity that will make it impossible for the acquired management group to move the company forward, if the entrepreneur leaves?

Executives should also consider the fit between the entrepreneurial company's culture and that of the acquiring company. How similar are the basic values in the two organizations, for example, about issues like accepted behavior, structure, and goals? (I am not thinking of a dramatic transformation but of a gradual shift.) Corporate executives should be equally open to change; cultural adjustment works both ways. In any case, executives need to consider whether the cultural differences are so great that a clash is inevitable.

Because of the wealth of product and market knowledge entrepreneurs usually have, separating them from their companies should be a last resort. If it quickly becomes obvious that an entrepreneur's need for autonomy overshadows everything else, it may be advisable to retain him or her only for a short transition period. As a rule, acquiring companies feel the need to impose their cultures on subsidiaries, and more often than not, entrepreneur-owners decide to leave.

Whatever executives or venture capitalists finally decide to do, they should keep in mind that entrepreneurs' personality quirks may have been responsible for the very drive and energy that made them so successful. Instead of fighting these idiosyncrasies, executives should regard developing them as a challenge.

ENDNOTES

The material for this chapter has been gathered from the following previously published sources:

- Zaleznik, A. and Kets de Vries, M.F.R. (1976). 'What makes entrepreneurs entrepreneurial?' *Business and Society Review*, Spring, **17**.
- Kets de Vries, M.F.R. (1977). 'The entrepreneurial personality: A person at the crossroads,' *Journal of Management Studies*, **14**.
- Kets de Vries, M.F.R. (1985). 'The dark side of entrepreneurship,' *Harvard Business Review*, November–December.
- Kets de Vries, M.F.R. (1996). 'The anatomy of the entrepreneur, clinical observations,' *Human Relations*, **49**: 7.

1. Shapero (1975) used Rotter's (1971) 'internal-external' scale to determine the locus of control of entrepreneurs. Entrepreneurs tended to be on the internal end of the scale. Internal people were defined as individuals who felt that they have some influence on the course of events in their life (as opposed to external people who felt dominated by outside forces such as luck or fate). For internal people, personal destiny comes from within and therefore they tend to be more self-reliant and more in need of independence and autonomy.
2. All names are fictitious.
3. The Oedipus complex is a concept from psychoanalytic theory referring to a stage of psychosexual development where a child of either gender regards the parent of the same gender as an adversary, and competitor, for the exclusive love of the parent of the opposite gender. The name comes from the Greek myth of Oedipus, who, unaware, kills his father, Laius, and marries his mother Jocasta.

CHAPTER 2

THE HYPOMANIC
PERSONALITY

I am hyperactive ... in an extremely hyperactive sort of way.
—Josh Lewsey

INTRODUCTION

Wouldn't it be nice if the people we work for and with, and those who work for us, were stable, well-balanced, and perpetually happy? Wouldn't life be simple if the emotional state of the people we encounter in the workplace were predictable and non-mysterious? Unfortunately, real life rarely matches that utopia. Although the expression of emotions by most executives falls well within middle range—high highs and low lows being rather rare—there are exceptions. Some executives act and interact in ways that puzzle, disconcert, and even disturb us, their emotional style occupying an extreme position on the emotional spectrum. Dealing with such people—people for whom there is no emotional middle ground—leaves us with a strange aftertaste. But that is not the worst of it: their emotions, and the behavior those emotions engender, have potentially dramatic repercussions (for better or for worse) on their co-workers and their organization.

In the course of a long working life, there is a strong possibility that we will be managed by, or will manage someone, at one extreme of the emotional spectrum or the other. Some of these people are proselytes of the psychology of elation, while others are disciples of the psychology of dissociation. While the first sweep us off our feet with charm and charisma, the others fill us with apprehension and dread through the apathy they exude. While the first possess the kind of infectious behavior that sparks enthusiasm and inspires action in the people around them, the others leave us ice-cold and can, in fact, be deadening. While we may be drawn to the first as moths to a flame, with the others we may experience only boredom and frustration.

The kinds of mood states represented at these two extremes of the spectrum have been widely described in the psychological literature. The people who make up the first set are characterized as 'hypomanics' (hypomania is a mild form of bipolar disorder), while those in the second set are known as 'alexithymics' (from the Greek, meaning 'no word for emotions'). In this chapter I will look at hypomanics, and their effect on the organization. I will turn to the alexithymics in Chapter 3.

THE DIONYSIAN QUALITY OF CHARISMATIC LEADERSHIP

Dionysus, son of Zeus—the god of wine, fertility, and ecstasy—has long been a controversial figure in the Greek pantheon. There are profuse and contradictory legends about him. In ages past, festivals were held in his honor. Orgiastic, manic behavior—enhanced by music, wine, dancing, and the eating of the flesh and blood of sacrificial animals—characterized many of these celebrations. During these festivals, the Dionysian cult worked themselves up to states of ecstatic frenzy. They hoped to merge their identity with that of the god and thus be liberated and inspired. According to legend, Dionysus was subjected to both great ecstasy and great suffering, symbolizing the struggle between creativity and madness. He was thought not only to be able to free humankind through wine and ecstatic frenzy but also to endow people with divine creativity.

Like Dionysus, some leaders have the ability to influence others by their mood state. The ebullience and energy they radiate can be downright contagious. That infectious behavior sparks enthusiasm in the people around them. Followers are irresistibly drawn to such people. Their attraction is such that everyone wants to be with them; they are singled out, and become the subject of identification. Because of their ability to touch and stretch their followers, they rise easily to positions of power. As they energize others, creating high commitment, their followers answer their summons and exert themselves beyond the call of duty.

The term 'charismatic leadership' is often used to describe this ability to draw excellence out of one's followers. German sociologist Max Weber is credited with introducing the concept of charisma in his description of various forms of authority. While Weber found concepts such as traditional or legal authority fairly easy to grasp, charisma was another matter altogether; it was not as clear-cut. Yet in analyzing the mysterious effect some leaders have on their followers, Weber saw a strong link between charisma and authority. Looking at historical figures, Weber observed that some individuals have an *inherent* authority—that is, the ability to influence by the nature of their personality—which seems to result in spiritual or inspired leadership. Great mystics, religious leaders, and political leaders, for example, generally possess this quality. In Weber's conceptual framework, charisma consists of:

> a certain quality of an individual personality by virtue of which he is set apart from ordinary men and treated as endowed with supernatural, super-human or at least specifically extraordinary powers or qualities. These are such as are not accessible to the ordinary person, but are regarded as of divine origin or as exemplary, and on the basis of them the individual concerned is treated as a leader. (Weber, 1947, pp. 358–359)

Charisma is a precious quality. Charismatic leaders know how to help people to transcend their normal way of doing things and make an extraordinary effort. Charisma is also a cause for concern, however. It has a darker side, as history has shown. Charismatic people can be like the Pied Piper, entrancing those around them and leading them to their doom. We have only to think of political leaders like Mussolini, Hitler, Stalin, Saddam Hussein, and Robert Mugabe to recognize the dangers of charisma. Many charismatic people engage in self-destructive behavior, and when—because of the power of their personality—they draw others with them, the consequences can be far-reaching and even deadly.

However, charisma has an enigmatic quality, in part because its origins are difficult to deconstruct. The effort is rewarding, however. If, in going beyond a purely descriptive level of charisma, we take more of a psychodynamic orientation, we can decode a great deal of the mystery. This particular orientation looks at charisma as a transferential process, an emotional confusion in time and place. Transference and charisma are closely interconnected. An understanding of the process of transference makes the concept of charisma less puzzling.

When transference is operative, a person reacts to others not according to the reality of the situation but as if those others were significant individuals from his or her past (Breuer and Freud, 1893–5). The foundation of this kind of behavior is the developmental need that all children feel to idealize the caregiver as a way of building up self-esteem; in the powerless child, idealization is a way of internalizing the caregiver's power (Kohut, 1971). Through this process of internalization, the basis is laid for the individual's sense of self.

So what ramifications do transference and idealization have in the workplace? Because the need for idealization is an omnipresent phenomenon—humankind's way of finding strength in an otherwise anxiety-provoking world—we often see followers responding to their leaders as they would have done to their parents or other authority figures while growing up.

In fact, this process of idealization is part of a general developmental matrix that repeats itself, to some extent, in most leader–follower relationships (Kets de Vries, 1995). It is more prominent when the leader is more energetic and visionary, however, because it is easier to imagine such a leader living up to the ideal. As the past is transferred to the present in the interaction between a dynamic leader and his or her followers, it sets the stage for 'charismatic attribution,' reactivating former developmental interaction patterns and bringing a hunger for the ideal to the fore once again. This hunger—this need for powerful people with whom one can identify—puts a lot of energy into the workplace. It makes for mutual identification, team play, and goal-directed behavior. Furthermore, the tendency toward the idealization of people in leadership positions often helps align and energize followers in pursuit of a common vision.

Important as this transferential component is in charismatic behavior, it alone does not determine charisma. Although leadership works partly because of the human tendency to idealize, very few leaders have a truly charismatic disposition. For leaders who really demonstrate this quality, we need to take a closer look at the 'psychology of elation.' People in that kind of elevated mood state will have a compelling, contagious influence on others. Not surprisingly, this behavior pattern can be highly advantageous in leadership situations.

CASE STUDY: HYPOMANIA IN ACTION

Although most of us have heard of bipolar disorder (what used to be termed manic-depression) and its devastating consequences to the sufferer, family, and friends, many are unaware of milder temperamental variants of this condition, including hypomania. These variants are often not as easily identified. Hypomanic people are prone to mildly manic states rather than the extreme highs and lows of full-blown bipolar disorder.

Being managed by a hypomanic is a challenge. There are pluses, to be sure. Colorful, stimulating figures, hypomanics make life anything but dull. Drawn into their magical sphere, a world of unlimited ideas and possibilities, in which success is assured, employees experience a sense of exhilaration. There is, however, a volatile undertone to this elevated mood state. Hypomanics can easily become dissatisfied, irritable, intolerant, and fault-finding when their demands are not met. When confronted with opposition, they can become pretentious, impertinent, and even verbally or physically aggressive. Trifling incidents can bring about open hostility and violent outbursts. Compounding that emotional irritability is the ever-present threat of depression.

Let's look at a case in point.

A few years ago I was contacted by Alex Young,[1] an acquaintance who was the non-executive chairman of Novorex, a large consumer products company. He was calling because the board had just forced the resignation of David Klein, a man in his mid-forties who had been the president of the company for just over three years. Initially, according to Alex, all the board members had been very pleased to have David at the helm of Novorex. He had been a highly attractive candidate for the position; everyone on the board had been taken by his charm, energy, and positive thinking. More importantly, he had been full of ideas for revitalizing the company, which had been in a slump for some years.

Soon after his arrival (with the board's approval), David had gone on an acquisition spree to improve Novorex's global product/market position. Although his logic for the different acquisitions was convincing at the time, the policy soon put Novorex in dire financial straits and loaded it with a portfolio of poorly matched enterprises. The expected synergies were not materializing.

Alex confessed somewhat sheepishly that he and the other board members felt a considerable responsibility for the present state of the company; they regretted not having been more vigilant in monitoring and questioning David about his intentions and actions. Alex explained that the board had been entranced by David's vision of the future, his intensity, his energy, and his self-assurance. David really knew how to inspire enthusiasm in other people, said Alex. As a result, the board had gone along with David until it was almost too late. Only recently, having commissioned an external consulting report, had the board members realized that most of David's acquisitions had turned out to be lemons. Because the envisioned complementarity of products had never materialized, the financial results over the last two years had been terrible. And the stock market had reacted accordingly, bringing their share price to an all-time low.

Alex explained that he and the other board members had waited for so long to intervene because they really wanted to believe David's claim that—in spite of poor financial results—a turnaround was just round the corner. However, a costly strike at their major distribution center, due to a number of poorly executed cost-cutting measures, had convinced them otherwise. That development meant another year of serious losses and a further fall in the share price. With some of their larger institutional shareholders becoming vocal in their concerns, the strike had left them no alternative but to pull the plug and ask for David's resignation.

It was clear from Alex's comments that his sense of responsibility extended beyond the company to the colleague who had been asked to resign. He implied that, by allowing themselves to be caught up in David's personal magnetism, they had failed more than just their shareholders. Alex felt that David, in his present state, needed some help and asked me if I would be willing to see him. I told him that I would be happy to do so. I received a call from David the same day, and agreed to see him later in the week.

On the basis of Alex's description, I had anticipated a very different type of person. It was not easy to recognize, slumped in my office chair, the energetic, self-assured individual I had been told to expect. As a matter of fact, David made exactly the opposite impression: he described himself as feeling sad and empty and having very little interest or pleasure in anything. As I probed a little further, David complained about his inability to sleep, his loss of appetite, and his general sense of fatigue.

David explained his present mood state as a consequence of his dismissal. Having had time to reflect on the matter, he acknowledged that the board's decision was not unreasonable—an acknowledgement that grieved him. His behavior and actions may have given them cause, he admitted: his acquisition policy may have been too bold; he may have painted too rosy a picture of the expected results; he may have been a bit too cavalier with the figures; he maybe should have heeded the advice of some of his more sober executives rather than attempting to sweep them away with his enthusiasm. He confessed that he had ignored a consulting report that showed much less attractive figures than the ones he had presented to the board and had rationalized as temporary the dramatic fall in share price.

It soon became clear from my discussion with David that he had been prone to mood swings since childhood. He mentioned that there had been many periods in his life when he had been wildly out of control—dominated by soaring highs and melancholy lows. To control his unstable behavior, he had finally, some years ago, consulted a psychiatrist, who had prescribed medication that had helped him for a time; it had made his life more balanced. However, he had found that life with lithium was not as rich as life without—it had made his existence more flat, less exciting; it had resulted in an emotional dampening of his experiences. Missing the highs of hypomania, he had stopped taking the medication. Not taking it confirmed his preference for the occasional state of euphoria (and the lows that were part of the package) to the more middle-of-the-road state he had attained with the help of medication.

David tried to explain his feelings when flying high. While in that state, he said, everything became much more intense. A simple thing like walking in the local park, for example, became an almost mystical experience. With all his senses fully operating, his awareness of all the objects in his environment was intensified. Whatever he did—looking at a tree or a flower, listening to a bird, or talking with an associate—he did more deeply.

It became clear from the conversation that David was addicted to his highs. An elevated state brought him a great deal of satisfaction. He felt that his highs benefited his work as well. After all, being high was exhilarating not only to him, increasing his productivity, but also to the people around him; his mood helped him to energize his colleagues and actualize the various projects they were involved in. He mentioned that getting others excited about his ideas made him feel alive. When that high-spiritedness left him, life had a dead and deadening quality.

Upon further questioning, David also indicated that before his marriage he had been something of a Don Juan, dating a steady supply of girlfriends. Women had seemed to flock to him, drawn by his ebullience. While not many stayed around long, he had enjoyed their company, craving the intensified sexual feelings he had experienced when in an elevated mood state. David's ability to attract women seemed to have had an addictive quality to it—the more women he dated, the more he felt the urge to meet new women—but it had also had a destabilizing influence, making him more prone to mood swings.

His marriage at the age of 23 had helped to balance his moods. His wife had given some stability to his life. Recently, however, with their children in high school, his wife had embarked on a full-time career. Their equilibrium had changed as they saw less and less of each other. With his wife preoccupied with professional concerns, David began to spend more time at the office and traveling, and he had affairs whenever tempted, making little effort to conceal the evidence from his wife. Gradually, his preoccupation with other women had eaten into their marriage. He and his wife had been separated for over a year, but he was only now coming to realize how much the decrease in interaction with his wife had affected his behavior.

It also became clear from the conversation that David was no stranger to substance abuse. He often turned to alcohol when he was feeling high, because alcohol prolonged and intensified the euphoric effects. When asked, he denied that he was an alcoholic, but he admitted that he drank a few whiskeys every day. He also admitted that he had experimented with drugs, especially cocaine.

Before joining Novorex, David had been the chief operating officer of another company in a related industry, working closely with the CEO—a man who seemed to have exerted a stabilizing influence on David's life. They had been very successful as a team, in part because their temperaments offset each other: the conservative CEO had modified David's expansive ideas into more manageable proportions. David had been lured away by a headhunter, however, and accepted the job at Novorex. He had thought that serving as CEO would give him the opportunity to show his true worth. And for a while it had; he really had been flying—until the present crash.

ELATION AND ITS VICISSITUDES

What can we say about David Klein? What, if anything, is wrong with him? How can we explain his attitudes and actions?

David demonstrates a relatively mild variety of bipolar disorder. Bipolar illness encompasses a wide range of mood disorders and temperaments, varying in severity from cyclothymia—which is characterized by noticeable (but not debilitating) changes in mood, behavior, and thinking—to full-blown, life-threatening manic-depression. What makes the behavior of people with any of the bipolar variants so special is the cyclical nature of their illness.

The German psychiatrist Emil Kraepelin, a pioneer in the classification of psychological disorders, described the oscillating nature of this type of disorder:

> [Bipolar illness] is seen in those persons who constantly swing back and forth between the two opposite poles of emotion, now shouting with joy to heaven, now grieved to death. Today lively, sparkling, radiant, full of the joy of life, enterprise, they meet us after a while depressed, listless, dejected, only to show again several months later the former liveliness and elasticity. (1913, p. 222)

In the handbook of psychiatrists, the *Diagnostic and Statistical Manual of the Mental Disorders, DSM-IV-TR* (American Psychiatric Association, 2000), mood disorders are listed according to their intensity. Broadly speaking, going from more to less extreme, a distinction is made between Bipolar I Disorder, Bipolar II Disorder, and Cyclothymia. True manic-depressive illness, or Bipolar I Disorder, is not something to be taken lightly. It is a disorder characterized by one or more manic epi-sodes. The mood disturbance of the true manic-depressive is sufficiently severe to cause a marked impairment in occupational functioning, social activities, and relationships. Some manic-depressives also experience psychotic episodes characterized by delusional thinking, hallucinations, and/or bizarre behavior. Occasionally manic-depression is extreme enough to require hospitalization, to prevent harm to the sufferer or others. Without medication, all manic-depressives have difficulty func-tioning normally. With medication, however, even those with a ten-dency towards psychosis generally do not become psychotic. Any bouts of madness they do suffer are generally temporary, seldom progressing to chronic insanity.

Of the three bipolar sub-categories, it is the other two that are more commonly found in organizational settings. Instead of engaging in truly manic behavior, with its increasingly explosive highs and potentially suicidal lows, Bipolar IIs and cyclothymics are prone to *hypomanic* behav-ior, or 'mildly' manic states. According to *DSM-IV-TR* (p. 362), the criteria that characterize hypomanic behavior include the following:

A   A distinct period of persistently elevated, expansive, or irritable mood lasting throughout at least 1 week (or any duration if hospitalization is necessary).

B   During the period of mood disturbance, three (or more) of the fol-lowing symptoms have persisted (four if the mood is only irritable) and have been present to a significant degree:
1   Inflated self-esteem or grandiosity
2   Decreased need for sleep (e.g. [the person] feels rested after only three hours of sleep)
3   More talkative than usual or pressure to keep talking
4   Flight of ideas or subjective experience that thoughts are racing
5   Distractibility (i.e. [the person finds his or her] attention too easily drawn to unimportant or irrelevant external stimuli)
6   Increase in goal-directed activity (either socially, at work or school, or sexually) or psychomotor agitation
7   Excessive involvement in pleasurable activities that have a high potential for painful consequences (e.g. engaging in unrestrained buying sprees, sexual indiscretions, or foolish business investments).

These hypomanic episodes alternate with depressive episodes (which can be identified using the *DSM* criteria applied to major depression and the depressive phase of manic-depression). During these depressive episodes, people lose interest and enjoyment in what are normally pleasurable events. They may experience a sense of emptiness and futility. This depressive state may be accompanied by changes in appetite or weight, problems with sleeping (too much or too little), decreased energy, apathy, lethargy, hopelessness, feelings of worthlessness or guilt, difficulty thinking, an inability to concentrate or make decisions, or recurring thoughts of death and suicidal fantasies. It should be noted, however, that these mood disturbances are not due to the physiological effects of drug abuse or medication.

While hypomanics in the depressive state are bereft of energy, the opposite can be said of them when they are in the manic state. It is easy to see how executives in a hypomanic mode can revitalize and move organizations. These people are energetic, flamboyant, and expansive. They are positive thinkers, defiant optimists in the face of adversity; their glass is always half-full. Furthermore, they rush in where others fear to tread; they assume risks easily and are willing to make bold moves. They crave stimulation, novelty, and excitement. Life is filled with meaning for them: they have a purpose, and there are many things to be done. They make an enormous effort to make their dreams come true and take others with them in their search for adventure (Fuller, Torrey, and Knable, 2002; Winokur, Clayton, and Woodruff, 1969; Campbell, 1953). Given their belief in ultimate possibility, it is not surprising that following the rules is not their forte. They know how to beat the system, finding creative ways around it. However, they often underestimate the effort needed to get projects on their way.

In their manic state, hypomanics usually have an inflated sense of self-esteem, as well as an unbending conviction of the correctness and importance of their ideas. Although this sense of conviction can be used for the good, their 'I'm always right' way of thinking and behaving disregards valuable alternatives and contributes to poor judgment. This, in turn, can lead to chaotic patterns of personal and professional relationships.

Hypomanics are also extremely social, ready to engage whomever they encounter. Consequently, they may get caught up in intense and impulsive romantic or sexual liaisons, even with workplace colleagues. Compared with more common mortals, hypomanics seem to need very little sleep; there are too many things to be done. Because their thoughts may race, often faster than they can articulate them, they may talk more loudly and rapidly than other people.

What are the consequences of hypomanic characteristics like these? The increased energy and expansiveness, intensified perceptual awareness, willingness to take risks, and fluency of thought associated with hypomania often result in highly productive and creative periods. As a result, hypomanics can be a real asset to their organization. They can be very imaginative and creative, and are generally high achievers. There is, in fact, a considerable body of research indicating a strong relationship between bipolar disorders and intellectual and creative achievement. A much higher than expected rate of bipolar disorders exists among exceptionally creative artists and writers. One study concluded that 38% of a sample of eminent British writers and artists had been treated for mood disorders (Jamison, 1993). Nonetheless, while extreme fluctuating mood states can contribute to creative imagination and expression, the research findings also show that they can be highly destructive. For example, a large percentage of people suffering from bipolar disorders have a history of some kind of substance abuse or dependence. Furthermore, people with bipolar disorders are also far more likely to be suicide-prone (Paykel, 1982).

The precarious balancing act of these people can also be observed in business settings. Their expansiveness, unwarranted optimism, grandiosity, impulsiveness, and poor judgment while in an elevated mood state can lead to the undertaking of extremely risky ventures. Caught up in their grandiosity, they overestimate their capabilities and engage in more activities than they can handle—more, indeed, than are humanly possible. Yet they do not take well to suggestions about cutting back. Indeed, they can become extremely irritable when their wishes are thwarted. Irritation may underpin their behavior across the board. Instability in mood state, alternating between euphoria and irritation, is frequently seen in hypomanics.

Interactions with hypomanics are further complicated by their tendency to deny that their behavior is problematic, and often to resist all efforts towards help. Because hypomanics put on a good front, they can be very convincing in assuring others that there is nothing the matter with them. They avoid unpleasant ideas and perceptions, along with the emotional consequences of reality—the anxiety that would overwhelm them if the warded-off depressive feelings and images were permitted to flood them—by immersion in a mood state that varies from good humor to exaltation; but only the good humor is readily apparent to outsiders.

MANAGING A HYPOMANIC

Managing a hypomanic is clearly challenging, as the next case study illustrates. Mary's story is told to me by her supervisor in the merchandising department of a Fortune 500 company.

Mary was one of our most prized people, responsible for more creative concepts than any other person in the firm's history. Her creativity and her capacity for work were legendary. When she was given a project that caught her fancy, she could really make it fly. In searching for solutions, she was indefatigable; she worked long into the night. Mary's excitement during such an effort knew no bounds. And she had a knack for getting others involved. Working the way she did, and inspiring others to help, she produced incredible results.

But Mary was also problematic. Her mercurial temperament got her into trouble more often than most of us cared to remember. And there were many occasions when the flurry of her ideas generated confusion rather than clarity—when her reality-testing seemed to be impaired. At times like that, Mary was out of control. It was as if she abandoned all caution, all social constraint. She'd make irrelevant intrusions in social conversation and tell jokes that were completely out of place. When she was in one of these odd states, there was a certain disconnectedness about her. For example, the original focus of a conversation would sometimes be lost along the way. She would jump from one subject to the other. And her confusion was just as contagious as her enthusiasm. If I tried to get her to back off when she was like this, to retreat long enough to pull it together again, she was extremely unpleasant, not only to me but also to her co-workers.

There were many anecdotes about her in circulation. I remember hearing about the number of times that she left the office early and went on a buying spree, stretching her limited financial resources. Once, acting on impulse after spotting a gem in a used car lot, she returned to the office driving an old Austin Healey. Another time she enthusiastically made it known to all and sundry that she had just acquired a speedboat. She mentioned that she'd always wanted to try water skiing. Predictably, given such extravagances, her finances always seemed to be on the brink of disaster. She was given to excess with drink as well. Lots of times she came back from lunch quite intoxicated. And her appearance could change dramatically from one day to the next. At times she looked downright radiant, exuding energy; at other times she looked extremely haggard, as if she hadn't slept for weeks.

On a number of occasions we were quite worried about Mary. When she was in one of her low moods, she was *so* low that we were afraid she had suicidal tendencies. When an overexcited mood state had passed, she reacted with such self-disgust. She was haunted by acute feelings of shame over her bizarre and inappropriate behavior, her drinking, her violent reactions, and her financial escapades. I talked to her a few times when she was low—that was the only time she was open to this sort of conversation—affirming her contribution to the organization but also pointing out inappropriate behavior.

Mary was both stimulating and difficult. I recognized her emotional instability, and I worried a great deal about it, but I also valued her prodigious creative work. It was a trade-off really: I tolerated her eccentricities in order to keep her talent. That wasn't always a popular decision, though. I had to protect her politically when things got bad, and I certainly turned a blind eye to inappropriate behavior often enough.

HYPOMANIA IN THE WORKPLACE

The practical consequences of hypomania include career derailment, job loss, estrangement from friends and family members, major financial problems, drug abuse, alcoholism, and even hospitalization and suicide (or attempted suicide). These consequences are sufficiently serious that anybody associated with hypomanics needs to be on guard. Yet people close to the victims of this syndrome tend to engage in a conspiracy of silence, ignoring the symptoms (see Box 2.1) and denying that a problem exists.

Box 2.1   The Warning Signs of Hypomanic Behavior

What are the major indicators of hypomanic behavior? How do we recognize when something is wrong? The following questions help to determine whether a person tends towards hypomania.

- Does the person have grandiose ideas, make unrealistic plans, and exercise poor judgment?
- Is the person overtalkative and given to seeking out others aggressively (to the point that those others feel intruded upon)?
- Does the person laugh inappropriately and make inappropriate jokes?
- Does the person verbalize feelings of excessive well-being?
- Does the person seem to possess an inflated sense of self-esteem?
- Is the person unusually distractible, jumping from one subject to the next and exuding a physical restlessness?
- Is the person quickly irritated, tending to become extremely combative and argumentative when things do not go his or her way?
- Is the person overactive, trying to do too many things at once?
- Does the person appear to have unlimited energy and a markedly diminished need for sleep?
- Is the person sexually preoccupied and inclined to engage in sexual indiscretions?

- Is the person engaged in irrational financial activities, including massive overspending and unwise investments?
- On 'down' days, does the person obsess over past actions, berating him- or herself unduly?
- Does the person have a problem with drugs or alcohol?

When things get so bad that friends, co-workers, and family members can no longer ignore the problem, those interested parties still have to convince the hypomanic him- or herself of the need for change. At these times it is often hard to convince them that some form of intervention is needed. That task is further complicated when spontaneous remission occurs (as is often the case). During remission, the severity and nature of manic episodes is minimized or even forgotten, creating the illusion—for victim and associates alike—that the problem is under control. It is easy to underestimate the seriousness of the situation. People with affective disorders—like hypomania—are far more likely to commit suicide than individuals in any other psychiatric or medical risk group.

POSSIBLE INTERVENTIONS

Let's return to David Klein and think about what might be done to help him. What are his options? What would be the appropriate form of intervention? As we consider treating this disorder, we have to take some things as givens. The origins of hypomanic behavior seem to be physiological, tied to defects in the neurotransmitter system. Due to some as-yet-unidentified form of genetic vulnerability, these defects render the system unable to dampen unwanted oscillations and provide regulatory stability. In spite of the genetic underpinning, however, environmental stressors also appear to play a role. Hypomania is a chronic condition; it will not simply go away, even with treatment. As suggested there seems to be a genetic basis to bipolar disorder, which has been demonstrated through twin studies. Data from identical twins show that if one twin is bipolar, it is very likely that the other, if not bipolar him- or herself, will have a cyclothymic nature (Bertelsen, Harvald, and Hauge, 1977).

Bipolar disorder is also relatively common. This is bad news, to be sure, but there is good news to balance it: no other form of mental illness has been more profoundly affected by advances in neurophysiological research than bipolar disorders. Lithium and related drugs are highly effective in controlling the devastating effects of this dysfunctional state's more serious forms, allowing people to lead relatively normal lives. Many people have taken these medications with good results.

As David's case shows, however, there is a caveat to taking medication. When hypomanics are on lithium, they discover that they are just like everyone else—a goal that is desirable only when the going is rough. To be middle-of-the-road is not attractive to a person who has been on the mountaintop. Life in a medicated emotional state may seem flatter, less colorful, and less fun. Hypomanics with this reaction may continually compare their present state with the former in its best moments—those times when they were at their liveliest, most creative, and most outgoing. Missing the highs of hypomania (and the lively people they themselves were under its spell) may lead them to stop taking medication. In other words, there is an addictive quality to the hypomanic state. Treatment is complicated because once lithium is effective, people taking it often believe that they are able to handle things without it and refuse further treatment. It is no easy task to make people who do not want to take medication do so. After all, there are no pills for people who do not want to take pills.

The hope is, of course, that taking drugs for the regulation of moods will not limit the creative abilities of people with bipolar disorders. With the flood of new medications being developed for bipolar disorders, we are a long way from hearing the last word about the extent to which creativity and productivity are affected (if at all). At present, research shows conflicting findings on the effects of medication on creative achievement.

However, although there are real problems in giving pharmacological treatment to people with mood disorders the consequences of *not* doing so are far worse. If nothing is done about bipolar illness, it will progress, the mood swings becoming increasingly frequent and severe. Depression may intensify, increasing the risk of suicide. Modern medicine permits relief from the extremes of despair and chaotic behavior, allowing choices that were not previously available.

Psychotherapy in combination with medication can be a very effective means of treatment. Medication frees the person from the devastation caused by extreme depressive and manic episodes. Psychotherapy, for its part, helps the person deal with the disorder, assisting him or her to understand the psychological implications of mood swings and their aftermath and persuading him or her of the need to take medication to prevent a recurrence. Therapy can also be seen as a form of preventive maintenance: the hypomanic client, as a life strategy, takes steps to mitigate the expected fluctuations.

Of course, suggesting therapy is easier than initiating it, because hypomanics are not always the best listeners. While in a hypomanic state, they rarely have genuine insight into their condition. Furthermore, whether high or low, they may not have a good sense of how they are perceived by others. It is worth repeating that denial is a frequent defense mechanism among hypomanics—a mechanism that seriously impairs their critical faculty. In the hypomanic state, they are reluctant to admit the maladaptive nature of their behavior. For the hypomanic, *tout va bien*, there are no problems. However, as Mary's story shows, in their depressed state they tend to be more realistic about their abilities and possess more insight; for that reason, they are more easily reached when down.

So, what can be done to help a colleague who exhibits hypomanic characteristics? Partners and business associates can take on the 'container' role; that is, they can psychologically 'hold' the person while he or she is on a high or low, reining him or her in when necessary. Partnering that person with a sober mind can make for a more effective team. An organizational role constellation whereby other executives can exert a balancing influence is also useful. Colleagues can then caution the person before he or she plunges into ill-conceived business activities. Even the hypomanic who resents such warnings may heed them. In the case of the hypomanic who heads an organization, the role of non-executive board members as a balancing power is essential.

SELF-HELP MEASURES

Hypomanic people can do a lot to help themselves. David would do well to familiarize himself with the nature of hypomania, and to work with a mental-health professional to put together a treatment package. He can begin with a couple of commonsense steps toward stability. First, given his vulnerability to mood swings, he should pace himself; the potential for drama in his life is great enough as it is. Second, in both his private and his public life, he should avoid situations that aggravate his condition and create situations that do not.

Alongside these self-help measures, psychotherapy or some form of coaching may be some help to David. Medication, while a more extreme measure, should also be considered if his severe mood swings continue. The combination of psychotherapy and medication may help him stabilize his life.

To synthesize treatment modalities, David should also evolve a life strategy that allows his wife to have a balancing influence. Taking that step, while easier said than done, is likely to expedite therapeutic interventions. If the marriage has broken down irretrievably, he should look for another life partner—someone who shares his wife's 'containment' capabilities and can bring him to earth when he is flying too high. At work, he needs checks and balances in the form of other executives, as I have noted—people who can calm him down when his hypomanic behavior takes over, who can exert a sobering influence without destroying his creative potential (see Box 2.2).

Box 2.2   Coping Strategies

Executives working with hypomanics may feel their options for intervening are very limited since the hypomanic is unable to 'hear' most feedback. Indeed, sometimes the only real alternative for an executive is letting the hypomanic go, and the only real alternative for employees is reporting disturbing behavior over the hypomanic's head and/or transferring him or her out. However, it is worth trying the following first.

- Colleagues can build coalitions with other people in the organization to keep the hypomanic out of harm's way. This strategy does not address the underlying disorder, but it helps to minimize damage to the individual in question and to the organization.
- Colleagues can create a supportive environment. (This intervention is more difficult when the hypomanic is a senior-level executive.) In the case of Mary, her boss and colleagues recognized the symptoms of her hypomanic behavior—her long hours at the office, her bizarre shopping behavior, and her drinking spells, for example—and were put on guard. They tried to help her by creating a supportive environment, praising her achievements and showing that they really cared for her. Then, having earned Mary's trust, they pointed out the inappropriateness of some of her behavior. Such interventions were a great help to her.
- Colleagues can collaborate effectively with hypomanics, helping them to achieve organizational success. Partnering hypomanics with even-keeled colleagues—colleagues who have the power to dissuade them from plunging into ill-conceived ventures—often results in highly effective teams. The spouse can also be brought into the collaboration, if colleagues are acquainted with him or her and feel comfortable sharing their concerns. If the hypomanic is the CEO of an organization, the role of non-executive board members in this collaboration is critical.
- Colleagues can consult with experts in the human resources department. They can take on a mediating role, helping to clarify

the nature of the person's condition and suggesting avenues of treatment such as a leave of absence or referral to the employee health-assistance program.

- Family members and friends can perform a balancing function. Changes in sleep patterns, unusual sexual or financial behavior, expansiveness or undue enthusiasm, involvement in an excessive number of projects, and changes in judgment—symptoms that would be obvious to intimates—are signs of impending affective episodes. Family members can be crucially important to the hypomanic in making early interventions, such as contacting the clinician. They can encourage the hypomanic to avoid situations that aggravate mood state and to choose partners and organizations that moderate his or her inclinations. (Family counseling and therapy may be called for to encourage this sort of familial collaboration, since early and aggressive treatment can go a long way in stabilizing this condition.)

- Colleagues, family members, and friends can help to educate the hypomanic about the disorder. Insight into hypomania is the foundation of preventive maintenance. If hypomanics themselves can recognize the early signs and symptoms of elevated or depressed episodes, they can help to avert disaster.

- Colleagues, family members, and friends can encourage the hypomanic to seek treatment. The current treatment of choice is medication in combination with psychotherapy. Psychotherapy helps the person understand the psychological implications of mood swings and their aftermath, and the importance of taking the medication required to prevent recurrence; social support creates containment and serves as an early-warning system.

THE PLUS SIDE FOR ORGANIZATIONS

Executives caught up in the frenzy of Dionysian ecstasy dance a fine line between creative achievement and business catastrophe. Their decisions and actions, interpreted as bold and imaginative at the outset, may become disastrous. However, hypomanics who learn from their mistakes, who nurture their reflective capacities, who are able to put on the brakes when the alarm bells ring, who create life situations that have a balancing influence, can be a great asset to any organization. Their capacity to dream and set high goals, their positive attitude in the face of adversity, and their ability to inspire and energize go a long way toward giving their organization a competitive advantage as far as talent is concerned.

Samuel Beckett, in *Waiting for Godot*, wrote, 'We are all born mad. Some remain so.' It is to be hoped that we all retain a touch of madness. Without it, life in organizations would be pretty dull. Moreover, such dullness would lead to complacency, making us less creative and unprepared to deal with life's discontinuities.

ENDNOTES

This chapter collates material from two published sources:

- Kets de Vries, M.F.R. (1977). The Dionysian Quality of Charismatic Leadership. INSEAD working paper.
- Kets de Vries, M.F.R. (1999). 'Managing puzzling personalities: Navigating between "live volcanoes" and "dead fish",' *European Management Journal*, **17** (1): 8–19.

1. All names are fictitious.

CHAPTER 3

THE ALEXITHYMIC EXECUTIVE

The best way to become boring is to say everything.

—Voltaire

INTRODUCTION

In Chapter 2, I focused on leaders whose symptomatology is centered on their highs—individuals who can be extremely charismatic but are sometimes problematic to work with. There is another type of leader who presents a completely different picture: for them it is the lack of feeling rather than the excess of it that gives rise to difficulties. It is this type that I will be considering in this chapter. These people are unable to relate in depth to others, evidencing instead an emotional detachment. This detachment extends beyond relationships to every area of life. Feelings of zest, enthusiasm, and passion are non-existent; emotions are flattened; there is very little, if any, pleasure. In the absence of emotion, such people live in a world permeated by formalities and ritual. When this detachment appears in the workplace—especially in those holding senior executive positions—it affects other colleagues' morale, spontaneity, and productivity.

THE 'DEAD FISH' SYNDROME

In psychiatry the word alexithymic is applied to people who have a 'dead fish' quality—individuals who either struggle, or are unable, to understand their emotions or moods, who are incapable of perceiving the subtleties of mood change. The term 'alexithymia' was first coined in the early 1970s by Peter Sifneos, a Boston psychiatrist working with psychosomatic patients. The term is made up from the Greek, meaning 'no word for emotions.' In spite of its recent labeling, alexithymia is rooted in a large body of consistent clinical and phenomenological observations that telescope a number of well-recognized features into an easily communicated term. In a nutshell, alexithymia refers to a cluster of characteristics that includes an inability to describe feelings verbally, an impoverished fantasy life, and over-pragmatic, unimaginative thought content.

Executives in the grip of alexithymia have the power to bring down organizations. Because they do not exude the dynamism, inspiration, and vision that a high-performing organization needs, they cannot motivate others to make exceptional efforts or stimulate in them a passion for learning and further development. Because they do not handle discontinuous change well, they impede organizational progress. Their emotional absence puts its stamp on corporate culture, discouraging creativity and strategic innovation, and contributing to a decrease in organizational performance.

IDENTIFYING ALEXITHYMIA

So, what sort of person could be described as an alexithymic? Have you ever met a person like the one described by this executive?

> For years I worked with a robot. It would have driven me crazy to have him as a boss; he was bad enough as a colleague. Sometimes you didn't know whether to laugh or cry. I could give you so many examples. He had a son, a year or so older than mine. The kid got into a great school. I said, 'You must be so proud of him.' He said, 'You gotta have qualifications.' Another time, I knew he'd been to a function where a famous violinist—an idol of mine—was present. I asked him if he'd met him, and he had. I said, 'What was he like?'—you know, real excited, and he said, 'Small.' Like I say, you didn't know whether to laugh or cry.

Peter Sifneos used the term alexithymia to describe a condition in which individuals were unable to find words to describe emotions, habitually used actions to express emotion and avoid conflict, were preoccupied with external events rather than fantasies or feelings, and had a tendency to give tediously detailed descriptions of the circumstances surrounding events rather than attempt to describe their emotional reaction to the events themselves. Pursuing their research, he and a colleague identified alexithymia as a kind of communication disorder (Nemiah and Sifneos, 1970; Nemiah, 1977, 1978).

Henry Krystal, another psychiatrist working independently with patients suffering from severe posttraumatic states, was coming to the same conclusion. He noticed that alexithymic individuals 'are unable to distinguish between one emotion and another' (1979, p. 17), but 'like the color-blind person, they have become aware of their deficiency and have learned to pick up clues by which they infer what they cannot discern' (1979, p. 18).

Krystal observed that emotionally color-blind people are super-adjusted to reality and can function successfully at work. However, he also noted that once one gets 'past the superficial impression of superb functioning, one discovers a sterility and monotony of ideas and severe impoverishment of their imagination' (1979, p. 19).

Krystal noted an impaired capacity for empathy among alexithymics, who characteristically treat others with cool detachment and indifference. There is an absence of the human quality in the relationships they form; love objects are frequently interchanged. Krystal's observations were supported by others, who reported being left with feelings of fullness, boredom, and frustration when dealing with alexithymic individuals (Taylor, 1977).

Preoccupied with the concrete and objective, alexithymics also have no use for metaphors, allusions, and hidden meanings; such verbal tools are a foreign language to them.

Alexithymics remain unperturbed by the ups and downs of daily life—even by events that others would find emotionally shattering. A death in the family, a partner's infidelity, a friends' betrayal, being passed over for a promotion—nothing seems to ruffle them. All experiences slide into a black hole of inexpressiveness and blankness.

ALEXITHYMIA AS A COMMUNICATION DISORDER

The following interview between an executive and an organizational coach illustrates what it can be like dealing with an alexithymic.

Consultant: Can you say something about the kind of work you do?
Executive: I'm in charge of the planning department—have been since September three years ago. I joined the company two and a half years before that. Before signing on here I worked

five years for a large department store chain. I've always done similar work. In my role as planning director, I ask for input from the people responsible in other areas. It means a lot of e-mail. I compile the data I receive from those people into an integrated plan. I remind the heads of the various departments and regions of a number of specific deadlines that we have to meet. For example, there's the September date. You can see that on the flow chart [pointing]. Another date important for the planning cycle is in October. See how the numbers relate to each other? Some consolidation of input takes place in November. Of course, the whole planning process starts much earlier. I remind people by e-mail way back in March and then June that they have to come up with some provisional information by certain dates.

Consultant: Do you find that people take an active interest in the plan? They find it useful?

Executive: I don't know. But every company needs plans.

Consultant: Do you like the kind of work you do?

Executive: We *need* a plan, as I said. Without a plan many processes in this organization would come to a halt.

Consultant: Does your work involve a lot of personal interchanges with colleagues?

Executive: It could, but I try to minimize such interactions. I'm interested only in facts. I find that e-mail and the occasional memo serve me well; they get the job done with no waste of time.

Consultant: Are there certain things in the organization that irritate you, make you less effective?

Executive: Not really. With the plan things work fine.

Consultant: Can you say something more about yourself?

Executive: What else would you like to hear?

Consultant: I heard that you weren't considered for promotion to the board. Instead, a person who used to work for you got promoted. How did you feel about that? Were you very disappointed?

Executive: I don't understand your question.

Consultant: Did you feel hurt? Were you upset that someone else got promoted?

Executive: Not that I remember. Life in organizations is like that. It has its ups and downs.

Consultant: What about your physical well-being?

Executive: I sometimes have asthma attacks. They come and go. I also have stomach problems.

Consultant: Do you have any idea why you get these breathing and stomach problems? Do you feel that they're related to your job?

Executive: Well, I don't know exactly how to explain them. They're bothersome, that's for sure. I always get this stomach pain somewhere around here (gesturing). At times, it moves a bit. It comes and goes. I don't feel sorry for myself, though. I can live with it. Pills seem to help somewhat.

Consultant: Do you have any interests outside work?

Executive: Not many. I'm building a garage, though. I like masonry, working with bricks.

Consultant: Are you married?

Executive: I used to be. My wife doesn't live with me anymore. One day she told me that she'd had enough. I still don't understand what was wrong. I thought everything was fine. She just started screaming at me one day and then left. She asked for a divorce, but I don't know what the grounds were.

Consultant: Do you ever dream or daydream?

Executive: No, I don't remember any dreams.

Consultant: Do you have wild fantasies?

Executive: What did you say?

Consultant: Wild fantasies—do you ever have them?

Executive: I don't understand.

Consultant: Fantasies about doing something completely different, for example. Take Gauguin, who decided to become a painter and left his family to live on a Polynesian island after working as a bank teller for years.

Executive: I still don't know what you mean.

Consultant: How do you feel now?

Executive: I don't know what you expect me to say when you ask me how I feel. I told you I have stomach aches.

WHERE DO THE ORIGINS OF ALEXITHYMIA LIE?

All the studies indicate that, as a communication disorder, alexithymia is relatively widespread. As with any clinical syndrome, however, estimates of its prevalence among the general population vary. For example, one study carried out among undergraduate students suggested that 8.2% of the men and 1.8% of the women could be defined as having alexithymic tendencies (Blanchard, Arena, and Pallmeyer, 1981), although the validity and reliability of the instruments used in this particular study are questionable. But whatever the exact proportion of alexithymics in the general population, there is considerable confusion about the etiology of alexithymia. Is it genetically or developmentally based? Is it a character trait or a situation-specific form of coping behavior? Is it the price that has to be paid for emotional labor and stress? Could it be both trait and state (Von Rad, 1984; Ahrens and Deffner, 1986)? No clear answer has been found.

A number of explanations have been proposed for this kind of disorder—some physiological, some psychological. Researchers offering a physiological answer see it as a deficit in the connection between the left and right hemispheres of the brain. They believe that something has gone very wrong with the 'wiring' between these two parts. Researchers, who see the origins as more psychological in nature, point to the person's early relationships with the primary caregiver. The origin of this behavior, the psychoanalyst Joyce McDougall speculates, is a particular style of parenting, whereby the mother tends to use the child as a 'drug' (1974, 1980, 1982a, 1982b) and is apparently out of touch with the child's emotional needs.

> Infants constantly send out signals to their mothers regarding their wants and dislikes. Depending on her freedom from inner pressures, a mother will normally be in close communication with her infant over these signals. If internal distress and anxiety prevent her observing and interpreting her baby's cries, smiles, and gestures correctly, she may, on the contrary, do violence to the tiny communicator by imposing her own needs and wishes, thus plunging the infant into a continuously frustrating and rage-provoking experience. Such an eventuality runs the risk of impelling the baby to construct, with the means at its disposal, radical ways of protecting itself against overwhelming affect storms and subsequent exhaustion. (McDougall, 1989, p. 26)

Because separation is discouraged by the mother, any desire the child shows for exploration or any form of initiative is nipped in the bud. Predictably, this sort of treatment has grave consequences for later personality development. In alexithymic individuals, the ability to differentiate and verbalize emotions never develops properly; this inability to recognize emotions in turn impedes the construction of the highly complex matrix of emotional signals on which we all rely for daily functioning and without which emotions are experienced as dangerous, potentially uncontrollable forces. Alexithymics ignore the distress signals given by their mind and body. Their fantasy life may become stilted; they are out of touch with their psychic world. Moreover, given the state of dependence to which they have become accustomed, they may become addicted to external stimuli as ways of giving structure to their world, unable as they are themselves to resort to their own symbolic representations, fantasies, or dreams to work through mental conflict. They need others to tell them how they feel.

In the case of these individuals, the general human tendency towards mirroring (seeing in others what we would like to see in ourselves) seems to have been carried *ad absurdum*. In McDougall's words, what they feel 'will appear in the people [they are] involved with. They are [their] mirror' (1982a, p. 88). They attempt 'to make substitute objects in the external world do duty for symbolic ones which are absent or damaged in the inner psychic world' (1974, p. 449).

In general, alexithymic people are preoccupied with the concrete and objective. Psychologically, they seem to be almost illiterate, lacking any capacity for empathy or self-awareness and resorting to action as a way of dealing with conflicts (Neill and Sandifer, 1982; Lesser and Lesser, 1983; Taylor, 1984; Taylor *et al.*, 1999). McDougall terms their behavior an 'activity addiction': 'a drug-like relationship to their daily work or to numerous other activities (which sometimes do not even interest them), with the unconscious aim of leaving no room for relaxation or daydreaming.' These people are continually involved in 'doing' rather than in 'being' or 'experiencing' (1989, p. 97). Given their capacity to negate and deny emotions, people with alexithymic tendencies do not experience, nor are they aware of, intrapsychic conflict. Their physical behavior can seem robotic, accompanied by stiffness of posture and a lack of facial expressiveness. External details seem to be used as a way of filling their inner deadness. They have never been permitted to experiment with their own feelings.

DEGREES OF ALEXITHYMIA

Alexithymia is not an all-or-nothing phenomenon. It exists along a continuum of affective experience and expression. Some researchers, however, make a distinction between primary and secondary alexithymia. The former implies a real deficit in experiential thinking. Because it is a relatively permanent condition, it is the more difficult one of the two to change. Secondary alexithymia, generally the result of certain developmental restrictions, manifests itself as alexithymic-like behavior. People belonging to certain national cultures may show these characteristics; we have only to think of stereotypical descriptions—cold, emotionless, reserved—that we apply to some cultures. In this sub-type, alexithymic reactions may also be a consequence of external influences at later life stages, including the workplace.

In some organizations—those that frown on any form of emotional expression—alexithymic-like behavior is a necessary survival strategy. In addition, certain industries or functional specializations may attract people with alexithymic-like tendencies. Because it is more circumstance-specific than primary alexithymia, secondary alexithymia is more temporary than its counterpart. It is also more prevalent; indeed, all of us might react in an alexithymic-like fashion in certain situations.

ALEXITHYMICS IN THE WORKPLACE

Many organizations offer environments that legitimize behavior that would be seen as strange in a different setting. In doing so, they give those with an alexithymic disposition a form of relief, in that they provide some kind of structure. This structure helps disguise alexithymic behavior and provides a 'containing' environment (Bion, 1961). Alexithymics are frequently extremely successful, particularly within large organizations where playing safe, making the right noises, predictability, and relative inconspicuousness are rewarded. Many organizations favor predictability over maverick and innovative behavior because people who do not take risks do not make expensive mistakes. However, employing such people not only creates the possibility of providing entirely the wrong sort of role model for other executives but also contributes to mediocrity, which drives out excellence.

Two types of organization seem to cultivate alexithymic behavior: the compulsive and the depressive. The compulsive organization is bureaucratic and tends to be inwardly focused. It usually has a rigid hierarchy, in which individual status is related to job title. The leadership dominates the organization from top to bottom, demanding strict conformity to rules and procedures.

The depressive organization is in many ways similar, but actually in worse shape. It frequently drifts with no sense of direction and is often confined to antiquated, so-called mature markets. Its survival depends on protectionist practices, and it is characterized by extreme conservatism, a vague set of goals and strategies, and an absence of planning. Structurally, these organizations are bureaucratic, ritualistic, and inflexible. There is a leadership vacuum, a lack of motivation and initiative, and an attitude of passivity and negativity. Many state-owned companies fall into this category, although they can often continue to operate in this way for considerable lengths of time because of government protection.

Both of these types of organization provide ideal camouflage for people with an alexithymic disposition because the expression of affect or emotion is not often readily permitted.

THE ALEXITHYMIC CEO

It is possible to identify several different types of top executive who demonstrate alexithymic tendencies.

The Detached CEO

Occasionally top executives experience great difficulty in dealing with emotions. To protect themselves from emotional involvement, these people develop a detached leadership style. Their emotional isolation, however, can have serious organizational repercussions. In one organization, the CEO was described as 'the Yeti, living at great heights and occasionally sighted in cold places.' This man was very much a loner, quite uncomfortable with other people, and appeared awkward, stiff, and humorless. This personal style would have mattered little if it had affected only himself, but unfortunately he was running a large organization. His detachment from the day-to-day functioning of the company had serious implications for corporate culture and the policy-making process. As his key executives were unsure what was expected of them, they withdrew into their own territories and began to create personal empires. The consequences were lack of co-operation, sub-optimization, escalation of internal conflict, and an inconsistent strategy—factors that seriously affected the organization's bottom line.

The Systems Person

For many people with communication difficulties associated with an alexithymic disposition, the technology revolution has been a tremendous facilitator. The internet has given many of these people a way of disguising their problems in communicating. Problems the individual might have in relating to others are disguised by his or her successful interaction with a computer. The systems person operates in an automaton-like way, clinging to fixed routines and avoiding real relationships with people. All relationships have a pseudo-quality. His or her direction is set by the terminal of a computer, which also seems to furnish all the stimulation such a person requires. Systems-oriented organizations provide a holding environment par excellence for these alexithymics; they can resort to jobs that are thing-oriented, where their attention is focused on abstractions, tasks, ideas, and inanimate objects. Their attachment to machines is a way of coping with the sterility of their inner world. Although many alexithymics can function extremely well in these circumstances, their often mindless and inflexible pursuit of routines means that curiosity and initiative are missing. They probably will not be sufficiently adaptable to cope with environmental changes, a deficiency that can have devastating repercussions for an organization.

The Social Sensor

> It's difficult to describe the atmosphere when he was around. He was like the grown-up who switches on the light in the nursery and all the toys, which were magically running around, freeze and turn into toys again. You'd see the effect on people new to the department. They'd start by saying how charming he was then after a while the uneasiness and bewilderment would set in. Getting to know him was like digging a hole in the sand. You keep hoping you're going to hit something but the further down you get, the more wet sand you find, and then the sides fall in and undo all your work. He seemed so interested in people, always asking questions, always laughing. After a while you realized the questions were his way of keeping you at a distance, and he laughed at everything just in case it was amusing, because he had no natural sense of humor.

These remarks made by a top executive about a colleague indicate the kind of atmosphere the social sensor creates. The social sensor is in many ways a chameleon, quick to pick up signals from the outside world and adjust his or her behavior accordingly. Predictably, social sensors fit very well in service-oriented industries, where prescribed emotions are the norm. However, despite all their efforts, and notwithstanding this superficial capacity for adjustment, their actions lack conviction. Although they may give an initial impression of complete normality and super-adaptability, under this veneer one rapidly uncovers a desperate shallowness and lack of real warmth. There will be a lack of authenticity. Changeability is their only fixed characteristic, resulting in pseudo-sincerity and pseudo-authenticity. Their super-adaptability and compliance have only one goal, which is to avoid having to deal with feelings. What appears as adaptability is really insensitivity to the feelings and reactions of people around them. The mask of extroversion is a disguise for the emptiness of their inner world, which handicaps their creativity and insight.

WORKING WITH AN ALEXITHYMIC MANAGER

The difficulties inherent in working with an alexithymic boss are obvious in the following example of Simon, an upper-level boss in an insurance company. Arthur, a newcomer and Simon's subordinate, describes the situation:

> From day one I tried to develop a relationship with Simon, but it felt like I was talking to a brick wall. Conversations with him were incredibly draining, because he exuded a stifling sense of dullness and boredom. In the beginning I wondered if something was wrong with *me*—if *I* was the problem. But I'd never had trouble building relationships in previous jobs. In talking with a number of colleagues, I learned that they'd had the same experience. They felt that communicating with Simon was like being face-to-face with a black hole that sucked up energy. They'd given him the nickname Tin Man, from *The Wizard of Oz*, because he seemed to find the expression of emotions so dangerous.
>
> True enough, Simon made all the right noises when I talked to him. He knew the terminology of business. But that's where it ended. His song had lots of words but no music. I could literally feel his emotional absence. He wasn't the kind of person who could get the best out of others. The words 'vision' and 'inspiration' seemed foreign to him, and as a result he couldn't 'stretch' employees. He just didn't know how to develop people. Feedback was another one of his weak points. He never once complimented me, or anyone else to my knowledge, for a job well done. The most people could expect of him was a rather sterile memo when targets weren't met.
>
> Simon believed that the organization had its set ways of doing things, and that those ways had to be followed. Deviation from the rules was dangerous. His preferred way of communicating was by e-mail, even though my desk was almost within arm's reach of his. He avoided direct interaction of any kind, even when we had conflict within the team. He'd either withdraw or refer us to obscure policies, leaving us to sort out the problem.
>
> In my entire working career, I've never had such a demotivating experience. Whenever I came up with a new business idea, Simon would tell me to be careful, warn me not to rock the boat. Dealing with discontinuities in the environment just wasn't his strength. You

might say that 'incrementalism' was written on his banner. It was extremely frustrating for me to see one opportunity after the other slip away. Eventually I gave up trying anything new. Simon's approach—not rocking the boat—may have been successful in the past, but by the time I came on board the industry had been transformed. His wait-and-see philosophy had become so dangerous that our competitive position was slipping.

After a while, this sense of stagnation on the job—the fact that I wasn't learning anything new and couldn't try anything different—began to haunt me. I finally made up my mind to try to get a position in another part of the organization, and I also put out feelers to a headhunter. When the headhunter came up with an interesting offer, I jumped at it. After all, life isn't a rehearsal. Any additional day of work under Simon would have been a complete waste of time. And I wasn't alone in that feeling; many other competent people also left the organization because they lacked stimulation.

MANAGING AN ALEXITHYMIC

People who are managed by alexithymics sense their dullness and boredom quickly, and they become frustrated when attempts at interaction fail. However, managing alexithymics is equally challenging. Let's look at the case of Peter. A senior vice-president of a large bank, he was wondering whether he should fire Richard, the leader of one of his project teams.

When I was put in charge of integrating a newly acquired bank with one of the main operations in our organization, I inherited Richard. He had been working in the acquired bank's research department; and since that department was being eliminated, I decided to test Richard's leadership abilities by putting him in charge of a project team studying the feasibility of private banking in Eastern Europe. The team's been on the job a few months now, but there's been very little progress. I asked for, and was promptly given, a progress report, but it detailed only the sketchiest of efforts. The only action I can see is people leaving: there's been a disturbingly high turnover rate among the members of Richard's project team.

I find it difficult to deal with Richard, in part because he always speaks and acts stiltedly. At first I attributed his speech pattern to shyness, and I thought that his formality might be a product of the more rigid corporate culture he came out of. But now, I think this is only partially true. Having gotten to know several other executives at the acquired bank, I realize that these behavioral characteristics are more idiosyncratic. I can't really put my finger on what makes Richard seem so lifeless, but sometimes I feel like kicking him just to see how he'd react. I get worn out just talking to him, because I work so hard to get a human response. Not even humor works. Getting a laugh out of him is a major achievement.

True enough, Richard makes all the right motions. He can generally be found busily scuttling around the corridors, for example. But where does he go, and what does he do? Having seen his report, I know he doesn't do much. And seeing those meager results, I've had a chat or two with the other team members. They obviously find him difficult to deal with too. I have the sense that he's stifling their creativity. It's almost like there's a negative contagion.

I finally talked to someone from the human resources department, and she supported the negative contagion idea. She mentioned having heard from other people about problems with Richard's team. In fact, she was of the opinion that it *isn't* a team. The only thing that binds these people together, in her view, is a common sense of resentment toward Richard. He's very inflexible in dealing with personnel problems, according to everyone she's spoken with. She mentioned one incident as an example—something I hadn't heard about directly. Apparently one of the members of the project team, a very good employee who was a single father, had a sick child at home. He asked Richard for a temporary leave, a few weeks at most, and the request was denied. He then asked to be allowed to do some of his work from home. Richard showed no understanding of the situation, no compassion. He told the man that since he himself was under great pressure to get his job done, he expected work at full throttle from everyone on the team. The rules applied to everybody, he said. The next day this man submitted his resignation.

That conversation with the HR person sort of clarified things for me. Although I don't see myself as a hard-nosed executive, I know now that I have to do something. I owe it to the remaining team members. Clearly, Richard isn't capable of running a high-performance team. But I don't know whether that means he has to go, or whether there's something I could do to help him become more effective in dealing with people to increase his emotional expressiveness. And if he does have to go, could we just move him into a more suitable position elsewhere in the organization? Or is he hopeless?

What, then, are the major indicators of alexithymia? Box 3.1 contains a list of typical warning signs.

Box 3.1   Warning Signs of Alexithymia

- Does the person have difficulty communicating with other people?
- Does the person describe details *ad nauseam* but never mention feelings?

- Does the person use action to express emotion?
- Does the person appear confused about the emotions he or she feels?
- Does the person describe the circumstances rather than the feelings surrounding an event?
- Is the person preoccupied with physical problems?
- Does the person suffer from an absence of fantasy and imagination?
- Do dreams and daydreams play a negligible role in the person's life?
- Does the person prefer movies with action over psychological dramas?
- Is the person's thought content associated more with external events than with fantasy or emotion?
- Does the person find life pretty boring most of the time, rarely exhibiting excitement?
- When talking with such a person, do you yourself become bored and frustrated, eager to get away from him or her?

SEARCHING FOR SOLUTIONS

The fact that some executives possess or are susceptible to the alexithymic disposition, whether primary or secondary, does not mean that the situation is unchangeable. However, breaking the vicious circle of emotionlessness is not easy, and, unfortunately, there is no quick remedy for the situation. If change is desired, if there is a wish to enliven organizational life, a sustained effort is necessary.

From an institutional perspective, the organization can make structural arrangements that encourage experimentation and participation. In order to foster such behavior, there is also a need for imaginative hiring, training, and development practices, which will, in turn, avoid the creation of organizations populated by clones. Enough flexibility should be built into organizational systems and culture to allow for continuous adaptations and developments. Organizations should do what they can to avoid alexithymic characteristics becoming part of their culture.

Coping Strategies

So how do we deal with alexithymics in the workplace? The answer depends on whether we are dealing with primary alexithymia (where the etiology seems to be associated with genetic neurophysiological or anatomical deficits) or secondary alexithymia (where developmental or socio-cultural factors play a greater role). The ideas given in Box 3.2 may be helpful.

Box 3.2 Strategies for Managing Alexithymic Staff

- *We can move people into jobs that highlight their strengths.* While this intervention applies whether the alexithymia is primary or secondary, it is restricted to lower-level employees rather than more senior executives—who have to do more people management. While we certainly don't want to include them in high-performance teams or in people management positions, there may be a place for them in jobs where emotional management is secondary. Every company has at least a few positions where a detail-oriented, mechanical approach is helpful and people contact is minimal—certain positions in data processing, for example.

- *Corporate cultures that encourage alexithymic-like behavior can be changed.* If people exhibiting alexithymic-like behavior join an organization after a stint with a firm that has a repressive emotional company culture, they can be 'cured.' It is an uphill battle, however, if the current organization is itself repressive, rewarding emotionless interaction. In such situations, senior executives (most likely coming from the outside) play an important part by providing an alternative role model. They can validate and encourage the expression of emotion, facilitating fun and creativity as well as allowing people to deal with anger and dissatisfaction. If the senior executives are convincing—that is, if employees believe that emotional expressiveness will no longer have negative consequences, that it is an important part of effective work behavior—they may inspire other executives and employees to rise to the occasion.

- *We can attempt to help secondary alexithymics become better at dealing with emotional issues.* We can team them with colleagues who have a more expressive disposition, assisting the former to become more daring with their emotions. Although change will take considerable effort—these patterns may be deeply rooted—it can be achieved. Alexithymics can discover the emotional poten-

---

tial hidden deep within them. Like the Tin Man, once he discovered that he had a heart, they will learn not to be afraid of expressing themselves. Such a change in relating goes a long way towards raising morale, inspiring, and getting the best out of people, making the organization a more exciting place to work.

- *We can encourage alexithymics (whether primary or secondary) to seek outside help.* Performance appraisal conducted via a 360-degree feedback system—that is, a system that gives feedback from superiors, colleagues and subordinates—is useful in this regard. The results of such an appraisal may indicate to the person in question that he or she has 'dead fish' behavior problems. If the appraisers present a consensus that the person's style is not effective, he or she may see the need for help. A host of therapies are available for people who have difficulties with emotional expressiveness. Psychodynamically oriented and supportive psychotherapy can be beneficial, for example, as can group and family therapy, in which group members and spouses lend assistance as educators of emotions. Through these various kinds of interventions, alexithymics can learn to recognize, tolerate, and verbalize different feelings, and they have the chance to practice their capacity for reflective self-observation. Behavioral techniques such as biofeedback, relaxation training, autogenic training, guided imagery, and hypnosis may also be of some help with both forms of alexithymia. These techniques give people a sense of control over stressful responses and increase their awareness of the relationship between bodily sensations and environmental events.
- *We can refer alexithymics to the human resources department.* HR people can play an important role in pointing out a variety of ways to tackle the problem. They might direct the person to selected leadership seminars of a more experiential nature with individual and group feedback, for example, or recommend a leadership coach. Feedback given at appropriate times by people in the seminar or by coaches could help these people to be more daring in their emotional expressiveness. Apart from these more easily accepted solutions, they might also outline the various therapeutic approaches cited above.

ENDNOTE

Material for this chapter has been taken from two published sources:

* Kets de Vries, M.F.R. (1993). *Leaders, Fools and Impostors*. San Francisco: Jossey-Bass.
* Kets de Vries, M.F.R. (1999). 'Managing puzzling personalities: Navigating between "live volcanoes" and "dead fish",' *European Management Journal*, **17** (1): 8–10.

CHAPTER 4

THE IMPOSTOR SYNDROME

The more gross the fraud the more glibly will it go down, and the more greedily be swallowed, since folly will always find faith where impostors will find imprudence.

—Charles Caleb Colton

INTRODUCTION

Throughout history, we have been fascinated by the figures of impostors. People leading fraudulent lives or engaging in fraudulent action always seem to have had a fatal attraction. One reason for their popularity may be that there is an element of recognition present in the encounter between impostors and their audiences. It often seems as if impostors show us something about ourselves that we may prefer not to see under normal circumstances. And to some extent (given the differences between the public and private self), we are all impostors, we all play roles (Goffman, 1971). Presenting a façade and misleading the audience is part and parcel of everyday life.

This stage role becomes more prominent when we move to a public setting such as an organization (Goffman, 1971). Entrepreneurs are more inclined than other business people to take on elements of the impostor role, given the inherent drama in the act of creation (in which they are trying to turn their fantasies into some form of reality). In their intense need to pursue a vision and convince others of their ideas, they may resort to distortion of facts, and be cavalier about what is reality. However, the enthusiasm they generate in selling their dreams, unrealistic or ill-defined as they may be, is important because it makes them catalysts of change and, if successful, a main source of economic development.

How, then, does one become an impostor? What do impostors want? Why do impostors behave the way they do? What makes them so fascinating? Why can they be so self-destructive? Is there an element of the impostor in all of us?

Defining Terms

The term 'impostor' actually has two connotations, which are often present concurrently. In the *Oxford English Dictionary* we find a description of the impostor as someone who imposes on others—a deceiver, swindler, or cheat. The other meaning is a person who assumes a false character or passes him- or herself off as someone other than he or she really is. However, we can find situations where the two roles are combined, in that a person takes on a false identity in order to swindle others. But we also encounter individuals who pass themselves off as someone else without obtaining any visible benefits. The situation in which a person assumes a false character in order to engage in some form of swindling is more common. Nevertheless, financial gain should probably be looked at as a means to an end, not as the principal reason for the impostor's actions. Psychological gratification often seems to be much more important. Moreover, imposture may be more universal than we might expect. Clinical investigation suggests that it may be a characteristic with a range going from feeling like a fraud without reason, to being actively involved in imposturous activities.

Impostors in Literature

Examples of imposture can be found in many different sources. The Old Testament story of Jacob's impersonation of Esau to win his birthright is perhaps the most famous. Another well-loved example of an impostor in early literature is Till Eulenspiegel. This German folk hero, whose name means 'owl mirror,' was a professional confidence man, jester, and self-styled philosopher reputed to be a real person who lived in the fourteenth century (Oppenheimer, 1972). Till Eulenspiegel's name is symbolic in that he 'wisely reflects' aspects of the audience's character—warts and all—at the same time as he is duping them.

Novelists also have been fascinated by impostors. Cervantes' Don Quixote de la Mancha is a famous literary example of a form of imposture. His is the story of an elderly knight confused by having read too many romances, who replaces reality with fantasy, acting out a life filled with delusion, fighting windmills along the way. Then we have *The Confidence Man* by Herman Melville (1954), which takes place in a fictional world populated by impostors where everyone seems to play a role. The naïve reader is deceived by the novel as much as the victims of the confidence man himself. A more specific example of the impostor in literature is the well-known *Confessions of Felix Krull, Confidence Man* (1969). This is Thomas Mann's uncanny description of the archetypal impostor, a person remarkable for his ability to win the favor and love of others by playing whatever role they desire, and taking advantage of everyone he encounters—seemingly without experiencing a trace of guilt.

Impostors in the Business World

A memorable example of imposture in a business setting was the case of Anthony De Angelis whose manipulation of millions of gallons of non-existent salad oil sent two Wall Street brokerage houses to bankruptcy, caused the failure of a subsidiary of the American Express Company, and led to plummeting futures prices on commodity markets in New York and Chicago (Miller, 1965). Although financial gain certainly played a role in this instance, De Angelis also created a remarkable world of make-believe to satisfy his need for recognition. He outsmarted dozens of the shrewdest bankers, brokers, and businessmen. While his scam was going on, however, nobody wondered how he could make money by selling salad oil at such impossibly low prices. Financiers rushed to lend him more money for the next deal. The wish to believe, fueled by greed, made even the most astute businessman suspend reality. Eventually, the financiers were holding papers for astounding quantities of salad oil, more than could be accounted for according to government reports about existing stocks. But still nobody was alarmed. Only after eight years of operation did the bubble burst, after De Angelis could no longer maintain his position in the future vegetable oil market and the authorities discovered that his salad oil tanks were empty.

Another unusual example of an impostor was Frank Abagnale—a con man who once was one of the most wanted fugitives in the world (Abagnale and Redding, 2000). His life story has been depicted in the film *Catch Me If You Can* (2002). At one time this impostor was wanted in 26 countries and 50 states. Abagnale successfully masqueraded as an airline pilot, a doctor, and a lawyer for nearly five years, while living luxuriously off the $2.5 million he cashed in forged checks. Most remarkably, he succeeded in doing all this before his twenty-first birthday. Aided by gray streaks in his hair and a belief that a uniform is the best prop in selling a scam, the 16-year-old Abagnale, who was raised in Bronxville, started posing as a Pan Am pilot. This disguise allowed him to travel the globe for free and aided his check-cashing con game. Abagnale was like a chameleon, able to adapt to any surrounding. Even when he was apprehended he would often find a way out. While being extradited from Sweden to the United States, he escaped from an airplane. Later, while serving time in an Atlanta prison, he escaped by talking his way out. Today, however, Abagnale is a legitimate businessman. One of the world's foremost self-taught authorities on fraud, he is a consultant for Fortune 500 companies, which he helps to keep up-to-date on scam technology. He has also been a consultant for the FBI.

Other Kinds of Impostor

There is a rather unusual psychiatric classification of imposture, the Münchausen syndrome, a condition named after Baron Münchhausen, a mythical German soldier–adventurer who lived in the eighteenth century and became known as the hero of many tall tales (Lehmann, 1975; Swanson, 1981). In this condition, the medical field is chosen as the stage on which these individuals play out their conflicts centered on aggression and dependency. The condition is characterized by repeated fabrication of clinically convincing symptoms and a false medical and social history. The affected person exaggerates or creates symptoms of illness in order to gain investigation, treatment, attention, sympathy, and comfort from medical personnel.

WHAT MAKES AN IMPOSTOR?

The earliest known clinical paper on the impostor was written by Karl Abraham (1955) who described the adventures of a conscript in the army. As an army doctor, Abraham was requested by a military court to make an investigation of the conscript. He wrote in his case history how impressed he was by the person's ability to gain the trust of others (including his jailers). Abraham was particularly struck by his 'genius at phantastic story telling' and his 'uncontrollable desire for aggrandisement' (p. 294). As an explanation, Abraham suggested that since this particular individual 'felt himself unloved in his childhood, he had an inner urge to show himself "loveable" to everybody ... to prove to himself and to show them soon afterward how unworthy he was of such feeling' (p. 300).

Abraham also pointed to the individual's longing for rich parents, symptomatic of what is called in clinical literature the 'family romance,' meaning the perpetuation of a relatively common childhood fantasy that one's parents are not one's real ones and that one is really of noble or royal descent. The parents are consequently viewed as frauds. The fantasy that somewhere out there, there must be some other, better, more understanding parents, lingers on. This feeling is triggered by the child's experience of parents who were not sufficiently responsive to its needs for recognition and independence. Family-romance fantasies are forms of compensatory narcissistic self-enhancement, attempts to regulate self-esteem (Kaplan, 1974). These fantasies contribute to the development of a 'personal myth' (Kris, 1975)—a fusion of early memories and fantasies that organizes later experience. Abraham also comments on the strong self-defeating streak in the conscript's behavior in that 'he never showed much aptitude for eluding the arm of the law' (p. 292).

In her discussion of impostors, Helen Deutsch (1965) inferred that they assume the identities of others 'not because they themselves lack the ability for achievement, but because they have to hide under a strange name to materialize a more or less reality-adapted fantasy' (p. 332). She suggested that 'the ego of the impostor, as expressed in his own true name, is devaluated, guilt-laden' (p. 332). No wonder such a person feels compelled to function under other, more glorious covers that are more in line with his or her magnificent ego ideal—i.e. his or her conception of how he or she really wishes to be.

Deutsch inferred from her case example that the unusual behavior of the impostor is caused by the emotional 'overfeeding' of the child by the mother, the former being smothered by all her affections. The father's behavior may have aggravated the situation, since he may have overburdened the child by making him or her recipient of his unfulfilled desires. In her discussion, Deutsch also referred to individuals who, after having achieved success, are troubled by the feeling that they are impostors. In the case of her patient she commented that 'the more effectively [he] functioned in reality, the more anxiety he developed ... he felt like an impostor in his new role, that of doing honest work' (p. 333).

Phyllis Greenacre (1958) postulated some basic constellations of disturbing symptoms in the case of imposture: 'first, the dominant and dynamically active family romance; second the intensive and circumscribed disturbance of the sense of identity, a kind of infarction in the sense of reality; third, a malformation of the superego involving both conscience and ideals' (p. 96). She commented on impostors' apparent need for self-betrayal, struck as she was by the discrepancy in their abilities, where 'skill and persuasiveness are combined with utter foolishness and stupidity' (p. 97). Greenacre recognized the necessity of the confirming reaction of the audience to help the impostor establish a realistic sense of self.

She traced the genesis of this behavior to a family background where the parents are at odds with each other and where the child is treated with extreme possessiveness by the mother, used as an item of exhibitionistic display, and not regarded as a separate person in his or her own right. At the same time, the mother may downgrade the father as being ineffective and disappointing. Greenacre postulated a serious imbalance in the Oedipal situation, with the child (in the case of a male impostor) seemingly superseding the father's role in the family. She argued that the child is forced into an adult role prematurely. In order to maintain this position and gain, and continue to capture, the admiration of grown-ups, the child will develop astounding talents in mimicry, i.e. the ability to imitate adult behavior. Unfortunately, the price of such a developmental track is often the lack of a well-formed separate self and a poor sense of identity and reality.

In his discussion of imposture, Finkelstein (1974) presented one of his patients, 'The Great Teddy,' as he called himself, who was busily acting out typical family-romance fantasies and demonstrating his narcissistic needs by, for example, elevating his parents' status. Finkelstein emphasized Teddy's great talents in the art of illusion and his ability to discover what his audience really wanted. The psychological defense mechanisms of denial, rationalization, and splitting enabled him to act out his unconscious fantasies (Klein, 1988; Freud, 1966). Moreover, because of these defenses, he was able to deceive his audience without experiencing any conflict with existing reality. In explaining Teddy's behavior, Finkelstein highlighted the role of the parents. He describes how poorly the mother was attuned to Teddy's needs and used him almost like an extension of herself, turning him into a demonstration piece. Her relationship to him was characterized by superficiality, as she had no concern for real, substantial issues. Outside appearances were all that mattered. In addition, in this family constellation, the mother–child interface had an element of seduction, which left Teddy with the impression that his mother very much preferred him to his father.

Teddy's parents instilled in him a highly unrealistic image of himself that became the basis for his later deceitful practices. In addition, lying and pretending were a common pattern among all family members. All of them seemed to live out the fantasy of being a wonderful family, whereas the reality was quite different. Consequently, quite early in life

Teddy became familiar with role-playing and imposture. To use Finkelstein's (1974) words, '[his] parents not only encouraged him to become
an impostor; they also provided characteristics for him to identify with,
particularly his mother's lying and her interest in superficial appearances
and his father's abilities as a glib talker' (p. 110). By being an impostor,
a liar, and a pretender, Teddy was in a way behaving and acting exactly
the way his parents wanted.

THE CREATIVE ARTIST AS IMPOSTOR

Someone in whom the crisis of identity, the power of language, and the
skill of myth-making met and combined with both creative and tragic
results was the eighteenth-century English poet, Thomas Chatterton.
Chatterton was the posthumous son of a Bristol schoolmaster and was
raised by his mother and sister. He was precocious and brilliant, and by
the time he was 16 had already written the poems on which his reputation rests. However, he passed the poems off as medieval manuscripts
that he had found in an old chest, producing further faked documents
to back up his discovery. When his fraud was exposed, Chatterton fled
to London, where, in misery and poverty, he took his own life at the
age of 17. What were Chatterton's poems about?

> Chatterton [fabricated] in his writings an imaginatively conceived family
> romance, which even included a perfected medieval city of Bristol, chang-
> ing it to a radiant 15th-century metropolis whose cultural centre was the
> very church in which generations of Chattertons had been the sextons.
> Written at what must often have been white heat, in an ostensible Middle
> English which was really his own neologistic invention, he idealized and
> fictionalized an actual 15th-century Bristol merchant and mayor into a
> saint-like philanthropist, warrior, and humanitarian, a man of the world
> who lived an exemplary religious life and who commissioned a priest-poet,
> Rowley, to write the chronicles and to eulogize the city's history. The
> evidence suggests that Rowley was a perfected projection of Chatterton
> himself, while the saintly merchant, Canynge, was his father. (Olinick,
> 1988, `p. 674)

Any writer of fiction can be said to be continually engaging in a form
of harmless imposture, requiring the willing collusion of his readers in
his fabrications. Chatterton pushed this mutual, consenting deception
over the moral boundary between fiction and fraud to satisfy some aspect
of his own injured narcissism. Deprived of a father-figure, perhaps forced
into a role he felt unable to sustain by the expectations of his mother

and sister, unsure of his own identity, deprecating and disguising his own talents, Chatterton fabricated and externalized a personal romance of extraordinary potency.

His reputation and verse have survived his exposure and humiliation; his tragic death has inspired other poets and artists. Beyond his appeal to the romantic imagination, the kernel of real genius in his writing was recognized by many. William Wordsworth described him as 'the marvelous Boy,' while John Keats declared him 'the purest writer in the English language.'

THE IMPOSTOR AS NATIONAL LEADER

In the context of societal turmoil there has been one outstanding example of a way of acting that contains imposturous elements, this time in a political context—and that is Adolf Hitler.

> One of the secrets of his mastery over a great audience was his instinctive sensitivity to the mood of a crowd, a flair for divining the hidden passions, resentments and longings in their minds ...
>
> One of his most bitter critics [Hanfstängl, 1957] ... wrote:
> [He] responds to the vibrations of the human heart with the delicacy of a seismograph, or perhaps of a wireless receiving set, enabling him, with a certainty with which no conscious gift could endow him, to act as a loudspeaker proclaiming the most secret desires, the least admissible instincts, the sufferings, and personal revolts of a whole nation ... His uncanny intuition ... infallibly diagnoses the ills from which his audience is suffering ... [He] enters a hall. He sniffs the air. For a minute he gropes, feels his way, senses the atmosphere. Suddenly he bursts forth. His words go like an arrow to their target, he touches each private wound on the raw, liberating the mass unconscious, expressing its innermost aspirations, telling it what it most wants to hear. (Bullock, 1962, pp. 373–374)

The seventh chapter of Alan Bullock's masterly biography of Adolf Hitler, from which this quotation is taken, is a study of a dictator's deception of an entire nation. In it, Bullock examines the almost incredible facility with which 'in the years 1939 to 1941, at the height of success, [Hitler] had succeeded in persuading a great part of the German nation that in him they had found a ruler of more than human qualities, a man of genius raised up by Providence to lead them into the Promised Land' (p. 410). Bullock finds the key to Hitler's success—and to his ultimate destruction—in the fact that he 'was a consummate actor, with the actor's and orator's facility for absorbing himself in a role and convincing himself of the truth of what he was saying at the time he said it' (p. 377).

This is the portrait of a man who managed to dramatize on a world stage his fantasies of domination and force, the cult of the hero and racial purity, the subordination of the individual and the supremacy of the state, leaving a trail of unprecedented horror behind him:

> In the Eyrie he had built ... above the Berghof ... he would elaborate his fabulous schemes for a vast empire embracing the Eurasian Heartland of the geopoliticians; his plans for breeding a new elite biologically pre-selected; his design for reducing whole nations to slavery in the foundation of his new empire. Such dreams had fascinated Hitler since he wrote *Mein Kampf.* It was easy in the late 1920s and early 1930s to dismiss them as the product of a disordered and over-heated imagination ... But these were still the themes of Hitler's table talk in 1941–2 and by then ... Hitler had shown that he was capable of translating his fantasies into a terrible reality. The invasion of Russia, the SS extermination squads, the planned elimination of the Jewish race; the treatment of the Poles and Russians, the Slav *Untermenschen*—these, too, were the fruits of Hitler's imagination. (pp. 374–375)

The devastating success of Hitler's imposture owed much to Hitler's cynical manipulation of his image, combined with his own growing belief in his self-created myth. As World War II continued, he succumbed more and more to megalomania. He had presented himself as Germany's savior, the player of a world-historical role, and exempt from the constraints that bound ordinary people, and gradually he began to believe in his own infallibility.

> When he began to look to the image he had created to work miracles of its own accord—instead of exploiting it—his gifts deteriorated and his intuition deluded him. Ironically, failure sprang from the same capacity which brought him success, his power of self-dramatization, his ability to convince himself ... No man was ever more surely destroyed by the image he had created than Adolf Hitler. (p. 385)

At a more profound level, far from being their longed-for savior, Hitler was strongly aggressive towards his people. Making a fool of the audience and using lies and deceit can be seen as aggressive acts, a form of retaliation—in Hitler's case, against what? His ineffective and violent parents? The sense of betrayal he felt at Germany's capitulation at the end of World War I and the end of the empire? He felt no scruples in demanding the sacrifice of millions of lives for the cause of Germany during World War II; equally, he was prepared to sacrifice Germany itself, in the final year of the war, rather than relinquish power and admit defeat.

Albert Speer, Reich Minister for Armaments and War Production, recalled Hitler's reaction when presented with Speer's conviction that the war was lost:

> In an icy tone [he] continued: 'If the war is lost, the people will be lost also. It is not necessary to worry about what the German people will need for elemental survival. On the contrary, it is best for us to destroy even these things. For the nation has proved itself to be the weaker, and the future belongs solely to the stronger eastern nation. In any case only those who are inferior will remain after this struggle, for the good have already been killed.' (Speer, 1970, p. 557)

Two days later, Hitler confirmed this attitude in his order to implement a scorched-earth policy in the face of the advancing allied forces:

> 'All military, transportation, communications, industrial, and supply facilities, as well as resources within the Reich' were to be destroyed. The message was the death sentence for the German people ... The consequences would have been inconceivable: For an indefinite period there would have been no electricity, no gas, no pure water, no coal, no transportation. All railroad facilities, canals, locks, docks, ships, and locomotives destroyed. Even where industry had not been demolished, it could not have produced anything for lack of electricity, gas, and water. No storage facilities, no telephone communications—in short, a country thrown back into the Middle Ages. (Speer, 1970, p. 560)

At the end of his life, Hitler was prepared to lay waste the country he had spent so much time and energy molding to his image of the most technologically and architecturally brilliant, militarily powerful, and culturally imposing on earth. The cynicism, deceit, and brutal exploitation that lay behind his imposture were finally exposed, fatally late in the day.

Yet the spell that this most seductive of Pied Pipers cast over his followers survived, battered but more or less intact, until the end. It compelled Speer, disgraced and demoted, to risk his life and return to Berlin to say a last goodbye to the *Führer*:

> The overpowering desire to see him once more betrays the ambivalence of my feelings. For rationally I was convinced that it was urgently necessary, although already much too late, for Hitler's life to come to an end. Underlying everything I had done to oppose him in the past months had been the desire to prevent the annihilation that Hitler seemed bent on ...

And yet that very expectation brought out once again my emotional bond to Hitler ... My feelings of pity for the fallen ruler were growing stronger and stronger ... On the one hand there was sense of duty, oath of allegiance, loyalty, gratitude—on the other hand the bitterness at personal tragedy and national disaster—both centered around one person: Hitler. (Speer, 1970, pp. 601–602)

It was many more years before Speer was able to come to terms with the ambivalence of his personal feelings and to grasp the full extent of Hitler's imposture on the German people—years of self-enforced introspection during the 20 years Speer served in Spandau jail:

August 24, 1960 ... Going over it all in Spandau, I have gradually understood completely that the man I served was not a well-meaning tribune of the masses, not the rebuilder of German grandeur, and also not the failed conqueror of a vast European empire, but a pathological hater. The people who loved him, the German greatness he always talked about, the Reich he conjured up as a vision—all that ultimately meant nothing to him. I can still recall the astonishment with which I read the final sentence of his testament. In the midst of an apocalyptic doom it attempted to commit us all to a miserable hatred of the Jews. (Speer, 1976, pp. 353–354)

THE IMPOSTOR: A CHARACTER SKETCH

If we look at common themes among the various descriptions of impostors so far and take into consideration other observations about this type of person, we can now see that potential impostors come from families in which there is often an ambience of shared deception, lying, cheating, and make-believe. Appearance, rather than substance, is what really counts. Relationships tend to be superficial; showmanship is all-important. Such individuals possess what might be described as an overstimulated or overburdened self (Kohut and Wolf, 1978). They have never learned to moderate their grandiose self-images or idealized parental images. They want the world to treat them according to their ideals, not according to their real achievements. The real and the imaginary are not well integrated.

Some of these children appear to have become proxies of their parents, entrusted with the mission of fulfilling many of the parents' unrealistic hopes and wishes. Moreover, some parents may have unconsciously encouraged amoral or antisocial behavior in their children (Johnson and Szurek, 1952); forbidden desires may consequently be acted out vicariously. In the family setting, mothers of future impostors may show off their children, using them to gratify their own narcissistic needs. At the same time, these mothers can be overseductive (Dupont, 1970). The fathers are frequently devaluated by the mothers and portrayed as ineffective. This particular family situation may create Oedipal problems, making for a lack of phase-appropriate identification (Gottdiener, 1982). Adult behavior is expected of the children at a stage of development when they are not physiologically ready for it. Such children may later be confused about their true abilities and become victims of self-deceptive narcissism (Kets de Vries and Miller, 1985).

Impostors learn early on to use mimicry and other techniques to imitate adult behavior, all ways to obtain and sustain attention. This talent continues to be present in adult life. Given this early training, the impostor becomes skilled at colluding with the audience to create an ambience of make-believe and appearing more grandiose than he or she really is. Impostors' behavior also has overtones of what sometimes is called 'pseudologica phantastica' (Fenichel, 1954; Deutsch, 1965) in which the content of the fantasies, usually elaborate fabrications to impress the audience, are really screen memories both revealing and concealing events that have actually happened. (Pseudologica phantastica and pathological lying are different from normal daydreaming, in that reality-testing is suspended long enough to allow the individual to act on his or her fantasies.) Fabrication of a new 'truth' also becomes a way of covering up painful psychological material containing grains of historical truths (Weinshel, 1979; Spence, 1982; Blum, 1983). Lies serve a self-protective function in compartmentalizing threatening inner conflict. Somehow, the personal myth has to be played out as an organizer of life experiences.

Clinical evidence suggests that impostors often feel much better when they assume the identity of someone else. Their own identity, in spite of their very real gifts and talents, is rejected or devaluated. They have never successfully negotiated the process of separation–individuation—becoming an individual in their own right: a crucial prerequisite to the development of a stable sense of identity (Mahler, Pine, and Bergman, 1975). Thus, impostors could be said to suffering from a severe form of identity crisis (Wijsenbeek and Nitzan, 1968). Moreover, for some individuals, becoming an impostor is the victory of a dreaded but, at the same time, extremely tempting negative identity, meaning an identity one has been warned not to become (Erikson, 1959; Gediman, 1985).

A corollary to this disturbance of the impostor's sense of identity is a deficiency in the acquisition of well-developed internalized standards and values. Façade and pretence will be substituted for real achievement. Impostors always seem to be on stage, relying on fiction for a temporary identity (Bursten, 1973; Martin, 1988). In acting the way they do, they have retained the make-believe quality of many childhood games, and the audience is needed to confirm their sense of identity and reality.

Impostors discover early in life the power of the word. Like the troubadours of bygone days, or writers of fiction, they know how to fabricate illusions. Langer (1953) refers to the 'mnemonic mode,' the ability 'to make that illusion convincing, i.e. make it, however far it may be from actuality, seem real' (p. 291). Structure, diction, imagery, the use of names and allusions are ways of making this happen. Descriptive expansion gives impostors' stories their vitality and encourages suspension of disbelief. Langer mentions how the troubadours' audiences would revel in their descriptions and ask for greater elaboration, building up, as it were, a three-dimensional painting. Impostors act in a similar way. Given their empathic responsiveness, their ability to react to the cues of his audience, they will weave those cues into their tales, creating an increasingly credible tapestry of illusions. Porter (1987), in his study of the language of quackery, gives some insight into the how fake physicians, a specific type of impostor, are able to fool their audiences. Quacks come across as verbal pyrotechnicians, combining flattery with assurance. They use pseudo-scientific terms to obfuscate. They resort to religious allusions and superstitions; they draw on the mystique of exoticism, of faraway places, and utilize, as another source of prestige, social cachet, alluding to their acquaintanceship with the high and mighty. The optimistic way in which they are able to describe the supposed success of their exploits and how this success will enhance the lives of others can be intoxicating to their audience.

Symbolically, one can argue that impostors take on the role of the archaic, all-caring mother, satisfying our oceanic longings, gratifying the almost-forgotten, but never really relinquished, wish for total attention that characterizes early childhood. To the impostor, the greediness of the audience becomes another level on which to operate. In this context, the comedian W.C. Field's statement—'You can't cheat an honest man'—rings a bell of truth. Between impostor and audience there is an element of mutuality, a kind of unconscious conspiracy. The audience is made happy, thinking it will get what it wants, while the impostor needs the audience to counteract a sense of inner emptiness and reaffirm some kind of identity. Of course, the audience is most

susceptible in times of upheaval, when imposture can occur on a grand
scale, feeding on the audience's need for a savior.

But to be constantly on stage, engaged as it were in a continuous
performance, can be very draining. The tension that accompanies deceit
brings with it occasional feelings of just wanting to give up. This may
explain the instability and self-destructive component we often find in
the behavior of impostors. Many of them are no strangers to masochistic
behavior. Frequently, there is a remarkable contrast between their skill
in creating situations of make-believe and their acts of stupidity that
bring about their exposure (Grand, 1973). The role of unconscious
guilt and the existence of disturbances in their sense of identity probably play a role in their failure to protect themselves adequately against
detection.

The Impostor as Entrepreneur

An interesting example of how elements of imposture can affect
a business enterprise has been the case of Refaat El-Sayed, the
disgraced former chairman of Fermenta, a Swedish biotechnology
firm. Before his fall, this Egyptian immigrant was able to dazzle
the Swedish financial and industrial establishment, the media, and
the public at large. El-Sayed became a folk hero to the man on the
street because of his unpretentious lifestyle and his indifference to
the trappings of wealth, despite having become the richest man in
Sweden. He would be photographed in his small apartment in a
suburb of Stockholm drinking Coca-Cola and eating pizza or be
seen playing soccer with an amateur league. Because of his activities
he became the inspiration and pride of Sweden's large immigrant
population. In 1985 he was voted 'Swede of the year' by Swedish
television. Unfortunately, what initially looked like a storm in a
media teacup—the revelation that he never, as he had alleged, held
a doctorate—turned into a full-fledged scandal when an increasing
number of irregularities were revealed. Fermenta stock, once the
darling of the investment community (having reached an incredible
price–earnings ratio of 56), plummeted more than 90% in one year,
damaging many individuals and Swedish institutions (Sundqvist,
1987; Wittebort, 1987).

Very little is known of El-Sayed's early days. He was born in
Egypt in 1946, the youngest in the family, and the son of a teacher.
His mother, who came from Czechoslovakia, died a year after his
birth. According to him, there were two sisters and another two

brothers in the family. Both the latter two are said to have died in the war with Israel. The father remarried and had nine more children. El-Sayed went to Czechoslovakia twice to participate in a youth camp. In 1966, he left Egypt for Sweden to study at a university. Before that, he had been enrolled at a school of agriculture in Cairo. While in Sweden, he visited Russia a number of times in order to go to summer camp. In 1972, he married a Swedish social worker.

Although fact and fantasy are mixed in El-Sayed's description of his personal background, one thing is clear; it must have been a very confusing and turbulent one. His mother died when he was very young. The fact that she came from a very different cultural background must have been a source of curiosity to him. To add to this sense of confusion there was, of course, the presence of a stepmother and more children. We can only conjecture about the role of the different female figures in his life, and not much is said about his father. But certainly, one male figure, his paternal grandfather, was important as a key transmitter of beliefs and values.

According to El-Sayed, he had to be self-sufficient and behave like a small adult from a very early age. One may infer from such a statement that age-appropriate development did not really occur. He must have learned very quickly how to be a survivor, not relying on anybody. He has described how from early on he knew how to take initiative, had the ability to capture the attention of others and assume a leadership role.

Although we will never really know the exact nature of the family dynamics, we may infer that his visits to Czechoslovakia and Russia and his eventual immigration to Sweden were ways of coming to grips with who he really was, all attempts to stabilize a confused sense of personal and cultural identity. His later behavior shows, however, that this sense of confusion may have lingered on and also demonstrates the difficulty he had in distinguishing fact from fiction. The 'wish to believe' may have become so strong that it marred his sense of reality.

Early in his business career, El-Sayed showed strong entrepreneurial inclinations. He worked as a consultant in microbiology and held several patents. In 1973, he started a company called Micro-Chem that brought him some of the contacts he found advantageous later on. In 1981, El-Sayed became interested in a penicillin factory owned by Astra, a Swedish pharmaceutical company. The factory, Fermenta, was losing money and Astra was willing to sell. Through ingenious representation of his financial solvency, since he didn't have any money, and a number of imaginative tax maneuvers, El-Sayed gained control over Fermenta, paying one Swedish crown for the shares. At that time, Fermenta was making the raw material for the production of penicillin, a depressed market with worldwide overcapacity. El-Sayed's original business idea was to turn the factory into a producer of cattle vaccine, a product that offered high margins. However, he never really pursued this idea, concentrating instead on buying various antibiotics firms.

Surprisingly, the factory started to make a profit, largely because of advantageous currency fluctuations. In 1984, El-Sayed decided to go public with Fermenta. In the issue prospectus, it was stated that he had a PhD in chemistry. The company went public at a time when the Swedish stock market was experiencing an unprecedented rise. There was also a lack of biotechnology companies in Sweden. The issue was 16 times oversubscribed.

The year 1985 was a period of rapid expansion for Fermenta. El-Sayed frantically bought new companies or entered into joint ventures or marketing arrangements with companies in related fields. His idea was to become a major player in the antibiotics field so that he could influence world prices. In the meantime, he had succeeded in attracting to his board some of the most reputable businessmen in Sweden.

From all descriptions, El-Sayed seemed to come across as a bundle of energy, a man in a hurry, totally future-oriented. Some portrayed him as a constantly moving target, a comment that implies he was hard to understand. His speech was rapid, fragmented, accented, and often incoherent. His mannerisms and unorthodox behavior were a puzzle to many. But, like Hans Christian Andersen's famous story about the emperor's new clothes, many labeled him a genius despite—or perhaps because of—their inability to understand him. In a Swedish context, this unconventional outsider left his audience completely spellbound.

El-Sayed was also extremely talented at reading people. There was a warmth and generosity about him that made him attractive. He had a great knack for appearing to give his audience what they wanted. He would dazzle others with his command of figures and tables. These qualities made him a very skilful negotiator.

Paradoxically, El-Sayed's self-cast role as antihero, not interested in the material rewards of being a successful businessman or the traditional trappings of power, brought him more attention than he might otherwise have received. It turned out to be a very effective way of satisfying his need to be in the limelight and to be liked. And in the end, as a spokesman for Volvo said, ascribing more deliberate planning to his actions than was probably the case, El-Sayed 'more or less fooled all of Swedish society—politicians, businessmen, financial analysts, financial journalists' (Wittebort, 1987, p. 96). In the aftermath, everyone realized that what he sold was dreams and promises, that the stock price of Fermenta rose to a large extent on air and not on substance, and that far from being a high-tech firm, his company was really a very ordinary factory. El-Sayed's persuasiveness, combined with the added inducement of the greed of others, enabled him to get the attention of everyone.

Meanwhile, Fermenta's stock price took off phenomenally. At the end of 1985, it was trading at 213 compared with an introduction price only a year and a half earlier of 21.25. With 44% of the stock (79% of the voting rights), El-Sayed had become the richest man in Sweden, at least on paper. El-Sayed reached the zenith of his career in January 1986 with the announcement of a spectacular deal. With Volvo's backing, Fermenta would take the lead in consolidating Sweden's pharmaceutical/biotechnology industry, thereby gaining control over some of the major players in the field. It was soon after this announcement that an innocuous-looking article in an obscure paper appeared questioning whether El-Sayed really had obtained a doctorate.

For many, this small deception was hard to take. After an initial reaction of disbelief, those involved started to take a closer look at El-Sayed's various activities. The Volvo deal fell through and the 'socialist dream,' as El-Sayed had been called because of his ability to play a capitalist game with a socialist touch, tumbled rapidly from his pedestal. An increasing number of irregularities were revealed, including long-term contracts with payments booked up front, capital transactions recorded as profits, buy-back arrangements of Fermenta shares at guaranteed profits, and loans given to El-Sayed himself for other questionable transactions. Industrivärden, an investment company affiliated with Svenska Handelsbanken, discovered that Fermenta's assets were vastly overvalued.

It was also discovered that some of Fermenta's profits were generated by deals that never existed. El-Sayed had taken a more than active role in managing Fermenta's stock price. A true master of the media, he had played his rags-to-riches story for all it was worth. Every journalist willing to listen had received stories about future deals, mergers, and acquisitions, announcements that influenced Fermenta's stock price.

However, it seems El-Sayed saw no wrongdoing in his actions. Like many entrepreneurs, he had had difficulty establishing the boundaries between what was his and what was the company's. He probably rationalized that what he was doing was in the best interests of the company. And, on one level of analysis, he may have been correct. (In spite of all his wheeling and dealing, he does not appear to have benefited personally from Fermenta.) In fact, El-Sayed's identification with Fermenta was so strong that he was unwilling to separate from it and enrich himself by selling out while a deal was still possible. The way he mixed fact with fancy seems to indicate that his capacity for reality-testing was marred. The lie about his credentials was certainly self-destructive, given the high likelihood, as such a public figure, that he would be found out.

When we look at his behavior more closely, we can see that El-Sayed demonstrates many of the characteristics of the impostor. We see it in his showmanship, his talent in playing on the greed of others, and his ability to suspend the disbelief of his audience and create excitement about the supposed success of his ventures. The protean quality of his sense of identity is demonstrated in the way he oscillated between playing the average guy and a business tycoon. In trying to resolve his own confusion, El-Sayed seems to have transgressed. His personal myth increasingly led him into trouble. His own problems and those of his business became too intertwined. Self-deception eventually led to his downfall.

The role of a hero is not very stable; many heroes end by being viewed as villains. The paradox of El-Sayed's story is that he got all the blame for his investors' shattered illusions. We could argue that Fermenta's investors were as much to blame, having become victims of their own greed. In the end, when he could no longer deliver, El-Sayed was turned into a scapegoat. Generally speaking, people like El-Sayed are the lifeblood of society, seeing new combinations that others miss and helping to re-evaluate existing patterns of behavior. The positive legacy of his particular story is that the scandal inspired lasting changes in the Swedish financial system. We might hypothesize that El-Sayed did not act intentionally, and was swept away by unconscious forces; but whatever the theories, he was found guilty on 14 counts of financial misconduct and jailed for five years (*International Herald Tribune*, 1989, p. 12).

In many respects, El-Sayed's behavior was little different from that of the typical entrepreneur. Similar behavior patterns can be seen in many entrepreneurs, particularly when the darker sides of entrepreneurship emerge (Kets de Vries, 1985). All entrepreneurs need dreams, but they are not always effective in distinguishing their dreams from reality—and there are limits to how far reality can be distorted.

The writer G.K. Chesterton once remarked that 'a really accomplished impostor is the most wretched of geniuses: he is a Napoleon on a desert island.' However, most impostors do not remain Napoleons for long. Eventually their all-too-human foibles take over and they unmask themselves.

The challenge for all of us in avoiding being duped by impostors is to maintain our capacity for rational thinking and not be swept away by emotional forces when the sirens promising instant love, wealth, and happiness are tempting us to respond to their call. But the wish to believe on the part of many people can be extremely strong. When greed takes over, rational thinking quickly evaporates, as many recent business scandals have demonstrated. It is not easy to resist an individual who says, in effect, 'Trust me, I will take care of all your needs.' It is particularly difficult to fight the formidable force that greed can be. However, when these powerful feelings arise, the time has come to distance ourselves, take another hard look, talk to outsiders, and work out what really is going on.

ENDNOTE

This chapter has been compiled from the following sources:

* Kets de Vries, M.F.R. (1990). 'The impostor syndrome: Developmental and societal issues,' *Human Relations*, **43** (7): 667–686.
* Kets de Vries, M.F.R. (1993). *Leaders, Fools and Impostors*. San Francisco: Jossey-Bass.
* Kets de Vries, M.F.R. (2005). 'The Dangers of Feeling like a Fake,' *Harvard Business Review*, **83** (9): 108–116.

CHAPTER 5

NEUROTIC IMPOSTORS: FEELING LIKE A FAKE

Your only obligation in any lifetime is to be true to yourself. Being true to anyone else or anything else is not only impossible, but the mark of a fake messiah.

—Richard Bach

INTRODUCTION

The mesmerizing individuals described in Chapter 4 are only one manifestation of imposture. Various writers have made a distinction between the 'true' and the 'neurotic' impostor (Aarons, 1959; Gediman, 1985). While the first refers to the sort of people described in Chapter 4, whose identity is built on impersonation rather than on accomplishment, the second is different, in that it describes successful individuals who nevertheless *feel* fraudulent and imposturous. This 'neurotic imposture' is not false humility. It is the flip side of giftedness and causes many talented, hardworking, and capable leaders—men and women who have achieved great things—to believe that they don't deserve their success. Often, they are labeled as 'neurotic overachievers,' a type of person commonly found in certain very demanding professions.

Neurotic impostors feel that they have fooled everybody and that they are not as competent or intelligent as others think. They attribute their success to luck, compensatory hard work, or superficial external factors, such as physical attractiveness or likeability. Some are incredibly hard workers, always overprepared. They cannot accept that they have real intellectual gifts and ability, and experience a constant fear that their imposturous existence will be found out, that they will not be able to live up to others' expectations and catastrophe will follow. We are reminded of Winnicott's (1975) description of people who develop a 'false self,' an attempt to hide and protect the inner core of their personality, an outcome of adaptive failure resulting in a deceptive false identity.

In describing the internal experiences of incompetence and phoniness among impostors, Gediman (1985) has suggested a continuum ranging from 'the psychopathic impostor who may assume a false identity for conscious and deliberate purposes of deception, through a heterogeneous variety of individuals who are vulnerable to a shaky identity sense' (p. 912). The 'neurotic' group seems to find it exceedingly hard to accept their own talents and achievements.

WHAT CREATES IMPOSTUROUS FEELINGS?

One of the tasks of childhood is to complete the separation-individuation process, when 'the infant's primary narcissism, the belief in his own and in his parent's omnipotence ... gradually recede(s), that is to say, it must be replaced by autonomous functioning' (Mahler, Pine, and Bergman, 1975, p. 226). Individuals who feel like impostors have usually experienced problems concerning the separation-individuation process, although to a much lesser extent than real impostors. Nevertheless, true separation has not been accomplished. These people never feel truly independent and lack a cohesive sense of self. Their achievements and capabilities are experienced as phony and hollow and cause guilt, fear, and stress. They view themselves as frauds (Clance and Imes, 1978; Clance, 1985). They make an incredible effort to prove these internal voices wrong.

My clinical interviews with CEOs and other high-level executives suggest that specific family structures can be breeding grounds for feelings of imposture. Certain kinds of dysfunctional families—particularly those in which parents have overinvested in achievement and where often human warmth is lacking—tend to produce children who are prone to neurotic imposture. Individuals who have been raised in this kind of environment seem to believe that their parents will notice them only when they excel. As time goes on, these people often turn into insecure overachievers.

Such people are unusually sensitive to experiences of rejection, excessively afraid of social failure and suffer from lingering dependency needs. It is as if they have incorporated the disproportionate expectations of their parents but never properly 'metabolized' them. In many instances, they may suffer from generalized forms of anxiety, lack of self-confidence, and depression.

Women Who Feel Imposturous

The term 'impostor phenomenon' was coined in 1978 by psychology professor Pauline Clance and psychologist Suzanne Imes of Georgia State University. In a study of high-achieving women, Clance and Imes discovered that many of their female clients seemed unable to internalize and accept their achievements. In spite of consistent objective data to the contrary, they attributed their success to serendipity, luck, contacts, timing, perseverance, charm, or even the ability to appear more capable than they felt.

Women who reach successful positions that conflict with their family of origin's way of thinking about gender roles are especially prone to feeling fraudulent. The gender socialization that women are often exposed to—for instance, being told that they should become nurses or secretaries when choosing a career—tends to augment their sense of imposture when their achievements rise above those expectations.

Inner confusion develops into genuine neurotic imposture for many women when they reach critical points in their lives—marriage, work, and children. Decisions around these areas are especially difficult for women who have been raised by traditional mothers, homemakers who raised the children and did not work outside the home. Consciously or not, women tend to compare their chosen role with the role their mother played. The fact that working women choose not to stay at home but to pursue a career—a lifestyle very different from what they witnessed as children—often makes them feel like bad mothers to their own children and bad wives to their husbands.

To take an example: a prominent female executive in Holland, where women used rarely to be found in top positions, described to me her experience of having both a career and family life.

> When I decided to go to university and study business economics most people looked at it as a passing whim, a few years of study at the most, a good way of finding a husband. I actually did find a husband but continued my studies and received a degree. To do that and have a baby as well was relatively unheard of at the time. I certainly got an earful ... But what really became an irritant to many was my decision to work. How could I do that as a mother? How could I live with myself? I think most people considered me quite irresponsible.

I was exposed to a lot of pressures and, of course, I had to deal with my own memories of the role my mother had played when I was growing up. She had been a typical housewife. Not staying at home and pursuing a career obviously made me a bad mother. Fortunately, it is now more common to have a career and a family life in Holland. But at that time there was a lot of pressure on me to quit.

In spite of my success in business and what I think has been a good family life, I still have my doubts about doing both. The symptom is that—in spite of all my efforts to fight it—I constantly feel guilty. I have always lived with the sense that I am not really good at anything. Men may find it hard to understand what I am talking about.

Gender-role socialization isn't the only thing that makes women more vulnerable than men to neurotic imposture. The fact that business-women have to function in an environment dominated by men compounds their insecurity, because when women are successful, they're not the only ones who suspect imposture. Many of their competitive male colleagues also assume that chance or an affirmative action program—rather than talent or skill—is responsible for female success. In addition, men—consciously or unconsciously—often exclude women from their informal networks. Though few men express the opinion of imagined 'special treatment' publicly, subtle insinuations from male colleagues add to a woman's fear that their 'luck' won't hold. As a result, many very gifted women fail to realize that they have superior talents. And, if they do realize it, they are more likely than men to hide those talents and play dumb as a strategy for dealing with others' envy and their own recurring feelings of self-doubt.

Clance and Imes (1978) hypothesize about the existence of two types of women who feel imposturous. According to their study, the first type is victimized by a family myth that designates one sibling the clever one, while the other is labeled the sensitive or socially adept one. In spite of the 'sensitive' girl's string of achievements, the family continues to attribute greater intelligence and ability to the 'clever' sibling, even when his or her (but it usually is 'his') academic performance is much the poorer. This leaves the other with a sense of doubt about her true abilities and the lingering question of whether her family may actually be right.

The second type experiences the reverse, and is mythologized as superior in every possible way, from her intellect and personality to her appearance. Anecdotes are told about her precocity as an infant. Yet, at the same time, she experiences situations where she has difficulty in achieving. Given the indiscriminate manner in which she is praised, she begins to distrust her parents' perceptions and consequently her own.

Men can suffer similar feelings, often related to an unconscious sense of guilt about doing better than their father, which finds it roots in childhood. There is also the saying that 'nothing grows in the shade of a great tree.' Having a formidable father doesn't always help. This may lead to anxiety because of fear never to be able to live up to the father's standards. In addition, if an effort is made, these talented youngsters struggle with the fear of the father's envy (and consequent retribution) (Schafer, 1984). These instances suggest that the Oedipal drama has never been successfully resolved for these individuals. Infantile fears like these, which may contain a kernel of truth, are often based on covert messages, and may linger on into adulthood (Kets de Vries, 1989). They will be exacerbated if an individual's success takes them into a different social or financial sphere from their family background, raising real fears of separation, estrangement, and rejection.

There is one important caveat worth mentioning concerning the issue of gender and imposture, and it relates to sexuality. While it is almost impossible for a man to fake orgasm, this form of imposture is relatively easy for women (Roach, 2008). Women who experience difficulties in reaching orgasm, and for various reasons take recourse to faking it, may also feel imposturous in other areas of their lives.

Like the true impostor, the person who feels imposturous adopts an inauthentic survival strategy to win approval from others. Sycophancy, intellectual flattery, and charm become means of deflecting anticipated social rejection. Telling the other person what he or she wants to hear becomes a strategy for gaining approval and postponing the dreaded moment of being revealed as an impostor.

Fear of Success

This way of thinking and acting is reminiscent of one of Freud's character types in his 1916 essay, 'Those Wrecked by Success,' a group of people who fall ill when a long-cherished wish comes to fruition. There are some differences, however. The people Freud describes may go further than merely feeling inauthentic and fraudulent, and actually engage in self-defeating acts, achieving, as it were, 'victory through defeat' (Reik, 1941). Their 'success neurosis' causes them unhappiness when they are faced with their own accomplishments, at least at one level of consciousness. Another perspective on this is to see their behavior as a form of rebellion, a continuation of an old determination not to submit to the expectations of their parents.

Both those 'wrecked by success' and those who feel inauthentic possess a strong masochistic, self-destructive streak and inflict pain on themselves by behaving in this way (Grossman, 1986; Simons, 1987). In the past, this behavior may have been a way of attracting attention or a form of negative identification with an abusing or abused parental figure. In this context, some authors have identified a 'Cinderella complex' (Dowling, 1981), a self-defeating tendency among some women of wanting to be taken care of or rescued from the responsibility of having to take care of themselves. However, waiting for a fairy godmother or glass slipper rather than taking control of one's own life can be a costly strategy.

Paradoxically, a predisposition to neurotic imposture is also quite common in individuals who are *not* expected to succeed. In socially disadvantaged groups (often with a blue-collar background), parents may withhold encouragement because their children's ambitions are inconsistent with family expectations. Children who manage to advance to positions of real power as adults often transcend their families of origin in such a spectacular way that a lingering insecurity remains about having become successful. Because of conflicting signals, these people frequently wonder how long their success will last. This fear of surpassing one's parents can cause feelings of neurotic imposture to persist long after the parents have died.

Birth order also influences the development of neurotic imposture. Feelings of imposture are more common among firstborn children, reflecting the new parents' nervous inexperience and greater expectations of the first child. For example, older children are often expected to help out take care of younger brothers and sisters and held up to younger siblings as models of maturity at a stage when they are feeling needy and insecure themselves.

THE NEUROTIC IMPOSTOR IN THE WORKPLACE

A few years ago, an executive in a telecommunications company came to see me. He had just been promoted to a senior management role. I'll call him Tobin Holmes.[1] A young Englishman, who had studied classics at Oxford before graduating in the top 5% of his class at business school, Holmes was very clever. But he feared he couldn't take on the responsibilities of the new job.

At the root of Holmes's dilemma was his suspicion that he was just not good enough, and he lived in dread that he would be exposed at any moment. Yet, at the same time, he seemed bent on betraying the inadequacy he was so anxious to conceal. In his personal life, for example, he indulged in conspicuously self-destructive behavior, such as public affairs with numerous women and a drinking spree that resulted in a disastrous car accident. At work, he found it increasingly difficult to concentrate and make decisions. He worried—with good reason—that his problems at the office would be noticed by the CEO and other members of the board. When would they realize that they had made a horrible mistake in promoting him to the senior executive team?

When the fear and stress eventually overwhelmed him, Holmes quit his job and accepted a junior position at a larger organization. Given his genuine talent, however, it didn't take long before he was asked to head up one of that company's major country units, a known stepping stone to the top. In this new role, Holmes' feelings of doubt resurfaced. Rather than risk being exposed as incompetent, he left the job within a year and moved to yet another company. There, despite his performance, top management looked at his employment record and concluded that Holmes didn't have the right stuff to make it to the highest levels of leadership. Holmes couldn't let himself move up to the most senior levels in an organization because, deep inside, he feared that he was an impostor who would eventually be discovered.

Listening to his tale of woe, I recognized the features of neurotic imposture. I felt that what he needed was to see the connections between his past and his present behavior and to realize that a certain type of behavior, which might have been quite effective at one stage of his development, was no longer working. He was no longer a child; he was an adult. He also needed to build up his self-confidence and have a more realistic assessment of his capabilities. I suggested that he should see a psychologically trained leadership coach, and at the same time take my top executive seminar, 'The Challenge of Leadership' (see p. 245). I felt that it would be a good experience for him to work together on individual and organizational issues with a group of senior executives for a significant period of time to build up his sense of self-efficacy. The discussions in the group setting were a revelation to him, making him realize that he was not alone in having imposturous feelings. Furthermore, these interactions also made him aware of the fact of how competent he really was. Considering how his career has progressed since, the intervention seems to have worked.

Neurotic impostors can be found at all levels of an organization. Typically, misgivings begin with the first job, right after graduation, when people are fraught with anxiety and particularly insecure about their ability to prove themselves. Promotion from middle management to senior management is another tricky time because an executive must negotiate the difficult switch from being a specialist to becoming a general manager. But neurotic impostors face their greatest challenges when they are promoted from senior management to CEO.

In my work with senior executives and CEOs, I've found that many neurotic impostors function well as long as they stay out of the number one position. Often, a leader's feelings of self-doubt and anxiety are less pressing when he is lower on the totem pole, because senior executives provide support and mentoring. He or she is not yet much in the lime-light. But once a leader becomes CEO, everything he does is highly visible. He is expected to stand on his own.

The incidence of neurotic imposture seems to vary by profession. For example, it is highly prevalent in academia and medicine, both disciplines in which the appearance of intelligence is vital to success. But people like Tobin Holmes abound in business. In my career as a management professor, consultant, leadership coach, psychotherapist, and psychoanalyst, I have explored the topic of neurotic imposture with both individuals and large groups of senior executives. My experience has shown that feelings of neurotic imposture proliferate in contemporary organizations: I encounter this type of dysfunctional perception and behavior all the time—particularly when working with executives in high-powered consulting firms and investment banking. Interestingly enough—and here I am thinking of strategic consulting firms—there also seems to be some kind of 'contagion effect' for people giving advice to top executives. The task of many of these consultants is to make what are frequently insecure clients 'heroes' or 'heroines' in the eyes of their various stakeholders. These people struggle with the question whether they are really good enough to give advice to what they perceive as 'glorious' clients.

HOW THE FEAR CAN BECOME A REALITY

How does neurotic imposture get out of hand? The trigger is often perfectionism. In its mild form, perfectionism provides the energy that leads to great accomplishments. Benign perfectionists, who do not suffer feelings of inadequacy, derive pleasure from their achievements and do not obsess about failures. Neurotic impostors, however, are seldom benign in their perfectionism. They are absolute perfectionists, who set excessively high, unrealistic goals and then experience self-defeating thoughts and behavior when they cannot reach them. They are driven by the belief that they could do better if only they worked harder. For this reason, perfectionism often turns neurotic impostors into workaholics. Fearing the exposure of their 'fraudulence,' they burden themselves with too much work to overcome their inner insecurity. Work/life balance is a meaningless concept to them. Neurotic impostors often collude in abusive, self-defeating situations in which others take advantage of them. They do not realize that they may be pushing themselves and others too hard, often to the detriment of long-term success. By exploiting themselves so brutally, they risk rapid and early burnout.

The vicious cycle begins when the impostor sets impossible goals. She fails to reach these goals, of course (because no one could reach them), then tortures herself endlessly about the failure, which incites further self-flagellation, accentuates the feelings of imposture, and inspires her to devise yet another unattainable set of goals—and the entire cycle of workaholism and fraudulence begins again. This is exactly what happened to Robert Pierce, another neurotic impostor who was an extraordinarily gifted trader at a highly prestigious investment bank, and who set ever-increasing goals of financial compensation for himself, to deal with his anxieties about being a fake. Initially, Pierce felt elated whenever he reached his goal but became desperate every time he learned that someone else earned more than he did. This kicked off an orgy of self-blame that did little to improve his career or his organizational effectiveness.

Because they are so ambivalent about their achievements, neurotic impostors often appear to be engagingly humble. Self-deprecation, of course, is a perfectly respectable character trait and from a career-management point of view can be a protective strategy. Underplaying your achievements diffuses other people's envy, directs their attention away from your success, and lowers their expectations of you. Self-deprecation also indicates of modesty, which can elicit encouragement and support from others.

But the neurotic impostor's humility actually stems from another kind of protective impulse: the need for an exit strategy. Failure (at least at a subliminal level) is a desirable way out. Think of the journalist who wins a Pulitzer prize at a relatively young age. What can he do for an encore? Great achievements have ruined many a neurotic impostor because they can lead to paralysis.

I said earlier that the heart of the problem for many neurotic impostors is the fear that success and fame will hurt them in some way—that family, friends, and others will continue to like them much better if they remain 'small.' As Ambrose Bierce wrote in *The Devil's Dictionary*, success is 'the one unpardonable sin against one's fellows.' Envy is a very powerful force. As the Greek playwright Aeschylus once said, 'It is in the character of very few men to honor without envy a friend who has prospered.'

Because of this, neurotic impostors can be quite creative at destroying their own successful careers. It is as if they want to be discovered. Perhaps assisting in their own unmasking is a proactive way of coping with anxiety.

Mike Larson, a senior executive I worked with some years ago, exemplifies this tendency. After a brilliant career as a medical researcher, Larson was offered the position of director of research in a global company specializing in over-the-counter drugs. When he embarked on this challenging new research agenda, however, Larson's incessant fear of exposure harmed rather than enhanced his performance. It was one thing to be a member of a team, but taking on the number one research position in the company was another thing altogether. The increased visibility made him increasingly anxious, contributing to his drive to do even better; but his inability to delegate and his tendency toward micro-management led to a great sense of malaise.

Larson realized that he was digging a hole for himself, but found it difficult to ask for help. He was afraid that doing so would give his colleagues proof that he was an impostor. To avoid being found out, he withdrew into himself, agonized over what his colleagues thought about him, worried about not living up to their expectations and procrastinated over every decision. The result was anxiety-filled days, sleepless nights, and an intense fear of making mistakes—a fear that made him unwilling to experiment, develop, and learn.

Like most neurotic impostors, Larson engaged in faulty reality-testing. This distortion in his cognition caused him to dramatize all setbacks—he blew small incidents out of proportion and cast himself as the helpless victim. Larson lived with the misconception that he was the only one prone to failure and self-doubt, and this made him feel even more insecure and isolated. Like other neurotic impostors, he focused on the negative and failed to give himself credit for his accomplishments. He also harmed his career by becoming a master of catastrophe—reaching exaggerated conclusions based on limited evidence.

It was only when Larson was awarded the top research position that he realized how much he missed the mentors he'd had at earlier stages of his career. They had helped him to deal with the pressures of his job and to maintain equilibrium under stress. But when he was promoted, he found it much harder to ask for advice and to find people who would challenge his faulty cognition. As a result, he executed a number of poor management decisions that contributed to his organization's ineffectiveness. Eventually, he was asked to step down from the position.

HOW NEUROTIC IMPOSTORS CAN IMPACT ON BUSINESSES

Neurotic impostors can actually damage the organizations they try so hard to please. Their work ethic can be contagious, but because they are so eager to succeed, they can become impatient and abrasive. Because neurotic impostors are extremely tough on themselves they are not predisposed to spare others. They drive their employees too hard and may create a gulag-like atmosphere in their organizations, which inevitably translates into high employee-turnover rates, absenteeism, and other complications that can affect the bottom line. Moreover, their intensity can intimidate others. And because they don't have what it takes to be effective leadership coaches, they are generally not good at leadership development and succession planning.

More damaging, however, is the effect a neurotic impostor's leadership can have on decision-making. Some executives who feel imposturous are afraid to trust their own judgment. Their fearful, overly cautious attitude can easily spread across the company. For instance, a neurotic impostor CEO may suppress the entrepreneurial capabilities of the people in his organization. If he doesn't trust his own instincts, why should he trust anyone else's?

Ironically (as many top management consultants feel like neurotic impostors), neurotic impostor CEOs are also likely to become addicted to soliciting the help of consulting companies because reassurances provided by impartial outsiders compensate for their feelings of insecurity. Of course, judicious use of consulting advice has its place; but neurotic impostor executives easily turn into puppets whose strings can be manipulated by advisers. Ralph Gordon, the CEO of a global engineering firm, suffered just such an experience. In a group session during one of my seminars, he explained that he hadn't really chosen engineering as a career—his father had chosen it for him. Gordon ceded to his father's wishes and entered the business world, where he never felt comfortable in a corporate role. When he reached more senior positions, Gordon began to rely on consultants, some of whom took advantage of his insecurity at a very high price. Not only did they charge Gordon's firm substantial fees for their services but their predatory behavior increased Gordon's feelings of dependency.

This type of behavior is exacerbated when neurotic impostors work in an organization that punishes failure. If the company culture does not tolerate mistakes, the leader's level of anxiety will increase, making neurotic behavior more likely.

Consider Lynn Orwell, who had a successful career at a consulting firm before accepting an offer from a prominent media company. In her consulting job, Orwell had functioned exceptionally well but this changed when she accepted an assignment to run the new firm's European operation. Although Orwell was an outstanding source of good ideas, her fear of failure led her to manage in ways that seemed countercultural. For example, in an organization that had always been decentralized, she decided to centralize many of the functions in her part of the business. But what really grated with many people was her determination to make most decisions herself. Her perfectionist attitude and need for immediate results meant that delegation was anathema to her, and her team's productivity and creativity were dampened. Orwell's co-workers started to worry about the abrasiveness that crept into her manner, and her prickliness about criticism—whether real or perceived—began to irritate a growing number of her colleagues. She reacted with defensiveness and hostility to comments about any of her proposals, reports, or decisions. Furthermore, anxious not to be found wanting, she took ages to prepare for meetings, trying to anticipate every conceivable question that could be asked. Such precautions extended her already lengthy working week into weekends, and she expected others to show the same commitment.

Orwell's sense of neurotic imposture affected the organization deeply. As time went on, many of Orwell's team members began to ask for transfers to other parts of the organization. Others quietly sought out headhunters. Those who stayed took a passive-aggressive attitude toward Orwell. Since they felt it was not worth the effort to reason with her, they let her make all the decisions but undermined them in subtle ways. As a result, her European division—once hailed as the flagship operation—increasingly became a liability. By the year's end, profitability for Orwell's division had fallen into a deep slump, confirming the company's belief that she was truly incompetent. Ultimately, the division was sold to a competitor. Orwell's neurosis had ruined not only her career but a perfectly robust business as well.

FINDING SOLUTIONS

Despite the somewhat gloomy picture given so far, neurotic imposture is not an inevitable part of the human condition, and it is avoidable. Early prevention, for instance, goes a long way to warding it off. Parental awareness of the downside of setting excessively high standards for children helps prevent later misery. But there is hope for late-diagnosed impostors as well. Experience has shown that psychotherapeutic interventions or leadership coaching can be very effective in changing distorted self-perceptions.

Yet the best—and often most appropriate—way for people to manage feelings of imposture is to learn to evaluate themselves. With the help of a leadership coach or psychotherapist they can begin a journey of self-discovery and change. A mentor or good friend can also help put things in perspective.

If executives seem unable to take the initiative to deal with their feelings of imposture, however, their boss will need to intervene. This was the case with John Stoddard, the division head of a large telecommunications company, who came to talk to me on the recommendation of his CEO. In our sessions, Stoddard wondered if he needed pointers on how to be a more effective executive. A 360-degree feedback exercise showed that he was inclined toward micro-management and perfectionism and that he possessed poor listening skills. Some of the written comments we received also noted that his impatience put intense pressure on his senior executives and that morale at the office was quite low. As we discussed the problem together, Stoddard began to realize the extent to which he had internalized the expectations of his extremely demanding parents, and he started to change. He began to experiment with new behavior in the office and received a surprisingly positive reception, which increased his sense of self-efficacy. When I met him a year later, Stoddard mentioned quite proudly how morale at the office had improved dramatically, how his division had become more profitable, and how his ability to let go of his controlling tendencies had contributed to these successes.

Like Stoddard's CEO, good bosses remain alert for symptoms of neurotic imposture in their employees, which include fear of failure, fear of success, perfectionism, procrastination, and workaholism. In performance reviews, bosses should signal (uncritically) any danger signs to their direct reports. They should also explain how anxiety about performance can take on a self-destructive quality, and should emphasize the value of work/life balance.

Above all, bosses need to point out that *everyone* in a responsible job occasionally feels unequal to the task and needs time to adjust and learn the ropes. The worst thing a neurotic impostor can do, especially in a new position, is to compare his abilities with those of seasoned executives. This is a guaranteed exercise in self-flagellation.

At the same time, leaders must strengthen the perceived link between positive achievement and effort. They can do this not only by offering praise when it is due, but also by acknowledging that making mistakes is part of a successful corporate culture. The wise organization does not punish 'smart' mistakes; indeed, to chance to 'fail forward' should be part of an organization's implicit cultural values. Mistakes offer great opportunities for learning and personal growth, and leaders need to help neurotic impostors understand that a fear of failure is normal and need not be debilitating.

When the CEO is a Neurotic Impostor

The situation is more complicated when the CEO is a neurotic impostor. Some of these executives find it hard to ask for support from mentors or from subordinates. For this reason, many high-performance organizations now have leadership-coaching programs to help their executives cope better. When leadership coaches recognize the signs of neurotic imposture, they are in a good position to give constructive advice, emphasizing self-efficacy. Being willing to talk about problems and accept peer support not only has a profound effect on leaders but also has a deep impact on the organization that the neurotic impostor has helped to shape.

It's often said that a person's strengths are also his weaknesses. The same is true for an organization. In most well-run organizations, senior executives remove low performers or develop them to become high performers. But the same executives are less effective in managing people who appear to be problem-free. By their nature, neurotic impostors are very hard to detect because the early stages of an executive's career are so conducive to high performance. It is, in fact, a rare leader who does not suffer from some degree of neurotic imposture. All the more reason, therefore, for executives to be on the lookout for it in themselves, their reports, and their potential successors. Failing to recognize and deal with neurotic impostors has serious consequences both for individual sufferers and for the organizations relying on them.

ENDNOTES

This chapter has been compiled from the following published sources:

- Kets de Vries, M.F.R. (1990). 'The impostor syndrome: Developmental and societal issues,' *Human Relations*, **43** (7): 667–686.
- Kets de Vries, M.F.R. (1993) *Leaders, Fools and Impostors.* San Francisco: Jossey Bass Publishers.

1. All names are disguised.

CHAPTER 6

THE ORGANIZATIONAL FOOL: BALANCING A LEADER'S HUBRIS

> The fool speaks, the wise man listens.
>
> —African proverb

INTRODUCTION

Hubris is a recurring theme in leadership, for the obvious reason that power is often accompanied by excessive pride and arrogance. Many leaders take for granted that they can transgress rules made for common mortals. But how does one go about pointing out the symptoms of hubris? How can a leader be prevented from getting trapped and seeing only what he or she wants to see? How can we fight the regressive forces inherent in leadership? And how can we tackle them in an organizational setting?

I would like to suggest that an effective way of dealing with these issues is a modern interpretation of an ancient role, that of the fool. In playing the role of mediator between leader and followers the fool can become the antidote for hubris in disseminating deep communication, that is, going beyond the directly observable, and consciously or unconsciously seeking out the basic significance of events and making them clear to all (Geertz, 1973, 1983; Kets de Vries and Miller, 1987).

THE ROLE OF THE FOOL

Historically, the person who took such a role vis-à-vis the king was the court fool. By this, of course, I don't mean an idiot, someone stupid or lacking in judgment. I am thinking of quite the reverse: the licensed figure of the fool in his transformational role of wise man. In this role, the destiny of the leader and the fool are intricately bound. The fool becomes the person who, through various means, reminds the leader of the transience of power and his fundamental humanity. He becomes the guardian of reality and, in a paradoxical way, prevents the pursuit of foolish action.

An early illustration of an institutionalized way of reminding the power-holder of the transience of his position is the ritual that surrounded the triumphant entry of a Roman conqueror into the capital. Clowns and satyrs would jump around his chariot and shout abuse at him. The slave who held the crown of Jupiter Capitolinus above the victor's head would whisper over and over that he should remember that he was only mortal (Willeford, 1969).

The role of the court fool is an acknowledged literary figure. In his handbook for rulers, *The Prince*, Machiavelli maintained that it was essential for a ruler to have trusted truthsayers to rely on:

> Courts are always full of flatterers; men take such pleasure in their own concerns, and are so easily decided about them, that this plague of flattery is hard to escape … For there is no way to protect yourself from flattery except by letting men know that you will not be offended by hearing the truth. But when anyone can tell you the truth, you will not have much respect. Hence, a prudent prince should adopt a third course, bring *wise men* into his council and giving them alone free license to speak the truth—and only on points where the prince asks for it, not on others. (1977, p. 67)

The philosopher, Erasmus (1971), came to a similar conclusion. In his *Praise of Folly* he examined why a licensed fool could be the favorite of kings:

> Wise men have nothing but misery to offer their prince, they are confident in their learning and sometimes aren't afraid to speak harsh truths which will grate on his delicate ear, whereas clowns can provide the very thing a prince is looking for, jokes, laughter, merriment, and fun. And, let me tell you, fools have another gift which is not to be despised. They're the only ones who speak frankly and tell the truth, and what is more praiseworthy than truth?
>
> … The fact is, kings do dislike the truth, but the outcome of this is extraordinary for my fools. They can speak truth and even open insults and be heard with positive pleasure; indeed, the words which would cost a wise man his life are surprisingly enjoyable when uttered by a clown. (pp. 118–119)

THE FOOL AS CULTURAL HERO

As a social type, fools are widely recognized. We have all encountered them and at times may have played the role ourselves. Moreover, we have also become familiar with fools from anthropology, myths, folklore, literature, and drama under many different names, such as trickster, jester, buffoon, comic, Harlequin, or Pierrot.

Anthropologists, in particular, have paid a considerable amount of attention to the role of the ritual fool. Elaborate descriptions of this social type can be found in their studies of African, Asian, Oceanic, North American, Mesoamerican, and South American tricksters (Steward, 1931; Bunzel, 1932; Charles, 1945; Radin, 1972; Makarius, 1969, 1970, 1973). The trickster is portrayed as a person with magical powers. He is both underdog and hero, a mirror to humankind, who provides order out of chaos by connecting the unexplainable to the familiar. He is a person with uncanny powers of insight and prophecy. Jung (1969) describes the trickster as 'a primitive "cosmic" being of *divine-animal* nature, on the one hand superior to man because of his superhuman qualities, and on the other hand inferior to him because of his unreason and unconsciousness' (p. 144). When we compare the role of this mythic creature in different cultures, we see how the trickster turns into a symbol of the human condition, parodying human drives, needs, and weaknesses, combining cunning with stupidity, and being simultaneously funny and scary.

As Willeford (1969) indicates, 'most of the people we recognize as fools experience the world and act within it in ways that indicate a fundamental abnormality, real or pretended, of psychic functioning' (p. 23). The misadventures of these characters provide the spectator with insight into all that is human through the transformation of wit into wisdom.

Anthropological research suggests that the trickster is a figure onto whom we can project our own foibles, ideals, and fears and as such plays an important social role. Welsford (1935) even goes so far as to call the fool an educator, 'for he draws out the latent folly of his audience' (p. 28). By setting a negative example, the fool emphasizes what is valuable and how best to act. The Zuni Indian tribal clowns, *koyemci*, exemplify this (Bunzel, 1932; Charles, 1945). The *koyemci* are not only clowns but also members of the priestly class that rules the village. In their ritual celebrations, the grotesque, obscene antics of these sacred clown–priests offer a cathartic expression of otherwise repressed fears and anxieties.

This role has been institutionalized in the professions of clown, buffoon, or court jester (Swain, 1932; Welsford, 1935; Klapp, 1972; Lever, 1983). The symbols of the fool's institutionalized role, his cap and stick, parodied the crown and scepter of the monarch. Under the guise of madness or stupidity (apparent harmlessness), the jester could speak the otherwise unspeakable. This is explicit in Shakespeare's *As You Like It*, where the jester 'uses his folly like a stalking-horse, and under the presentation of that he shoots his wit' (Act 5, Scene 4). Clumsiness, exaggeration, absent-mindedness, concealment, pantomime, and botched acts were used to get the message across (Bergson, 1928). Kris (1938) calls the jester a living caricature. He or she becomes the vehicle to express what under other circumstances would be considered destructive social information.

Perhaps the most famous illustration of a person playing such a role is the fool in Shakespeare's *King Lear*. Although seemingly half-witted, only he has both the wisdom and the courage to recognize and tell the truth. This sage–fool quickly sees through the various hidden agendas to apprehend the foolishness of the king's action in giving away his kingdom. The court jester becomes the privileged critic, a paradoxical figure both depreciated and appreciated. He is the disinterested truth-sayer who speaks frankly about how things really are. Humor is used to cushion the otherwise unspeakable, in this case, to iterate the king's self-deception about the true natures of his daughters.

What both Erasmus and Shakespeare indicate is that the power of the king needs the folly of the fool. They are like twins who keep each other in psychic equilibrium. The king–fool duality illustrates the Janus-like nature of power. The proverb 'fools rush in where angels fear to tread' has more than one meaning. The sage–fool is often the only one who can put a brake on the king's hubris. Equally important, the sage–fool (or, as he or she is sometimes called, *morosophe*, from the Greek meaning 'fool' and 'wise') (Lever, 1983), can play an important role in preventing leadership pathology. The fool will play the role of the 'insultant'.

THE BENEFITS OF HUMOR

Humor deals with conflicted imagery in a gentle way, preventing sudden explosions of tension. It can be a formidable weapon against those who, under other circumstances, would refuse to recognize and accept the true nature of things. It helps to maintain a sense of proportion about events and puts a brake on our tendency to take ourselves too seriously. It also has an unmasking function, releasing unconscious material, so can be a sort of safety valve. In this function, it can be used to control potentially destructive outcomes of leadership.

Humor is often a good way of highlighting signs of hubris. It is also a covert way of approaching taboo topics. Humor can be used to change a strained situation into a pleasant one. The psychiatrist George Vaillant (1977) once said, 'Humor is one of the truly elegant defenses in the human repertoire. Few would deny that the capacity of humor, like hope, is one of mankind's most potent antidotes for the woes of Pandora's box' (p. 116). Something said in jest does not carry the same weight as it does in ordinary communication. Consequently, greater risks can be taken in getting a difficult message across.

Their behavior and actions suggest that fools know, consciously or unconsciously, the power of the one-down position. They realize that humorous self-depreciation may make others feel better. Fools' antics enable us to unload our feelings of inferiority onto them. By so doing, we may feel virtuous compared with such misfits. Of course, there are risks involved in taking on this role. The fool runs the risk of becoming a scapegoat, representing an evil or malignant force that has to be expelled. Danger has always been an occupational hazard for the fool.

The anthropologist Radcliffe-Brown (1952) sees joking relationships as a form of permitted disrespect, a way of managing potential conflicts in society. Freud (1905) came to a similar conclusion. He noticed that people used humor as a socially acceptable way of releasing anxiety-provoking wishes of an aggressive and sexual nature. In particular, humor allows the expression of aggressive and vengeful feelings that otherwise would not be tolerated (Levine, 1961; Rose, 1969). But laughter can also mask many other emotions, such as sadness, despair, fear, regret, triumph, and hate.

Freud (1927) also identified the fact that 'humor is not resigned; it is rebellious' (p. 103). In many instances, joking behavior is used as a way of getting back at figures of authority. The fool turns into an anarchist, using humor to make the breaking of rules and regulations less objectionable (Goffman, 1967). However, his sort of rebellion has a tame, covert nature, and is a form of non-violent resistance (Bergler, 1937). But in this way, humor also becomes a safety valve (paradoxically, given its rebellious origin), an instrument of social control and regulation (Levine, 1961; Berlyne, 1964; Block, 1987). In spite of their ridicule of the established order, fools are actually engaged in setting outer limits to what is permitted. The break from day-to-day conventionality remains only temporary. As Pollio and Edgerly (1976) indicate in their research on humor, 'in this role of moralist-in-reverse the fool acts as a control mechanism stressing what he violates by emphasizing what is beyond him. To call a non-fool, *fool*, is to put social pressure on that individual to conform to a social value' (p. 216).

WHAT MAKES A FOOL?

To understand what motivates clowns or jesters to want to capture the audience's attention, it is important to examine their own preoccupations. In a study of professional comedians and clowns, using projective and other tests, Fisher and Fisher (1981) discovered a number of recurring themes in their inner world. According to their study, true comics 'deny that things are as bad or threatening as they seem,' they are 'fascinated by size ... particularly sensitive to smallness,' and they 'are sensitive to the dimension of up-down' (p. 35). Comics associate these patterns with a specific childhood situation where, from an early age, they had to learn to take care of themselves, having come to the realization that there was little emotional support to be expected from their parents. Fisher and Fisher suggest that by being ridiculous, comics conveyed the message that they had been treated in a ridiculous way.

The main dilemma for many future clowns or jesters seems to be that they were prematurely pushed into the adult roles while still children. This lack of congruency between their own capacity and the expectations of others may have led to preoccupations of feeling small, powerless, and unworthy. These feelings are hard to accept, so comedians may be acting the way they do, due to a life strategy of denying the unpleasant. Humor is a very effective all-purpose tool for this strategy (Fry and Allen, 1975). It is a form of defense, a way of dealing with anger about the absurdity of their situation. It is also a way of blunting depressive feelings and, by attracting attention, of proving that they are not as inadequate or bad as they may seem. Comics are fundamentally preoccupied with equalization. And, when they are through with their antics, all differences between good and bad, small and big, adult and child, or up and down are blurred—everyone ends up at the same level.

THE ORGANIZATIONAL FOOL

In organizational life, there are many ways to create checks and balances as a form of protection against the abuse of power. Aspects of the organizational infrastructures and suprastructures can be used as levers. Certain rules and regulations have a boundary function. In addition, given the role of the organization's many stakeholders, power can be distributed among a number of constituents.

But, notwithstanding these safeguards, the bottom line is that most organizations are not true democracies. Many important organizational processes are decided on in secret by a few senior figures. So, help is sometimes needed to prevent the abuse of power in organizations and shield against the loss of reality-based decision-making. This kind of help can be provided by a courageous individual who is willing to challenge the organization's leadership and help them see things from another perspective, free from the distortions of sycophancy.

Just as the *morosophe* played with fire when giving unpleasant news to the king through his foolery, it is a risky business to articulate the hidden agendas in organizational life, through dramatization, exaggeration, and humor (Malone, 1980). Bringing unconscious material to the surface in organizations can at times be explosive.

From early on Freud (1910) struggled with this issue in his paper on 'wild' psychoanalysis. He thought that two conditions had to be filled if informing another person of unconscious material were to have a positive outcome and not lead to intensification of conflict:

> First, the patient must, through preparation, himself have reached the neighborhood of what he has repressed and secondly, he must have formed a sufficient attachment (transference) to the physician for his emotional relationships to him to make a fresh flight impossible.
>
> Only when these conditions have been fulfilled is it possible to recognize and to master the resistances which have led to repression and the ignorance. Psychoanalytic intervention, therefore, absolutely requires a fairly long period of contact with the patient. Attempts to 'rush' him at first consultation, by brusquely telling him the secrets which have been discovered by the physician, are technically objectionable. (p. 226)

What Freud is really saying is that, in order to ease the surfacing of emotionally charged material in the context of psychotherapy, a working alliance must first be established between the two parties in question. To accomplish this, a certain amount of trust is needed. Furthermore, doses of insight have to be well-timed and carefully measured (Kets de Vries and Miller, 1985; Kets de Vries, 2006). Similarly, in playing the role of truthsayer, the sage–fool must realize that there are limits to the amount of conflict-ridden information the leader can accept at any given time. Fortunately, humor can play an important role in relieving tension when the truthsayer is trying to make a point about a sensitive issue. It short-circuits resistances and improves the readiness of the party toward whom the communication is directed to listen to what is being said.

A good example of the role of the sage–fool in a certain form of organizational life can be found in the novel *The Good Soldier Svejk* by the Czech author Jaroslov Hasek (1972). In one of the greatest masterpieces of satirical writing, Hasek describes the misadventures of his seemingly idiotic hero, making fun of the decaying Austro-Hungarian Empire and its war machine. In a certain way, Svejk stands for anybody trapped in the cogs of bureaucracy. His idiocy is really a subterfuge for wisdom and wit. He is a careful observer of humanity and his penetrating commentary makes others realize the absurdity of their actions. Svejk is an excellent example of the sage–fool. Using double-talk and the literal execution of orders, he demonstrates the foolishness of many rules and regulations. Through his behavior and actions he brings figures of authority down to size, having an uncanny ability to deal with any superior. He becomes the perfect antidote to hubris.

The role of the sage–fool in organizational life can be taken either by a person within the organization or by an outsider. In general, it is more difficult for an insider to take on the role, as the risks tend to be greater. The king's fool had to be careful not to go too far and forfeit his life, and the organizational fool has similarly to tread gently: dealing with highly sensitive material and telling it how it is can be prejudicial to career advancement. Whistle-blowing (standing up to figures of authority in an organization, for example, objecting to unethical or illegal practices), usually spells a bad end for the individual who initiates the process.

> When I realized what was happening, I was furious. It wasn't illegal, it wasn't criminal, it was irresponsible. Every day the papers wrote about cutbacks in funding [the service], nearly every day I got reminders about cost savings, and here were resources being mismanaged and squandered so obviously it was beyond belief. I went to my superiors but it was like talking to a brick wall. So I went to the papers myself. I didn't have much to lose, I was down for early retirement, but I did it anonymously anyway. All hell was let loose, somehow they found out who I was, I had the press and TV outside my house, and at work the atmosphere was unbearable. And in the end nothing happened. It was a five-minute wonder for the press. It all got lost in the bureaucratic mess of the service. (Interview with public service worker, UK)

When communication is blocked within an organization, or when an individual feels isolated and without support, it is tempting to turn to outside entities, such as the media, to air grievances. It is virtually impossible for the individual to escape the resulting fallout and hostility from all sides, especially as an organization exposed in this manner is hardly likely to provide the support and protection that the whistle-blower needs—the lack of which probably precipitated the action in the first place. The painful irony for whistle-blowers is that their personal integrity and trustworthiness, which motivate their actions, are put into doubt, and they frequently end up being blamed for the very things they expose. This is the classic reaction of killing the messenger who brings bad news. Whistle-blowers are fools working without protective clothing.

Enron employee Sharon Watkins became the most spectacular example of recent corporate whistle-blowing when she exposed former Enron chairman and CEO Kenneth Lay's very questionable accounting practices in 2002. Thousands of employees lost their retirement and savings plans while corporate officers ran off with the store. While testifying for a congressional committee, Watkins told how she met with Kenneth Lay, the founder of Enron, after taking to heart his encouragement that Enron employees could bring any problems directly to him. Within two days after her session with Lay, when she alerted him to accounting irregularities within Enron, the company sought legal advice on the consequences of terminating her employment. Enron's lack of response to her concerns ultimately led her to seek help from the media (McLean and Elkind, 2003).

In organizations, the role of the sage–fool is frequently assumed by a consultant. It is one of many roles a consultant is asked to play, not necessarily explicitly. Often, both parties remain unaware of the function that the consultant is fulfilling, and also of the importance that role has in keeping the organization firmly tied to reality. Occasionally, however, senior executives realize the value of having a 'corporate jester.' In my work in organizations I have encountered companies that use consultants for the specific purpose of staging short, satirical sketches in order to transmit difficult messages. In general, however, it appears that such messages are directed to middle management more often than to the top echelons.

Consultants frequently realize that the real problem presenting in an organization is very different from the problem the client originally defined. There can be a large gap between what clients say they want and what they need. Clients usually find it easier to talk about the role of others in creating problems than about their own contribution to them. There is often great reluctance to raise and confront the real issues. Bringing some of the contributing factors out into the open (with the consultant in the catalytic role of the fool) can be extremely important for clarity and insight (Kets de Vries and Miller, 1984; Kets de Vries, 2006).

This does not mean, however, that someone internal to the organization cannot take on this role. At times, a trusted senior executive will play the part. Some organizations even make attempts to institutionalize the role, casting internal consultants, some kind of ombudsman (following the Scandinavian tradition), or a senior executive without a specific portfolio in the part. With certain skills of dramatization, a less senior manager may occasionally play the organizational fool. Some organizations may actually prefer to have someone at a less elevated level, a Mr. Everyman, or Svejk, in the part.

In general, however, it is easier for an outsider to assume such a difficult role as the worst that can happen when the feedback becomes too disturbing is a prematurely terminated consultancy relationship. Indeed, the role of the external adviser and that of the fool seem to be made for each other. By playing dumb and asking seemingly naïve questions, the consultant can further the understanding of a particular organizational problem and take on the role of the agent for change. Here humor can be of great use, particularly when testing options and making recommendations.

Sometimes a CEO will recognize the need for regular input from external opinion in order to keep in touch with reality. The French financier, entrepreneur, and politician Bernard Tapie identified this as a principle of his leadership. In his autobiography, *Gagner* (*Winning*), he wrote:

> Even the most intelligent and shrewd of leaders surround themselves with people who surrender their individuality and spirit of opposition when face to face with their boss ... They say nothing, even when they see the leader leading the company astray, because they don't dare to ... A great leader will of his own volition institute a culture of deliberate irresponsibility. For me, frank discussion and what I call creative tension are absolutely fundamental. For this reason I have a network of friends whom I consult just as much as I consult my team. They are journalists, businessmen, a mixture of very different people who are completely independent of me, who aren't my employees, and who will tell me where to get off—and that's crucial. If you haven't got people around who'll tell you when to take a running jump, you're not a proper boss ...
>
> In order to choose the right sort of people to have around, the sort who also want to be 'winners,' you have to know yourself; to be open to contradictory opinions, to be able to work out where your own strengths and weaknesses lie. (1986, pp. 126–127)

In one company in the automotive supply business, the role of the sage–fool was played by the vice-president for manufacturing and operations. This individual, a self-made man who had risen through the production route, was intimately familiar with the internal processes of the organization. He was extremely effective in his job and highly respected because of his pragmatism. Given his background and the fact that the company was very marketing-driven, he had risen as far as he could. That did not seem to worry him, however, as he obviously liked the position he was in. Since he posed no direct threat to any of the other senior executives—power games were the least of his concern—his counsel was eagerly sought. Although the company had a director of human resources, the VP for manufacturing and operations informally played a very important role in that area.

When the CEO retired and a successor was appointed from within the conglomerate of which the organization was a part, the VP began to assume an even more prominent role for a number of reasons. In the first place, the new CEO was not very knowledgeable about the company or the industry, having worked in a very different sector. Second, he was quite abrasive when dealing with subordinates. When things were not exactly to his liking he was quick to cut them off or silence them completely with sarcastic remarks. Tension in the company rose with the dismissal of two old-timers after a heated executive meeting. Executives were increasingly at a loss to know how to deal with the new arrival. His mercurial temperament deterred them from arguing with him even when they felt he was making decisions that were not in the best interests of the corporation.

In order to cope with the prevailing state of anxiety and re-focus the company's strategy, the VP for manufacturing and operations began to play an increasingly visible role at executive meetings. In a humorous way, he was able to calm emotions but also to tell the CEO what he felt would be the right course for the company, reflecting the not-publicly-expressed consensus of the group.

His self-effacing but humorous style had a calming effect on the CEO, who was experiencing a considerable amount of anxiety about how to tackle his new job. Under the influence of the vice-president, the executive meetings were transformed. Having important issues portrayed in a humorous manner allowed them to be viewed with a more balanced perspective. Gradually, the other executives became sufficiently courageous to express their own opinions freely. When aspects of the CEO's abrasive style re-emerged, the VP was quick to neutralize the situation.

In another organization, an external consultant took on a similar role. He had been brought in to rationalize the work flow in the design department. He suggested it should be organized in a different way, with the establishment of some kind of 'skunk work,' in this instance, a design project group located elsewhere. This proved highly effective and created a burst of activity throughout the organization. Because of its success, the consultant was asked to help design and implement a new perform-ance-appraisal system. The CEO, normally a rather aloof individual, difficult to approach, very much appreciated the work of the consultant and began to take him into his confidence.

Since the CEO was not completely satisfied with the way executive meetings operated, he asked the consultant to sit in on some of the sessions and recommend ways to improve decision-making. The consultant quickly realized that the CEO's awkwardness was responsible for the rather painful discussions and stifled the free flow of information and creative ideas. Some form of action was needed to make the sessions more productive. He decided to ask for pseudo-naïve clarifications of the different issues at hand and to use humor. His regular attendance at the meetings proved extremely useful. His interventions helped to break the ice, while putting across important points. Gradually, all the executives loosened up and the discussions became much more of a give-and-take where people would listen to each other and build on each other's ideas.

THE VALUE OF THE FOOL

These examples illustrate how organizational sage–fools can take on a complementary role. When the sage–fool becomes the counterweight of the person in power, a kind of executive role constellation is formed (Hodgson, Levinson, and Zaleznik, 1965), which can be highly effective as a safety device in preventing organizational pathology. Through humor, the 'fool' and the 'king' engage in a form of deep play dealing with fundamental human issues like control, rivalry, passivity, and activity. There is an intricate link between the roles of the two: leaders need fools and vice versa.

George Bernard Shaw once said that 'every despot must have one disloyal subject to keep him sane.' That is what the sage–fool is all about. He or she plays an essential role in keeping an organization on track, maintaining its ties to reality, and most important of all, fighting the forces of hubris.

ENDNOTE

This chapter has been collated from material published in the following sources:

- Kets de Vries, M.F.R. (1990). 'The organizational fool: Balancing a leader's hubris,' *Human Relations*, **43** (8): 751–770.
- Kets de Vries, M.F.R. (1993). *Leaders, Fools and Impostors*. San Francisco: Jossey-Bass.

PART II

THE PATHOLOGY
OF LEADERSHIP

INTRODUCTION

Someone suggested to me that this section might be titled 'When Leaders Go Bad,' which is a crude but not wholly inaccurate way to describe the main themes of the chapters in Part II.

Some years ago I saw a cartoon of two fighting children being pulled apart by their mother. One child points at the other, protesting, 'She called me a CEO first!' In the past, business leadership was viewed as an essentially benign activity, with leaders working for the good of the organization and all its stakeholders. Most studies of leadership emphasized its positive, transforming aspects, assigning an almost moral dimension to the task—a calling to a higher plane. But this is no longer the case. Those 'outmoded' studies avoided confronting the dark side of leadership, the part that flourishes on the power that comes with the role. This 'Darth Vader' side, which grows out of personality traits like self-aggrandizement and entitlement, thrives on narcissism, self-deceit, greed, distrust, and the abuse of power. In the psychopathology of leadership, the combination of a dysfunctional personality and personal power can, and almost inevitably does, create social and business disasters.

Working with executives, you quickly realize that they don't behave rationally all the time. In fact, irrational behavior is common in organizational life and business leaders are much more complex than the usual run of subjects that psychologists study. People with mental illness are actually relatively easy to understand because they suffer from extreme conditions. The state of mental health of senior executives is much more subtle. They can't be too crazy or they wouldn't have made it to a senior position—but they are nonetheless extremely driven people. When I try to understand them, I usually find that their behavior springs from childhood patterns and experiences that have carried over into adulthood. It should be said that executives are not usually very pleased to hear this; they like to think that they are completely in control and are almost insulted to think that they might have an unconscious. But we all have blind spots and the non-rational personality needs of people who make decisions can seriously affect the management process and the organization itself.

I find that many executives are trying to compensate for narcissistic injuries—wounds to their self-esteem that were inflicted in childhood by parents who were, too distant, too inconsistent, or too indulgent. People with narcissistic injuries have a great hunger for recognition and external affirmation. To counteract their feelings of helplessness and lack of self-worth, they are always in search of an audience. And generally—part and parcel of their reluctance to admit that they might act in response to unconscious dynamics—I find that they have no idea that narcissistic wounds underlie their behavior. To make executives and leaders aware of their vulnerabilities (they are very good at hiding them from themselves and others), I sometimes ask them to describe the most critical negative voice that still plays in their heads from childhood. They all hear one: even the most successful will admit to a lingering echo of someone saying, 'You're not as good as you think you are. You will not amount to anything. You're an imposter.' That voice—perhaps the voice of a critical parent, perhaps the voice of the child who realized it couldn't live up to its parents' estimation—will influence the actions and relationships of an individual on a daily basis.

Once someone harboring a narcissistic injury reaches a position of power, funny things start to happen. Because such people are often highly charismatic, employees start to project their own grandiose fantasies onto the leader, and suddenly everything becomes surreal. This means, of course, that followers are in a vulnerable position as well. Dependency reactions take over.

I discovered this process for myself when I was about 14. My brother and I were at a youth camp in the Netherlands where we went every summer. Like everybody else, we usually went for only three weeks but this particular year we were sent away for the whole summer holiday. After three weeks there was always a transition between the old group and the new intake and my brother and I decided to liven up the changeover by creating an initiation ritual. We put a bathtub full of freezing water in the middle of a field and told all the new arrivals that it was an old camp tradition that everyone had to dip themselves in it. I shall never forget the sight of 60 boys—most of them much bigger than us—lining up obediently and one after the other climbing into the tub. Then the camp director happened to walk past … He brought our reign of terror to an abrupt end by pointing out to the boys that there were 60 of them and only two of us, and my brother and I got what we deserved. But I was left with a lasting impression of just how far people are willing to go to obey what they perceive as authority.

The fact is that people with even scant authority can get away with murder, literally and figuratively. I have been in some companies so permeated with insecurity and fear that they trigger images of concentration camps. I once met an executive who told me, 'Every day I walk into the office, I can make the lives of 10,000 people completely miserable by doing very, very little.' Now why would you want to do that?

The answer lies in the perpetual dilemma that has faced tyrants of all kinds throughout history. In spite of all their possessions, in spite of all their power, they are constantly on their guard against threats in their environment. I have been curious for years about what makes despotic leaders tick. What is the personality construct of a Caligula or a Hitler? What makes them behave in the way they do? How did they become so cruel? Why do the Mugabes of this world derail and slide into despotism? And on a lesser, but more common scale, what is happening in the inner world of ruthless leaders in the workplace? Why do some executives seem to lose their sense of humanity? Why and how do they create terror in their organizations? In this section, I highlight some of the psychological forces that make leaders prisoners of leadership. These psychological pressures may cause stress, anxiety, and depression, which may in their turn provoke irresponsible and irrational behavior that affects an organization's culture and decision-making patterns.

Tyranny in any context is inseparable from power. Thomas Jefferson once wrote: 'Whenever a man casts a longing eye on offices, a rottenness begins in his conduct.' Power can be a disease, contaminating those who come into contact with it; and it can be a narcotic, turning the power-hungry into addicts. Many people who seem otherwise quite sane suddenly engage in pathological behavior when they are given power. We all have a dark side, one that shows itself only in certain situations—like my and my brother's opportunistic and short-lived foray into despotism. I suspect that most of us will have been surprised by the recognition of the potential for violence within us.

Luckily very few of us will realize that potential to the extent that Shaka Zulu did. When I was studying in the stacks of the Harvard Library more years ago than I like to remember, I came across an article in *Scientific American* about the ways in which the infamous African king, Shaka Zulu, had modernized warfare in the nineteenth century. The article intrigued me. I saw Shaka, who is still held in awe in southern Africa, as the prototype of leaders who go off the rails. Much of his behavior reminded me of Saddam Hussein and, to a lesser degree, Robert

Mugabe. One thing led to another, and before I knew it, I had written the basis of a book from which Chapter 9 is drawn.

In that chapter, I explore the unusual relationship between leaders and followers in despotic regimes, and the self-destructive cycle that characterizes them. I highlight the price paid in the form of human suffering, the breakdown of the moral fabric of society, and the levers used by such regimes to consolidate their power base. I review the role of ideology, the illusion of solidarity, and the search for scapegoats. There are many valuable lessons for contemporary leadership to be learned from Shaka's story. I end with a number of suggestions about how despotic leaders might be prevented from gaining power—and looking up and ahead, the chapters in Part III of this book look at the sort of leaders who walk into the office every day determined to make the lives of their people very, very happy.

CHAPTER 7

PRISONERS OF LEADERSHIP

An army of a thousand is easy to find, but, ah, how difficult to find a general.

—Chinese proverb

INTRODUCTION

In the previous chapters I have presented different types of executives. I have looked at 'live volcanoes' and 'dead fish.' I also reviewed the phenomenon of imposture in organizational life. In addition, I have looked at the wise fool as a possible countervailing force to keep senior executives focused on reality. And the reality-testing abilities of senior executives can be a serious problem in organizational life. To be in a position of power can do strange things to people. Hasn't it been said that 'Whom the gods would destroy, they first make mad with power'? Abraham Lincoln was not far from the truth when he wryly remarked, 'Nearly all men can stand adversity, but if you want to test a man's character, give him power.' To understand what happens when people get power, we have to enter the inner world of the leader.

In most instances, the inner world of a leader remains largely an enigma to researchers, making it difficult to engage in thematic analysis of their behavior or isolate salient patterns. But given the importance of leadership to society at large, persevering in trying to understand the inner world of top executives will be well worth it. In trying to demystify the forces at work, a number of questions warrant our attention. For example, why do some people derail when they reach the top? Why do executives who seems bright, likeable, and well-adjusted, suddenly resort to strange behavior when they become CEO? What can go wrong when someone becomes a senior executive? There are no simple answers to these questions. First, however, consider an example that illustrates the kind of irrational behavior to which I am referring.

The case of Robert Clark

Before Robert Clark[1] assumed the presidency of the Solan Corporation, he had always been well-liked. His supervisors had been impressed by his capacity for work, his helpful attitude, his dedication, and his imaginative method of solving problems. He eventually crowned his seemingly brilliant career by being selected to succeed Solan's former CEO.

In the period immediately after Clark assumed his role he received many accolades for taking a number of long overdue steps. Gradually, however, after the initial enthusiasm had passed, many of his old colleagues concluded that he seemed to have undergone a personality change. He had become less accessible; his widely acclaimed open-door policy and advocacy of participative management had disappeared. He had become increasingly authoritarian, impatient, and careless of the feelings of others. Subordinates who did not share his opinion found themselves out of favor or even fired. Being the bringer of bad news became an increasingly risky proposition, while yea-sayers were welcomed.

The effects of Clark's transformation on the organization quickly became clear. In their desire to please him, key executives would jostle for his attention and waste time and energy on power games and intra-company squabbles rather than making strategic decisions. Dealing with the reality of the business became less and less important. Company morale sank to an all-time low, and the financial results were deteriorating.

What happened to Clark is that certain psychological forces—his own, and those of his followers—came into play, creating a multitude of problems. These occurred for three reasons:

- Succession to the top leadership position in an organization is necessarily isolating in that it separates leaders from others (who now directly report to them) and leaves them without peers. As a result, their own normal dependency needs for contact, support, and reassurance rise up and overwhelm them. The increasing isolation may make them anxious.

- Whether consciously or unconsciously employees expect their organization's leaders to be exceptionally capable—almost gifted with magical powers. Leaders have a hard time refusing these positive 'projections' of their subordinates, and may start believing that they are as infallible and powerful as their subordinates think they are. Reality-testing may suffer when this occurs.

- Troubled by guilt feelings about their success and fearful that it may not last, some leaders become anxious about the envy of others and may unconsciously cause themselves to fail. Some leaders may engage in self-sabotage. They may become so anxious that they cannot make decisions. The expression 'snatching defeat out of the jaws of victory' is all too true.

To some degree, every human being suffers from these reactions and feelings. History has provided us with many examples of leaders whose behavior became pathological in the extreme once they attained power: political leaders such as King Saul, Caligula, Adolf Hitler, and Stalin, or business leaders such as Howard Hughes, Conrad Black (Hollinger International), and Michael Eisner (former CEO of Walt Disney).

I am not suggesting that all business leaders resort to pathological behavior upon reaching the top of their organizations. What differentiates those leaders who crash from those who don't is the latter's ability to stay in touch with reality by creating a vibrant culture of open discourse in their organization and to take these psychological forces in their stride. Many leaders are very good at handling the pressures that leadership brings; indeed, some individuals who may previously have been rather colorless turn into great leaders when they attain positions of power. However, some leaders just can't manage; the regressive pulls simply become too strong.

But what psychological effects are at work between leader and followers? The answer to these questions can be found—using clinical insights—by looking at psychological defensive processes, transferential relationships, primitive group processes, and dysfunctional ways of managing anxiety and aggression.

The case of Frederick the Great

During the night at Münsterberg I had a strange dream—I don't know why, but I have the same dream very often. Anyway I dreamed my father came into my room at night with six soldiers and ordered them to tie me up and bring me to Magdeburg. 'But why?' I asked my sister who lives in Bayreuth. 'Because you have not loved your father enough.'

And I awoke dripping with sweat as if someone had dipped me in the river. (Koser, 1900, p. 45)

The story of Frederick the Great provides unusually rich material about the inner world of one particular leader. It shows us how specific anchor events, and a significant dream, can affect a leader's subsequent behavior. We also see clearly in this the developmental and motivational role of fear, anxiety, rivalry, guilt and envy, as well as the importance of objects of identification and how these affect a leader's later adult behavior.

Frederick the Great, King of Prussia, had this dream on January 19, 1760 when he was 48 years old. In a condensed form, this dream signals the conflicts that were critical in molding Frederick's personality and that contributed greatly to his later way of behaving and acting.

Dreams have a tendency to telescope events in time (Freud, 1900, 1933), and this is what seems to have happened here. Although it is the quality of sustained relationships that eventually determine an individual's personality make-up, important scenes in a person's inner theater can often be discerned from the way in which they handle specific key events. It is very likely that the dream described above referred to memories of a significant event that had occurred in Frederick's life 30 years earlier when, as a young prince, he seems to have experienced some kind of inner metamorphosis.

This key event in Frederick's life came after his attempt to escape from his father's tyranny and flee Prussia. This act was the culmination of a rebellious attitude toward his father who, albeit well-meaning, had been oppressive in his attempts to mold his son in his own image. The regimentation to which the young Frederick had been subjected had been intense. The responsibilities of his tutors were laid out in the minutest detail, with the threat of capital punishment as a deterrent to any deviation from them. Nothing was left to chance; the slightest breach of the rules had to be reported. Frederick's father wanted, at all costs, to make a soldier out of his son and, moreover, to make him love soldiering. He considered Frederick's interests in the fine arts, which had been generated by his mother and an older sister, to be effeminate, and forbade him to pursue them. Frederick's subtle sabotage of his father's stifling demands were met by violent attacks of rage about his mental and physical abuse, to paranoid fears of being assassinated, and to states of deep depression.

In his father's eyes, Frederick's attempt to flee the country was part of a malicious plot. Political intrigues by senior officials and the machinations of his wife may have added to this paranoid notion (Asprey, 1986). As might be expected, his son's clumsy escape efforts during a nightly stopover led to his arrest by his father's soldiers. He was incarcerated by his father and kept incommunicado in a small fortress near Berlin. Only then did it dawn on the young crown prince how seriously his father looked at his rather impulsive, innocent act. This was made quite clear when he was exposed to a brutal, horrifying scene. Under instructions from his father, Frederick was forced to watch the beheading of his 'accomplice,' an intimate friend. The deprivation caused by the incarceration and the shock of watching this execution seriously affected his mental state and marked a turning point in his relationship with his father.

From then on, a remarkable transformation took place in his behavior (Lewy, 1967). Rebelliousness seemed to have given way to submission and partial identification with his father. Frederick's resort to this and other defense mechanisms is demonstrated in the way he later rationalized this probation period as being invaluable for his training as king. The outbursts of great grief he showed when his father died can be taken as another indicator of defense mechanisms at work, 'identification with the aggressor' being the most likely (Freud, 1966) (see p. 139).

Soon after he became king, Frederick seemed ready to prove himself to the world—craving prestige and glory after having been kept in bondage by his father for so long. And his early actions as monarch quite clearly signaled the qualities of leadership and decision that would characterize his later reign.

When Frederick rose to power, he turned his army from an unruly group of soldiers into a well-oiled war machine. His behavior showed quite clearly his ability to externalize the conflicts of his private life and act them out on the public stage. Just as he had been drilled as a child, now it was his turn to drill his soldiers. And just as his father had done, he left no detail neglected. Standardization of equipment and specialization of tasks became the means to accomplish ultimate control over his men. To make his troops obey, Frederick was convinced that the men must fear their officers more than the enemy, a concept that must have been very dear to him, given the kind of relationship he had had with his father. At the same time, the courage and concern he showed on the battlefield must have been very inspiring to his men, and this particular leadership style did, indeed, seem to work—as his invasion of Silesia and his success in vastly expanding Prussian territory demonstrated. Without doubt,

Frederick's military tactics exerted a great influence on the art of warfare at the time.

In sharp contrast with the strong discipline he imposed on his army, in his role of enlightened despot Frederick instituted important legal and penal reforms, set up new industries, and encouraged educational innovations. He corresponded with Voltaire, wrote poetry, and completed prose work on history, politics, military service, and philosophy. He played the flute and composed marches and concertos.

Although we will never know the exact dynamics of Frederick's sudden transformation after his incarceration, he was subsequently somehow able in a very creative way, to combine soldiering with these so-called effeminate interests. His resolution of his particular inner conflicts made him a truly effective leader. Under his charismatic leadership, Prussia transformed dramatically. A great king and general, an imaginative statesman, and certainly deserving the description charismatic, he eventually earned the title Frederick the Great at the age of 33—a turn of events that would possibly have surprised his father.

EXTERNALIZING INNER CONFLICTS

For leaders to be effective, some kind of congruence is needed between their own and societal concerns. What gives truly effective leaders such conviction and power is their ability to articulate the underlying issues of a society. According to Erik Erikson (1958, 1969), using such dramatic examples as Martin Luther and Mahatma Gandhi, such leaders try to solve for all, what they originally could not solve for themselves; internal, private dialogues are transformed into external public concerns.

This identification of the connection between a public and a private crisis had already been made by the political scientist Harold Lasswell (1960) in his seminal work *Psychopathology and Politics*. According to Lasswell, the distinctive mark of *homo politicus* is the displacement of private motives onto public objects and, at the same time, the rationalization of these motives in terms of public interest. These people's intrapsychic conflicts are acted out on the public stage. The effectiveness of this process of externalization depends, however, on:

> the leader's ability to draw upon and manipulate the body of myth in a given culture and the actions and values associated with these myths to

> legitimize his claims by associating with himself the sacred symbols of the culture. (Willner and Willner, 1965, p. 77)

Thus, collective symbols are made proxy for self-symbols (Lasswell, 1960, p. 186). Part of the leadership phenomenon therefore seems to be a myth-making process whereby the leader's role in the myth is to make sense by creating continuity between past, present, and future.

One aspect of leadership seems to be 'cultural management, in part conscious and deliberate, in part probably unconscious and intuitive' (Willner and Willner, 1965, p. 83). Speeches, ceremonials, and rituals are some of the vehicles used to make this a successful process. And within cultural management, the mass media has an enormous influence on contemporary leadership. We can observe how the manipulation of propaganda techniques and the use of opinion polls have become critical to leaders, and the procedures employed are no different from those used in the creation of movie, theatrical, or television plays.

THE SEARCH FOR AUTHORITY

With the exception of Harold Lasswell, most political scientists failed to pay sufficient attention to the psychodynamic processes at play between leader and followers. Some of Sigmund Freud's later writings on societal issues can help us understand this topic better, however. According to Freud (1921), the appeal of leaders is that at a symbolic, unconscious level they represent the return of the primal father. What seems to happen psychologically is that, in fantasy, the followers replace their own ego ideal (the vehicle by which they measure themselves) with their unconscious version of the leader's ego ideal. When this occurs, the leader facilitates reconciliation between the two agencies of the mind, the ego (how we perceive ourselves) and the ego ideal (how we would like to be). Reconciliation between these two agencies of the mind reduces tension and can lead to a sense of euphoria. With their own demands and prohibitions dissipated and transferred to the leader, followers feel a sense of community between themselves and the leader. The leader turns into the conscience of the group. The followers no longer feel harassed by prohibitions; they have no more pangs of conscience. A group ego ideal comes into being, which serves all—and with that will come an abdication of personal responsibility. Followers now identify not only with the leader but also with each other in that they share a common outlet of identification. Freud noted:

We know that in the mass of mankind there is a powerful need for an authority who can be admired, before whom one bows down, by whom one is ruled and perhaps even ill-treated ... that all the characteristics with which we equipped the great man are paternal characteristics ... The decisiveness of thought, the strength of will, the energy of action are part of the picture of a father ... but above all the autonomy and independence of the great man, his divine unconcern which may grow into ruthlessness. One must admire him, one must trust him, but one cannot avoid being afraid of him too. (Freud, 1939, pp. 109–110)

Freud compared the bond between leader and followers to an act of falling in love or to the state of trance between hypnotist and subject. When this identification process occurs, followers will indulge in an orgy of simple and strong emotions and may be swept along by the leader's appeal. Although Freud does not discuss this explicitly, at the heart of this psychological process is the dynamic of transference. Leaders facilitate transference reactions.

Transference

The phenomenon of transference, which is touched on in Chapter 2, can be described as a kind of 'false connection' (Breuer and Freud, 1893–95), a confusion in time and place between people. A person perceives and responds to someone else as if that person were mother, father, sibling, or another important figure from the past. Thus, transference creates a modified version of an old relationship (Greenson, 1967; Langs, 1976). We rarely act toward other people as though they are a clean slate. In most situations, past experiences influence the present ones. As the case of Frederick the Great demonstrates, all our present reactions are colored by those in the past. Transferential characteristics are present in all meaningful relationships; all human interactions consist of a mixture of realistic and transference reactions.

As authority figures, leaders are prime outlets for these types of emotional reactions. Leaders easily revive previously unresolved conflicts followers have had with significant figures in the past. In these situations, regressive behavior may occur: followers endowing their leaders with the same omniscience and omnipotence that in childhood they attributed to parents or other significant figures. Transference reactions can be acted out in different ways and affect both leaders and followers. Conceptually, we can distinguish between three types: idealizing, mirror, and persecutor reactions (Kets de Vries and Miller, 1984a).

Idealizing Transference

As the heart of this process is a lingering striving to recover a state of lost perfection. This belief in 'Paradise lost' stems from the time when the early childhood illusion of absolute self-sufficiency and contentment gave way to the recognition of dependence and feelings of inferiority. As a way of combating feelings of helplessness there is a need for a state of merger with an apparently omnipotent and perfect other person (Kohut, 1971; Kohut and Wolf, 1978). To have a relationship with others whom they can admire makes those who behave in this way feel much better. To project our own opinions and values on others and identify with them becomes a way of affirming our own existence and enhancing our self-esteem.

Mirror Transference

It is very hard to imagine, unless one has experienced it, what it means to be the object of excessive admiration by followers—even in those instances where some of it may be warranted. Too much admiration can have dire consequences for a leader's mind; he or she may eventually believe that they really are as perfect, as intelligent or as powerful as others think. This belief may be intensified by the fact that leaders frequently have the power to turn some fantasies into reality. Of course, the distinction between mirror and idealizing reactions is only a conceptual one. In practice, these processes occur simultaneously.

No leader can really sustain the primitive idealization of the followers. There are always going to be frustrating experiences. The outcome of not meeting the tacit promise is predictable. Followers are fickle; they change their minds easily. There seems to be no middle road. Angry about the frustration of their dependency needs, and perhaps aggravated by callous, exploitative behavior, the subordinates of such leaders may react by engaging in hostile, rebellious acts against them. The leader can then be the target of a considerable dose of overt and covert aggression.

The Persecutory Transference

When subordinates unload their anger onto their leaders, the latter may counterreact. Given the pressures placed upon them, leaders may begin to feel persecuted, look for victims, and retaliate. As has been said, paranoia is the disease of kings.

In the context of these three interdependent transference reactions, the defense called 'identification with the aggressor' will often appear (Freud, 1966; Kets de Vries, 1980). This defense mechanism explains why followers continue to be attracted to leaders in spite of their abhorrence, and at another level, in spite of the leaders' violent acts. At the core of it all is the followers' illusion, which they cling to as a way of overcoming their own fears, that through identification they can incorporate into themselves aspects of the perceived omnipotence of the leader.

The followers' unconscious wish behind this merger is that they will become as powerful as the aggressor. Hence, an illusory transformation occurs whereby instead of being the helpless victim the follower convinces him- or herself that he or she is in control. Thus, followers may behave as insensitively toward outsiders as their leaders do, having appropriated the latter's particular symbols of power. Meanwhile, their feelings toward their leaders will alternate between love, affection, and fear. Naturally, followers who adopt this defense mechanism share the outlooks of their leaders and support them even if they engage in unrealistic, grandiose schemes or imagine the existence of malicious plots and enemies.

The move from these transferential patterns and defensive processes to group situations is only a small step.

REGRESSIVE GROUP PROCESSES

Group behavior can often be quite regressive. Black-and-white thinking dominates and scapegoating becomes common. The capacity for moderation and reflection will be absent. To quote Freud:

> A group is extraordinarily credulous and open to influence, it has no critical faculty, and the improbable does not exist for it. It thinks in images, which call one another up by association (just as they arise within individuals in states of free imagination), and whose agreement with reality is never checked by any reasonable agency. The feelings of a group are always very simple and very exaggerated. So that a group knows neither doubt nor uncertainty. (Freud, 1921, p. 78)

It was the research of the psychiatrist and psychoanalyst Wilfred Bion (1961) however, that shed most light on the regressive potential of groups. From his observations, he arrived at two common aspects of group behavior.

- Groups have an overt, specific task to perform that necessitates cooperation and effort from their members, a task that requires contact with reality. Here, leaders fulfill a function by providing the group members with a focus and a set of values with which to work.

- Groups are also affected by the 'basic assumptions' tendency. These basic assumptions, like transference reactions, are derivatives of an individual's way of coping with the various forms of anxiety generated by different life situations.

Whereas the work aspect of the group is more oriented toward reality, the basic-assumption aspect operates at a far more primitive level. Bion divided these basic-assumption characteristics of groups into three categories: pairing, dependency, and fight–flight. Interestingly enough, there seems to be considerable similarity between the transferential patterns described earlier and these basic assumptions (Kets de Vries and Miller, 1984b). Basic assumptions are, in fact, probably derived from transference reactions. For example:

- Pairing has elements in common with mirror transference. A utopian ideal is kept alive that somewhere there exists a person who will deliver the group from hatred, destructiveness, and despair. The individuals chosen as part of the pair are assigned the mission to deliver this state of bliss to the group. They become the alter egos, the bearers of the group's feelings of grandiose omnipotence (Kohut and Wolf, 1978), and they will reflect what is desired.
- In contrast, the dependency assumption is related to the idealizing transference reaction. Because of being in a group, the individual experiences a sense of loss of identity and irrational feelings of fragmentation. When this occurs, a sense of helplessness may follow. The desire may emerge to be nourished and protected by a leader, the followers having illusory wishes about his or her power.
- Finally, the fight–flight assumption and the persecutory transference reaction go together in that the fantasy emerges that there is an enemy somewhere, making defense or escape a necessity. But the fight–flight reaction will not only be directed toward an external enemy. There will be many internal enemies that qualify, including the leader, whose perceived imperfections may set off such a reaction. Thus, when the leader does not live up to the followers' unrealistic, excessive demands, anger follows.

A movement can be observed in these three basic assumptions from dependency to fight–flight to pairing (Klein, 1977). When a leader does not live up to the excessive expectations of the group members a revolt may occur. We should not forget that the emotional state of the followers is very changeable. Consequently, the group members may fall back into a fight–flight mode. Eventually, given the anxiety aroused by this particular culture, the group members may seek refuge in pairing as a defense against the fight–flight environment they have created.

These distorting reaction patterns and regressive group behavior are in fact major contributing factors to the strange, irrational behavior we sometimes find among leaders (Jaques, 1955; Menzies, 1960). Such reaction patterns are semi-dormant tendencies that revive easily in crisis situations and some leaders find it very hard to withstand their pressures.

The case of Ted Howell

To illustrate how these psychological forces can affect a leader, consider the following incident. As a result of the unexpected death of his predecessor, Ted Howell was appointed president of the Larix Corporation, a company in the electronics equipment field. Howell had been found with the help of a headhunter, who had highly recommended him. He had previously held a senior staff position in a company in the same line of business; Howell's knowledge of the industry had been a key factor in persuading the Larix board to take him on.

Soon after his arrival, Larix board members saw signs that Howell was having difficulties dealing with the pressures of the job. A number of rash decisions made in his first week at the office were the first indications of trouble. But despite these mistakes, everything initially turned out better than expected. First, one of the company's main competitors went out of business, which freed up an important segment of the market. In addition, one of Howell's employees came up with an excellent marketing idea that he quickly adopted and that proved very successful. Although some executives were disturbed because their colleague never received credit for his idea, nevertheless these two factors helped to get Larix back into the black.

Unfortunately, success went to Howell's head and he embarked on a dramatic expansion program, ignoring cautionary remarks made by his employees, consultants, and bankers. Other steps were taken, including the relocation of the company's headquarters to what Howell thought were more suitable surroundings and the acquisition of an expensive company plane. These two actions put a heavy strain on the company's finances. Those executives who expressed disagreement or concern about the new moves were fired; consultants who suggested that Howell change course suffered the same fate. In the end, only sycophants who were willing to agree to his grand schemes and accept his aggressive outbursts were left.

As expected, these unrealistic plans and high expenditures put the company into the red. However, Howell was unwilling to admit his role in the debacle. When questioned at directors' meetings, he would become defensive and deny any responsibility for the losses; instead, he would blame them on faulty moves made by his predecessor or on vindictive action by executives no longer in his employ. In his opinion, a turnaround was just around the corner. To an increasing number of board members, however, Howell's behavior was becoming unacceptable. Eventually, having become impatient with the continuing losses and with Howell's imperious, paranoid behavior, they managed to remove him.

As in the case of Robert Clark, here was an individual who was apparently well-adjusted and who had performed well in his previous job. After his promotion, however, when he was subjected to the pressures of being a leader, this same individual began to behave irrationally. Overwhelmed by all the attention that he was suddenly receiving, Howell apparently allowed his sense of reality to become distorted and seemed to assume that some of the qualities ascribed to him were true. When he couldn't deliver, and members of his board questioned his decisions, he reacted with anger and began to show signs of paranoid behavior.

DISTANCE AND AGGRESSION IN LEADERS

Being a leader inevitably implies a certain amount of loneliness—it is the nature of authority—the kind that, paradoxically, can be experienced when surrounded by a sea of people. A major reason for this is that leaders have to make decisions that cannot always be pleasing; they sometimes have to hurt people. Therefore, to facilitate neutrality in decision-making, they sometimes find it easier to keep their distance. Naturally, this adds to the atmosphere of mystery surrounding leaders. Followers will project their own fantasies on the leader. And some leaders enhance the process by creating the illusion that they need no one.

But achieving distance comes at a price. While leaders may be able to satisfy temporarily the dependency needs of their followers, they have to contend with the frustration of their own dependency needs (Kernberg, 1978). For some leaders, coping with these feelings is difficult. The need for affectionate bonds and attachment is a universal human characteristic (Harlow and Harlow, 1965; Bowlby, 1969). When this need is frustrated, separation anxiety may be reactivated, making for a strong regressive pull. And as if this regressive pull is not enough, leaders also are the recipients of their followers' transferential reactions, impacting their inner world. Many leaders don't have a sufficiently secure sense of who they are to help them deal with these forces. Illusions of grandeur, delusions of persecution, and paranoia will raise their ugly head. Consequently, leaders may resort to one of the more primitive defense mechanisms mentioned earlier: splitting, having an oversimplified view of the world, and searching for scapegoats. Moreover, being in a leadership position makes it more likely that their frustration is acted out on a public stage.

MANAGING LEADERS' BEHAVIOR IN ORGANIZATIONS

Given the dramatic impact leaders can have on their organizations, the regressive forces that affect leadership warrant serious attention. Apart from the unrealistic idea of having leaders submit to regular mental health check-ups or setting definitive time limits for top positions, what can be done to limit the excesses of power?

One suggestion is to build safeguards into the organization's structure, setting boundaries that will lead to the dispersion of power in an organization. To prevent regressive processes from getting out of hand, key power positions can be distributed over a number of persons. Such dispersion of power calls for the creation of more organic organizations. Flat, flexible structures that allow lateral communication for continuous consultation and the exchange of ideas help defuse excessive transferential manifestations.

A corollary to implementing such flat structures is the need for innovative human resource practices that tolerate diversity. A corporate culture needs to be created where there is a healthy disrespect for the leader; a culture where people can speak their mind. In addition, regular re-examination of organizational practices can create a culture of change. To foster such an environment and to make such internal auditing possible, it can help to bring in consultants who, generally speaking, are not subject to intra-organizational myopia.

Top executive management development programs (including the kind of group coaching practiced at INSEAD and the European School of Management and Technology) are another way to prevent regressive forces becoming prevalent (Kets de Vries, Korotov, and Florent-Treacy, 2007). Such programs offer participants the opportunity to exchange ideas, give and receive feedback, and discuss various courses of action in a relatively non-threatening setting. Doing so enhances reality-testing.

Boards of directors can play a critical role in monitoring the distribution of power and authority in an organization. With the increasing legal accountability of board members, acting merely as a rubber stamp has become a risky business. More than ever, board members are in an ideal position to become the countervailing force to check the excesses of leadership. Their role in planning for orderly management-succession can be crucial in defusing the pathology of power. Other countervailing powers that can prevent the excesses of leadership are stakeholders such as large institutional investors, the government, the press, unions, and even bankers.

Despite the existence of possible countervailing forces and organizational inertia, we should not underestimate the regressive pulls described earlier. Leaders can wield enormous power and can easily find ways to sidetrack these preventive measures. Moreover, paradoxically enough, these regressive forces that may give rise to irrational, even pathological behavior and which in normal circumstances would be the cause of disqualification, will in specific situations be exactly the qualities needed for leadership.

The leader's limited view of reality, the unrestrained abandonment to a certain aim, distorted as it may be, or his or her way of acting out aggression, at times, may be very functional. Paranoid reactions, the notion of a threatening menace that warrants struggle and sacrifice, can feed very well into this type of situation.

But such circumstances are highly unusual and may lead (at least in the long run) to questionable results. In general, it is therefore essential that sufficient safeguards are in place to prevent excess. And here the burden is on both leader and followers. Both parties have a tremendous responsibility to monitor their own behavior and, in spite of the operation of defensive processes, should make efforts to recognize their own particular way of acting. Individuals who are unable to do so are very likely to become prisoners of their own leadership. Leaders should never forget that their primary task is to define reality. To paraphrase Winston Churchill, quoting an old Chinese proverb, 'Poor leaders ride on hungry tigers they dare not dismount.'

ENDNOTES

Most of the material for this chapter has already appeared in print under the same title in the following publication:

- Kets de Vries, M.F.R. (1988). 'Prisoners of leadership,' *Human Relations*, **41** (3): 261–280.

1. All names and organizations are pseudonyms.

CHAPTER 8

THE SPIRIT OF DESPOTISM: UNDERSTANDING THE TYRANT WITHIN

The people have always some champion whom they set over them and nurse into greatness ... This and no other is the root from which a tyrant springs; when he first appears he is a protector.

—Plato, *The Republic*

The possession of unlimited power will make a despot of almost any man. There is a possible Nero in the gentlest human creature that walks.

—Thomas Bailey, *Leaves from a Notebook*

INTRODUCTION

Throughout the ages, autocratic governments have been more the rule than the exception; in fact, democratic forms of government have been relatively rare. Despots from the past such as Caligula, Nero, Tamerlane, Vlad the Impaler, Shaka Zulu, and Ivan the Terrible were followed in the twentieth century by the likes of Joseph Stalin, Adolf Hitler, Mao Zedong, Pol Pot, Idi Amin, Nicolae Ceausescu, Saddam Hussein, Fidel Castro, Kim Jong Il, Muammar Qaddafi, and Robert Mugabe. Although some of these leaders have been lionized as nation-builders despite the atrocities they committed, most stand out for having instigated the worst kinds of horror humans can inflict on other humans, and some, such as Hitler, Stalin, Mao Zedong, and Pol Pot, left tens of millions of dead in their wake.

Leadership by terror achieves its ends and gains compliance by the use of arbitrary power beyond the scope permitted by law, custom, and tradition. It is lust for power that pushes true despots beyond the boundaries of their mandate to rule, causing them to abandon respect for human rights and individual freedom, and to behave in ways that prevent others from living their lives with dignity and self-respect. In a nutshell, tyrannical leadership is the arbitrary rule by a single person who, by inducing a psychological state of extreme fear in a population, monopolizes power to his or her own advantage (unchecked by law or other restraining influences), exercising that power without restraint and, in most cases, contrary to the general good. Despots hamper justice, the right to fair process, excellence, and the development of the human potential of a population.

My objective in including this kind of material in this chapter is to foster a better understanding of despotic regimes and the reasons behind the continued of existence of leadership by terror—hitherto a largely unexplored domain. Because prevention of such phenomena requires knowledge, my hope is that assisting in the understanding of the mechanics of terror will be a modest step in the fight towards preventing despotic leaders and totalitarian regimes from gaining, and remaining in, power in future generations.

Clarifying Terminology

In contrast to much other writing on this subject, I use the terms 'dictatorship,' 'despotism,' 'tyranny,' 'authoritarianism,' and 'totalitarianism' somewhat interchangeably, since specific classification of such words would be a whole article in itself. It is useful, however, to acknowledge efforts by other writers to classify non-democratic forms of government as specific positions on a spectrum, according to the degree of mind-control enforced—putting at one extreme traditional, relatively benevolent authoritarian regimes, and at the other, totalitarian governments of the Nazi and Soviet variety (Walter, 1969; Reich, 1990; Chirot, 1994; Herschman and Lieb, 1994; Glass, 1995; Robins and Post, 1997). Although many of the observations made in this article will refer to both positions, special attention will be given to the extreme, most intrusive position: totalitarianism.

Totalitarianism

This term is used by the afore-mentioned writers to refer to the most dangerous extreme of the control spectrum—that is, regimes under which a population is completely subjugated to a political system aspiring to total domination of the collective over the individual. Such forms of government are typically permeated by a secular or theocratic ideology that professes a set of absolute values propagated by the leadership. Repression of individual rights and loyalty to that ideology are their salient characteristics. Totalitarian regimes strive to invade and control their citizenry's social, economic, political, and personal life. Because such governments seek to transform human nature, they exercise thought-control and control moral education. In other words, repression is carried out not only against people's actions but also against their *thoughts*.

Such regimes can retain control only so long as the terror of such totalitarianism is all-pervasive. Thus any objection to governmental control is viewed as a danger to the regime, a threat to its delicate equilibrium. As a result, such regimes are more likely than others to 'eat their own'—that is, to do away with (by exile, imprisonment, or death) government supporters tainted by the merest suspicion of rebellion. These regimes need the sacrifice of an endless stream of new 'enemies' to retain their focus (Friedrich, 1954; Arendt, 1973).

Authoritarianism

These regimes are perceived by those who make this distinction as being less invasive. Although repression of the populace takes place, there is no intrusive ideology. Such regimes do not profess the benefits of a future utopian state; they do not seek to transform human nature. The goal of authoritarian leadership is much more mundane: simply that of retaining power. The amassing of wealth, the betrayal of social reforms, the development of a military power base, and rampant paranoia are characteristics associated with authoritarianism. Authoritarian rulers strive to keep the riches and privileges that come with holding on to power, and they exert whatever level of repression it takes to do so (Boesche, 1996).

Although both types of regime can be extremely brutal to their political opponents, in an authoritarian state, the government's efforts are directed primarily at those who are considered political opponents. The government lacks the desire (and often the means) to control every aspect of each individual's life, and thus intervention in the day-to-day life of the citizenry is limited. Grounded in greed rather than ideology, authoritarian leadership does not claim to represent a specific historical destiny or possess the absolute truth; it is not in the business of creating a new type of social life or a new kind of human being. Russia under Stalin would be a good example of a totalitarian regime, while Zimbabwe under Robert Mugabe can be considered to be a more authoritarian example.

SETTING THE SCENE FOR TYRANNY

Whenever people gather in groups, there is the potential for the abuse of power. The early civilizations that grew up along great rivers such as the Nile, the Tigris, the Euphrates, the Yangtze, the Yellow River, and the Ganges clamored for leaders to give the management of these public water supplies a modicum of centralized direction. A brief look at history tells us, however, that centralized leadership can easily become perverted. For example, ancient Egypt, Mesopotamia, China, India, and the pre-Columbian Central and South American cultures all positioned an absolute, often despotic ruler at the center of their ruling bureaucracy. We also can observe, however, the rise and inevitable fall of such regimes.

Despots are often leaders with the foresight to take personal advantage of a chaotic situation, such as situations of war or class war. An obvious example here is Germany after World War I, dealing with a sense of national humiliation and a class struggle verging on civil war— the situation in which Hitler gradually rose to power. Consider China, still haunted by the affront of Western powers intruding in their sovereignty, a process that started in the nineteenth century. The lingering memory of such indignities creates typical breeding grounds for tyranny. Societies in which democratic traditions and institutions are still lacking or are poorly developed, societies with weak political systems and/or an ineffective judiciary, and societies in severe economic distress, seem to be particularly vulnerable. These social conditions, especially occurring together, facilitate a power grab by a power-hungry despot.

Nations just emerging from colonial or communist rule have been particularly vulnerable—as demonstrated in the emergence in the twentieth century of some of the most brutal and oppressive regimes in history. Such nations have had institutions imposed on them—institutions not rooted in their original culture—making them susceptible to subsequent despotism. Many such examples can be seen in the history of Africa, Asia, and the Middle East. The proliferation of recent, new dictatorships in countries formerly belonging to the Soviet Union and increasingly, the 'new' Russia, provides further illustration of this vulnerability.

When formerly colonial or communist countries become independent, people generally have sky-high expectations about the future, which are often followed by deep disappointment once the gap between hope and harsh reality becomes clear. Deep contrasts between wealth and haunting poverty, both within nations and between nations, and the prevalence of corruption (now more visible through the media), add to this state of discontent.

All the above social conditions create alienation within a society, and that alienation paves the way for tyranny. When social institutions disintegrate, and when there is little to hold on to, people search for messiahs who promise economic and political salvation from the hardships they are currently experiencing. People in this situation are seeking the 'containment' that they hope a strong leader offers—they are looking for what psychoanalyst Donald Winnicott termed a holding environment to contain their existential anxiety and deal with their sense of alienation, dislocation, and aloneness (Winnicott, 1975). They can find all these things in one mass movement or another. Mass movements, whatever their ideology, typically offer solidarity, an end to loneliness and anxiety, and hope for a better future.

WHAT MOTIVATES TYRANTS?

Much has been said, and written, about absolute rulers—particularly by philosophers. Plato, for example, was one of the earliest recorded observers of tyranny. Tyranny evoked, for him, associations of disharmony and disease, and he viewed tyrants as individuals governed by out-of-control desires. According to Plato, 'drunkenness, lust, and madness' differentiate the tyrant from other people. A tyrant 'becomes, in reality, what he was once only occasionally in his dreams, and there's nothing, no taboo, no murder, however terrible, from which he will shirk. His passion tyrannizes over him, a despot will be without restraint or law' (Plato, 1955, p. 348). In other words, tyrants act out in the light of day what most of us only dare to dream about at night. Plato concluded that to act on such dreams—to satisfy one's darkest desires—leads the tyrant into an unending, spiraling cycle of desire, gratification, and more desire.

HOW TYRANNIES OPERATE

The terror and violence that characterize despotic regimes take two forms: outwardly directed (to a country's enemies outside its borders) and inwardly directed (to members or groups within the country's own population). Both forms often lead to mass murder and genocide.

- Outwardly directed terror is used to intimidate, or even exterminate, enemies outside one's borders. Typically, enemies are viewed by despots as forces of darkness that need to be destroyed by a force of light. They are described in derogatory terms and depicted as less than human. This dehumanization makes the administration of violence more palatable to members of the enforcement arm of the government. After all, it is only the enemy—no more than a subspecies—upon whom violence is inflicted (Volcan, 1988).
- Inwardly directed terror heightens considerably the fear and anxiety of living under despotic regimes. Using violent acts against the despot's own population, inwardly directed terror results in subjugation of the citizenry, classification as a subspecies of one part (or multiple parts) of the population, loss of various freedoms and, ultimately, the suffocation of the mind.

The ability to enact terror—whether against an external enemy or against one's own people—is viewed by many tyrannical leaders as a special prerogative. To despots, boundaries of acceptable behavior apply only to others. Living in a narcissistic self-delusional 'soup' with little concern for the needs of others, despots perceive few restraints on their actions. They believe that divine providence (however they construe divinity) has given them power over life and death. In other words, they believe that they have the *right* to act as they do. This sense of entitlement is especially frightening when it spreads: the specific psychology or psychopathology of a leader can become institutionalized (as with Hitler, Stalin, Pol Pot, and Bin Laden), so that the common people come to support the distorted and dangerous ideology articulated by the leadership (Kets de Vries, 1989).

Leadership by terror succeeds only in the hands of a despot skilled at the fine art of boundary management. If, on the one hand, terror is taken to its extreme and executed too forcefully, there is soon nothing left to terrorize: all the objects of terror are destroyed. If, on the other hand, terror is applied too lightly, it does not result in the desired compliance. Maintaining the devilish bond between the terrorized and the tyrant requires a delicate balancing act: traditional mechanisms in society need to be modified but cannot be destroyed.

HOW DESPOTIC REGIMES ARE MAINTAINED

One interesting question is why it is that some societies can pass through an initial despotic phase into freedom while others become mired in despotism. How does the process of despotic rule evolve?

Niccolò Machiavelli viewed the despot's role as a natural phase in nation-building—one that would, of necessity, last until the nation-builder had achieved his or her primary goals (Machiavelli, 1966). However, many leaders take on the role of tyrant without hesitation, and then fail to temper their violence or modify their rule after they have consolidated their power base. Unable to make the transition that Machiavelli believed to be possible, many rulers have unleashed powers that then they could not ultimately control. They turn into the sorcerer's apprentice. Because of that intemperance, such countries never become societies based on the rule of law.

Nonetheless, many political scientists share Machiavelli's outlook that dictatorship is simply a transitional phase that many countries have to go through on their way to democracy (Boesche, 1996; Friedrich and Brezezinsky, 1965). Those who support this view argue that non-democratic political configurations do not thus deserve the harsh condemnation they receive from democratic idealists. Like it or not, they remonstrate, simplistic Western political formulas do not suit certain societies at an early stage of development. Given the mindset of the people in these developing societies, democratic structures would probably be highly ineffective—worse, in the end, than a transitional tyranny. The people in these societies are simply not ready to deal with the freedom that democracy not only offers, but also demands.

While acknowledging the darker side of dictatorship, these proponents are quick to point out the advantages of being ruled by an autocratic government. Although despots repress their citizens, they also protect the population from outside dangers, reknit a society torn apart by violent upheaval, put an end to internal strife, introduce law and order, and eradicate certain forms of corruption. Some despots even create a new prosperity (or at least the illusion of prosperity) by embarking on great public works and by providing such services as schools, housing, hospitals, and roads.

What these Machiavellian adherents fail to acknowledge is the likelihood that autocratic leadership will turn into all-out tyranny. I would argue that, positive contributions notwithstanding, shadow sides of power-based leadership will almost inevitably come to the fore. As time passes, most leaders with despotic tendencies are likely to feel increasingly entitled to do whatever they want as their feelings of entitlement sway behavior and increase their narcissistic tendencies, Mugabe of Zimbabwe being one of the more recent examples.

THE DESPOT'S TOOLBOX

It is useful now to analyze what other means (beyond the obvious one of violence) tyrants use to remain in power, and to succeed in continuing to subjugate an entire population. Probably the strongest weapon other than violence is that of ideology.

The Enchantment of Ideology

To Hannah Arendt, a major tool of the totalitarian despot is the introduction of an ideology with supreme values—a political religion that replaces traditional religion (Arendt, 1969). Such an ideology usually claims to provide the answer to all-important social and historical dilemmas. To use the words of the sociologist, Robert Jay Lifton:

> Behind ideological totalism lies the ever-present human quest for the omnipotent guide—for the supernatural force, political party, philosophical ideas, great leader, or precise science—that will bring ultimate solidarity to all men and eliminate the terror of death and nothingness. (Lifton, 1961, p. 436)

Frequently, the promise is a laudable, utopian-like solution to the human condition, but the ideological goals of totalitarian systems vary. For example, while the Soviet Union under Stalin and the People's Republic of China under Mao Zedong sought the universal fulfillment of humankind through the establishment of a classless society, Germany under Hitler's National Socialism attempted to establish a thousand-year reich based on the superiority of the so-called Aryan race. Ironically, in the process of universalizing their goals to improve society, despotism often destroys the moral fabric of that society. Frequently, the leaders of such totalitarian entities create huge bureaucratic machines to institutionalize their allegedly virtue-based worldview.

Although the outside world often views despots as the instigators of evil regimes, in fact the belief system that supports them is often in place before they take the reins. Often this has developed initially through alienated and frustrated intellectuals and/or theocrats in such a society developing and speaking of a particular vision of utopian society. They typically establish a pseudo-scientific or extremist religious base to undergird their 'formula' for the perfect society. Through their convoluted ideology, they offer a form of salvation to a select group of true believers—those who are chosen to attain the Promised Land. As a test to determine entry into such a promised land, followers are challenged to overcome a number of obstacles posed by non-believers. These opponents are depicted, at best, as evildoers, at worst, as 'sub-humans' (Erikson, 1963; Des Pres, 1976) and followers are encouraged to fight these evil adversaries with whatever force is necessary. As time evolves and the group of followers grows, a political party (either established or new) embraces the ideology, with believers unquestioningly parroting its tenets. And out of that party emerges the leader, the high priest, who will turn vision into tyranny.

By facilitating conscious and unconscious dreams of togetherness, of shared purpose, ideology creates a false sense of group solidarity, and a resulting abdication of autonomous functioning. Because individuation (the process of becoming a person in one's own right) starts early, the family is viewed in totalitarian societies as an important training ground—a forum for building patterns of obedience to authority. After all, someone who knew no freedom in childhood is less likely to protest a lack of freedom later on. Given the importance of such early indoctrination, many totalitarian governments also use pre-school and later schooling to eliminate any undesirable attitudes that the parents may have passed on. Some totalitarian regimes have even taken children away from their parents. The Soviet Union, for example, experimented with raising children in communal houses in the 1920s and the 1950s. Likewise, during the war with Afghanistan during the 1980s, the Soviet Government forcibly took tens of thousands of young Afghan children to the USSR to be raised away from their families. Movements such as the *Hitlerjugend*, the Pioneers, the Komsomols, the Red Guards, and the Khmer Rouge were all tools used to brainwash young people, gain their support for the prevailing ideology, and even make them spy and inform on their parents.

Leaders of ideology-based totalitarian states will do anything to win new converts. They want to spread their creed—though only to people 'worthy' of conversion. They are convinced that sharing their ideology, whether secular or theocratic, will bring enlightenment to the masses. There is a sect-like intensity to this need to convert others: the fragility of the ideology demands constant validation from others, to bolster faith in the worldview, create solidarity, and reinforce the righteousness of the cause. People who resist conversion threaten the ideology and make the converted uncomfortable. They remind true believers of the shakiness of their belief system, often triggering anger and violence.

Whichever party adopts the totalitarian ideology, it generally attempts to give the appearance of propriety. For example, it typically makes participation in politics, especially voting, compulsory. As we all know, though, under totalitarian rule the right to vote does not mean the right to choose. The only real choice is the party and the party's leader. The lack of choice is enforced through political repression. The ruling party and its leader restrict the rights of citizens to criticize the government, the rights of opposition parties to campaign against the government, and the rights of certain groups, associations, and political parties to convene (or even exist). The citizen's duty to the state is thus the primary concern of the community. All legally recognized buffers between the leader and his subjects need to be eliminated. This means that tyrants subvert existing institutions, particularly the judiciary, to make their control absolute. Traditional groups such as labor unions, political parties, an independent press, and other associations of any kind, are destroyed. Meaningful participation in a vibrant political community cannot be tolerated, though participation (actually *imprisonment*) in ideologically correct institutions and in front organizations is allowed, encouraged, or even mandated.

Because divine authority is a particular threat, totalitarian regimes typically combine spiritual and secular guidance, gaining a monopoly on correct interpretation of both secular and religious thought. The totalitarian state's ideology then becomes the nation's religion, as it did in Nazi Germany, Stalin's Russia, and Mao Zedong's China.

Using a State Within the State

Another means by which despots maintain control is by using their country's police and armed forces to spread fear in the general population and to assist with imprisonment, internment in hospitals and camps, torture, and execution of government opponents. In truly despotic regimes, the secret police become like a state within a state, suppressing freedom in the name of law and order but holding its own actions above the law, free from accountability. As despots thus use one segment of the population to keep another in control this often becomes a vicious circle, with those who carry out purges one day being themselves purged.

We have all heard how the Gestapo and the SS in Hitler's Germany, the NKVD in Stalin's Soviet Russia, and the Khmer Rouge in Pol Pot's

Cambodia were used to paralyze their country's populace. The Ministry of Intelligence and Security, the Ministry of Interior, and the Revolutionary Guards in Iran have used similar tactics to shore up an unpopular theocratic regime; and during the regime of Saddam Hussein his Special Republican Guards maintained an iron grip on the population.

The Role of the Media

Distorted mass communication is another hallmark of any despotic, totalitarian regime. While in ancient societies indoctrination by despots was rather crude, contemporary totalitarian leaders now use all available forms of modern propaganda techniques to brainwash their subjects. In today's totalitarian states, information flowing from the party is severely censored, with distorted discourse and 'news-speak' sanitizing corruption and abhorrent acts. Absolutely no honest, open debate is permitted; any moral or spiritual authority, independent of the leader or contrary to party doctrine, is prohibited. Rote memorization of the party line is encouraged, and people who engage in critical inquiry or speak out against the party line are arrested, or worse. Ideological jargon and magical celebrations replace open discussion as the party and its leader engage in verbal acrobatics to hide the reality of the situation.

The Illusion of Solidarity

Another important tool used by despots to maintain power is that of isolation. The very idea of totalitarianism implies the breaking of lateral relationships between individuals—the original sense of community—in favor of strong ties to the state. This dissolution of the ties between people creates helplessness, dependency, and loneliness.

Despots well understand the psychological vulnerability of humans, knowing that people are more easily manipulated when they feel isolated and powerless. The prevalence of human anxiety explains why totalitarianism and authoritarianism have been with us since the dawn of time. Lacking other people to exchange opinions with and who can act as reference points, isolated individuals gradually lose their common sense and their ability to think independently. Regressing to a state of passivity, they become increasingly helpless. And in that state, they become more open to a leader apparently endowed with omnipotent qualities—qualities promoted and continually reinforced by the state propaganda department.

Thus, tyrants go to great lengths to break up traditional relationship patterns, prohibiting all associations between citizenry that could lead to free debate. To ensure that the populace cannot coordinate any form of political opposition, they rely on an elaborate network of spies and informers (many of whom are happy to turn in friends and associates in the hope of saving themselves), reinforced by police terror tactics.

Having destroyed existing relationship patterns, tyrants then encourage their subjects in the fantasy that they as leaders are wise, noble, kind, and understanding. They offer evidence that they are doing whatever they can to create a perfect society—one in which, according to the propaganda machine, there will be justice for all, everyone's needs will be met, there will be meaningful work for everyone, and hunger and poverty will be eradicated. The result, they promise persuasively, will be a just, humane society, a society in which children can grow up safely.

The Search for Scapegoats

Another potent tool of the despot leaders is finding someone to blame for the injustice and misery they themselves create. A typical tyrant might, when 'learning' of an incident of cruelty or injustice, announce that he did not know of the problem; if he had, of course, he would have handled things differently. It was some key person or group that was actually responsible for people's privations. This is, of course, not true. The very definition of a totalitarian state is that nothing can be done without the leader's knowledge and say-so. If the inner circle or the military behaves cruelly, it is because he tells them to. He selects his henchmen; he dispenses orders and permission; he rewards obedient behavior. And the henchmen oblige. They follow his wishes, sometimes even exceeding his demands to show their loyalty (especially if they 'identify with the aggressor'; see p. 139).

Because the leader sets the tone for the whole society, his unwillingness to take responsibility then creates an entire culture of blame. Each henchman passes on blame to his or her underlings, but somewhere in that cascading blame game, the responsibility has to finally come to rest. Thus, scapegoating comes into play. The 'non-believers' described earlier—forces of evil (as designated by those in power)—are seen as posing a great threat to the purity of society and the well-being of 'believers,' and are thus deserving of elimination. The Jews in Nazi Germany, the kulaks and capitalists under the Soviet regime, the educated elite in Pol Pot's Cambodia, the non-Arab Christians and animists in southern Sudan, and the Muslims in Kosovo were all victims of scapegoating, being blamed as the source of all the problems their countries were experiencing.

As mentioned earlier, enemies—real or imagined—are essential to tyrannical regimes (Volcan, 1988). With the help of propaganda, despots inspire intense hatred for their chosen scapegoats. In so doing they often succeed in creating a sense of belonging in their followers, giving them a sense of purpose, and distracting them from the real issues of the day. Indoctrinated by a constant stream of propaganda, people become willing to inform on neighbors, friends, and family members.

But there is an even uglier side to scapegoating: it has a genuine attraction to people. Scapegoating works in the same way as participating in violent spectator sports: it helps people to overcome their own fears. Violent participation is, for many, a way of dealing with their own anxiety and feelings of doubt about the regime. It is a form of insurance as well: people hope that by showing commitment to the regime and its policies of violence they can save themselves. Even those who only stand at the sidelines are affected, feeling bound together by shared guilt over not putting an end to the violence.

THE ECONOMIC COSTS OF TYRANNY

History shows irrefutably that enduringly great societies have been built on freedom of spirit and expression. Such freedoms cannot flourish in the absence of basic standards of morality, civic virtue, and justice for *all,* fairly administered. Far-reaching restrictions on freedom inevitably result in economic decline. Thus freedom in the economic sphere makes for individual initiative and entrepreneurship, creates employment, and helps eradicate poverty, thereby supporting all the other freedoms. Someone with a job and three square meals a day feels freer to express his/her opinion than someone dependent on others for survival.

Totalitarian governments, with their gigantic bureaucracies, are not conducive to the spirit of entrepreneurship. Inefficiency, corruption, and uncertainty, combined with the lack of individual freedom and human rights, sap the energy and weaken the moral fabric of a country. Creating special rights for some people, as despotic regimes do, undermines individual freedom and civil rights, and thus undermines civilization itself. A government that does not hold itself accountable cannot create a foundation for economic growth. As totalitarian states mature, their practices become greater and greater obstacles to economic development.

Unemployment, poverty, and hunger typically result, as was seen in the regimes of Mengistu Haile Mariam of Ethiopia, Joseph Désiré Mobutu of the Democratic Republic of Congo, and Robert Mugabe of Zimbabwe. Although they may enjoy a temporary honeymoon period, despots usually bring on economic decline.

They also destroy a country's cultural institutions and sense of national pride. The discontent that grows in a populace around inequities and lack of freedom eventually turns even an environment of creativity and free thought into a breeding ground for the disenfranchised. In their anger and desperation, seeing enemies and conspiracies everywhere, citizens begin to commit desperate terrorist acts. Unable to touch the leader, they strike out wherever they can, destroying their own society in the process.

Once people embrace a theological or secular belief system that has no room for compassion, goodness, and hope, it is only a matter of time before violence sets in. And once violence takes hold, civilization itself is condemned. Dictatorships and totalitarian governments kill civil society. Thus, it is necessary for people to combat despots *before* totalitarian states are totally established. People need to be able to dream of a better society for their children and for future generations, and to incorporate their dreams into positive goals, both individual and collective. Without meaningful work, close ties to family and friends, and reasonable hope of a positive future, people quickly become alienated. That alienation becomes universal when totalitarianism deprives people of these essential rewards, and an entire population loses its sense of humanity and compassion.

THE NEED FOR DEMOCRACY

If dictatorships are one-way streets, then democracies are clearly two-way: in the latter, the people have a voice. That does not mean, however, that democracy is perfect: life in freedom is not always easy. After all, having choices implies having responsibilities. Moreover, democratic decision-making can be cumbersome and slow. Democratic leaders are often unwilling to bite the bullet and make unpopular but necessary decisions, because they are concerned more about being re-elected than about the good of the country. Short-term decision-making may prevail; not the bold moves that a country may need. Furthermore, compromise and coalition politics do not always lead to the best outcome. The latter, for example, sometimes results in a paradox of voting whereby the least attractive candidate wins the election. Winston Churchill is reputed to have said that 'democracy is the worst form of government, except all the other forms that have been tried!'

And yet the alternative to democracy is not really an option. While benevolent autocracy is a theoretical possibility, rule by a solitary leader typically ends in servile obedience to authority and abuse of human rights. In contrast, democracy (though flawed) is more likely to safeguard human dignity, protect individual freedoms, assure free choice, and give people a voice in decisions that affect their destiny, allowing them to work for a better future for their children. Humankind's desire for *justice* and fair play makes democracy possible. Humankind's capacity for *injustice* makes democracy necessary.

Democracy requires well-entrenched social systems of checks and balances to protect against humankind's destructive potential. Only political diversity, a well-established legal code, and freedom of expression and economy can ensure democratic rule. But, furthermore, individuals must have a civilized personal code of conduct and endorse a civic mindset that supports democratic social structures. In other words, the populace has to internalize a civic culture that protects against the abuse of power. That internalization comes from learning the fundamentals of democratic government at home and in school, seeing democratic government at work in daily life, witnessing open and honest elections, and hearing respected adults support human rights (and question authority when it restricts those rights). The case of Iraq has demonstrated what can go wrong when this internalization process never took place.

THE DANGERS OF POWER

Since all leaders are susceptible to the darker side of power no individual should ever be in sole control of an organization, community, or society. Human susceptibility to cruelty and violence turns people in high positions into villains with alarming frequency—the words of the old Latin tag, *Homo homini lupus* ('Every man is a wolf to every other man,' a Roman proverb attributed to Plautus) still ring true. However admirable leaders may be when they first take the scepter, however enlightened they may be, however much they may resemble Plato's philosopher–king, none are exempt from the pull of psychological regression.

Perhaps the best test of any person's character is to put him or her in a position of power. Power is so intoxicating, so addictive, that only the hardiest individuals can survive it without psychopathology. Even those on the receiving end of power feel its psychopathological effects and often become dangerously overdependent. It is bad enough when an ordinary citizen becomes intoxicated by power but when that intoxication strikes a national leader—someone reading his or her lines on a world stage—the consequences can be devastating. Paranoid fears that others will seek to overthrow them makes leaders resort to what psychologists call 'protective reaction'—that is, they take the aggressive initiative, attacking before they can be attacked. If their protective reaction gains a base in reality (if, for example, dissidents from their own regime form an alliance with external forces), it is as if oil has been thrown on their paranoid fire. Even when their paranoia alone does not argue for war, despots are motivated into combat by the sense of purpose and solidarity it gives the people, and the distraction it offers from the despot's own misdeeds.

Power and reason cannot coexist peacefully, and reason is always the loser. Excessive power blurs the senses, triggers delusional paranoia, and corrupts reality-testing. And paranoiacs do not take their delusions lightly. Many a reign has been steeped in the blood of enemies more *perceived* than real; many a ruler, from Aztec rulers to modern despots, has been more executioner than diplomat. And in every case, those who are carried away by power eventually self-destruct—but not before sacrificing countless victims on the altar of their ambitions.

The history of many despotic regimes is a string of cautionary tales, reminding us that every culture needs to build and maintain strong checks and balances against the abuse of power. Without these safeguards, any regime, no matter how benign, can give way to despotic rule. Thus power retained should always be a check to power conferred.

WHY DESPOTISM MUST BE FOUGHT

What makes despots so dangerous for the world community is not so much their tendency toward violence as the ease with which that tendency can be indulged. Starting a war—engaging in *any* form of violence, for that matter—is so much easier for despots than for democratic leaders. Despots do not need to ask permission from various executive and legislative bodies. Despots do not have to convince the populace. The most they have to do—if that—is to get an official-sounding agency to rubber-stamp their war effort. They have the power to do pretty much as they wish.

It goes without saying that wars come at an incredible price in human suffering for the citizens involved. But the visible costs of war—death of soldiers and civilians, homelessness, privation, economic disaster—are only the tip of the iceberg. There are hidden effects of war that can take generations to rebuild—for example, the loss of self-respect and national pride, and the obliteration of a civil culture and the spirit of creativity. These desolating consequences are a persuasive argument for humankind to rid the world of dictatorships—even if, paradoxically, it takes war to do so. Certain regimes are so corrupt and destructive that they have to be restrained, no matter what.

Just as despots are the instigators of war, so they can sometimes be its victims. After a career of villainy and deception, some despots are brought down, regime in tow, by victors in battle. Others survive a losing war only to be brought down by segments of their own population who, seeing the devastation that accompanied defeat, decide that enough is enough and mount a successful insurrection.

Sometimes, what brings a despot to ruin is rot within the regime. The idealism that flourished when the regime was first put in place gradually turns to cynicism as the ideals lose their meaning. Those true believers who once fought for an ideal now fight only for the perks that loyalty brings. With the onset of corruption, any regime loses two of its most powerful sources of control: moral authority and political legitimacy.

The Case of Ceausescu

A good illustration of a regime brought down by inner rot was the decades-long reign of Nicolae Ceausescu of Romania. His secret police, the *Securitate*, maintained rigid controls over free speech and the media, tolerating no internal opposition. He encouraged an extensive personality cult and appointed his wife, Elena, and some members of his family to high posts in the government. Despite the glowing promises of the early years, his regime was marked by disastrous economic schemes that led to great suffering for the populace. Over time, his regime became increasingly repressive and corrupt. After years of agony, that regime finally collapsed. The catalyst was his order, given to his security forces, to fire on antigovernment demonstrators. A December 1989 uprising of the people, in which the army participated, led to his arrest, his trial, and sentencing (by a hastily assembled military tribunal), and his execution. His wife and other key figures were also put to death.

UNJUST DESERTS

The execution of Nicolae Ceausescu is a rare exception; few despots are ever held accountable for their evil acts. The tragic paradox of history is that those individuals who murder *one* person are more likely to be brought to justice than those who plot the genocide of *millions*. Despots who commit crimes against humanity far too often go into quiet retirement rather than being brought to justice. A small sampling of the many examples available:

- More than nine thousand people disappeared during the 'Dirty War' (the state sponsored violence against trade unionists) in Argentina that started at the end of the 1970s, to end at the beginning of the 1980s. Most of the perpetrators are living happily ever after.
- Syria's late dictator, Hafez al-Assad, also had a happy ending to his life, although he ordered the death of at least ten thousand people in the city of Hama after an insurrection, and then bulldozed over the city.
- The late North Korean dictator, Kim Il-Sung, who kept a tight rein on his totalitarian state, advocated what he called a 'self-reliance policy' that caused the starvation of millions of his people. He also lived happily ever after, and died peacefully in his bed.
- Few people recall the holocaust inflicted by the Ottoman Empire on Armenians in 1915, although more than a million people died. Nobody was ever held accountable for this mass murder. In fact, the Turks never even acknowledged that it happened.

JUDICIAL REMEDY

This pattern of denial is changing, however. Since the milestone International Military Tribunal at Nuremberg in 1946, at which war crimes and crimes against humanity were prosecuted, resulting in the execution of a number of former Nazi leaders, the world has been taking increasing notice of despots. That tribunal, and the subsequent tribunal in Tokyo (which reviewed war crimes committed by the command of the Japanese Imperial Army during World War II), established a precedent for holding the leaders of a country accountable for crimes committed by that country. Unfortunately, none of these trials led to the immediate establishment of a permanent international court that would be specially empowered to deal with crimes against humanity.

In fact in the decades just after these two large tribunals, the prosecution of war criminals lessened significantly again—most likely due to the effects of the Cold War—and power politics froze any meaningful decision-making. During (and because of) this passivity, the despot Pol Pot, a criminal responsible for the deaths of over two million Cambodians (during the years 1976–1979), was never brought to justice.

Since the fall of the Berlin Wall and the end of the Cold War, however, the United Nations has acted to take more positive action against despots. One of the primary objectives of the United Nations is securing universal respect for human rights and fundamental freedoms of individuals throughout the world. Its reluctance to intervene against war crimes and other crimes against humanity—to halt them immediately, rather than condemn them later—had come to haunt the institution. Many politicians and military strategists believed that if the UN had taken preventive action in hot spots around the world, considerable violence could have been avoided, millions of lives could have been saved, and many countries could have avoided political and economic ruin. Eventually shamed into action by the tragic events in former Yugoslavia (during the Bosnian war of 1992–1995) and Rwanda (the murder of Tutsis in 1994) the Security Council established two specialized ad hoc tribunals.

The first, the International Criminal Tribunal, set up in The Hague in 1991, began by bringing to justice the instigators of various crimes against humanity in Yugoslavia, convicting a number of the key players, the most important one being Slobodan Milosevic. Similar steps were then taken to bring to justice the people responsible for the genocide in Rwanda. The second International Criminal Tribunal, convened in Arusha, sentenced Jean Kambanda, former prime minister of Rwanda, to life imprisonment (the harshest penalty available under the UN tribunal) for supporting and promoting the massacre of some 800,000 Tutsis, when the Hutus briefly held power. Although these results have been encouraging, more still needs to be done. The serious political, practical, linguistic, and financial difficulties presented by the international tribunals need to be overcome, and without delay.

Difficulties notwithstanding, these tribunal convictions act as a warning to dictators everywhere that the world is changing and that they can no longer expect to escape consequences. Another positive step is the willingness of many national courts to bring charges against dictators. The court in Chile, for example, acted against Augusto Pinochet, former president of that country, for human rights abuses that occurred during a period when many members of the political opposition disappeared. The same happened in Iraq, where his fellow citizens had

Saddam Hussein executed in 2006. Such indictments are a signal by and to the world community that nobody stands above the law.

The mass media have also played a huge role in the shift, awakening the conscience of the world. In this day and age, atrocities are more difficult to conceal. The work done by a despot's henchmen today may be broadcast tomorrow on CNN or BBC World News. That visual awareness of human atrocities, projected by television into billions of homes, has helped many of the world's key decision-makers—under pressure from their citizens—to recognize the exponential costs in human suffering of standing by as spectators. These leaders have seen that preventive action would be a bargain, in cost–benefit terms, compared with an after-the-fact salvage operation.

The disastrous attacks on the Twin Towers in New York on 9/11 (2001) was another wake-up call to the world. Those attacks succeeded in weakening the isolationist position of the United States by making it clear that acts of terror do not honor national boundaries. Although we have long known that despots will not hesitate to alienate whole segments of their society, destroying their civil, civic culture in the process, it is now clear that those alienated citizens—unable to find a level playing field in their own society—will readily look for scapegoats outside. It is now clear if we want to prevent further 9/11s, we have to get to the root of the problem: alienation and brutalization of any population must be stopped at all costs. The activities of the Taliban, Al-Qaeda, and Iraq's ruling elite have made it clear that sometimes the only way to get rid of despots and totalitarianism is through outside intervention.

THE INTERNATIONAL CRIMINAL COURT

In 2002 the Rome Statute saw the establishing under the auspices of the United Nations, an independent International Criminal Court (ICC). This is a permanent, international, judicial body, specifically set up to try individuals for genocide, crimes against humanity, and war crimes.

Unfortunately, the United States was unwilling to ratify the treaty, fearing that US service members and officials could be brought before the court in politically motivated cases. Legal specialists have argued, however, that this fear was unwarranted since the treaty stipulates that the ICC will take on only cases that national courts are demonstrably unable or unwilling to prosecute, and it includes numerous safeguards to protect against frivolous or unwarranted prosecutions.

The ICC was given a much wider jurisdiction than the earlier tribunals, being a complement to existing national judicial systems, but only stepping in if national courts are unwilling or unable to investigate or prosecute crimes falling under the mandate of the ICC. The ICC was also tasked with defending the rights of groups that often have little recourse to justice, such as women and children. The establishment of this court was more than just a symbolic move and was a much-needed step in the direction of universal, global, criminal justice.

The ICC aimed to make international standards of conduct more specific, to provide an important mechanism for implementation of these standards, and ensure that potential violators are brought to justice. Because it can investigate and begin prosecutions at an early stage, it is also expected to shorten the span of violence and hasten expedient resolution of conflict. Furthermore, it is hoped that it will have a positive impact on national laws around the world, because ratifying nations will want to ensure that crimes covered by the ICC can be tried within their own borders. It is the wish of the international community that the ICC will ensure that future Hitlers, Pinochets, Pol Pots, Mengistus, Amins, Savimbis, and Mobutus will face a day of reckoning. In this context, it is interesting to see how in 2008 the ICC charged the Sudanese President, Omar Hassan Al-Bashir, with genocide, given his contribution to the bloodshed in his country's Darfur region. He should have listened to the words of Mahatma Gandhi: 'I object to violence because when it appears to do good, the good is only temporary; the evil it does is permanent.'

ENDNOTE

Material from this chapter has already appeared elsewhere, published as:

- Kets de Vries, M.F.R. (2004). 'The spirit of despotism: Understanding the tyrant within,' *INSEAD Working Paper Series*, 2004/17/Ent.

CHAPTER 9

LEADERSHIP BY TERROR: FINDING SHAKA ZULU IN THE ATTIC[1]

The best political weapon is the weapon of terror. Cruelty commands respect. Men may hate us. But, we don't ask for their love; only for their fear.

—Heinrich Himmler

INTRODUCTION

In this chapter, I try to enter the despotic mind to understand better the behavior of tyrannical leaders and explore the collusive relationship between despots and their followers. Why and how do people become accustomed to violence and go along with the practices of a despotic regime? I look at cultures characterized by paranoia, obedience to authority, identification with the aggressor, and dehumanization of the enemy, and examine the psychology of regressive group behavior. How do a despot's subjects experience the terror enacted by a tyrannical regime?

In twelve short years, the South African warrior-king Shaka Zulu— sometimes called 'the Black Napoleon' or 'the African Attila'— conquered a territory larger than contemporary Western Europe. A proxy for all tyrants throughout human history, his life allows us to better understand the timeless motivations and manifestations of despotism.

THE LIFE AND DEATH
OF AN ABSOLUTE DESPOT

Shaka was born about 1787 in the region now known as KwaZulu Natal. His father, Senzangakhona, was the chief of a small Zulu tribe; his mother, Nandi, the daughter of the chief of the neighboring eLangeni tribe. Oral and written accounts about the way his parents met and conceived Shaka differ widely. One account tells that Senzangakhona saw Nandi bathing in a stream. According to this version, the two young people were immediately attracted to each other and engaged in *ukusoma* ('thigh sex')—a form of sexual play without penetration that was a socially acceptable way for young unmarried people to release sexual tension. But they lost their heads; Nandi became pregnant; and the families of both were disgraced (Isaacs, 1836; Fynn, 1950; Stuart, 1976, 1979, 1982, 1986, 2001).

Another account maintains that when Zulu elders were told of Nandi's pregnancy they indignantly dismissed the claim, suggesting instead that she was suffering from an intestinal parasite called *ishaka*, which was alleged to suppress menstruation and enlarge the belly. The elders were unwilling to accept that their chief would have disgraced himself with an eLangeni woman. Remembering the insulting way she had been treated, Nandi later called her son Shaka, or 'parasite.'

The illegitimate birth was not the only taboo that the couple broke, however. In conceiving a child, Senzangakhona and Nandi transgressed kinship rules about proper social behavior. Marriage and sexual play of any kind were not permitted between members of the closely linked eLangeni and Zulu clans. This social convention carried such weight that both clans were publicly humiliated by the baby's birth. The stigma of this double dishonor—illegitimacy and the violation of exogamy rules—extended to the child.

Senzangakhona's affection for Nandi cooled and eventually he abandoned her and their children. Nandi returned to the eLangeni, who grudgingly took her in. Shaka hated living with his mother's family. Despised by his mother's clan, he had to endure many humiliations, and was bullied by other children, who referred to him as 'the fatherless one.'

In 1802, a persistent drought threatened the eLangeni's survival: there was no food to spare for unwelcome clan members and Nandi and her children were thrown out. With no wealth and no husband or family member to stand up for her, Nandi was an outcast; she and her children had to fend for themselves. This rejection affected Shaka profoundly. He became revenge-focused, vowing never to forget what had been done to them.

When Shaka was in his early twenties, he became a warrior for King Dingiswayo, the chief of the nearby Mtetwa tribe. Dingiswayo soon recognized his extraordinary fighting ability and decided to train him as a future Zulu chief. If Dingiswayo could control the Zulu through his 'disciple,' Shaka would act as a buffer against the forces of his main rival in southern Africa, King Zwide. Shaka rose quickly through the ranks of the Mtetwa army and soon became their commander.

When his father died, Shaka (with Dingiswayo's military backing) seized control of the small Zulu clan. Once chief, he took immediate revenge on those responsible for his childhood torment, ordering the execution of large numbers of eLangeni and Zulu. He then decided to turn his small group of warriors into a fighting machine. Shaka trained the Zulu soldiers rigorously, punishing the slightest sign of hesitation with death. He commanded his army to be celibate, created an all-encompassing regimental structure, and instilled his own fighting spirit in his warriors.

Shaka built on Dingiswayo's experiments in social engineering. Dingiswayo had replaced traditional puberty rites involving circumcision with a system whereby young men were organized into age-based military regiments. Under Shaka, coming of age meant being inducted into a regiment (under direct control of the king) and stationed away from home. Once part of a regiment, every male earned his manhood by accomplishments on the battlefield. The young men were required to 'wash their spears' in blood. Through such interventions, Shaka reorganized the Zulus into a formidable fighting force, turning them into an army more Spartan than the soldiers at Sparta—a force unchallenged in southern Africa.

Shaka revolutionized Zulu weaponry and military tactics. Using the *assegai* as a stabbing rather than a throwing spear, his men were able to retain their weapons and advance toward their enemies behind protective shields. He also perfected several complex battle formations that outflanked and confused his enemies.

When Dingiswayo was murdered by his old rival Zwide, Shaka stepped into the vacuum. In 1819, after a series of inconclusive battles, he finally defeated Zwide and took over his territory. Conquering tribe after tribe, he assimilated all his conquests into the Zulu nation. When a chiefdom was conquered, it became a territorial segment of Shaka's kingdom-at-large. The warriors became part of his royal army and were drilled and fought beside combatants from other chiefdoms. Tribes that resisted were annihilated. The Zulu did not take prisoners: old people were killed, and young men and women were incorporated into existing regimental systems. To reinforce his reign, Shaka established a large number of military settlements that served as centers of administration.

The only threat to Shaka's absolute power came early in his regime, from the so-called diviners, go-betweens between the world of the living and the dead. Unable to oppose him directly, a number of diviners accused some of his closest military officers and counselors of witchcraft, an offense punishable by impalement. Shaka did not take this challenge to his power lightly, but he had to move carefully to prove that the diviners were frauds and extinguish their power. The story of how he did it has passed down through generations of oral history.

One night Shaka splattered the outer walls and grounds of the royal kraal with ox blood. The next morning, his subjects were horrified by what they perceived as a blasphemous act. A huge 'smelling out' ceremony was convened to find out who was responsible. More than 150 diviners were invited by Shaka to identify the guilty, and they obliged. Working as teams, they accused more than 300 people of witchcraft. However, three of the diviners deduced that Shaka himself was responsible and with great astuteness pronounced that the blasphemy had been 'done by the heavens above' (Stuart, 2001, p. 45). They were the only diviners whose life was spared. All the others were slowly tortured to death by the people they had falsely accused.

As the combined effects of unbroken victories, unparalleled wealth, absolute and unchallenged power, and extraordinary physical strain began to take their toll, Shaka became increasingly domineering and grandiose. His temper became more and more volatile: he would erupt in rage at the slightest provocation. If someone angered Shaka for any reason, he or she was ordered to be killed, generally by impalement. Executions were capricious and frequent.

As time went on Shaka's isolation and loneliness increased with his growing power—and so did his paranoia. His reality-testing became seriously defective. After the death of his mother, he ordered an orgy of killing for those who did not show sufficient grief and issued a series of bizarre edicts, including the imposition of a year's sexual abstinence on his increasingly bewildered population. Women found pregnant were killed with their husbands, as were thousands of cows in calf. These bizarre acts suggest that he may have suffered a full-fledged psychotic episode.

Toward the end of his reign, Shaka's destructiveness increased. He chased his army from one battle to the next, and his treatment of his enemies became increasingly outrageous. In 1828, at the age of 41, Shaka was murdered, the victim of a palace coup by his half-brothers and chief counselor. He had no children. He had never married, and any women in his harem who became pregnant had been killed. In the absence of a direct heir, one of his half-brothers ascended the throne.

Shaka's military genius and leadership transformed a chiefdom of 100 square miles into an empire that extended to over a million. In a period of ten years he succeeded in building a vast kingdom and a powerful sense of national identity that is retained even today. He swiftly passed into legend as the founder of the Zulu nation. However, it is estimated that Shaka was directly or indirectly responsible for the death of more than two million people. When white settlers arrived in Zululand Natal, they found the desolate landscape littered with skeletons.

DECONSTRUCTING THE DESPOT'S INNER THEATER

When a despotic leader takes charge of a country, the demons that populate his inner theater are reproduced in wider society. The despot's desires, ideals, and hatreds become the fears and wishes of his subjects.

It has been argued, from an ethological point of view, that aggression is needed for the survival of the species (Lorenz, 1966; Tinbergen, 1968). While it is likely that a certain level of aggression is both inherent in and necessary to the human race, a case can be made for a 'malignant' type of aggression that is characterological rather than instinctually programmed (Fromm, 1973). The salient characteristics of this form of aggression are interpersonal abrasiveness and the attainment of narcissistic satisfaction through intimidating and humiliating others. Shaka typifies a leader in whom malignant aggression patterns were so thoroughly internalized that they influenced not only his own behavior but also that of his followers.

Malevolent Antisocial Behavior

We have all known people who show signs of antisocial behavior. Although they are unpleasant to be around, they function adequately in the world of work, if less successfully in the social sphere. Fortunately, few of us know, or will ever meet, someone with the most extreme form of antisocial behavior: malevolent antisocial personality disorder.

Malevolent antisocial personalities, whose behavior shows elements of sadism, extreme aggressiveness, narcissism, and paranoia, are the least attractive among people with antisocial tendencies; they demonstrate extremely callous, vengeful, belligerent, and brutal behavior (American

Psychiatric Association, 2000; Millon, 1996). They like to be in control, and because they care very little about the feelings of other people, they are ruthless in gaining mastery. They take pleasure in victimizing those they control, although they fear being controlled by others and are prepared to go to great lengths to prevent this from happening. Because they perceive the world as hostile, they anticipate betrayal and punishment, and favor pre-emptive aggression. They are driven to avenge any perceived mistreatments in the past.

Just as Shaka engaged in role reversal, taunting the weak as he had been taunted as a child, so malevolent antisocials generally try to make amends for the injustices and deprivations of childhood. Believing themselves to have been victimized, they now feel entitled to be the aggressor. Their provocative behavior can be seen as a form of mastery, a way of coming to terms with their deepest fears, of overcoming the experience of narcissistic injury and recapturing long-lost feelings of omnipotence. Paradoxically, although malevolent antisocials feel that they are entitled to transgress boundaries, they make an enormous effort to control others, setting rigid boundaries and ensuring that they are respected.

Malevolent antisocial personalities, or 'sociopaths,' generally function adequately in intellectual dimensions, despite their socially repugnant behavior and inability to differentiate between what is socially acceptable and unacceptable. Because they have no sense of boundaries, social or otherwise, the role of tyrant comes naturally to them.

Malevolent antisocials' lack of empathy is another defining characteristic (Millon, 1996). Because they cannot identify with their victims (or do so only briefly and opportunistically), the latter can be destroyed and discarded at will. Malevolent antisocials have a strong sadistic streak and no moral qualms about destroying their victims or impounding their possessions. On the contrary, they feel a sense of entitlement.

Vindictive Gratification

A core belief of malevolent antisocials is that they should look out for themselves, regardless of the cost to others. Having once been the victim, they want to make sure they never again find themselves under another's control. The best way of ensuring this is to do the victimizing themselves, so their preferred operating mode is uncontrolled and intimidating aggression. Lacking proper parental controls while growing up, antisocials never learned how to moderate their aggression. Now, as adults, they feel secure only when they are independent or in control of those they fear could harm or humiliate them. With the power to live out their childhood fantasies, they gain vindictive gratification from humiliating and dominating others. When blocked in that or any other endeavor, they exhibit a violent temper that can flare up quickly without regard for others.

Lacking the compassion, ethics, and moral values that characterize most humans, malevolent antisocials experience only superficial and shallow emotional reactions (despite their occasional empathic façade), and their relationships have little depth. Their only emotional strength is hostility.

Malevolent antisocials tread a thin line between adventurousness, recklessness, impulsiveness, and unruliness. Sometimes their creative, non-conforming explorations lead to novel solutions; more often, though, they transgress the limits of acceptable behavior, bringing malevolent antisocials into conflict with established mores and inflicting great pain on others. Because malevolent antisocials do not care what others think (although, given their narcissistic predispositions, they do enjoy the attention of an audience), they forge ahead regardless of the world's disapproval.

Cruelty as a Control Device

Expressing superiority through sadistic behavior is one way malevolent antisocials try to overcome feelings of self-contempt (Stekel, 1929; Horney, 1945). People characterized by what psychologists call the sadistic personality are typically irritable, argumentative, abrasive, malicious, and easily provoked to anger. They nurture strong hatreds and experience a persistent need to destroy and dehumanize people they see as a source of their frustration (Bursten, 1973; Kets de Vries and Perzow, 1991; Kernberg, 1992; Reid Meloy, 2001). They are generally extremely dogmatic, closed-minded, and opinionated, rarely giving in on any issue even when evidence supports another view. Believing that force is the only way to solve problems, they use physical violence and/or verbal cruelty to establish their dominance and achieve their will. Worse, they take pleasure in the psychological and physical suffering of others; they enjoy humiliating and demeaning people in the presence of others. They are fascinated by violence, weapons, martial arts, injury, and torture (Shapiro, 1981; Millon, 1986; American Psychiatric Association, 2000). Despite these inclinations, sadistic types often remain unaware of the impact of their activities.

Children who have been physically or psychologically abused, like Shaka, often engage in abusive behavior as adults. Shaka developed a paranoid outlook, initially with good reason: people really *were* after him; his playmates *did* torture him; he *was* an outcast. Eventually, though, his vigilance ran rampant, and he responded to perceived threats as actual threats, spoiling for a fight even when there was no need. By the time he was an adult, this kind of behavior had become his main operating mode; he had become a sadist who enjoyed inflicting violence.

Although in some individuals constant belittlement leads to depressive behavior, Shaka stood up to his tormentors and fought back and as each successful counterattack built up his confidence, his psychological balance gradually shifted from impotence to power. But even as Shaka's growing power counteracted his earlier sense of powerlessness, his fear of being regarded as a cowardly nobody lingered—one possible explanation for his need to kill his regular quota of cowards when he was in a position to do so.

Because of the violence that individuals like Shaka experience in early childhood, they have little understanding of the good qualities in others. Kindness is viewed as weakness, inadequacy, and unreliability. Sadistic people believe only in might: they identify with powerful, cruel figures and derive pleasure from the suffering and destruction of the weak. As a result, they create a fearful world in which the biblical injunction to 'Love your neighbor …' is reversed to 'Fear your neighbor as you fear yourself.' When this injunction is the motto of a leader, the expectation that others will act in a hostile manner becomes a self-fulfilling prophecy: others follow suit, responding with hostility.

Sadists try to overcome feelings of self-contempt by expressing superiority (Stekel, 1929; Horney, 1945). As Erich Fromm noted, the core of sadism is 'the passion to have absolute and unrestricted control over a living being' (Fromm, 1973, pp. 288–289). As each new victim— each instance of 'unrestricted control'—takes sadistic personalities closer to the omnipotence they seek, they feel the aggressive satisfaction noted earlier.

Sadists also feel an element of righteousness. They rationalize their cruelty by saying that it is for the victims' own good: they are simply laying down socially helpful rules and encouraging people to follow them carefully. They are convinced that the weak need to be devalued and deserve degradation. Shaka often justified his behavior with a grounding in righteousness.

Certain anecdotes about Shaka suggest, however, that a considerable number of his subjects believed that he really cared about them. This apparent blend of kindness and malevolence is common in sadistic types, but it is *only* apparent. Perceived kindness is actually deceit, a form of playacting designed to manipulate the audience. Lacking any center within themselves, sadists play different roles, depending on the particularities of the situation. They make a compensatory attempt to show that they are capable of genuine friendliness and concern, that there is more to them than mere coldness. Such behavior often succeeds, in the eyes of the sadist: it puts others off-guard, encouraging them to say things that they pay for—and regret—later.

Because sadists are unable to see the potential for good in the behavior of others, they are always suspicious of what others say. They are extremely sensitive to perceived insults in anything from comments about the weather to comments about their person. It is as if they are expecting insults—and indeed they are. With their talent for manipulation, they distort the most innocent remark into a barb, responding with fury, scorn, and vindictiveness.

The Paranoid *Weltanschauung*

Healthy suspiciousness is an adaptive mechanism for leaders. Vigilance in the presence of perceived or likely danger is simply an extension of any leader's wish to survive. Suspicion must always be moderated by a sense of reality, however, lest it slip over into paranoia. Effective leaders ground their behavior in sound political practices that limit and test danger, and rely on trusted associates to help them stay safe and sane.

While most of us can distinguish real danger, some see danger everywhere and hostile intent in everyone. Paranoid leaders fall into this category. Persecutory paranoia and paranoid grandiosity are common ingredients in power and politics. Paranoia is the disease of kings. Paranoid individuals distort information and engage in delusional thinking and faulty reality-testing. In their efforts to deal with perceived dangers, they create what looks to them like a logical world. But while their reasoning may be rational, the assumptions on which their logic is based are false.

Leaders with a paranoid *Weltanschauung* typically question the trustworthiness of everyone around them and suffer from delusions of conspiracy and victimization. Fearing that others may do them harm, they listen for—and find—hidden meanings in even the most innocent remarks. If a cursory check proves their suspicions wrong, there is no relief; instead, they search deeper for confirmation. If that effort fails, they may claim to have special knowledge of the inner experiences of the potential offender. In other words, lacking proof, they create it. Over time, their suspiciousness becomes their prevalent, habitual mode of thinking (Shapiro, 1965; Meissner, 1978; American Psychiatric Association, 2000).

In most instances, a person has a limited arena in which to exercise his or her conflicts. Shaka, on the other hand, could extrapolate the emotional conflicts and deprivations of childhood, his resentment toward specific children and adults, onto social situations. His aggression found a perfect outlet in war, which gave him an opportunity to test the limits of the forbidden. And because he respected no boundaries, his cruelty and callousness toward human life became his lasting signature. In that legacy, he joins a long line of other despots, such as Caligula, Tamerlane, Ivan the Terrible, Adolf Hitler, Joseph Stalin, Pol Pot, Kim Il-Sung, Saddam Hussein, and Robert Mugabe.

Primitive Group Formation

Leaders who are governed by a paranoid, malevolent, antisocial outlook are extremely talented at engaging their subjects in a cosmic battle of good against evil. Their paranoid leadership encourages the development of two of the most basic emotionally regressive states to be found in groups: the fight–flight orientation and the dependency orientation as described in Chapter 7 (Bion, 1961). These basic orientations—which take place at an unconscious level—create a group dynamic that makes it much harder for people to work together constructively on the task at hand. They encourage pathological regression in groups to more archaic (that is, primitive) patterns of functioning. These regressive processes are ways of dealing with feelings of fear and anxiety. Freed from the constraints of conventional thinking, groups subject to such regression retreat into a world of their own. The result is often delusional ideation—in other words, the development of ideas completely detached from reality—a fertile soil for the proliferation of totalitarian ideologies. Encouraged by the leader, an infectious dynamic occurs, contributing to shared madness between leaders and followers (Kets de Vries, 1989).

When regressive group processes take place—such as fight–flight and dependency—people subjected to them readily give up their autonomy when help is at hand—an unburdening process that is easy for people living in a collectivistic society like that of the Zulu. Their unquestioning faith in their leader brings focus, goal-directedness, and cohesiveness, but it also it impairs critical judgment. While they are willing to carry out their leader's directives, it is up to him or her to take all the initiative, to do all the thinking.

Shaka encouraged regressive group processes. Feeling in himself the urge to regress to these archaic forms of functioning, he built on the same weakness in others. By simplifying his complex world into distinct us-and-them categories, he defined a clear path out of chaos; by making his people anxious and uncertain, he made them dependent on him. Riding these waves of regression helped him combat the demons of his inner world and build a powerful nation.

The battlefield was the ideal stage on which to play out these regressive group processes. By harnessing general feelings of anxiety, Shaka transformed a private war with his inner demons into a real war. What better way to deal with aggression than by blaming an outsider—by vanquishing a foe? What better way to act out paranoia than by attacking the enemy within, killing one's own people? And if the cause of a setback was unclear, there was always witchcraft to blame.

Shaka's paranoid operational code was highly contagious. During his relatively short reign, he created a culture that left no options: either you participated, or you were eliminated. Participation meant propagating still more suspicion and mistrust, creating (and killing off) still more scapegoats. Ironically, that shared task of finding and destroying scapegoats facilitated group identity formation among the Zulu.

Shaka's readiness to deal swiftly with known enemies and suspected conspirators gave him the upper hand. But he had an additional trump card: he was the 'chief diviner.' He played that card often. Having a great dread of sorcery, and believing that sorcerers were everywhere, he was quick to accuse others of witchcraft. In the early part of his regime, Shaka had kept his war doctors busy working magic against the external enemies the clan was fighting, and relied on his own witchdoctors to 'smell out' the enemy within. But he was uncomfortable with the autonomy this gave the witchdoctors—their ability to 'smell out' his personal favorites was not appreciated—and eventually limited their power, at which point he became de facto the only diviner in the country. With a virtual monopoly on magic, he followed the route of many totalitarian despots before him: total mind-control. Achieving the triumph of paranoia over reason, he made his subjects believe that he could read their thoughts and see their most secret actions.

A Culture of Conspiracy

The tyrannical leader and his followers create a common culture characterized by shared delusions of grandeur and persecution (Kets de Vries and Miller, 1984a; Kets de Vries, 1989). The leader encourages his subjects in the fantasy that he loves them all equally, that each of them is especially chosen. The followers, for their part, engage in an interactive process that psychologists call mutual identification (Freud, 1921). Essentially a recognition of the self in the other, this process fosters the feeling among members of the populace that they are not alone and thus encourages the process of group cohesion and solidarity. This cohesiveness is especially appealing in a society in a state of upheaval—as southern Africa was in the time of Shaka Zulu. In the chaos of political upheaval, a paranoid message disseminated by an absolute despot makes for attractive listening. The despot's tendency to engage in dichotomous thinking—to present his dreams of the future in stark, black-and-white terms—introduces certainty into an otherwise unpredictable world. With friends and enemies clearly differentiated by the despot, choices can be made without hesitation. Thus paranoia is not only a disease; it is also the perceived cure for the disease, granting both leader and subject (spurious) clarity. The despot's subjects experience a new sense of purpose; they gain a sense of direction. They know where to go, what to do, and whom to fight.

In times of crisis, anxiety and confusion make people more susceptible to regressive pulls. Feeling lost, they submit to the lowest common denominator of emotional impressions. Caught up in that emotional whirlwind, they become less selective in both thought and action; in short, they become more gullible. When social and cultural institutions are disintegrating, the illusions of powerful leadership are tempting. Manipulative leaders, adept at simplification and dramatization (and well aware of the gullibility of their followers), take advantage of the situation and present themselves as merchants of hope.

Unfortunately, followers who relinquish autonomous psychological functioning and buy into the collective fantasy of a despotic leader rarely recognize the destructive path they are on. They want so desperately to believe the proffered images of unlimited power, regal grandeur, and awe-inspiring majesty that they fail to see what the leader really stands for. They cheerfully cement a Faustian bargain, not recognizing the high price that will eventually have to be paid. They are blind and deaf to a future of self-destruction, social disruption, and economic decline.

Shaka's presence at a historical moment in southern Africa's history created a situation of complementarity between the script in his inner theater and the pre-eminent concerns of a society in transition (Erikson, 1963). The changes taking place in the physical and political landscape of southern Africa, and the death of Dingiswayo, gave Shaka the chance to act out the script of that inner theater on a much larger public stage.

The Zulu hunger for leadership facilitated his rise to the top; the population was predisposed and willing to transfer to him all the power he needed.

When Shaka consolidated his empire, he transformed a loosely constructed federal structure into a totalitarian, highly centralized state, keeping all the levers of power within his grasp. No appointment could be made without his approval and no decision without his consent. Every official in his empire reported to him. Every transgression in his domain, however slight, was brought to his attention and dealt with promptly. It was as if Shaka feared that condoning little offenses would open the floodgates to loss of control.

Shaka made himself the senior executive, sole source of the law, ultimate court of appeal, commander-in-chief, and high priest. Thus the executive, judiciary, and religious functions were all concentrated in his hands. By opting for total centralization, the traditions of the royal Zulu house became the traditions of the nation, the Zulu dialect became the language, and every inhabitant of Shaka's realm was dependent on his whims.

THE COLLUDING MIND

Shaka orchestrated his symphony of terror brilliantly, knowing just which notes to play to create and sustain fear. Building on existing cultural themes, he forged a military state that exerted total physical and ideological control; and in the process he re-educated the psyche of the population.

The Tools of Thought-Control

Shaka was in an excellent position to use many tools of thought-control (Lifton, 1961) against his people. Because he was the chief diviner of the nation, they believed he could communicate directly with the ancestral spirits, secure the fertility of their land, protect their cattle from disease, and bring the much-needed rains.

Speaking to Shaka through his dreams, the ancestral spirits provided him with a rationale for his actions and absolved him from responsibility for his horrendous acts of violence. Having wrested the monopoly of magic from the diviners, he had the final word. Whether Shaka really believed that he had special powers in dealing with the spiritual world is questionable, but his well-documented superstition and the conviction with which he apparently made his pronouncements suggest he might have done.

Family life was fundamentally changed by Shaka's military innovations. Personal attachments had to give way to loyalty to the crown and that loyalty was rigorously tested: people were asked, for example, to execute close family members to honor the king—and to sing the king's praises while doing so. No important decision could be taken without Shaka's approval. The right to marry became part of his elaborate reward structure. His social manipulation meant that the demands of the regiments took priority over family life. Defining the 'evil' outside gave him and his followers a sense of purpose. As students of groups have observed, demonizing others can bring satisfaction and play an important role in identity formation (Volean, 1988). When they experience a sense of superiority over others, people begin to feel better about themselves.

Shaka had no trouble identifying targets, and he showed no reluctance in dispatching them. He created a very dangerous world—one in which any sign of independent thought could (and more often than not did) lead to death. Tremendous conscious and unconscious self-censorship evolved as a result. Blind, unthinking obedience to authority (supported by the patriarchal structure of Zulu society and by the cultural scapegoating of evildoers) became the distinguishing feature of Shaka's regime. To be good was to obey; to be bad was to be disobedient—and rewards and punishments were expected to ensue accordingly. The overall culture of terror laid the foundation for those tactics. Knowing that Shaka needed to feed his aggression with victims, people were sorely and frequently tempted to offer up others to save themselves.

Divide-and-Conquer Leadership

Like many despots, Shaka knew the value of information, and manipulated it astutely. He was adept at playing people against each other, using a divide–and–conquer policy to prevent his inner circle from uniting against him. For example, he often gave his senior people assignments with incomplete or overlapping authority, creating intense competition. They soon learned that one way they could garner more authority was by betraying each other. As a result, Shaka had an elaborate espionage network of private and public information sources. Unfortunately, what he thought they should have said, or what he had expected them to say, was generally more important than what they really said.

The consequence of such information (mis)management was that Shaka's followers divided themselves into factions that fought among each other constantly, weakening their own positions. This was exactly what Shaka had planned. By bestowing favors on one group, then on another, he made sure that none of the factions got the upper hand. With this delicate balancing act, he monopolized all the decision-making power, effectively destroying any internal opposition to his rule.

Shaka rotated his key advisors, reshuffling them whenever he thought they were becoming too comfortable. This kept them from learning too much about any one thing and prevented them from building their own regional power base. In order to keep people in positions of power under his thumb, he summoned district chiefs to be members of his council at the royal kraal. With their family left behind, vulnerable to Shaka's long arm, they would think twice before harboring any subversive thoughts, and many times more before acting on them.

While Shaka appeared to seek the counsel of his advisors, in reality their role was purely perfunctory. In the manner of all despots, he would state his opinion and expect his advisors to agree. On the rare occasions when there was opposition to his plans, he would convene another council to get the feedback he wanted. As we saw earlier, council meetings could not be held without his presence, since that would be an invitation to conspiracy. Shaka's advisors went along with this, as they did with everything else he did. They knew too well the cost of disobedience.

Shaka manipulated his military advisors as much as his civil advisors, using the same divide-and-conquer technique with his generals to prevent them arriving at a common opinion that could be used against him. As far as Shaka was concerned, the generals' only function was to execute his orders. Any opposition to his way of leading the nation was quashed immediately. As a result, most members of his inner circle—military or otherwise—applauded Shaka's actions and even encouraged him to be more violent.

By playing one constituency against another, Shaka made sure that no single person or group ever knew exactly what was happening in his regime. His ability to form and shift alliances depending on the expediency of the situation, his talent at eliminating actual and imagined enemies, and his aptitude for maintaining overlapping networks of spies to discover, intimidate, and undermine any form of opposition served him well. The divide-and-conquer leadership style that these combined strategies comprised—the style favored by despots everywhere—put Shaka, like a spider, in the middle of a web of information.

A Capricious Operating Mode

Not only do despotic leaders create structures and use divisive tactics to keep their populace in check, they also specialize in random terror. Shaka made sure that the only predictable element in his leadership style was cruelty: everyone knew that sometime, somehow, somewhere, someone's neck was going to be broken, or someone was going to be impaled, or someone's family was going to die. Nobody could feel safe.

Deliberate, unpredictable violence has a devastating effect on those who witness or hear of it. The horror plunges people into a psychological abyss, breaking their will and enforcing total subjugation. A review of totalitarian regimes—like that in North Korea—suggests that when a certain degree of submission has been reached, the populace is prepared to accept anything. They come to believe that their leader is entitled to do whatever he wants. Once that submission point has been reached, saying 'Bayete!' ('Hail to the king!') is the only option open to them.

Shaka made terror part of his daily routine. He kept a group of executioners as part of his regular retinue, their sole purpose to kill at his command. The victims were often nobodies, but important figures were no safer. On many occasions Shaka selected two or three of the counselors in attendance at a meeting and ordered them to be killed on the spot.

At first glance, this behavior seems highly irrational, but in the context of absolute, totalitarian leadership it is rational in the extreme. Shaka's random executions—like those of Joseph Stalin, Mao Zedong, Idi Amin, Pol Pot, Saddam Hussein, and others—kept the people in check. As king, Shaka had the right to kill and if he failed to exercise that right routinely, he might give the impression that his power was waning. People might disdain or even rise up against him. Thus the whimsical killing had to go on.

That Shaka could so blithely inspire fear suggests that cruelty came naturally to him. A true malevolent antisocial, he saw people as things, devoid of emotional value. Like cattle, people were a lower form of animal that could be disposed of at his pleasure. His words could kill people or save them. Unfortunately, his subjects' reactions of awe and terror, their perception of him as all-powerful, omniscient king, fed his delusions of grandeur and he became more brutal still, his early impotence transformed into omnipotence. But as Shaka came to understand, the experience of absolute control over other human beings is a narcotic: as time passes, larger and larger infusions of the drug are needed. He pulled others into addiction with him. Those people who were asked to participate in executions were bonded to his atrocities; they shared in the guilt, even if, like Shaka, they felt none.

We can only imagine how Shaka's inner circle must have felt, constantly subjected to his whimsically tyrannical behavior. It was obviously far too dangerous to offer an honest opinion. But given Shaka's unpredictability, even flattery had its dangers. It tended to make the king suspicious and often triggered a paranoid response. That left only total submissiveness and passive dependency; and often even these were not enough. The *assegai* in Shaka's hand moved more quickly than thought, it seemed. Toward the end of his reign, that spear of death spoke as loudly in the royal kraal as it had earlier spoken on the battlefield.

A TYRANNY OF SELF-DECEPTION

Given the danger of mere proximity to Shaka, the obvious question is, why did his henchmen hang around? Why did they not flee rather than become active collaborators in his terror? The most likely answer is that they had very little choice. If someone was asked to be part of Shaka's entourage, refusal was not an option. Any transgression of the king's wishes invited execution. Fleeing the territory as a whole was not an attractive proposition either. First, Shaka had created such a large nation that it was difficult to get beyond its range of power. Second, he had created a wasteland around his empire. Where there were people at all, the barren territory had forced some to resort to cannibalism.

Crumbs of Power for the King's Dogs

Still, when things were at their worst, why was there not a united rebellion against Shaka's atrocities? The answer lies in human nature. There were benefits to be had from being close to the king. Shaka's activities gratified a number of psychosocial needs in those followers who earned the king's favor. The royal kraal may have been a place of high risk, but it was also a place of great reward. A hub of exciting action, it offered great contrast to the rather humdrum, pastoral existence that the Zulu had been born into.

The royal kraal was the place to be seen. There were drills, social events (including dances), courtships, and other interesting activities. As in the heyday of Louis XIV's Versailles, to be somebody, one had to be part of the inner circle. Exclusion from the royal kraal was equated with oblivion; it was as if the person did not exist. Best of all, the royal kraal housed the great king, who rolled the dice of life and death. What more exciting game could there be?

With all these enticements, the royal kraal attracted a large number of people in search of power, honor, fame, glory, and wealth. People of rank did not have to till the land or take care of cattle; on the contrary, they were taken care of at state expense. They were often shown enormous generosity by the same regal hand that meted out death. Shaka shared with his favorites of the moment the bounty that came to him through raids and the cattle that were seized at the executions of the less fortunate.

Furthermore, Shaka was leading his people on a glorious adventure. There was terror, yes—but the tedious herding of cattle or cultivating land were no longer the only options. Freeing them from petty concerns, Shaka gave his men exciting roles in a great historical drama; he led them into battle and brought them out again victorious. Dangerous as war is, it appeals to basic human motivational needs. Being part of a regimental structure gave the struggling Zulu people a sense of purpose and meaning, a reason for living. Fighting for an imagined just cause, they rose above the trivia of daily existence. They experienced comradeship and sexual adventure, and they felt alive. Marching against an enemy created a sense of righteousness and dispelled any sense of alienation that individual warriors may have felt. The young men felt good knowing that they were on the side of the angels, that they were superior to the enemy, with its deceitful, treacherous behavior.

War also provided Shaka's warriors with an ideal outlet for their aggression; the ultimate definition of manhood, it tested their mettle. Flexing their muscles both literally and figuratively gave them a collective (and addictive) euphoria. Allowed to engage in the most violent acts without consequences, they explored their capacity for evil—a capacity that lies barely submerged in all of us. They experienced a godlike power over life and death and found it extremely seductive. They could spare lives or take them, with honor rather than guilt.

Furthermore, Shaka's men were granted sexual liberty. Like many conquering armies throughout history, they were given permission to rape. Relatively chaste at the kraal, they were allowed to have full sexual intercourse after battle, to ward off any negative effects associated with killing. Participating in rape and massacre created feelings of group solidarity among the men; they shared a collective complicity that negated alienation and contributed to nation-building.

Shaka's men had been trained for killing from youth. Although Shaka set the process of leadership by terror in motion, he had willing followers in his warriors, who had been schooled in war during their years in the regiments. Eager to 'wash their spears' in battle, they wanted to practice their profession. Shedding blood was the culmination of their years of training. Having been rigidly controlled during their training, on the battlefield they could let go of their inhibitions and experience war as a sort of catharsis.

In Shaka's regimental system, his men found a new way of life: comradeship, a sense of purpose, colorful dress, flashy weaponry, and permission to indulge in violent behavior. They wanted the wealth, prestige, power, and glory that battle could bring them. They wanted to advance in the military or civilian bureaucratic system and become one of the chief advisors to the king. They wanted to be attractive to women and hear their praises sung after battle; they wanted to earn the right to marriage. Eager for all these rewards, they urged Shaka, at least during the early part of his rule, to send them on one campaign after another. Sharing his fantasies of grandiosity and majesty, they clamored for war.

This kind of collusion between leader and followers is the despot's major source of power. Totalitarian rulers cannot act alone; they need people who are prepared to participate in their cruelty.

Indoctrination into Violence

The training to become a Zulu warrior glorified violent killing and involved a process of gradual brutalization and desensitization, which progressed from watching experienced colleagues commit violent acts to participating in violent acts oneself. This process involved divesting target groups of human qualities (for example, Shaka belittled old men and cowards). Researchers have demonstrated that violent socialization of this sort makes people more prepared to commit atrocities (Von Lang and Sibyll, 1983; Athens, 1992; Grossman, 1996; Rhodes, 2002). We have seen ample evidence of that fact in concentration camps in Hitler's Germany, Stalin's Russia, Mao's China, and Karadzic's Bosnia.

In fact, the socialization of the regiments was so effective that Shaka and his generals had to work hard to control the violence; they had to orchestrate activities, specifying that violence was permitted only at certain times and certain places. How explosive this form of brutalization could become is well-illustrated by the mass violence that erupted when Shaka's mother died.

Although Shaka's men lived with violence every day, they felt protected by the cruelty they inflicted on others. Shaka convinced his men that 'washing their spears' would help them overcome their own fear of death—or even free themselves from death. Thus violence and terror became the warriors' guardian angels. The men were helped in this belief by Shaka's role as supreme spiritual leader. When Shaka rationalized mass killings by invoking predestination and divine mission, the warriors believed him, accepting their assigned tasks as sacred duty. What he thought was right, must be right—so said their patriarchal, superstitious worldview. In validating Shaka's construction of reality, the Zulu people increased his influence, weakening the individual dissenter's hold on reality.

LEADERS AND FOLLOWERS

Totalitarian societies invade every citizen's private, inner world. There are many psychological difficulties associated with such an invasion, as the individual struggles to maintain a modicum of uniqueness. Many people lose that struggle, swept away by the leader's charisma and tactics of intimidation.

The Group Mind

There are peculiar intrapsychic and interpersonal psychological dynamics at work in leader–follower relationships. A good example is the Milgram experiment, a socio-psychological investigation that explored obedience to malevolent authority (Milgram, 1975). In this experiment, subjects were led to believe that they were giving electric shocks to a test-taker, who pleaded desperately (but fictitiously) for the shocks to stop. The results, based on a random sample of the population, showed that people are remarkably willing to yield to individuals in a position of authority. The 'collaborators' abandoned their humanity and abdicated responsibility for that choice. Allowing the authority figure to absolve them for their actions, they delegated their guilt to others. Although they knew that what they were doing was hurtful and unnecessary, they lacked the will and courage to act on their convictions. Going along with the authority figure, relaxing their conscience, and rationalizing their behavior was easier than taking a stand and protesting to the shock treatment.

When reflex-like obedience to authority becomes a way of life in a given society, a collective mindset emerges. Collective pathological regression makes people revert to archaic patterns of behavior and absolutist forms of thinking. We have all seen, in group settings, how individual judgment and behavior can be influenced by the forces of group dynamics. People in a group typically do not feel responsible for the decisions made by the collective, and they are reluctant to question the appropriateness of any given decision. An unquestioning belief in the righteousness of the group's actions allows individuals to overlook, support, and rationalize atrocious acts.

The Process of Dehumanization

Groupthink is one way of explaining regressive, violent behavior patterns. Used in conjunction with dehumanization of the 'other,' groupthink is a formidable weapon in the despot's arsenal. Dehumanizing the enemy paves the way for leadership by terror, because it allows ordinarily humane people to become active participants in the regime's atrocious acts (Erikson, 1963; Des Pres, 1976). This complex psychological process, which combines defenses such as denial, repression, depersonalization, isolation of affect, and compartmentalization (i.e., disconnecting related mental representations and walling them off from each other), facilitates the use of terror. To perceive another person as human requires empathic or vicarious reactions based on perceived similarity. Dehumanization shuts off empathy by implying that the victims are not individuals in their own right. The argument is made that these people are not like us—people with feelings, hopes, fantasies, and concerns. Instead, they are subhumans or demonic forces bent on destroying what the perpetrators hold dear. Something that evil clearly requires different treatment and unusual methods. Any atrocity that addresses the problem is permitted. Defenses such as these help bypass the moral inhibition against killing. When the enemy is a subhuman or non-human—an inanimate object, as it were—its destruction need not be hindered by the restraints of conscience.

As the Milgram experiment demonstrated, people are eager to please those in authority. Psychologists talk of the 'idealizing transference' and submission to an overpowering, uncompromising force, but what it comes down to is this: when we please the leader, we feel a sense of oneness with him or her (Kohut, 1971, 1985; Kets de Vries, 1993). There is an illusory merger between leader and led that allows underlings to feel a temporary sense of omnipotence. For a moment, they know what it is to have the power of the leader. They feel absolved of any moral responsibility—that lies with the leader—and they feel bonded with both the leader and the other group members by their shared action, even if that action is cruel and deadly. When the leader is a despot, the identification that followers feel leads them to imitate his violent acts. What he did to them, they can (and should) do to others.

Ways of Coping with Terror

Psychological defenses do not offer much protection against tyranny, but sometimes they are all that the victims (and those co-opted) have to rely on. Some of these defensive reactions imply colluding with the despot; others are flight reactions; and still others, adopted by individuals prepared to take a stand regardless of consequences, involve proactive efforts to overthrow the despotic regime.

Identification with the Aggressor

Some people, in an effort to cope psychologically with despots, resort to the defensive process known as 'identification with the aggressor' (Freud, 1966) (see p. 139). When people find themselves in situations of great distress, they feel a basic need to retain an element of psychological security. A tyrannical regime and the violent and unpredictable behavior of the leader strike terror and paranoid anxiety into the hearts of his followers. To cope with these feelings, some of the followers develop an ambivalent relationship with their leader. They feel frightened by them, but attracted too, and lured by the protection they seem to offer.

In full-fledged identification with the aggressor, individuals impersonate the aggressor, assuming the aggressor's attributes and transforming themselves from those who are threatened to those making the threat. These victims (or victims-to-be) hope to acquire some of the power that the would-be aggressor possesses. The more extreme the actions of the leader, the more aggressive the self-defense must be—and the more tempting it is for subjects to gain strength by becoming part of his system and sharing his power. Victims become informers, for example, or underguards in concentration camps, and in those roles sometimes act more barbarically toward their fellow prisoners than the real guards do, resorting—though they know well the pain—to psychological and physical torture.

Violence and submission are closely intertwined in identification with the aggressor. The victims of a despot's violence hold their hostility in check by excessively subservient behavior toward the aggressor. If they turn the aggressor into a 'good' person, they reduce their feelings of fear and helplessness. This defense is an illusory attempt to gain control over an uncontrollable situation. The hostility does not simply go away, of course; it comes out eventually, transformed and displaced toward people out of favor (Adorno *et al.*, 1950).

Identification with the aggressor is a sinister pact between a 'mirror-hungry' leader, who never can receive enough admiration, and 'ideal-hungry' followers, who clamor for an all-wise, all-powerful leader to guide them (Kohut, 1971, 1985). Because of the anxiety created by social unrest and the violence of tyranny, the despot's subjects are prepared to suspend independent thinking and go along with the whims of the leader. They are willing to participate in whatever atrocity he chooses to enact, knowing that resistance will be met by violence; what he does (or did) to them, they will do to others. Their principal rewards are survival, solidarity, and social cohesion.

Dissociative Thinking

Throughout history there have been abundant candidates for the posts of assistant despot and deputy conqueror. We can surmise that we all have a dark side capable of cruelty; *we all have a Shaka Zulu in the attic*. Likewise, we all possess a number of defenses against cruelty in our arsenal.

Some people resort to dissociative thinking to handle the violence and terror of a totalitarian regime. Dissociation is a common mechanism by which people cope with overwhelming, stressful experiences (Steinberg and Schnall, 2000). As an occasional tool it can be lifesaving: when faced with a tiger in the wild, for example, it is wise to stand back and assess the situation without emotion. As an everyday coping device, however, dissociation is excessive: people who rely on dissociative thinking as a way of life disconnect themselves from the world.

Dissociation is a schizoid resolution to the human condition. It is effective at defusing anxiety, but it results in feelings of uncertainty or conflict about one's being and purpose. It also creates a sense of unreality, a subjective experience of deadness, disconnection from others, and internal disintegration. Dissociative people act out a charade, putting on a bland mask in public to cover the turmoil within.

Fleeing into Despair

While some victims and henchmen of tyranny take refuge in dissociation, others flee—but not far enough to do any good. They become depressed and give in to feelings of helplessness and hopelessness. People who take this route engage in non-stop self-recrimination. Despairing of a life free from violence and cruelty, they become morose, tearful, joyless, fatalistic, and hopeless about the future. Devoid of their former vigor and focus, and seeing themselves as worthless and inconsequential, they are unable to initiate action. They expect the worst, which is usually what they get. Eventually, they either become resigned to the situation, withdrawn and apathetic, or they welcome violent acts against them by the regime as a way of stopping the work of worrying.

Fighting for Freedom

And yet, as we so often hear in the world of sport, the best defense is a good offense. In a society of sheep served by a government of wolves, there are generally a few citizens who are unwilling to baa with the others and are prepared to stand up to the demagoguery of the despot.

People who assume the 'fight' position have realized that they have been asked to make a Faustian bargain—material advantages in exchange for dishonesty, hopelessness, cruelty, and destruction. Some freedom fighters are swayed initially by the lure of a utopian ideology but stand up for freedom once they see the excesses of their leadership; others recognize the new order for what it is from the outset. However they reach their determination, they stick with it: at great risk to self and family, they defend their convictions. Many heroic examples—most of whom died for their efforts—can be found in Nazi Germany, Stalinist Russia, and Maoist China. Such people resist exploitation, defend the right to liberty for all, and believe that all people should be able to follow their own dreams. People with this mindset are catalysts for the creation of new, more democratic societies out of the rubble of tyranny. By defending principles of personal responsibility and individual liberty, they bring human dignity to all.

SHAKA'S LEGACY

Despots can be builders, creators of great empires. However, the seeds of self-destruction lie dormant in the beliefs and practices on which their empires are founded. Shaka both built up and tore down the Zulu people. He created a powerful nation, but he did so by legitimizing violence, weaving it throughout the entire social structure. Shaka's inability to form attachments, his incapacity to connect with others, were transformed by hardship into a desire to destroy others. By institutional-izing that desire, Shaka destroyed the moral fiber of a formerly relatively benign society. And as we can see in other totalitarian societies—like Russia, Romania, Bulgaria, and Ukraine—it takes a long time to rebuild a civic society.

By the end of his reign, not only his warriors, but also his subjects, were willing to kill others ruthlessly—even women and children, close friends and family members—if the king desired. Thoroughly socialized to violence, they cognitively and emotionally restructured the moral value of killing, absolving themselves of any wrongdoing. Loyalty to the system created by their leader took precedence over all other considera-tions, and loyalty protected them from moral liability for actions exe-cuted in the line of duty. But when morally abhorrent conduct is enacted by what seem to be decent people in the name of a leader or a secular or theocratic ideology, the absolution of conscience is generally only superficial and temporary; the emotional cost is itself often deadly.

Although Shaka never had a formal day of reckoning, he was locked in a psychic prison of his own making. Though unrestrained physi-cally—with no boundaries to constrain him, no countervailing powers to control him—he was never able to combat the psychological forces of narcissism and paranoia. Eventually those forces sent him across moral boundaries from which he could not return. His craving for admiration, affirmation, and power prompted such extremes of cruelty that he even-tually overreached himself, destroying his own power base. By the time of his assassination, the Zulu nation had been transformed into a military parasite terrorizing outlying clans.

Because of Shaka's endeavors, or despite them, southern Africa was left with several powerful nations, including the Matabele, the Basuto, and the Swazi. But the most powerful of them all, for a long time, was the Zulu. Notwithstanding all his shortcomings, Shaka established a state system robust enough to last a further 50 years, in spite of the rule of two incompetent successors. Shaka's Zulu kingdom became his monu-ment, and it has continued to be a source of pride for the Zulu since his death.

ENDNOTE

1. My account of Shaka's life is based on the writings of two European traders, Henry Francis Fynn and Nathaniel Isaacs, who were both in close contact with Shaka (Fynn, 1950; Isaacs, 1836). Other source material about Shaka's

birth, childhood, and early career comes from collections of oral history (with that genre's poetic embellishments) gathered in the James Stuart Archive (Stuart, 1976, 1979, 1982, 2001). Because writers of many ideological persuasions have elaborated this source material, it is sometimes hard to distinguish between myth and reality in Shaka's story. Most of this material can be found in my book, *Lessons on Leadership by Terror: Finding Shaka Zulu in the Attic* (2004). Cheltenham, UK: Edward Elgar.

PART III

TRANSFORMING LEADERSHIP

INTRODUCTION

After the chapters in the previous section, it is a relief to turn in this part of the book to leaders who use their power very differently and more or less get it right, get the best out of their people, and construct great places to work. What makes a great place to work? I always look for two elements—trust between executives and employees and value-driven leadership. Great places to work show a strong commitment from CEO and senior management, a genuine belief that people are indispensable for the business, active communication throughout the entire organization, perception of a unique culture and identity ('we are not like the others'), an articulated vision and values that are lived and experienced at all levels of the organization. In addition, and most importantly, the CEO and the members of the executive team are role models of integrity and honesty. But even if many executives know how to define a great place to work, they may fail in their attempt to make one happen. So why do these organizational characteristics—in theory quite obvious—seem to be so elusive in practice? How do organizations become and remain best places to work? What does a leader have to do to motivate people to create a better organization?

Transformational leadership style is played out through two main roles: charismatic and architectural. The charismatic role involves envisioning, empowering, and energizing people; the architectural role involves designing organizations that encourage the kind of connecting behavior that contributes to a common vision and group identity. Furthermore, because knowledge management is a major competitive advantage, you need to be able to hang on to the people in whom knowledge is embedded—which means you need to know how to keep them on your side and working creatively for you. To do that, you need EQ—emotional intelligence—and a culture of trust. Organizations in which trust is compromised cannot be truly creative and innovative: loss of creativity is an early victim to a regime of fear and anxiety. In this chapter I look at some very distinctive leaders who possess what I like to call the 'teddy bear' factor—something in them and the way they operate that helps people manage their anxiety and work creatively.

It is probably stretching readers' credulity to suggest that Alexander the Great, the subject of the first chapter in this section, had a Winnie the Pooh side, although he might seem distinctly cuddly in comparison to that other great military innovator, Shaka Zulu—his leadership style was very different. Alexander the Great has always fascinated me. He can probably be viewed as one of the greatest leaders of all time. Accounts of his exploits show that many of the soundest principles of leadership are actually very old—principles of leadership that are vaunted now date from the time of Alexander. For me, exploring Alexander's life has been a fascinating journey into the history of leadership. As a conqueror, Alexander represents the dictum that nothing is impossible for those who persevere. Alexander is an example of someone with unlimited ambition, who wanted to have it *all*—and then worked relentlessly to achieve that ambition. He was a man with a dream who spoke to the collective imagination of humankind. In Chapter 10, I summarize some of the lessons of leadership that Alexander presented. He certainly set a good example. He did not walk behind his troops; he led from the front. His troop deployment on the battlefield was innovative and he was a tremendous inspiration to his soldiers. He held pep-talks for his officers and men before a battle, telling them how brave and successful they were. He made his people feel special and had a keen understanding of symbolic leadership. Admittedly, he was ultimately prey to the fallibilities attendant on great leadership and toward the end of his life declared himself a god—but his journey to that point was one of unparalleled achievement.

I have always been interested in leaders who make a difference and on the lookout for exceptional leaders. When I came back to Europe from Canada, I very much wanted some personal accounts from top organizational leaders, so I wrote everyone I could think of, asking for an interview. Only one person replied (by telex) and he just said, 'Hi, Manfred, please come.' That was Richard Branson. I have spent a long time following Branson's career, watching him achieve folk-hero status in the UK, and become a role model for young people wanting a career in business. He is one of three leaders whose style I examine in Chapter 11. There has been almost too much written about Jack Welch, one of the most influential business leaders of the twentieth century. Welch turned General Electric into one of the largest and most admired companies in the world, with a market value of about $500 billion, when he stepped down as its CEO 20 years later, in 2000. He has been a master in utilizing talent management to drive change through GE's vast organization. I have also been fascinated by the career of Percy Barnevik, the former CEO of ABB, a real organizational innovator. To unleash energy and creativity and to minimize the stifling effects of bureaucracy, throughout his truly global organization, he created 5000 separate 'responsibility centers'.

All three men have very different styles. In his early years as chairman, Welch was known as 'neutron Jack,' a reference to his dramatic way of transforming a company that suffered from organizational arteriosclerosis—the buildings were left standing but the people were dead. Although he fired many people, he revitalized a very sleepy company, ending up hiring many more people. Richard Branson has a warm personality and is very accessible, encouraging his employees to approach him personally with ideas or problems. Percy Barnevik, by contrast, is more reserved but always placed a high priority on 'walking the talk'—acting on your principles. He is probably more 'left-brain' orientated (analytical, logical, and precise) than Branson, who displays many of the qualities of 'right-brain' thinking: emotional, intuitive, and imaginative.

'Right-brain' thinking is characteristic of highly creative people, the sort who often find it difficult to fit into an organizational framework but who are essential to its well-being and continuation—the kind of people who need to have room made for them. In the last chapter in this section, I touch upon the question on how to manage creative people, and how to create workplaces where these potentially rewarding people can be at their best. We all know that managing creative people presents a huge challenge. They need to be nurtured and may require special treatment. The leadership in many organizations is not always very adept at this. In this chapter I also look at people who are extraordinarily creative. What makes them so special? What characteristics do they demonstrate? And are there associations with mental illness for people who are exceptionally creative?

As to the theory that a leader's influence on an organization is illusory—that leaders are actually like passengers in a bus over which they have no control—I am convinced that leaders are more proactive than that. Leaders can be change agents. It's not always an easy process—it requires vision, initiative, courage, decisiveness, resilience, and a lot of patience—but all of us possess some of these qualities to a greater or lesser extent.

There is an old story that illustrates the way in which a visionary, charismatic, and architectural leader can inspire everyone in an organization. There were once three bricklayers who were asked what they were doing. The first bricklayer said, 'I am laying bricks.' The second said, 'I'm working to feed and house my family.' But the third said, 'I am building a cathedral'—which goes to show that we all have the capacity to wake our inner Alexander.

CHAPTER 10

'DOING AN ALEXANDER': LESSONS ON LEADERSHIP BY A MASTER CONQUEROR

There is nothing impossible to him who will try.

—Alexander the Great

I am not afraid of an army of lions led by a sheep; I am afraid of an army of sheep led by a lion.

—Alexander the Great

INTRODUCTION

The aim of this chapter is to explore what makes for effective leadership and what contributes to leadership derailment. For the purpose of elucidation, I have selected one of the most famous leaders of all times: Alexander the Great of Macedonia, who, more than any other single person, changed the history of civilization. I cover his life story in some detail as a means to illustrate the psychological forces that generally come into play in the making of a leader and to highlight a number of leadership lessons that can be learned from his life story. Included are: the need for compelling vision, the role of strategic innovation, the creation of an executive role constellation, the management of meaning, 'praise-singing,' training and development, succession planning, and the importance of instituting well-structured systems of organizational governance.

THE LIFE OF ALEXANDER

Alexander the Great was one of the most celebrated conquerors of the ancient world, one of history's greatest warriors, and a legend of almost divine status in his own lifetime. He falls into the category of individuals who changed the history of civilization and shaped the present world as we know it. He accomplished greater deeds than any other leader before or, indeed, after him (Kets de Vries and Engellau, 2004).

Before Alexander, the world's civilization had been dominated by eastern cultures—by Persians, Egyptians, and Babylonians. Alexander radically changed that picture. The first great conqueror to reach Greece, Egypt, Asia Minor, and Asia as far as western India, Alexander stretched the limits of what was considered the inhabited earth. Within less than 12 years, Alexander conquered almost the entire known world of his era. At the height of his power, his realm stretched from the Ionian Sea to northern India. Not until the voyages of the Portuguese and Spanish explorers in the late fifteenth century would Europeans be able to say that they had finally explored farther than Alexander had.

Alexander the Great was born in 356 BCE in Pella, the ancient capital of Macedonia, the area around present-day Thessaloniki in northern Greece. He was the son of Philip I, King of Macedonia, and Princess Olympias of Epirus (now Albania). His father, a brilliant ruler and strategist who turned the Macedonia army into a formidable fighting force, conquered most of Greece in just a few decades. His mother, Olympias, was a woman known for her temper and willfulness. These traits, coupled with her great intelligence, made her an extremely difficult person to live with. Her quarrelsome nature put her at war with Philip (and him at war with her) for most of Alexander's childhood (Hogarth, 1977; Lane Fox, 1994; Baynham, 1998).

Education and Training

At the age of seven, Alexander stepped from under his mother's wing to undergo rigorous training by Leonidas, a relative of Olympias. Leonidas taught him the physical skills—such as horseback riding and sword fighting—necessary in a warrior-king. To further refine his education, at the age of 13, Alexander became a student of the Greek philosopher Aristotle, who instructed him in rhetoric and literature and stimulated his interest in science, medicine, and philosophy.

Through his mentor, Alexander learned the Greek way of life and the ideals of Greek civilization. From him, he also acquired a love for the works of Homer. Alexander's final tutor was Lysimachus, and through him, the young man learned many cultural aspects of the world around him, acquiring an appreciation for fine arts such as drama, poetry, and music, and learning to play the lyre (Cawkwell, 1981).

Aspiring to Greatness

This education made Alexander aspire to greatness from an early age. Encouraged by his mother, he was taught to believe that on her side he was descended from Achilles, the mythical hero of the *Iliad*, while his father was said to be descended from Zeus's son Heracles. Heroes, indeed, to look up to! The role models that eventually occupied Alexander's internal world—role models that help to explain the 'stretch goals' he set for himself—included one ruler (Cyrus the Great), two gods (Zeus and Dionysus), one demi-god (Heracles), one epic chronicler (Homer), one hero (Achilles), and one philosopher (Aristotle).

As portrayed in works of antiquity, even as a young boy Alexander was fearless, strong, tempestuous, and eager to learn. Father and son were both extremely ambitious and highly competitive. Alexander was like a racehorse in his enthusiasm and competitiveness, keen to emulate, and then surpass, the conquests of his father. As a youngster, he is said to have complained to his friends that his father overshadowed him in everything. He feared that there would be nothing truly great left for him to do, nothing spectacular for him to show the world.

Alexander's upbringing at the court in Pella, where at a young age he met many leading statesmen, philosophers, and artists, turned him into a precocious child. That precocity, along with his mother's influence, fueled his fervor to surpass the others. The intensity of his need to stand out is illustrated in a famous story. When his father bought a beautiful horse named Bucephalus, it proved to be so wild that nobody was able to ride it. Philip was about to get rid of it when Alexander made a wager that he would be able to tame the beast. When approaching the horse, the younger man noticed that it appeared to be afraid of its own shadow. Facing it toward the sun to keep the shadow behind it, Alexander managed to get on Bucephalus and was able to ride him. King Philip's famous statement to the 16-year-old Alexander—'My son, you must find a kingdom big enough for your ambitions. Macedonia is too small for you'—was supposedly spoken in reaction to that event

(Plutarch, 1973, p. 258). Having won the wager, Alexander got to keep the horse and later rode him all the way to India. When the horse died there, Alexander founded a city and named it Bucephala after his beloved animal.

When Alexander was 16, he was sent to serve as regent of Macedonia. In that role, he had to deal with an uprising in a wild region of what is now Bulgaria while Philip was away at war. Alexander and his troops managed to subjugate the rebellious Thracian tribe, and he established his first city (of many to come), Alexandropolis. In naming it after himself, he was following his father's example as, after a recent victory, Philip had named a similar outpost Philippopolis.

The Succession

In 336 BCE Philip was assassinated, and Alexander ascended the throne of Macedonia. The leaders of the Greek city-states saw Philip's murder as a godsend, an opportunity to rid themselves of Macedonian interference in their affairs. To their surprise, Alexander quickly showed his talent as an incisive strategist and brilliant tactician by putting down uprisings in Thrace and Illyria. To set an example, after subduing Thebes he destroyed the city and sold the inhabitants off as slaves. This draconian act sent a strong message to the other city-states and quashed any further attempts at rebellion. Alexander united the Greek cities and formed the League of Nations, of which he became the leader.

Although Alexander made use of the well-trained army created by his father, he pushed the limits of Macedonian and Greek power to levels nobody had previously dreamt of. Under his guidance the celebrated 'Macedonia phalanx'—an impenetrable fighting wall made up of rows of soldiers holding 5–7m spears (each soldier protected by the shield of the person next to him)—reached the height of deadly effectiveness.

After subduing the remaining opposition from various Greek city-states, Alexander, in the spring of 334 BCE, embarked on an Asian campaign—a war originally planned by his father. The 'party line' (or reason that he handed out for popular consumption) was that the campaign was necessary to redress the insult of the Persian invasion by the great King Xerxes 150 years earlier. More likely was that he needed the riches of the Persian king to support his costly war machine. Still another reason (perhaps the deepest motivation) was the urge to best his father.

See the Conquering Hero Comes

The series of conquests Alexander then carried out proved to be the greatest in history. His main opponent during this time was the Persian King Darius III. At the time, the Persian kingdom was an empire of epic proportions, stretching from Egypt and the Mediterranean into India and central Asia—an empire that had dominated the ancient world for over two centuries. The story goes that when the army reached land after crossing the Hellespont (separating Europe from Asia), Alexander leaped from his ship in full regalia and, hurling his spear ahead, declared that he accepted Asia from the gods.

In spite of being greatly outnumbered, Alexander defeated the Persian army during three major engagements (Dupuy, 1969; Arrian, 1971; Bosworth, 1988; Fuller, 1989; Fildes and Fletcher, 2001). The first encounter came in 334 BCE when Alexander swept away a Persian defense force sent (but not led) by King Darius III at the Granicus River (located in present-day Turkey). On the banks of that river, Alexander quickly defeated the Persian troops who had been waiting for him. This victory made the rest of Asia Minor extremely vulnerable to his military might. That might was accentuated, symbolically at least, when he severed with his sword the Gordian knot, which (according to legend) would make the person who could untie it the ruler of the world.

In 333 BCE Alexander marched into Syria. Even though King Darius had raised a large army, he was unable to withstand Alexander's powerful infantry, cavalry, and phalanx. The entire region soon submitted to Alexander. Following this victory he went on to Egypt, where he was welcomed as a deliverer from oppressive Persian rule and crowned as pharaoh. There he founded the famous city Alexandria, which bears his name and which went on to become a world center of commerce and learning. While in Egypt, he went to the oasis of Amon (now in Libya), where he was acknowledged as the son of the god Amon-Ra, an act that may have contributed to a conviction of his own divinity.

After the stay in Egypt, Alexander reorganized his forces and started for Babylon. In 331 BCE he again defeated Darius in the decisive Battle of Gaugamela, after which Babylon surrendered. Subsequently, Darius was killed by one of his generals, a murder that gave Alexander the opening to declare himself King of Asia. Alexander then forced his way to Persepolis, the Persian capital, allowing his soldiers to sack the city. He did not rest for long, however, having already set his sights on India.

Alexander went on from what is today Afghanistan into northern India. In the spring of 327 BCE Alexander defeated King Porus (a formidable opponent equipped with, of all things, war elephants) at the River Hydaspes. After this difficult victory his Macedonian soldiers rebelled, refusing to go farther. Having little choice, Alexander ordered the return to Babylon, where he spent about a year organizing his dominions and completing a survey of the Persian dominions and the Persian Gulf in preparation for further conquests. Those who returned safely with Alexander had covered over 20 000 miles within a period of roughly ten years.

Alexander was now at the height of his power, with an empire stretching from the Ionian Sea to northern India. However, despite his troops' desire to call it a day and head home, Alexander was far from satisfied. He felt compelled to explore more territory, pushing back the borders of known civilization. He also wanted to combine Asia and Europe into one country and name Babylon the new capital. In order to unify his acquisitions, he encouraged intermarriages, did away with corrupt officials, and spread Greek ideas, customs, and laws into Asia.

However, Alexander's many plans came to an abrupt end when, while in Babylon, he contracted a fever. His war-ravaged body could not combat the illness effectively, and he died in 323 BCE aged only 32. He is supposed to have complained, as he lay ill, that he was dying from the treatment of too many physicians. Though his first wife, Roxanne, was pregnant Alexander had left no provisions for a successor, and eventually his empire was divided between his generals. There was, however, a lasting legacy of his conquests: the bringing together of Greek and Middle Eastern civilizations.

Alexander the Strategist

As he built his empire, Alexander saw himself as the propagator of Pan-hellenic ideas, customs, and laws in new lands. Using both military and administrative techniques, he tried to integrate the various peoples he had conquered into a unified empire by devising localized forms of rule in each region (Hammond, 1993; Stewart, 1993). As much as he could, however, he kept intact indigenous administrative systems. In Egypt, for example, he became the pharaoh. In Mesopotamia he became the great king. Regardless of the role he played, he tried to rule in a fair manner. If he heard that some of his provincial officials were ruling unjustly, he replaced them. He also founded hundreds of new settlements, encouraging his men to marry local women and setting an example by himself marrying a Persian princess and a Bactrian woman. He made the army multicultural as well, by including soldiers from all conquered regions.

He introduced a uniform currency system throughout the empire and promoted trade and commerce. Exceeding the bounds of conventional rulers, he manipulated the local religions to legitimize his own rule by having himself named a god.

As a leader, Alexander was without peer. He could be magnanimous toward defeated enemies and extremely loyal toward his friends. As a general, he led by example, giving directions from the front, suffering the same wounds as his soldiers. He was extremely concerned about his soldiers, encouraging one or another whenever possible (Green, 1991; Ashley, 1997).

Seeds of discontent

Though these traits encouraged loyalty among the men, Alexander was also known for his ferocious temper. He once, in fact, killed a close associate in a drunken rage. His adoption of Persian ways and his attempt to be seen as a living god became bones of contention within the administration and on the front lines, creating estrangement. His vision of empire based on tolerance—that is, on giving equal status to the Persians and other conquered peoples—caused increasing resentment among his own people. In particular, his Macedonian officers objected to his attempts to force them to intermarry with the Persians. They were also troubled by how brutally Alexander put down an imagined conspiracy, and by other instances of harsh treatment.

A victim of His Own Success?

Alexander was clearly a multifaceted personality, with his compensatory strivings, his quest (actively encouraged by his mother) to do better than his father, his recourse to 'flight into action' to ward off feared depressive reactions, and his cyclothymic characteristics (his tendency toward radical mood swings) (Millon, 1996; Solomon, 2001). In addition, he was in great need of positive 'mirroring' for affirmation, using his close friend Hephaiston as alter ego to establish greater psychological security. Moreover, like many leaders before and after him, Alexander became a victim of hubris—succumbing to excessive arrogance and pride. The combined effects of unbroken victories, unparalleled wealth, absolute and unchallenged power, extraordinary physical stress, alcoholic bouts, and isolation began to take their toll. As his advisers grew less and less willing to state their mind for fear of the consequences, Alexander's system of reality-testing crumbled.

As time passed, Alexander's behavior was increasingly domineering and grandiose. His particular tragedy was not only the breakdown in his reality-testing but also the display of paranoid outbursts that created a vicious circle of isolation and loneliness. Eventually, with no one willing to challenge his self-created reality, his world became a house of mirrors and he could see only what he wanted to see.

Nevertheless, despite his darker side, the constructive parts of Alexander's personality more often prevailed, and it was these that enabled him to go from victory to victory, and triumph to triumph.

ALEXANDER'S LEGACY

Alexander's main accomplishments can be summarized as follows.

- He brought Greek ideas, culture, and lifestyle to the countries that he conquered and assured the expansion and domination of the Hellenistic culture, which, together with Roman civilization and Christianity, constitutes the foundation of what is now called Western civilization.
- He marched for 12 years over 20,000 miles and never lost a battle.
- He united an area of over 22 million square miles.
- He adopted Persian dress and customs, married Bactrian and Persian princesses, and required thousands of his Macedonians and Greeks to wed Persian women.
- He proclaimed himself god-king in Egypt, Greece, and other parts of his empire for the alleged purpose of unifying his realm.
- He took scientists along on his expeditions to gather data about biology and geography.
- He made Greek the prevailing language of the near East for all matters of government, learning, and commerce.
- He established many new colonies and cities (70 of them named in his honor).
- He started a great experiment in acculturation by sending many children of Near Eastern families to Greece to be educated.
- He trained and used Persians in his army and used Greeks, Macedonian, and Persians in his administration in an attempt to unite East and West.
- He revolutionized international trade by setting up a common system of currency for the entire realm. (The economic system that

began to take shape after Alexander's reign remained virtually unchanged until the Industrial Revolution of the nineteenth century.)

LESSONS IN LEADERSHIP À LA ALEXANDER

In addition to his concrete achievements, Alexander's life left the world a number of important lessons on leadership, from which leaders today in business and politics can still learn much about what leaders should (and should not) do:

- Have a compelling vision that speaks to the collective imagination.
- Develop a creative strategy responsive to enemy strengths.
- Create a well-rounded executive role constellation.
- Model excellence.
- Encourage and support followers.
- Invest in talent management.
- Consolidate gains.
- Plan for succession.
- Create mechanisms of organizational governance.

Have a Compelling Vision

Alexander's actions demonstrate what can be accomplished when a person is totally focused—when he or she has a magnificent obsession. Effective leaders clearly convey what the existing situation is and where they want people to be headed. From early on, Alexander knew what he wanted to accomplish. His leap onto the beach after crossing the Hellespont and his statement about becoming the ruler of Asia made this quite clear. Through these dramatic gestures, he spoke to the collective imagination of his people. His army was going to make things right: they were going to demand retribution for Xerxes' slight to the Greek world, and it was Alexander's rhetorical skills that helped his followers buy into this greatest of all adventures. Alexander knew where he was going and how to get there. Unfortunately, he did not know how or when to stop (to the great confusion and dissatisfaction of his troops).

Develop a Creative Strategy Responsive to Enemy Strengths

Alexander not only had great vision, he also knew how to make that vision become reality. His use of strategy is unsurpassed in the annals of history. On the battlefield he knew how to take maximum advantage of any situation, adapting quickly to the tactics of his opponents due to sophisticated competitive analysis. He was comfortable in any battle situation, from standard combat to guerrilla warfare, and was always prepared for the unexpected.

He maintained an excellent information system and knew how to interpret his opponent's motives. Because he was a master at coordinating all parts of his military machine, perfect execution on the battlefield became his competitive advantage. Furthermore, no other military leader has ever used speed and surprise with such skill. He knew the true value of the statement, 'One is either quick or one is dead!'

Create a Well-rounded Executive Role Constellation

Alexander also knew how to shape a committed team around him (Hodgson *et al.*, 1965; Kets de Vries, 2006). He created an 'executive role constellation' by which each of various commanders could build on the others' strengths. Parmenion, Alexander's main commander, played an essential role on the battlefield, and Antipater, his regent in Macedonia, kept his home base in order, while Alexander's other key commanders each superintended particular domains. Their teamwork created the extraordinary coordination that made for Alexander's success on the battlefield. Only in later years did his relationships with his key people deteriorate.

Model Excellence

Alexander set the example of excellence with his leadership style; he walked the talk and wasn't an armchair general. He led his troops quite literally. Many times, he endangered himself by being too much in front. And given the symbolic role of the leader, his death would have been catastrophic. Furthermore, during the early years, unwilling to enjoy the comforts of his position, he lived a soldier's life, sleeping in simple tents and eating mess food. When his troops went hungry or thirsty, he went hungry and thirsty; when their horses died beneath them and they had to walk, he did the same. This situation changed only when he was seduced by the luxury of Persian court life.

Encourage Innovation

Alexander realized the competitive advantage of strategic innovation. Because of his deft deployment of the phalanx, his support for and reliance on the creativity of his corps of engineers, and his own logistical acumen, his war machine was the most advanced of its time. He knew the importance of understanding his adversaries, so he used reconnaissance to maximum advantage. Alexander's creativity and innovation were not limited to the military field, however. His curiosity about biology, zoology, and medicine, and his support for the scientists on his expeditions, led to further developments in these areas of research.

Manage Meaning to Foster Group Identification

Alexander had a propaganda machine, and he used it effectively. His oratory skills, based on the simple language of his soldiers, had a hypnotic influence on all who heard him. He made extensive use of myths, metaphors, analogies, and stories, evoking powerful cultural symbols and eliciting strong emotions—his jumping on the beach in full regalia to claim Asia and his cutting the Gordian knot being good examples. When he felt that his case needed strengthening, he knew how to use his diviners to reframe various incidents as tokens of destiny; and he used symbols and rituals (such as sacrifice to the gods) to great effect. These 'meaning-management' actions, combined with his talent for leading by example, fostered strong group identification among his troops, and motivated the men to exceptional effort.

Encourage and Support Followers

Alexander was a praise-singer: he knew how to encourage his people for their excellence in battle in ways that brought out further and greater excellence. He routinely singled people out for special attention and recalled acts of bravery performed by former and fallen heroes, making it clear that individual contributions would be recognized. He paid attention to his men's needs, visiting and helping the wounded, arranging for elaborate ceremonies for the fallen (and providing for their widows and children), and rewarding his troops handsomely. He had the ability to be a 'container' of the emotions of his people and could also be an excellent listener.

Invest in Talent Management

Extremely visionary for his day, Alexander spent an extraordinary amount of time and resources on training and development. He not only trained his present troops but also looked to the future by developing the next generation, schooling young Persians in the ins-and-outs of Macedonian warfare and striving to bring Greek language and mores to Asia.

Consolidate Gains

Paradoxically, three of Alexander's most valuable lessons were taught not through his strength but through his weakness. The first of these is the need to consolidate gains. Alexander failed to put the right systems into place to integrate his empire and thus never really savored the fruit of his accomplishments. Captive to the demons in his inner world, he could not rest and enjoy but felt compelled to go ever forward. It was as if he had no choice; the trumpets of rivalry never gave him a rest. His temperament, personal development, and an historical moment in time combined to make him who he was: a man destined to succeed in battle and to win a vast empire. They also limited him, however, and formed the walls of a psychic prison containing demons of the past (the main themes of his inner script) that constrained him from consolidating his domains. Conquest may be richly rewarding, but a leader who advances without ensuring the stability of his or her gains stands to lose everything.

Plan for Succession

Another lesson that Alexander taught (and the second that he taught by omission) is the need for a viable succession plan. Alexander was so focused on his own role as king and aspiring deity that he could not bring himself to think of the future when he was gone. (Of course, it can be argued that his young age when he died played a role in this lack of planning.) As a result, political vultures tore his vast empire apart after his death. Power is an easily ignited explosive that must be transferred with care. Great leaders realize that they are taking care of an heirloom that should be left behind in better shape than it was received. To do so, they need to ensure competent succession. Alexander's narcissistic disposition didn't permit him to look beyond his own rule.

Create Mechanisms of Organizational Governance

The final lesson that the case of Alexander illustrates (again by omission) is the paramount importance of countervailing powers. Leaders have the responsibility (weighty though it may be) to put proper mechanisms of organizational governance into place. Checks and balances are needed to prevent faulty decision-making and the abuse of power (see Chapters 8 and 9). Alexander began his reign as an enlightened ruler (given his time and circumstances), encouraging participation by his 'Companions'—loyal soldiers drawn from the noble families in Macedonia—and others. But like many rulers before him, he became addicted to power. As time went on, he tolerated nothing but applause from his audience, so his immediate circle kept their reservations to themselves. With candor muted in those around him, he began to live in a world of his own. Only a crisis, such as happened when his soldiers rebelled and refused to march further, could bring Alexander into the real world. Being out of touch with reality was another contributing factor to his failure to consolidate his empire.

CONCLUSIONS

It is hard to say which of these lessons we can learn from Alexander is the most important because an empire's (or an organization's) needs change throughout its history. Though all these lessons are important, Alexander taught the last three most forcefully through the crumbling of his empire. Though his realm was huge and wealthy, his hubris was greater still. He shared the view that would later be expressed by one of his successors in the field of empire-building, the 'Sun-King,' Louis XIV. *'Après moi le déluge,'* Louis said, apparently unconcerned about what he would leave behind. But Alexander, in spite of his failure to provide for effective succession, left his footprint indelibly on the world as we know it.

ENDNOTE

The material in this chapter has already appeared elsewhere in print, under the same title, in *European Management Journal*, **21** (3): 370–375, June 2003. In addition, another resource was the book: Kets de Vries, M.F.R. and Engellau, E. (2004). *Are Leaders Born or Are They Made: The Case of Alexander the Great.* London: Karnac Books.

....

CHAPTER 11

LEADERS WHO MAKE
A DIFFERENCE

*Don't tell people how to do things, tell them what to do and let them
surprise you with their results.*

—George S. Patton

INTRODUCTION

This chapter addresses the question of which factors make for vanguard
companies. I start by identifying effective leadership as one of the key
points that helps create high-performance organizations, and then consider the two roles leaders can have in an organization: the charismatic
and the architectural. In the architectural role the leader plays the role
of organizational designer, putting into place appropriate structures and
systems. Envisioning, empowering, and energizing are characteristics of
the charismatic role.

To illustrate these factors I examine the style of three CEOs who
have received considerable notoriety because of their huge success in
business. Richard Branson's Virgin gives the opportunity to look at a
fast-growing entrepreneurial company. The case of Jack Welch of
General Electric provides an example of one of the few leaders who has
been able to transform a corporation suffering from organizational arteriosclerosis. Finally, I look at Percy Barnevik of ABB who took up the
challenge to create a truly global organization integrating numerous
companies and national cultures. In spite of having very different histories, these three companies have many characteristics in common and
can be viewed as a paradigm of what companies are going to look like
in the twenty-first century.

THE EFFECTS OF LEADERS
ON THEIR ORGANIZATIONS

Some organizational observers argue that the leader's role is not very significant and that the importance of leadership is highly overrated. To them, an organization is mainly influenced by the environment in which it operates. Leaders are subjected not only to many internal organizational constraints in the form of structures, procedures, and political processes, as well as to numerous external constraints; they are also prisoners of immutable environmental strictures.

It is not surprising that the theory of impotent leadership has its proponents. After all, adding a leadership dimension to the business equation does muddle things up: if leaders really make a difference, then a host of complicated human factors must be taken into consideration. Advocates of this point of view reduce the complex person–organization–environment interface to a limited number of simple variables supposedly influencing a firm's strategic direction and performance.

Clearly environmental forces do play an important role in organizational life, but underestimating the human factor is a mistake. Without the character of King Henry, Shakespeare's historic account in *Henry V* wouldn't make any sense. The English would certainly have lost the Battle of Agincourt if they had underestimated the importance of the leadership factor. I would argue that any astute observer of organizations will notice that CEOs have a considerable impact on their companies, for better or worse. And the quality of leadership is particularly relevant in situations of strategic transformation and change. A good leader has the capacity to transform strategic constraints into new challenges.

The significance of the leadership factor can be demonstrated by looking at the stories of three contemporary business leaders who now, or in the recent past, regularly grace or graced the front pages of the major business journals: Richard Branson of Virgin, Jack Welch of General Electric, and Percy Barnevik of ABB. These CEOs, although quite different in personal philosophy and leadership style, continue to have a major impact on the way we view organizations (Kets de Vries and Florent, 1999; Welch and Byrne, 2001; Welch and Welch, 2005).

So, what is it that these three individuals have done to change our way of looking at organizations? What is it about their particular way of running their companies that has made them unique?

DIFFERENT LEADERS, SAME RESULTS

Virgin is now one of the top five brand names in the UK. Its chairman and founder, Richard Branson, has become an international celebrity, the subject of numerous profiles in gossip magazines, the business press and television programs. He became one of Britain's richest people before he turned 40, running an empire that encompasses travel (Virgin Atlantic), communications (books, radio and television stations, computer/video games), retail (Megastores), and hotels.

Jack Welch, the former Chairman and CEO of General Electric, used to run one of the world's largest corporations. From the time he took the reins in 1982, he rebuilt the company into a $60 billion conglomerate of diverse businesses, including medical systems, aircraft engineering, plastics engineering, major appliances, NBC television, and financial services. During his term as chairman, Jack Welch has succeeded where many other CEOs of large companies fail. He turned a plodding dinosaur into a lean, sharply focused leopard of a company.

In 1987, Percy Barnevik surprised the business community by announcing the creation of the largest cross-border merger in modern history. In record time he combined ASEA, a Swedish engineering group, with Brown Boveri, a Swiss competitor. Since that announcement, by adding more than one hundred companies in Europe and the USA, he created a $30 billion giant with a portfolio covering global markets for electric power generation and transmission equipment, high-speed trains, automation and robotics, and environmental control systems.

At first glance, there may appear to be few obvious similarities among these three organizations, and even fewer among the three CEOs. Virgin, run by a flamboyant, intuitive, disarmingly friendly entrepreneur, has a corporate culture that highly values creativity and innovation. General Electric is a relatively ancient US company that used to be run by a highly technical individual with a doctorate in engineering. For many years Jack Welch featured in *Fortune* as the toughest executive in North America. In comparison, ABB is an assembly of companies with many different nationalities. Its former CEO, Percy Barnevik, is a soft-spoken, very intense, philosophical Swede, a business-school graduate and a specialist in data-processing and information systems.

These three men also differ fundamentally in their predominant operational codes. Richard Branson is a *builder*. He has created an organization completely from scratch. Jack Welch can be viewed as the high priest of business process re-engineering, a highly regarded *transformer* of organizations (a change-catalyst), while Percy Barnevik was hailed at the time for assembling the ultimate global organization, and was seen as a highly effective *integrator*—an individual with a great strategic vision. Despite these basic differences, there are, however, many similarities in their outlook towards organizational design and the way they view their role.

Initially, all three were dissatisfied with the way organizations are traditionally run, and so were motivated to experiment with new ways of making their organizations more effective. Searching for alternatives, each one developed a new concept of how a corporation *should* be run and a vision of where they wanted to take their organization in the future.

Their beliefs and values were an integral part of their vision, motivating them to spread their message with passion and conviction. Observing Welch, Barnevik, and Branson in action, we see three people who knew how to create the kind of enthusiasm and commitment that inspired others to join them. They recognized the importance of their roles as strategists, change agents, coaches, and mentors. They wanted to change the way people work in their respective companies by changing their attitude. Moreover, these three CEOs wanted to instill in their employees a kind of pride that would go beyond the numbers game. They wanted to contribute something to society. Through their collective effort, they hoped that their companies would be perceived as changing the world in a positive way. Just as Alfred Sloan of General Motors was once the master architect of the 'modern' corporation—a model that held up for many decades—these three executives became the designers of a new prototype more in line with the postindustrial age.

THE ARCHITECTURAL ASPECT OF LEADERSHIP

So what makes these three men so different from many other executives? First, and most importantly, all three acted as organizational architects, and redesigned their corporate culture to inspire people wherever they happened to be positioned in the organization to get them involved. They wanted to foster a sense of *ownership* in their people.

Flat Structures, Not Tall Hierarchies

It has been a strong belief of all these three leaders that strategic awareness should not be limited to the top echelons of the organization but should be pushed deep down. The organization of the twenty-first century has to be more horizontal. Tall structures are out, flat structures are in, encouraging lateral rather than vertical communication. Barnevik pushed authority, responsibility, and accountability far down into the organization, with never more than five people between himself and the shop floor. Welch has been called the 'master of delayering,' obsessed by finding ways to cut layers out of his organization. Where once there were nine organizational layers between himself and the shop floor, there would now be around five. The lack of hierarchy in Virgin has also become legendary. The company is as flat as any organization can be. Also, all three executives designed their respective organizations to be as simple as possible. They wanted to minimize the potential for confusion in the decision chain. They realized that the right organizational structure can be a competitive advantage.

New Ideas for New Times

Barnevik, Branson, and Welch realized that creating behavioral change would not be easy. They understood that young employees entering organizations today had very different attitudes toward the organization compared to their parents. The corporate culture of the postwar generation—was typified by the organization man, the loyal individual who strongly identified with his or her company and made a commitment for life. This kind of person had become a liability in the current climate of leveraged buyouts, merger mania, corporate downsizing, and business re-engineering.

Whereas the traditional command-and-control style of management and organization was designed for an unskilled labor base, the three CEOs realized that the future of the high-performance organization would consist of self-managed virtual teams run by people who didn't have to be continually prodded to do things. They looked for people who set their own standards and rewards. They wanted people in their organizations to be internally motivated. They tried to attract the kinds of people who would set very high standards for themselves; who would criticize themselves when they didn't live up to these standards. They were looking for individuals capable of learning and adapting, with a high tolerance for ambiguity. Decentralization and operational autonomy was a sine qua non for the creative and high-performance atmosphere found in these three companies.

The design of this type of structure was very much in line with the realization on the parts of Barnevik, Welch, and Branson that people wanted to have some control over their own career. These three CEOs also realized that the employees that worked for them were impatient. These people were not prepared, as their parents were, to wait in line for eventual recognition. They wanted responsibility and rewards now. Consequently, they would be attracted to organizations that would offer exciting, immediate challenges. They were looking for companies in which they would be stretched, where senior executives were willing to take a gamble on them and give them the room to learn. Learning and the permission to make mistakes seem to be very closely linked. Thus they were searching for organizations in which employees would be allowed to make mistakes. After all, people who don't make mistakes haven't made any decisions!

That doesn't mean, however, that employees were not held accountable for their performance. Accountability was driven deep down the organization. It is impossible to be part of a winning institution without making a distinction between excellent and mediocre work. Thus constructive feedback about performance is very much part of the culture of these three organizations. There is compassion, but there is a limit to excuses.

Small is Beautiful

All three CEOs knew that while size means more possibilities, it can also become a serious impediment. Economies of scale are not without serious diseconomies of size. These executives were very aware of the fact that when organizational units become too big, employees would become less involved. They could experience a sense of alienation and depersonalization, with obvious negative repercussions on creativity, innovation, and entrepreneurship.

To challenge their employees and give them a sense of ownership, Branson, Welch, and Barnevik went to great lengths to create in their large corporations the small-business atmosphere of a high-performance workplace. Branson has been overheard saying that when there are more than 50 to 75 people in a building, they lose their sense of identity and belonging. When that happens, it is time to spin off the unit to create a new business in another building. Branson has applied his philosophy religiously: his organization consists of a large number of small autonomous units. His organization is like an amoeba, continuously dividing and reproducing. Virgin has turned into a subtle network of interrelated companies with a mutuality of interests, all of which can be mystifying to outsiders. To some extent his company has become like an imaginary organization given the existence of a myriad of alliances that make up the company. In a similar vein, Welch has noted on many occasions that General Electric is a company made up of small companies where people are very much encouraged to take on intrapreneurial challenges. The outlook of Barnevik has been very similar.

In this new type of organizational structure, large head offices, which were previously needed to exert control over the operating companies, would no longer be required. Branson doesn't really have a head office. Significantly, his head office used to be a houseboat, not a place that one can load up with people.

Barnevik's aversion to large head offices has been infamous. According to ABB's 'policy bible,' an important guideline for acquiring companies during his time at the helm, was the '30% rule.' In newly acquired companies, this meant a dramatic cut of 30% of personnel to eliminate some functions, another 30% cut to decentralize certain functions into profit centers, and yet another 30% reduction to create service centers that would invoice services at market rates. Implication of the 30% rule means that only 10% of the staff would remain. To illustrate this rule in action, when Barnevik took over, he reduced ABB's head office to a mere 150 people (before the merger Brown Boveri had 4000 people in Baden, Switzerland, while ASEA had 2000 people in Västerås, Sweden).

Barnevik, Welch, and Branson were well aware of the fact that the 'psychological contract' between their employees and their organizations had been changing. With merger and acquisition mania and the passion for business process re-engineering, job loyalty had gone out of the window. Job tenure and security were no longer to be expected. All three executives realized, however, that a new form of security has to be offered to make their organizations attractive. What these three executives could offer was employability. They provided their executives with portable skills. If the day would come when the organization no longer needed the services of a particular employee, that person would be better equipped to find a position elsewhere. The implication of this new psychological contract was, however, that companies needed to offer learning opportunities (see later under 'All Change').

Structuring for Success

Welch talked about the 'boundary-less corporation,' meaning a structure without the stifling costs of bureaucratic controls. The loose organizational architectures of Virgin and ABB would be of a similar nature.

218 REFLECTIONS ON CHARACTER AND LEADERSHIP

During Barnevik's tenure, ABB had a sophisticated global matrix structure with enormous fluidity between business area managers and country managers. Virgin resembles an assemblage of loosely linked companies in which employees have the possibility to constantly rewrite their job definitions depending on the kind of new challenges they are prepared to undertake.

All three executives created a centralized/decentralized structure. They strongly believed in decentralization, but at the same time they kept a close watch on a number of key performance indicators to stay informed about what was happening in their various strategic units.

The Role of IT

Being big and small at the same time, breaking up a large company into a number of small, loosely connected companies while maintaining the organization's cohesiveness only became feasible with the revolution in information technology. Sophisticated information systems have become a major force pulling geographically dispersed employees together. It is now possible for top executives to decentralize without losing control. Naturally, success in these new structures requires literacy in modern information and communication technology.

Information technology made it possible for Barnevik to say, 'We want to be centralized and decentralized, big and small, global and local.' Similar comments, although not as extreme, have been made by Branson and Welch.

Minimizing Bureaucracy

In all three organizations bureaucracy is a dirty word, and the three CEOs would make a great effort to avoid turning their organizations into paper factories. One of Welch's solutions was to introduce the concept of company 'work-outs' at General Electric. Meetings were set up where all members of an organizational unit (irrespective of position) would have an opportunity to review existing procedures, approval systems, measurement systems, reports and meetings, and decide whether these still added value. If not, radical surgery would take place. The executives at Virgin and ABB would use a minimum amount of paper. Virgin and ABB executives prefer to use the telephone, email, or to manage by flying around and seeing people in person.

Nurturing Creativity

These three CEOs were trying to create a climate for innovation whereby they very much played the role of sponsors. They knew that new ideas are like delicate flowers; without a considerable amount of nurture, they would quickly wilt. Consequently, these three CEOs would give not only strong financial but also emotional support to get projects off the ground. They would like to see a continuous stream of new projects and products in their portfolio. And all three have been extremely successful in doing so. For example, rarely a week goes by without an announcement by a Virgin spokesman or its flamboyant chairman of again another project that is off to a flying start. Similar statements can be made of General Electric and ABB. They want a considerable part of their product portfolio to be new each year.

The principle behind Barnevik's, Branson's, and Welch's way of designing organizations is that when people have a sense of control, they feel better about what they are doing; they will be more creative. Moreover, research on stress has shown that when people feel that they have the perception of control over their lives, when they do not experience a sense of helplessness, they show fewer stress symptoms (Zaleznik *et al.*, 1977). And unless a person has a masochistic disposition, the absence of stress tends to have a positive effect on their productivity at work.

Also, when people feel a sense of ownership for a particular part of the organization, they are more committed. Equally important, they will have more *fun* doing their job. Most people who have fun work harder, a connection that Welch, Branson, and Barnevik have thoroughly understood. In all too many organizations the word 'fun' seems to be dirty word. Many top executives seem to have forgotten its importance. They don't make an effort to let people 'play' in the organization. And as students of creativity will tell you, playfulness and creativity are closely intertwined.

These three executives also realized that the high performers of today can be compared to frogs in a wheelbarrow: they can jump out any time. Thus imaginative talent management systems needed to be found to keep them committed to the organization. As well as giving these people the opportunity to spread their wings, attractive material rewards needed also to be put into place. But these new employees want tangible rewards beyond salary increases. They want to be rewarded according to their contribution. Gain sharing is a way of tying high performers to an organization. The executives attracted by these companies preferred organizations willing to provide them with a piece of the action in the form of stock options, bonuses, or some other profit-sharing plan. Share ownership plays an important role in retaining the best people in a company.

Branson has been overheard saying that he is in the business of making millionaires. He makes it quite clear that he doesn't want his high performers to leave Virgin to start their own companies elsewhere. He makes sure that the key players have the possibility of becoming millionaires under the Virgin umbrella. Under Welch's rule, General Electric has seen an explosive growth in the number of employees who have been granted stock options. As he observed, when the share price of General Electric goes up it really gets employees' adrenaline going. Of course, this way of rewarding employees also adds to the creation of a sense of ownership.

Valuing Customers

Another critical theme in the design of these organizations is that they are customer-centered. Close customer contact for everyone in the organization is a major pillar of the three CEOs' business philosophy. The only oracle to listen to is the customers. Superior customer satisfaction colors the design of all the organizational processes. In these high-performance organizations, customers are not merely an abstraction or a distraction. In this, the three executives would set the example by devoting a considerable part of their time to dealing with customers. And again, the small-business size helps here, too, by enhancing the possibility of contact and improving the feedback loop.

Swifter than Light

Apart from organizational form, another characteristic of the high-performance organization is speed. Product life cycles are growing ever shorter, and speed to market has become increasingly important. Too many companies have invented great products, only to lose out in the process of market introduction. These three executives recognized the importance of speed, creating dynamic, fast-paced environments in which employees would be continually challenged and could expect quick action and results. At General Electric, speed is considered part of the company's core philosophy. Welch himself continually would stress this value.

One of the key success factors in Branson's organization has also been his ability to act fast. As he says himself, 'I can have an idea in the morning in the bathtub, and have it implemented in the evening.' Speed would also take an essential place in Barnevik's management philosophy. In his policy bible, was recorded that 'It is better to be roughly right than exactly right with respect to speed.' He made it very clear that it was permissible to make mistakes due to speed. He did expect his executives to have an 80% betting average. Not taking action and losing opportunities because of a reluctance to make decisions would be the only non-acceptable behavior in ABB.

All Change

An important component of Virgin, General Electric, and ABB's corporate cultures would be continuous change. Nurturance of a positive attitude toward change was going to be critical because of the danger of complacency in the face of external danger signs. As the saying goes, 'Nothing kills like success.' Employees of these companies needed to realize that change would be a permanent aspect of their organizations, not a temporary state.

The three executives were very cognizant of the fact that successful change and adaptation to uncertainty in the highly competitive business world would be more likely to occur when there was a sufficient and appropriate learning culture in an organization. All three executives have therefore created organizations that would provide world-class learning opportunities for employees at all levels. It would be the responsibility of the employees, however, to use these opportunities to their maximum advantage. To observe this notion of employability in action one only has to look at the number of executives that have been poached by competitors. A graduate of General Electric or ABB has an undeniable attraction to headhunters.

Creating Good Corporate Citizens

These three executives have also recognized that there are two kinds of glue that work in loosely structured organizations, one being sophisticated information systems as discussed earlier, and the other kind being provided by the way in which Branson, Welch, and Barnevik manage their corporate cultures. Sharing common values goes a long way towards ensuring cohesiveness. These three CEOs (implicitly or explicitly) wanted each organizational participant to share certain values specific to their respective corporations. In General Electric and ABB, these key values would be summarized in 'policy bibles.' In Virgin, these values are more subtly instilled. Everyone, however, is expected to be familiar with the values of their organization. The values are reaffirmed in workshops, seminars, and meetings. People are expected to internalize these values and behave accordingly, with a positive payoff: the internalization of corporate values would mean less need for external controls.

Also, as culture guardians, these three executives would make an enormous effort to let people speak their mind; they would encourage contrarian thinking. They have taken General Patton's comment, 'When everyone agrees, somebody is not thinking,' to heart. They realized that when people do not have the confidence to say what they mean, the CEO receives filtered information. One of Welch's 'cultural' rules was, 'Be candid with everyone.' He was famous for his directness in dealing with his people, and he expected the same thing from them. Barnevik also would acknowledge the risk of not getting enough feedback. He went to great lengths to encourage people to speak their mind. Branson has an open-door policy. In some ways he plays the role of 'ombudsman' in his organization. He welcomes critical comments about ways to improve the operation of his companies.

Branson, Barnevik, and Welch knew that the key ingredient for encouraging people to speak their mind and be frank was trust. Creating an atmosphere of trust in their respective organizations became an extremely high priority. They knew that factors such as competence, credibility, consistency, support, respect, and honesty were key parts in the trust equation, but the most important factor in creating trust in the organization would be communication. Of course, killing the bearer of bad news would also be the way to kill trust in the organization, and this is something these three leaders would avoid doing. On the contrary, they handled such situations constructively. And they would set the example with respect to openness. They would make an enormous effort to practice what they preached. They would take their roles as coaches, cheerleaders, and mentors very seriously.

What these three CEOs were also trying to do was to make good corporate citizen behavior an essential part of their value systems. A factor that made these companies so successful was that employees were prepared to go out of their way to help each other and to preserve the integrity of their organizations. In contrast to what can be found in many other organizations, their employees wouldn't take a parochial attitude to their job. They wouldn't say when something needs doing, that it was not their job to do it. Instead, they would always be prepared to go beyond their particular job requirements. What would be important to them was the greater good of the organization. And to make this happen, the leadership would set the example by acting that way themselves. They would ensure a sense of passion and pride in the organization.

Know Thyself

What also contributed to the effectiveness of these three organizations was the fact that all three leaders had the emotional intelligence to have a realistic grasp of their own weaknesses, and find people with corresponding strengths to compensate. Branson has had a series of strong managers to compensate for his weaknesses. Barnevik would depend on a number of colleagues who had been working with him for a long time, some giving him advice on long-term business developments, the others giving him tactical support. Welch had two vice-chairmen with whom he would form a team. He was also a regular participant in GE's now-famous 'work-out sessions,' which would give employees a safe way to taste empowerment and criticize standard operating practices.

THE CHARISMATIC ROLE OF LEADERS

So far we have seen how Percy Barnevik, Jack Welch, and Richard Branson handled the architectural role in the way they designed their respective organizations and set up the proper control and reward systems. But there is also another essential part of what leadership is all about: the charismatic role, which has to do with the envisioning, empowering, and energizing elements of leadership. Without alignment between the charismatic with the architectural dimensions of leadership, an organization will flounder. Unfortunately, in far too many organizations, alignment is missing.

The Overriding Vision

What made these leaders and their organizations so successful is that all three had a strong picture of what they wanted to do, and where they wanted to go. They provided focus; they knew how to set the direction for their organization, and how to build commitment to following that direction. They wanted their people to feel proud of their organizations; they wanted them to experience their organizations as something special. And by pushing responsibility down the line and encouraging dialogue throughout their organizations, they facilitated a commitment to their way of looking at things.

Vision is important in that it provides a road map for the future, generates excitement, creates order out of chaos, and offers criteria for success, but it is useless if it is not shared by all members of an organization. Branson, Welch, and Barnevik all recognized the importance of impression management—the need to communicate their respective visions in an effective way. For example, Branson has a showy, almost exhibitionistic style, Welch is an aggressive, confrontational, 'cowboy,' and Barnevik is more rational but also humanistic. Although they differed in style, all three would exude enthusiasm and radiate self-confidence when talking about what they were trying to do, and where they wanted to go, and this made their vision contagious.

One of the values Welch introduced in his organization was, 'Don't manage, lead.' And to make this statement more precise, he told everyone in General Electric that he wanted them to be number one or number two in whatever business segments they were in. If they were not number one or number two, they should ask for the resources to get there. Otherwise, they should get out, or 'disengage,' to use his particular terminology. Branson's vision is one of fostering entrepreneurship. He is looking for people with innovative ideas to start new entities, people who are willing to be the best in what they are doing, be it entertainment, communications, airlines, hotels, store management, or even beverages. Barnevik's vision was of creating the world's number one engineering group.

Barnevik, like other extremely effective business leaders, was very good at creating meaning. He would say that he was motivated by a desire to create a better world by creating employment (particularly in Eastern Europe, where—at the time—he was the largest investor), and help ensure the world remain inhabitable by providing clean energy and transportation. This vision of engaging in good works, of looking beyond the bottom line, performance with purpose has been a very effective way of motivating and challenging the people who worked for him. For Branson, too, this social concern is an important part of corporate philosophy. He has put his money where his mouth is on many occasions.

Power-Sharing

I have already indicated ways in which these three CEOs created organizational structures that empowered people. They realized that one does not become powerful by hoarding power. On the contrary, it is the CEO who pushes power down the line who benefits in the long run. Although letting go of power can be difficult in the short run (after all, power has an addictive quality), eventually the whole organization benefits. Employees become more productive, and as a result of the organization's productivity the CEO becomes more powerful. These three CEOs avoided the trap that many other executives would step into, whereby short-term psychological benefits would overrule the longer-term tangible ones. These CEOs knew how to postpone the gratification of their more immediate power needs.

In this empowerment process, they would set high-performance expectations. They would strongly express their confidence in their executives. They knew that high expectations are likely to motivate capable people.

Harnessing the Energy Within

In all too many organizations the general rule is that garbage goes down and credit goes up. All too many senior executives engage in conflict avoidance, micro-management, or abrasive behavior. Such practices lead to the arousal of strong negative emotions. Welch, Barnevik, and Branson knew how to harness the affectionate and aggressive energy of their people, another critical component of the leadership tool kit. They also knew how to create an emotional holding environment. One often neglected part of leadership is the role of 'psychiatric social worker.' These visionary leaders were very good in expressing affection when needed. They would be active listeners; they had excellent interpersonal skills, and as a result (as this particular way of behaving cascaded down in their organizations), they would get the best out of their people.

These three CEOs encouraged their people to direct aggressive energy outwards. They knew that inner-directed organizational aggression leads to excessive politicking, turf fights, lack of team work, and morale problems. To avoid this, they would set clear boundaries to prevent such behavior, and at the same time, direct this energy toward the competition. Having a strong, common 'enemy' gets the adrenaline flowing in an organization, and is an ideal way to give it a sense of focus. Jack Welch would say that he doesn't want his people to fight with the person at the next desk. He wants them to fight competitors such as Westinghouse or Dupont. Percy Barnevik constantly reminded his people of enemies such as Siemens and General Electric. And the nemesis of Virgin Atlantic has been, of course, British Airways.

CONCLUSIONS

A good summarizing metaphor for the kind of workplace that these three CEOs were trying to create is that of a jazz combo—a place where all musicians work together to play harmonious music. For each player, however, there is ample room to improvise as a soloist.

As described earlier, the era of the highly structured organization is past. Rigidity in organizational design, hierarchical structure, and power-hoarding are now recipes for corporate disaster. Organizations that do not integrate the individual or maximize the potential of today's executives will lack the kind of creativity and imagination needed to survive in the global business world of the twenty-first century.

Clearly, some executives may not be able to deal with the ambiguities that this new kind of networking, boundary-less organization entails—the external boundaries in an organization can be removed fairly easily, but the boundaries inside people's heads are more difficult to dissolve. Weaning some leaders away from their need for authority, structures, and controls may take considerable time and effort. In the long run, however, it will be well worth it. Eventually, they will enjoy their work more, and be more effective.

Equally, many organizational leaders are deficient in nurturing the creative potential of their people and don't understand how to create the kind of learning culture that proactively transforms itself (as opposed to being changed by outside intervention). They would create organizations in which people don't anticipate, they would just react. But leaders like Branson, Welch, and Barnevik knew that if people get the opportunity to spread their wings, they may really take off. They knew how to nurture the creative spirit in their organizations. They would go to great lengths to make life in organizations a meaningful experience where people really enjoyed what they were doing.

A wit once said that there are three kinds of people in this world: some of them make it happen, some of them see it happen, and some wonder what has happened. Branson, Welch, and Barnevik seem to have realized that belonging to the latter two groups of people doesn't augur well for organizational longevity.

ENDNOTE

Some of the material in this chapter has appeared in print elsewhere, under the same title in: *European Management Journal* (1996), **14** (5): 486–493.

REAPING THE WHIRLWIND: MANAGING CREATIVE PEOPLE

The creative process is a cocktail of instinct, skill, culture and a highly creative feverishness. It is not like a drug; it is a particular state when everything happens very quickly, a mixture of consciousness and unconsciousness, of fear and pleasure; it's a little like making love, the physical act of love.

—Francis Bacon

INTRODUCTION

In this chapter I try to give the reader a whirlwind tour on the topic of creativity. When I insert the word creativity at Amazon.com almost 200,000 results come up. Obviously, a whirlwind tour it will be. I will touch upon some of the salient aspects of creativity and its effects on organizations.

Managing logical and orderly left-brain-oriented people is usually a pleasant experience. The organizational world suits their specifications. They like analyzing anything and everything; rules and regulations make them feel secure. They do what is proper and correct; they conform. In contrast, creative right-brain people are a pain in the neck; their drummer is slightly off-beat. Their way of doing things is disorderly, unorthodox and unconventional, and their playful, intuitive methods can wreak havoc in a by-the-book organization. Their thought patterns are divergent, relational and associative; they deal with problems by circling them in a zigzag, erratic fashion until they come upon a solution.

But before concluding that the successful organization should root out all right-brain oriented people like bad weeds, consider this: if you want your organization to go places, if you want to succeed in the global corporate Olympics, you need to include these creative types. Organizational mavericks are often a source of innovative products or processes that will help you do better than the competition. In this chapter, I consider what makes creative people different and look at the challenge of transforming their unorthodox methods into constructive organizational action.

CHARACTERISTICS OF CREATIVE PEOPLE

What differentiates creative people from common mortals? How can you recognize them? How can you acquire them and nurture them in your organization?

Nowadays it is hard to know what creativity really is because the word is overused. The potential for creativity is attributed to just about anyone. It is considered derogatory to label someone as 'uncreative.' After all, anything is feasible in an age of self-help books and seminars. The power of positive thinking is virtually guaranteed to boost creativity, for only a small amount of money down and low monthly payments.

There is something to be said about the populist notion of creativity insofar as most individuals do possess a certain amount of unrealized potential and could be more productive, given the right circumstances— skills can be improved, talent developed (Miller, 1998; Birch, 2000; Von Krogh, 2000; Monahan, 2002; Lucas, 2003). However, in my experience, genuine creativity is a rare, and often fleeting, quality; something to refer to with a capital C. Truly creative people experiment constantly and apply their knowledge in very novel ways, or throw out preconceived ideas altogether. This type of creativity goes beyond innovation, or the implementation of good ideas; in fact, established patterns are often shattered to produce new paradigms (Koestler, 1964; Gardner, 1993; Simonton, 2004).

I believe that truly creative people possess a considerable amount of conceptual fluency, in that they are able to produce highly unusual ideas very quickly. Wherever a problem may lead, they will follow, and in fact are often able to make mental leaps to imaginative solutions. They have an enormous amount of energy and willpower. They are also very independent in their judgment, non-conformist, have a sense of playfulness, accept their own impulses, and possess a rich, sometimes even bizarre, fantasy life.

Creative people demonstrate some key characteristics:

- They are very inquisitive.
- They are also intuitive (intuition is just another form of reasoning, albeit one that depends on unusual channels of information).
- Their heightened intuition makes creative people very sensitive to stimuli around them. They notice things that would be unconsciously screened out by others. This is partly explained by the fact that they are able to handle cognitive complexity; they can visualize forests, and at the same time, recognize individual trees.
- Creative people recognize patterns where others hear cacophony.
- They internalize their impressions and make connections.
- There is a visionary element to their behavior. They are driven by a 'magnificent obsession' toward distant goals.
- They are persistent and compulsive, and not afraid to take risks. Although their work may seem effortless to an uninformed observer, it is often the outcome of a long series of advances and setbacks.
- Truly creative people are also very autonomous and independent, daring to be different. They do not feel a need to 'fit in.'
- Creative people are characterized by a high tolerance for ambiguity; they do not aim for premature closure. They can tolerate the tension and suspense that comes with leaving questions temporarily unresolved.
- Conversely, they are prone to anxiety, perhaps because they are always dissatisfied with what they produce.

As these characteristics show, the creative person is a paradox: a rebel against conformity, but at the same time very attuned to whatever is happening in the environment. Creative individuals are extremely sensitive to the changing needs of their art or science. When there is dissatisfaction with the status quo, they are often the first to recognize a need for revision. Not only that, they do something about it. The truly creative person is like the Greek god Prometheus (whose name means 'wise before the event'). Creative people sometimes seem to have a form of prophetic power to look into the future.

A number of researchers have shown that there is a higher degree of mood disorders among creative people than is the case for the general population (Jamison, 1993; Hershman and Lieb, 1998). Interestingly, the link between mood disorders and creativity may explain some of the characteristics that contribute to extraordinary talent. Among other things, people who suffer from mood disorders have a higher degree of emotional reactivity—that is to say, they are highly sensitive to external and internal stimuli. Moreover, they have a greater capacity for absorption. This may give them superior concentration; they often have an unusual intensity of focus. In addition, their thought patterns are less structured. This quality gives them free-flowing access to their own unconscious, and facilitates novel associations.

STIMULATING CREATIVITY

So what about the rest of us? Is it possible to be creative to a small degree and make the most of it? Evidence shows that there is some hope for us all (Runco and Pritzker, 1999). Attempts to stimulate the process of less-gifted mortals can yield positive results, for example, more divergent (associative) thinking processes in contrast to more analytical (convergent) thinking. Divergent thinking tends to be much more fluid and flexible, and is associated with creativity.

Some of the more valid techniques for encouraging creativity include:

• Brainstorming—generating new ideas by asking a group of people to temporarily suspend critical judgment in order to produce a wide range of ideas;
• Attribute listing—studying all the basic attributes, properties and specifications of a problem and searching for alternatives or modifications;
• Synectics—using analogy and fantasy to make the unfamiliar familiar, and vice versa;
• Lateral thinking—rearranging information into new patterns.

It is hard to differentiate precisely between these various techniques. What they seem to have in common is a suspension of premature critical judgment to enable the free flow of associations.

It is well known that some people advocate using mind-expanding drugs as a way of stimulating creativity, and that doing so sometimes can lead to interesting results. The nineteenth-century English poet Samuel Taylor Coleridge maintained that his poem 'Kubla Khan' was inspired by an opium-induced dream; and in *The Doors of Perception* (1954) the novelist Aldous Huxley described his experiments with LSD.

Researchers trying to distill the essence of creativity have suggested that there is a sequence of steps in the creative process. According to them, the evolution from idea to eventual outcome involves a number of distinct phases (Runco and Pritzker, 1999). First, there is the preparation phase (gathering information about the problem); then the incubation phase (mulling over unrelated bits of information, allowing the unconscious to work on the problem); followed by the illumination phase (think of Archimedes running through the streets of Syracuse screaming 'Eureka!' after figuring out how to weigh the king's golden crown); and the last step is, of course, the verification process (testing the findings).

Some people have described the process even more succinctly as the three 'Bs' of creativity. The three 'Bs' refer to situations that stimulate the creative flow:

1. **Bed:** in the twilight zone between falling asleep and waking up, or dreaming, when the mind is cut loose from preconceptions and really starts to float. The German scientist August Kekule claimed that he had figured out the composition of the benzene ring as a result of dreaming about a snake with its tail in its mouth.
2. **Bath:** where Archimedes worked out the theory of buoyancy.
3. **Bus:** or any form of public transport where one can think one's own thoughts. Kekule, again, recounted that his theory of structure came to him on the top deck of a London bus.

These three situations create an almost hypnotic ambience. They represent the kind of setting where bi-sociative thinking—making connections where none existed before—is most likely to occur (Koestler, 1964).

On closer examination, the creative process is littered with 'accidents.' Discovery often requires an element of serendipity. Creative people see possibilities in chance occurrences that others might let slip by. No breakthrough in twentieth-century medicine was more driven by opportunism than the discovery of penicillin, which happened when the first detected penicillin spore was borne by a random London breeze through an open window into one of Alexander Fleming's dishes. Fleming made sense out of the strange mould that resulted because he was ready for discovery, after working for years almost exclusively on this type of experiment. There is a saying: 'If your mind is a hammer, everything you see looks like a nail,' or as Louis Pasteur put it, 'Chance favors the prepared mind.'

PLAYING IN A TRANSITIONAL WORLD

So how it is that some people acquire Creativity with a capital C? What singles them out? Is it a question of inheritance, determined by biological law? Or is it more a result of the kind of developmental experiences to which these people were exposed? An interesting corollary is the connection between creativity and madness—given a creative person's often unorthodox behavior, it is understandable that this association has grown up. This begs the question of where we draw the line between genius and madness.

Without getting too deeply into the nature–nurture controversy, we can safely assume that genetic factors play some part in this. We all start with a certain biological endowment but superimposed on this biological matrix are our developmental experiences. Even with similar biological endowment, our early experiences lead to differences between individuals. There will be specific factors in a creative person's upbringing that contributed to their genius (Gardner, 1993; Simonton, 2004).

Think back to when you were growing up. You may now be aware that, as a child, you dealt with two worlds: there was the everyday world with all its demands (the things you were expected to do and the ways in which you were expected to do them) and an intrapsychic world, a world of inner reality, where your drives, wishes, and needs prevailed. These outer and inner worlds would later become separate and distinguishable, but as a child, a third world existed for you: a space of fantasy and illusion, a place where connections were drawn between the two spheres.

Do you remember the way you played and created an imaginary world? This illusionary place between reality and fantasy has been described by the psychoanalyst and pediatrician Donald Winnicott as a world occupied by 'transitional objects' such as blankets, dolls, and other playthings: familiar objects that help a child link their outer and inner realities (Winnicott, 1975). To Winnicott this world is the intermediate area of experience between the thumb and the teddy bear. The capacity to explore and investigate, the development of an inner sense of cohesion and an external sense of reality, had its beginning in this illusionary space.

Winnicott argued that transitional space plays a major role in our development in a very basic way by helping us establish a sense of self-esteem. For most of us, the transitional world is part of the process of resolving the developmental tasks of childhood to arrive at adulthood and maturity with a unique sense of self. For creative people, however, there is a difference. For most of them, this process never reaches closure, and so they do not give up their transitional world. Consequently, their involvement in the transitional space will continue to affect their behavior throughout their lives.

Parents can play a substantial role in this 'play area' of the mind—they can be encouraging and help the free flow of associations, or they can stifle it by not giving the developing child enough psychic space. If they are not willing to join in the illusionary processes, they may damn up their child's free play of fantasy and illusion. However, if parents encourage a child's transitional world, it becomes an incubator for creative thought. This is where symbolization, make-believe, illusion, daydreaming, playfulness, curiosity, imagination, and wonder all begin. Every human being has these qualities to some extent, but truly creative people are able to re-enter this world as adults much more easily than the rest of us. Consequently, they are familiar with the irrational in themselves and are more in touch with their unconscious. And they never really outgrow this capacity for introspection. As adults, they are able to reach into this transitional world to find unorthodox ideas and solutions. In this context psychoanalysts have written about the notion of 'regression in the service of the ego,' meaning the ability to move back and forth between these different worlds, and make the most of the interface.

TWO ROADS TO CREATIVITY

Broadly speaking, a creative person will follow one of two paths: either developing a constructive form of creativity or, in the case of the less fortunate, a more reactive form. Although in both instances, we are dealing with people who are unwilling to give up their transitional space, there is an important difference between them.

Constructive Creativity

In the case of constructive creativity, we see a situation where play was encouraged when the person was a child. Parents of this type probably played language games with their children. They took the child's transitional objects seriously, not treating them as something that needed to be cleaned or thrown away. Furthermore, the parents took part in the child's games and applauded curiosity and inquisitiveness. The creative child's parents accepted imaginative and irrational communication; they enjoyed their child's nonsense. They rewarded independent achievement and didn't ridicule their child's mistakes. They gave their child credit for accomplishments. Frequently we find that these parents were also role models for their children in that they were autonomous and imaginative themselves.

Of course, parents can push a child too hard, and overemphasize creativity to the point that the child feels inadequate. This situation often occurs when a parent has grandiose ambitions for their child in an area in which they themselves have felt frustrated. They want their child to succeed in their place; they may send their child on 'mission impossible.' But, in general, gentle, supportive encouragement can help develop this constructive creativity.

Reactive Creativity

For people who are reactively creative, however, the situation is quite different. For them, the transitional world is a refuge from the painful reality of the external world. As John Milton expressed it in *Paradise Lost*:

> The Mind is its own place, and in itself
> Can make a Heaven of Hell, and a Hell of Heaven.

Typically, we find that people who are reactively creative are trying to cope with various forms of traumatic experience. Their environment somehow causes them to be chronically anxious. Giving free rein to their creativity is often their only method for coping with their inner turmoil.

The catalyst for their creative preoccupation is frequently something that happened early in their life, at a time when they were most susceptible. For example, the death of a caretaker or another child in the family, serious illness, deformity, excessive sibling rivalry, and external events such as war or being uprooted can be extremely traumatic for a child. Later life experiences, often of a similar nature, may preoccupy the creative adult. Outbursts of creativity seem to help this type of person manage free-floating anxiety and depressive feelings. What stands central is their need for reparation, to find a creative solution to their internal struggle.

There are many examples of creative attempts at reparation in the arts (Jamison, 1993). A common manifestation of this struggle is found in reproductions of internalized body images. Painters' self-portraits, for example those of Munch, de Chirico, Schiele, or Kahlo, are usually a good 'projective indicator' of their state of mind. Edvard Munch once said, 'Disease and insanity were the black angels at my cradle.' Witnessing the death struggle of his mother when he was young had a devastating effect on the painter and may explain his brooding and cataclysmic style of painting. Egon Schiele depicts himself in castrated, deformed, and mutilated states in his paintings. A probable explanation here is his troubled childhood, punctuated by the deaths of his father and four of his siblings, and a difficult relationship with his mother. Frieda Kahlo, bedridden and incapacitated for long periods of her life (due to the aftereffects of an accident, and to polio contracted at a very young age) focused her work on distorted representations of the body. Depression and depersonalization were major elements in the personality of Giorgio de Chirico and his estrangement from himself is reflected in his paintings, in which themes of departure, melancholia, strangeness, eerie emptiness, and stillness predominate. His work was also probably influenced by his sister's death and his mother's rejection. Not much commentary is needed to explain the tragedy of self-fragmentation reflected in the work of Vincent Van Gogh. The emotional deprivation Van Gogh experienced as the child of a woman mourning her stillborn first son, also named Vincent, and his knowledge that he was a replacement child, born to fill the emptiness left by his brother's death, had a devastating psychological after-effect. Francisco Goya's illness, experienced later in life, had a dramatic impact on his painting. A gruesome reminder of his change in style is reflected in his painting of Cronos eating his own children.

Many writers and composers also try to master their internal struggle in their creative productions. Franz Kafka's story, 'The Metamorphosis,' which describes his transformation into a disgusting, monstrous insect, certainly did not result from empathic parenting. His *Letter to his Father* details the perceived terrors he suffered during childhood. The father of Edgar Allan Poe, master of the macabre, deserted the family when Edgar was two and his mother died of tuberculosis the following year.

The parents of the composer Johann Sebastian Bach died when he was only nine years old, and few of his seven siblings survived childhood. Themes of death and resurrection are frequent in his compositions. Gustav Mahler's *Songs on the Death of Children* are settings of poems by Friedrich Rückert, written after the poet had lost two of his children in the space of two weeks. Mahler lost his own daughter four years later and wrote to a friend, 'I placed myself in the situation that a child of mine had died. When I really lost my daughter, I could not have written these songs any more.' The Swedish film-maker Ingmar Bergman had always struggled with inner antagonists, a result of his stiflingly restrictive upbringing. This struggle led to highly neurotic but also extremely creative behavior, although in an interview with a Swedish television channel in 2004, he admitted that he found his own work depressing, saying, 'I don't watch my own films very often. I become so jittery and ready to cry. ... and miserable. I think it's awful.'

CREATIVE MANAGEMENT

Creativity, whether reactive or constructive, is not limited to the world of the arts. It extends to the natural and the social sciences: the construction of the first automobile, the discovery of quantum physics, and the design of the Eiffel Tower undeniably involved creative genius. Business, too, has its share of creative characters, although major contributions to the corporate world do not generally create the same excitement. Creativity in organizational design tends to be of a much more subtle nature. Does anyone remember the inventor of double bookkeeping? And what about the first designer of the divisionalized organizational structure or the matrix organization? All of these were, in fact, creative steps.

There is another reason why creativity in business is less recognized. Artists and scientists often work in splendid isolation but this is rarely practical in a business setting, since organizations are composed of groups. And with groups come group dynamics. The much touted ideal of team spirit in organizations can create problems, particularly for more creative types who do not easily conform. A kind of Gresham's Law of Creativity might apply: not bad money driving out good, but conformists driving out creative people. In many organizations creative people are seen as troublemakers, and as a result get into trouble and leave.

So how can one manage these mavericks and avoid the loss of potentially valuable people? What can organizational leaders do to attract, develop, and keep creative people in their organizations? Perhaps they need to begin thinking in terms of *creative management* (Robinson and Stern, 1998; DeGraff and Lawrence, 2002; Byrd and Brown, 2003; Mauzy and Harriman, 2003; Shavinina, 2003). This involves translating the maverick's spontaneous and impulsive behavior into constructive organizational action. Just as parents should encourage their children's imaginative play, senior executives have to develop conditions that stimulate innovation and unorthodox methods in their organization.

Richard Branson, the charismatic chairman of Virgin (see Chapter 11), an empire best known for its highly profitable airline and Megastore retail chain, is an extremely creative leader with a creative leadership style (Kets de Vries, 1999). His way of running his empire has been extraordinarily successful. He is not only one of the richest people in the world but also an international celebrity. In the United Kingdom, Branson has been hailed as a role model not only for teenagers but also for their parents. He has been nominated for many awards for enterprise and been voted the most popular businessman of the year. As an organizational designer he is highly unusual. He has no real corporate headquarters (although he used to use a houseboat on the River Thames in London), something you would not expect from someone who employs 6,000 people in more than 15 countries. Status and the trappings of power are not for him.

To Branson, decentralization is a religion. The company's operating style is characterized by informality, casual dress, a lack of hierarchy, a comfortable environment, and an absence of conformity. Branson makes it a point to attract mavericks to his company, a role he plays himself as his crazier exploits, such as his transatlantic ballooning and powerboat adventures, illustrate.

In Virgin, lateral communication is the norm. Branson likes the idea of the boundary-free organization. He encourages people to move around; he does not want them to become stuck in narrowly defined jobs. He believes in organic growth, not in raiding other businesses for market share. When someone has a creative idea, he makes sure there are resources available to him or her to realize it. In that respect he serves as a project champion, nurturing others to develop ideas and bring them to fruition.

Basically, in his company Branson is trying to create a community of people where everyone collaborates and helps each other and at the same time has fun and excitement. Having fun is a central value of the corporate culture and as a well-known prankster he often sets the example. In emphasizing the importance of fun, he is following a simple school of thought that happy people are more creative and productive. Whatever Virgin is involved in, he wants the company to be the best, but not necessarily the biggest. By setting high-performance expectations, he encourages his people to rise to the challenge. His airline, Virgin Atlantic, is a good example of this philosophy.

So what can we learn from the Virgin case as far as stimulating creative management is concerned? It demonstrates that a number of organizational, cultural, and leadership steps have to be taken to manage creatively.

Organizational Factors

We need to look at the organizational variables that make for a creative workplace—for example, the structure. Is it bureaucratic or organic? Is it centralized or decentralized? Obviously, a decentralized, fluid, less rigid, boundary-free structure is to be recommended, since a highly formalized environment tends to have a stifling effect on creativity (Kelley and Littman, 2000; Goldenberg and Mazursky, 2002; Hesselbein and Johnston, 2002). Decentralization is linked to accountability, responsibility, and direct feedback, and as a result people gain a feeling of control. Having a perception of control over one's environment makes people feel better. Feeling good has a positive effect on one's work. The key to getting the best out of people is a high degree of freedom. To enhance creativity, people need to feel that they are in charge of their work and ideas. Excessive reporting and standardized procedures are counterproductive to this.

The company should also have performance evaluation and compensation systems that reward innovation. An appropriate reward system will single out the creative people behind a successful project for recognition and offer them a share in the consequent bonuses or other forms of reward in appreciation for their contribution. However, creative people are not principally motivated by rewards. It is much more important for them to see their ideas realized. Furthermore, giving successful contributors a piece of the action can do wonders for their sense of equity.

There are many ways to stimulate learning and new ideas. There should be frequent and easy lateral communication in the organization. 'Bypassing' should not be a dirty word: people should not be forced to communicate through specific or hierarchical channels. Jobs should not be narrowly defined. Task interdependency and job rotation can also be useful; knowing the details of other jobs leads to a broader point of view. Multidisciplinary project teams are also an advantage.

Talent management is another critical organizational area. Diversity should be embraced and there should be openness to non-conformists in the organization. These non-conformists may ask awkward or unusual questions, but they may also be the people who identify new product niches or come up with more effective ways of organizing. In general, diverse groups may take longer to arrive at decisions, but there is a greater likelihood that these decisions are creative.

Other organizational issues worth considering are physical facilities. Is the workplace the kind of environment that stimulates creativity? Or does it resemble the kind of Stalinist structure that used to characterize Eastern European architecture?

Last, but certainly not least, it is very important for a company to have the necessary slack resources—financial, material, and human. Are facilities or funds available for work that initially appears unprofitable or unrelated to the company's vision? Are these resources relatively easy to come by? A person who has continually to fight for resources and time for a project is mentally boxed in and unlikely to produce much.

Organizational Cultural Factors

The corporate culture introduces another set of variables. What are the organization's value and belief systems? Is there a risk-taking ethos in the company? Are people allowed to make mistakes? Can people fail forward? People who are not allowed to make mistakes will not make decisions or take risks either. Creative people do not last long in this situation.

Access to information is also important. A company culture of secrecy will build paranoia rather than a co-operative and collaborative atmosphere. This is not the kind of ambience that encourages people to help each other. On the contrary, it is more likely to lead to turf wars.

Many of these factors can be summarized as 'trust.' If there is no sense of trust in an organization, if people are preoccupied with self-protection, the psychological contract between individual and organization will break down, and creativity will be one of the first casualties.

A culture that builds in a fun factor, and a light-hearted attitude toward work, like Virgin, avoids the accumulation of stress and tension. People who have fun are more creative and usually work harder.

Finally, a key value of corporate culture should be openness to change. Executives have to create a protean organization, one that has the capacity to learn and change. Where there is no change, there can be no creativity.

Leadership Factors

The third variable that can stimulate creativity in organizations is leadership. What is the organization's leadership style? Is it democratic and participative, or autocratic? Naturally, creative people feel much more at ease with the former (Hesselbein and Johnston, 2002; Kets de Vries, 2006). Autocratic leadership will kill creativity. People do not question the way things are done in an autocratic organization; they do as they are told.

What about shared vision? Do people have a good idea of what the organization is trying to accomplish? Are the goals clear enough? But goals need not be very detailed. Some form of general direction is needed, however, and can often be provided by role models, mentors, or idea champions.

Training and education play important roles in the generation of new ideas. A creative outcome might look accidental, but usually it is the result of a lot of preparation and years of hard work. Of course, there is always an element of luck involved, but as people like Alexander Fleming discovered, the harder you work, the luckier you get. Not only must a person be well-prepared, but also willing to try and try again, despite setbacks.

Creative people should be challenged and made to feel essential to the organization. Top executives must empower their people by expressing an expectation of creative work. Leaders should be prepared to nurture the ideas people come up with, including the crazy ones. If you set high expectations and provide the necessary resources, people will try to oblige.

WATCHING FOR THE DANGER SIGNS

Creativity in organizations is a very delicate flower and fairly easy to kill off. If you are not careful, your creative people will leave—or, even worse, will not be attracted to the organization in the first place. Organizational leaders should be aware of the attitude disseminated in the organization and remember that they are the ones who set the tone. For example, a prescriptive culture that says that there is only one way of doing things, and only one right answer to a problem, will by definition preclude creativity. Leaders who cultivate a 'not-invented-here' culture can have a very negative effect on the organization. A related problem is the kind of parochialism where people say that something is 'not their area.' Venturing out on uncharted ground is seen as too risky. These attitudes should be interpreted as danger signs. Nothing will kill creativity as much as negativity.

Some leaders I have met feel that play is frivolous, that there is no room for foolishness in the organization. I advise them to bear in mind the creative person's need for transitional space. To stimulate creativity, organizational leaders must be willing to accept underdeveloped ideas and bend the rules. They should be able to tolerate ambiguity and show empathy. And they should be willing to make quick decisions, rather than composing elaborate committees or task forces to study ideas.

Above all, leaders should allow their people to make mistakes (and not dwell on them). Chaos breeds life, while order breeds habit. While your habits will be very easy for your competitors to copy, the creative talent in your organization will be a unique asset.

When Alexander the Great visited Diogenes and asked whether he could do anything for the famed teacher, Diogenes replied, 'Only stand out of my light.' Perhaps someday we shall find the key to heightened creativity. Until then, one of the best things we can do for creative men and women is to stand out of their light.

ENDNOTE

Some of the material for this chapter has appeared elsewhere in the following publication:

Kets de Vries, M.F.R. (1994). '*Reaping the whirlwind: Managing creative people.*' INSEAD working papers, 94/09/ENT. Fontainebleau: INSEAD.

PART IV

LEADERSHIP IN A GLOBAL CONTEXT

INTRODUCTION

The ways in which people from different national and cultural backgrounds differ are so numerous, and frequently so subtle—making interactions of any kind so fraught with possible misunderstanding, offensiveness, and social gaffes—that the growth of global business over the last 50 years might justifiably be seen as an extraordinary human anthropological achievement. There are huge differences in national character, culture, and verbal and body language. Some people are serious, inexpressive, and undemonstrative; others will clasp you in their arms, kiss you on both cheeks whatever your gender, raise their voices, and gesticulate. I once amused myself with a 'time and motion' study to see how often people meeting in a café would touch each other. In one hour in Puerto Rico, four people touched each other 70 times. In my local café in central Paris, four people touched each other 50 times. In London the number was five. In some cultures, personal relationships have to be established before effective communication and interaction can take place; in others, people want to cut the crap and get down to business. Attitudes toward time can cause great confusion. In some cultures, 'She's always late,' represents a serious criticism, while in others it is a greater social solecism to arrive early—or even at the appointed time.

Understandably, leadership styles differ radically as well. Leadership style lies on a wide spectrum that ranges between consensual, technocratic, autocratic, political, centralized, democratic, and patriarchal. Leadership style will be reflected in organizational form. I have always been interested in the relationship between personality, leadership style, organizational culture, and organization. Organizational structure in some countries is tall, in others flat. Yet, in spite of all these differences, somehow we all have to find ways of talking to each other and working together—and as companies' reach becomes increasingly global, we have to mold and develop leaders who can deal with these problems and run these enterprises. It is not always easy to appreciate or understand that what people do, mean, and say varies from one culture to the next, but without that understanding, it is impossible to lead in another culture. In a corporate context, there are differences in the way people view things like power, status, hierarchy, authority, and control. Do global leaders require a set of skills entirely different from those needed by their domestic counterparts? What are the main issues leaders have to deal with when they move beyond domestic markets? I have spent many long hours talking to leaders of these organizations about the choices they have to make.

Going outside your home market means having to deal with a multiplicity of new issues related to different cultural, legal, regulatory, and economic systems. It's about operating in multiple environments trying to achieve a common objective. It's about the allocation of power and resources. What kind of organizational structure should the organization have? What decisions are made at headquarters and which are made at the country level?

Leaders of European or global firms have to revisit many of their assumptions about things they would normally take for granted. Leaders who are most effective operating outside their home markets engage in an interesting balancing act. Being global doesn't mean that people will understand you if you speak in English but just a little bit louder. It means appreciating the fact that every country is so different—that attention needs to be paid. But while national culture is important, individual personality traits play a role, and so does company culture. In these organizations, senior leadership needs to make sure the management team they have at the local level is making the right decisions at the right time. In addition, they need to put into place mechanisms that will help other people in the organization to learn from these decisions. Global organizations are far too vulnerable to 'not-invented-here' syndrome.

While finding people who have a sense of cultural relativity is important, close attention also needs to be given to the leadership pipeline that operates in global organizations. Through the high-level executive seminars that I run, I have been closely involved in creating the kind of experiences that will help develop a firm's next leaders. In particular, my CEO seminar ('The Challenge of Leadership') and my coaching and consulting seminar ('Consulting and Coaching for Change') have been used to create the kinds of leaders needed for global firms.

From my childhood, when I first fell in love with its literature, I have always been interested in Russia. During my student days, I spent a considerable amount of time reading the Russian classics. This love affair continued, and my position at INSEAD has luckily put me in a position to start to build bridges with the Russian business community since the country has opened up. Over the years I have worked closely with Russian academics and business people. To help me better understand the Russian 'soul,' I have had many interactions with Russians in the role of consultant. I wanted to obtain an informed understanding of the way Russians deal with organizations and approach leadership style. I was also trying to better understand the personality make-up of the Russians, and the salient factors that make them the people they are. I was intrigued by Russia's turbulent history, its contribution to a paranoid *Weltanschauung* and anarchistic streak. I was also trying to explain the evident national yearning for strong leadership and the existence of paternalistic practices.

However, it took a unique insight into coping with personal disaster in a huge country with a hostile environment and unreliable infrastructure to reveal most about life and leadership in Russia. My deep interest in the outdoors has led me to travel in some of the most remote areas of the country. On a trip in the mountains of Kamchatka in 2008 to look for bears with the Koryaks (the local inhabitants), I was thrown from a snowmobile, breaking my spine in two places. I couldn't have found a worse place to be repatriated from. The five-hour journey back to the tented base camp, pulled over the snow strapped to a sledge, is an experience I do not care to remember, and would not want to repeat. I learned more about pain than I ever want to know. My return journey to Paris from Petropavlovsk (the capital of Kamchatka) was an interesting study in logistics. It contributed to my understanding of the country, its people, and its philosophy of life and suffering.

Given the major transformations occurring in Russian society today, some of the themes I discuss in Chapter 15 are currently in a state of flux. They will evolve and prove fruitful for further research. But many of these themes have the kind of robustness that will endure, retaining their significance for those attempting to understand and deal with the Russian people. However, much of the riddle that is Russia will remain—at least for me. As the country reaches out to the rest of the world in some ways, while reviving the old Cold War rhetoric, perhaps we should consider the old Russian proverb: 'It's good to be visiting, but it's better at home.'

CHAPTER 13

THE DEVELOPMENT
OF THE LEADER WITHIN
THE GLOBAL CORPORATION

> Many business leaders today view their jobs as entailing responsibility
> for the welfare of the wider community. These individuals do not define
> themselves as profit-making machines whose only reason for existing is to
> satisfy escalating expectation for immediate gain.
> —Mihaly Csikszentmihalyi

INTRODUCTION

The globalization of business is increasing at a phenomenal rate, accelerated by a breakdown of some of the past barriers to international
trade—the continued growth of the European Union and Eastern
Europe, and the development of China, India, and Brazil. As companies
seek to globalize their operations, they often run into a number of
barriers, many of which have their roots in cultural differences. All this
raises the question of whether a new kind of 'global' leader will now be
needed—someone who can play the role of catalyst, who is sensitive to
and adept at managing cultural diversity, and who functions effectively
in different cultural environments.

The extent to which leadership must be culturally adaptive if an
organization operates in multiple cultural environments is not yet completely clear. However, it's probably safe to presume that adaptability
will be an asset. So what qualities are needed to make good future global
leaders? What kind of management development and training enhances
cultural empathy and adaptability? In what organizational context does

global leadership thrive? And, finally, what can be said about career-path management in the global corporation?

A CASE STUDY IN INTERNATIONALIZATION

In studying the question of global leadership, we encounter the problematic area of the interaction between corporate and national cultures and, inevitably, the issue of cultural adaptiveness. A number of companies have tried to cope with these challenges, one example being Schlumberger—a highly successful international organization in the oilfield-service industry that operates in about 80 countries with about 84,000 people of 140 nationalities. What is salient about Schlumberger is the emphasis placed on research and technology—very much a part of the Schlumberger corporate culture. People who want to work for this quiet giant are expected to subscribe to its orientation. But, although the company is very technology-driven, there are other values that have to be taken into consideration. The late Jean Riboud, a former CEO of Schlumberger, touched upon these values when describing the company's 'spirit' during his reign:

1. We are an exceptional crucible of many nations, of many cultures, of many visions.
2. We are a totally decentralized organization ...
3. We are a service company, at the service of our customers, having a faster response than anybody else.
4. We believe in the profit process as a challenge, as a game, as a sport.
5. We believe in a certain arrogance; the certainty that we are going to win because we are the best—arrogance only tolerable because it is coupled with a great sense of intellectual humility, the fear of being wrong, the fear of not working hard enough. (Auletta, 1984, p. 160)

Life at Schlumberger is different from that in many organizations. A supervisor of a rig in Ireland can receive a phone call at noon on Friday directing him to close down operations there by five o'clock and report for work in Northern Thailand at eight o'clock on Sunday morning. Upon arrival at the airport in Bangkok, he will find a jeep and the name of a place a day's drive away that he has to get to; no map, no instructions. It is very much up to him to make it happen, to make his assignment a success.

Although when describing his company, Jean Riboud did not explicitly talk about the making of a global leader, certain subtle mechanisms having to do with selection and the creation of the right organizational ambiance are clearly at work at Schlumberger to make its people so successful. Not only does Schlumberger choose people who fit a certain profile, there are other factors that also play an important role.

The headquarters of Schlumberger is very small, and although overall strategic direction is largely determined there, the company has a strong regional structure, and career progression does not depend on time spent at the head office. A great deal of operational autonomy is given to the people in the field. 'Space' is provided for each national culture. At each location, the management team is made up of people from five or six different nationalities; there is no single dominant national culture but, rather, a group of people from different cultures who have internalized a common set of values. And this shared outlook is an essential factor in assuring coordination among the many different units of the organization.

Schlumberger is only one among many companies now dealing successfully with the increasing globalization of business. How do they, and other organizations, do it? Let's take a closer look at what it takes to be a global organization.

FORMS OF GLOBAL ORGANIZATIONS

It would obviously be foolish to suggest that there is an ideal structure, suitable for all organizations and national cultures. Different types of organizational structures have developed from very different beginnings, and there are numerous kinds of global enterprises, international joint ventures, parent–subsidiary relationships across national borders, and other forms of alliances. However, there are certain structural factors that can enable an organization to make good use of its global advantages, and it is those that I will consider next.

Concepts of Globalism

If we look at the evolvement of organizations, we can see a development of evolution from ethnocentrism via polycentrism to geocentrism (Perlmutter, 1969; Hedlund and Kverneland, 1985). In the ethnocentric orientation, key positions are occupied by home-country nationals. Foreign subsidiaries take on a subservient position. In polycentric companies, foreign subsidiaries are run by local nationals and have a great amount of autonomy as long as there are results. The head office takes a more 'hands-off' position. The regiocentric orientation differs in that the action takes place in various regional headquarters. Finally, in the case of the geocentric orientation, a complex network of interdependencies exists between headquarters and subsidiaries. Generally, observing how these companies are structured, we notice flatter structures with less emphasis on hierarchy, greater lateral communication, complex networking systems, and loosely coupled, interdependent organizational units with innovative human-resource management practices.

A key trend in these types of global organizations is getting away from a headquarters mentality, that is, the urge to intervene and give directions. More and more frequently, the corporate center is split into a number of relatively autonomous regional headquarters with a set of shared values as common denominator. In these global organizations careful management of the corporate culture becomes essential. These deeply internalized, commonly shared core values of the corporate culture have become the new control device—it is the 'glue' that holds the organization together.

Movement of executives among different parts of the company will be common; it is a way of building up the 'nervous system' of these global organizations. To enable this development, certain global companies follow a policy of having their managers who will have a global role work for several years abroad followed by several years at headquarters (e.g. Philips, Shell, IBM, Proctor & Gamble, Rhone-Poulenc). This pattern serves various purposes: it creates a more consistent corporate culture than when people remain in only one country or one region, and brings into headquarters a dose of global experience.

Some of these global organizations seem to have several levels of executives: those who operate only within their own countries, those who are assignable within their regions, and those who are assignable globally. The more ethnocentric a company is, however, the more this last category tends to be made up of parent-country nationals. Many of these global organizations use some form of periodic assignment to headquarters for their high potentials, and also rotate assignments within regions.

Interdependence in truly global organizations is reciprocal; products, know-how, financial resources, and people flow in complex, interdependent patterns, not from the core to the periphery as in the ethnocentric firm. The interdependencies in these organizations are demonstrated in the following ways:

- They have worldwide centers of excellence with a great degree of independence of the original home country.

- Their strategy focuses on global integration and national responsiveness.
- Their country units contribute to integrated worldwide operations.
- Their organizational structure is highly interdependent, a network configuration being the norm.
- Those with high potential from anywhere in the world are developed for key positions wherever needed.
- Governance is mutually negotiated between units.
- Communication is both vertical and lateral.
- Cultural complexity is the name of the game; many different perspectives and approaches have a voice in the structure and decision-making patterns of the organization.

BP (British Petroleum) is an example of such a geocentric organization. It considers the very complexity of its network of relationships around the globe—customers, supplier, governments, non-governmental organizations, communities, and so on—to be a distinctive asset. These relationships are seen as being long-term and based on mutual advantage; assets that help BP endure and remain strongly competitive.

Some of the best-performing global organizations are in fact so geocentrically focused that they prefer to have no national identity at all. ABB is a good example: what was originally a merger between a Swiss and a Swedish company has become a truly global organization. The diverse composition of the executive board, the size of investment and number of employees outside the original home countries, and the considerable power vested in the subsidiaries are giveaways. BP is also distancing itself from its national identity. In an advertising campaign, the company downplayed the word British in its new slogan: 'BP—Beyond Petroleum.'

The last barrier that remains, however, in global organizations, is the placement of non-parent-country nationals on the board of directors. One of the indicators that an organization is truly global is the number of nationalities represented on its executive board. Most US organizations with global operations still have boards composed almost entirely of Americans. Many European and Asian corporations have equally homogeneous, home country oriented boards. But a mixed-nationality executive board sends a clear message to the outside world that the organization is committed to globalization and is determined to integrate varying perspectives. Such a message is a powerful antidote to ethnocentricity within the organization. It also demonstrates that the top jobs are not the exclusive bailiwick of certain nationalities. Most important, a truly global board can effectively make decisions based on many diverse perspectives.

What can be said about career path management in these geocentric, global organizations? Is their way of managing people different? What steps should companies take to make the expatriation–repatriation process seamless? Let's have a look at observations from the field.

Career-path Management in the Global Organization

In most cases, an international assignment is initially seen as a step up a career ladder. That being said, expatriation remains a difficult issue and what makes it so is the way companies deal with re-entry.

In a number of the global organizations I have studied the following practices could be observed. To start with, an obvious method in dealing with the expatriation–repatriation issue is the establishment of a talent databank for the purpose of making an inventory of an organization's human talent. The companies more effective in dealing with this issue set up a special monitoring unit (e.g. as at Philips, IBM, Unilever, Sony, or Shell) to take responsibility for their key people, and in particular, the expatriate executives. Such a unit would play a major role in career-path management by assisting in succession planning with the expatriate executive prior to departure—a process that considers length of stay, projected responsibilities when abroad, systematic management reviews, and subsequent job position on repatriation.

If companies put a monitoring unit in place, it would report to someone at a sufficiently senior level in the organization to make sure that the expatriate's visibility would be maintained. What most expatriate executives fear is that they will lose touch with the center of action and be overlooked for promotion at the corporate center or centers. To minimize such fears, top management in these companies have to make very clear in word and deed that an international assignment to key markets is a major factor for eventual selection to senior leadership positions.

What I also observed is that such a monitoring unit would also engage in regular reviews of positions to be vacated because of retirement or resignation and changes of assignment for development reasons. The need to recruit outside candidates would be assessed periodically. Much attention would be paid to succession planning. To engage in such evaluation practices of high potentials, ranking systems were often utilized to enable their identification.

In these companies, headquarters found it essential to be kept informed of expatriates' achievements while they were away; otherwise the latter's work may go unrecognized, not giving these executives opportunities for promotion. Given the advances in communication systems (the internet), extreme degrees of isolation are now probably rare. However, a feeling of isolation can be very real for people returning to an organization after a gap of some years. With increasing executive mobility, they may no longer know the top level of management personally. The environment at headquarters may have become very different compared to the time they were there. In addition, as individuals, they may have been changed by their experiences in another culture (Adler, 1991). All told, the 'fit' may be quite different. The re-entry shock of return may not be that easy to overcome. The question becomes, what can be done to facilitate this process?

Facilitating Return

To facilitate return, a 'social contract' in some form or shape may be helpful. For example, companies such as IBM have 'on loan from the home country' policies that guarantee a position upon coming back at least at the same level as the position vacated when taking on the assignment. Numerous firms also organize support networks, involving communication through travel and company newsletters. Some Japanese companies have institutionalized a mentoring relationship. The mentors, who often have gone through the same experiences, coach their charges and serve as an additional source of support to monitor the executive's career trajectory. Other companies may have internal consultants who take on a mentoring role. Smooth repatriation and reabsorption into the corporate hierarchy are essential—even just one casualty can be a major setback for a corporation through giving a bad example.

The question of what makes expatriation successful brings us to the issue of the qualities needed to be successful as a global executive. What qualities are we looking for? Are there differences between being successfully locally compared to globally?

QUALITIES NEEDED IN GLOBAL LEADERS

For too many companies, the primary criterion for choosing someone to work abroad is technical competence (Adler, 1991; Zeira and Banai 1981; Mendenhall, 2006; Mendenhall, Dunbar, and Oddou 1987; Tung, 1988a, 1988b, 2001). If an executive in the home country has done a good job, the assumption is that he or she will automatically be able to repeat the successful performance in another country. This happens particularly in cases where people are sent to oversee the setting up of a plant, the establishment of an oilrig, or the expansion of a factory—tasks that are basically technical in nature. There may be very little preparation for variations in cultural approaches. After all, an executive is supposed to be someone who has the confidence to sort out any problems that deviate from usual working procedures—if something goes wrong, he or she should be able to fix it.

For such assignments, it cannot be denied that technical skills are necessary, but they are not sufficient: it is much more difficult, however, to assess the interpersonal qualities and attitudes that can make an assignment a success or a failure. But not doing so is risky. The cost of failure for a company can be very high, not to mention the loss of business and prestige due to poor leadership. In addition, there are the psychological costs of failure for the individual and family involved. It is clear that other, non-technical qualities will be required to make expatriation a success, particularly when one reaches higher-level leadership positions.

Broadly speaking, these qualities fall into three categories: general leadership qualities, cultural adaptability, and upbringing and personality.

General Leadership Qualities

Clinical research on leadership (Zaleznik, 1989; Kets de Vries, 2001, 2006), building on and complementing the work of others (MacGregor Burns, 1977; Bennis and Nanus, 1985; Tichy and Devanna, 1986; Kotter, 1988) shows that the following qualities are consistently cited as likely to be necessary in a global leader.

The Capacity for Envisioning

Envisioning means being able to set future direction in an increasingly complex environment and frequently depends on the person in question having a strong operational code in their interior world that can drive such a vision (McDougall, 1991; Leites, 2007). To understand the concept of operational code, imagine it as an onion, with the more superficial levels on the outside, and the more fundamental ones on the inside. Taking this onion metaphor one step further, visions can range from more prosaic preoccupations (such as a belief in the feasibility of a new product or the entry into a new market) to much deeper concerns, such as ethical issues or environmental consciousness.

The nature of our relationships during childhood with significant others (i.e. parents, siblings, other family members, teachers) determines the kind of cognitive and affective 'maps' (the scripts in our inner theater) that we internalize, and forms the basis for our operational codes. These personal operational codes have to be balanced with specific societal concerns—the vision can diverge from the existing preoccupations of the group to which it is applicable so long as this isn't too marked a divergence. And in order to match personal agenda with 'historical moment' (Erikson, 1975)—to create this catalyst for change—the leader's responsiveness to what is happening around him or her is essential. In addition, he or she will also need to be able to articulate a vision with conviction in order to get others to align themselves with it, which leads on to the next point.

The Ability to Empower Others

Empowerment is the process of increasing the capacity of individuals or groups to make choices and to transform those choices into desired actions and outcomes. It also implies having decision-making power of one's own. It also means giving people access to information and resources for taking proper decisions. The ability to empower others is an important characteristic of effective leadership. By communicating high-performance expectations, leaders can enhance the self-esteem of their followers, having these followers meet the challenge.

The Ability to Build and Maintain Organizational Networks

This is something that necessitates considerable sensitivity to the dynamics of power and dependency, as well as strong interpersonal skills in negotiations and coaching. These human resource management skills will be even more important in our global world. One key reason these skills are now so essential is that the management of alliances has taken on an increasingly critical role in today's organizations.

'Pattern Recognition'

Global leaders especially need to be able to manage cognitive complexity in order quickly to sort out relevant from irrelevant information and recognize major themes. They have to be masters in sense-making, in bringing order out of the chaos that surrounds them. They also need to know how to prevent themselves from being swamped by sensory and informational overloads. Without this skill, fast and accurate decision-making is hampered.

Hardiness

Hardiness is a quality identified in stress literature (Kobasa, 1979). The global company in the information age puts incredible stresses on its leaders: regular travel through different time zones, the massive exposure to information mentioned above, long hours, and so on. Hardy people (those more able to cope with these strains) are resilient; they possess a sense of internality, a belief that they can control and influence the events in their lives. They are of the opinion that they can make a difference, as opposed to believing that whatever happens to them is dependent on fate or luck. Hardy people tend to be deeply committed to whatever activities they are engaged in and anticipate change as an exciting challenge to further development.

Cultural Adaptability

There are also a number of values or assumptions that indicate that a person has a propensity for cultural adaptation, another factor in the success of a global leader. The most obvious, perhaps, is the person holding the belief that every culture has developed its own way of managing and that one (his or her own) country's way is not necessarily superior. Another is the belief that cross-cultural learning is enriching. Yet another may be the feeling that 'home is where I am, rather than where I come from.' The understanding of where one's roots are— whether in oneself, one's family, or one's country of birth—can greatly affect the ease with which a person can move from culture to culture.

Unfortunately, recommendations made by many researchers interested in the question of what qualities are found among people who are culturally adaptive can be excessively broad. Some of the characteristics most often listed are:

- Open-mindedness
- Self-confidence
- Ability to deal with ambiguity

- Ability to relate to people
- Curiosity.

With respect to cultural adaptability, the Jesuit order can be singled out as having been extremely effective in selecting people with the right qualities. Their *Weltanschauung* made them very successful in 'conquering' the world. Jesuits have successfully grappled with challenges that test great companies like forging seamless multinational teams, motivating performance, being open to change, and staying adaptable. The success of the Jesuits is very much due to the selection and training of people prepared to be guided by four principles:

- Self-awareness: understanding your strengths, weaknesses, values, and worldview.
- Ingenuity: confidently innovating and adapting to embrace a changing world.
- Love: engaging others with a positive, supportive attitude.
- Heroism: energizing yourself and others by embracing ambitious goals and a passion to excel.

Apart from the criteria used by the Jesuits to prepare them for success, there have also been lists of criteria of what is important for global executives compiled by researchers and practitioners. Among them, Michael Harvey (1985) has made probably one of the more heroic efforts. He suggests some 30 characteristics (including mental flexibility, stability of marriage, social and cross-cultural exposure, and physical and emotional stamina), each weighted according to country and type of job.

I have learned from experience that the greater the consideration paid during the selection process to a candidate's emotional intelligence, the higher the success rate in the assignment. What is open to question, however, is whether these selection criteria are specifically applicable to executives on international assignments. Some of the factors—emotional intelligence being key—probably increase effectiveness whatever the context may be. Obviously much more research is needed to refine these selection criteria.

According to Zeira and Banai (1985), the criteria for selection for cultural adaptability are all too frequently developed in a vacuum. The advice of the host-country nationals—the people who are to work with the expatriate manager—is rarely sought at the selection stage. They suggest that in fact the better the fit between the stakeholders' expectations and the expatriate manager's behavior, the less the inter-role conflict. Expectation management seems to be a salient factor in ensuring that assignments in other countries are successful. Research in this area confirms that another critical success factor in expatriation. can be their having had early exposure to other cultures and management development for global assignments.

The Reaction of the Family

Another extremely important element of an expatriate executive's success or failure is the experience of the spouse and children. The most frequent reason for an executive's failing to complete an assignment in another country is the negative reaction of his or her spouse. Apparently, in the majority of cases, family circumstances account for expatriate failure. Despite this, only 50% of American companies interview spouses during the selection procedure, and a far smaller percentage include spouses in training programs (Tung, 1988a, 1988b). Although I realize that the role of the spouse is only one factor considered among others, the failure to recognize it can be a costly omission for both the company and the family.

In a situation where the executive risks finding him- or herself cut off from other relationships, a supportive spouse and family can be the essential factor in enabling him or her to make the necessary cultural adjustments. Of course, actually marrying into another culture provides a person with intensive long-term experiential training in cultural empathy and diversity!

Upbringing and Personality

With the coming of a 'flat world'—the increased movement of people due to greater ease in travel and communications—there is an ever-growing number of individuals rooted in more than one culture. The more intercultural experiences children have early in life, the more likely they are to develop the kind of cultural empathy necessary for leadership effectiveness in a global setting. Exposure in childhood to different nationalities and languages can be a determining factor in how well an adult deals with cultural diversity later in life. Children of mixed-culture marriages, bilingual parents, diplomats, or executives who move frequently also have an advantage because of their exposure to diverse cultural contexts.

Children who have changed countries several times when young have a very different sense of belonging than those who are born and grow up in the same place. Given the impact of childhood socialization on adult development, it is to be expected that such early exposure will be a determining factor in how successful the individual is in dealing with cultural adaptability later in life. Competence in more than one language at an early age adds another layer to perception and cultural sensitivity.

'As If' Qualities

In psychological terms, global leaders require a personality that combines some slightly paradoxical characteristics. On the one hand, they need to have what has been described in another context as an 'as if' characteristic (Deutsch, 1942)—that is, they need to be able to conduct themselves in a chameleon-like way. They need to be individuals who have a plastic readiness to pick up signals from the external world and mold themselves and their behavior accordingly, easily adapting to whatever culture they find themselves in. In the true 'as if' personality, the advantage of such adaptability, however, is usually counterbalanced by a shallowness in relationships, an absence of genuine feelings, and a lack of a strong sense of identity (making for transient identifications and kaleidoscopic shifts in behavior).

On the other hand, global leaders need as a part of their inner script a set of resilient core values that will guide them and provide support in whatever environment they find themselves—core values that are compatible with those of the corporate culture. The challenge becomes to combine qualities of resiliency with those of plasticity. This does not necessarily have to be a contradiction. 'Going native' is not the answer, but neither is staying aloof from the host culture. A middle position is to be recommended.

Those who lack a strong set of inner values may feel threatened and act defensively, resisting the benefits of cultural exposure. However, individuals with a cohesive sense of self and a set of core values can allow themselves to rework and build on earlier experiences without becoming anxious about being swept away into the unknown if they adopt aspects of another culture. These individuals will recognize the potential for creative synergy in doing so. They are the ones who will successfully populate the organization of the future, going beyond narrow ethnocentric concerns and making the world a true 'global village.'

Narcissistic Development

Another essential element in the foundations of an effective leader is having successfully dealt with the trials and tribulations of narcissism (Kohut, 2000; Kets de Vries, 2006). Narcissism is the matrix from which derives a person's ambition, achievement, and self-confidence. Successful narcissistic development is what determines an individual's later capacity for empathy—the ability to put oneself in the psychological frame of reference of another so that the other person's thinking, feeling, and acting are understood. Such a capacity is clearly essential when trying to experience and understand another culture. Extreme narcissists, however, lack this capacity because they are preoccupied with themselves.

So, what kind of management development and training enhances cultural empathy and adaptability? What can companies do to facilitate this process?

TRAINING, TRANSFER, TEAMWORK, AND TRAVEL

International executive training courses have become almost a requirement for future global leaders. Many organizations send promising young executives to an international MBA program outside their home country—fertile ground for developing cultural relativity. For example, at INSEAD, the international business school located in France, Singapore, and Abu Dhabi, students work in mixed-nationality teams over their 10-month program. For those executives who continue working in their organization, there are Executive MBA programs available. Much of the work in all these programs is done in study groups that are composed of people of many different nationalities. A typical group might include an American, a Belgian, a Russian, a Japanese, a Swede, and a Brazilian. Participants must work closely together on a variety of projects; to succeed, they must develop a cross-cultural mindset. This process effectively minimizes ethnocentricity.

On-the-job training offers education of another sort, and is no less vital. Exposure early in one's career to international leadership experiences—that is, concrete project responsibilities in other countries—is important. These experiences should include working in multicultural teams. Experiences of this nature hone a person's capacity to cope with difficult leadership challenges later in the career cycle. Travel for pleasure or business is also essential. This kind of early international experience is a good test of a young executive's global leadership potential.

Transfers stretch young executives in new ways, especially if they occur in conjunction with an organizational support system conducive to the long-term management of global careers. Unfortunately, I still see far too many leading global firms using their foreign subsidiaries as parking lots for redundant employees when times are lean at home, with no guarantee of a job in their home country when the foreign assignment is finished. As I mentioned earlier, truly global companies make foreign experience a requirement for reaching more senior leadership positions. Transfers should be handled by a globally oriented human resource system that takes into consideration the family situation of the global executive and helps transferees prepare for reassignments abroad.

Companies can do more to prepare people for international assignments through company-specific executive education. An increasing number of companies have set up a corporate university to facilitate this process. Others have created company-specific programs with the help of business schools, even going so far as creating degree programs. Unfortunately, and too often, most of the training concerning cross-cultural issues that are carried out seems to be based on cognitive approaches: language training and information about the country, culture, and style of living. In addition, many of these executive programs seem to focus on the development of analytical skills and neglect the less quantifiable intuitive processes, such as stimulating a sense of cultural empathy. The enhancement of right-brain capabilities—the domain of emotional intelligence—(e.g. judgment, intuition, 'gut feeling') has often not been satisfactorily introduced into the traditional left-hemisphere, more logical, business environment.

Experiential Training

In some cases, however, affective training is also undertaken to prepare people for situations they may encounter using case studies, simulation, outward-bound situations, and role-playing. Global business schools such as INSEAD pay a great amount of attention to the skills necessary for working in a multinational environment. For example, at the INSEAD Global Leadership Center, much energy is devoted to integrating the cognitive with the affective domain. A main vehicle to accomplish cross-cultural sensitivity is to engage in joint problem-solving through group coaching in multicultural groups.

Clinical interventions have demonstrated that basic values, beliefs, and attitudes do not change overnight, however. On the contrary, change requires a lengthy process of working through and overcoming resistance (Kets de Vries, Korotov, and Florent-Treacy, 2007). But it can be argued that some executive programs—if the right parameters are used—can be instrumental in setting a process of change in motion. The subsequent success in reshaping a person's inner representational world and acceptance of a new reality greatly depends on a further, sustained effort on the part of the individual concerned.

A FRAMEWORK FOR ANALYZING THE DEVELOPMENT OF THE GLOBAL LEADER

The various factors that contribute to the making of a global leader are summarized in Figure 13.1. This figure highlights that there are three

CHILDHOOD DEVELOPMENT ADAPTABILITY FACTORS
- Narcissistic development
- Cultural diversity in family
- Early international experience
- Multilingualism
- Multiple roots
- Some 'as if' qualities

LEADERSHIP FACTORS
- Self-confidence
- Responsibility
- Curiosity
- Imagination
- Hardiness
- Decision-making skills
- Networking abilities
- Envisioning
- Communication skills
- 'Core values'
- Career goals and expectations

PROFESSIONAL DEVELOPMENT TRAINING AND EDUCATION
- Analytical skills
- Professional skills
- Study in another culture
- Study in international environment
- Languages
- Emotional intelligence

EXECUTIVE DEVELOPMENT
- Early responsibility
- Variety of tasks
- Early international experience
- Corporate values

PERSONAL DEVELOPMENT
- Supportive spouse
- Adaptable spouse
- 'Movable' children
- Variety of interests

PERSONALITY SCREEN

ORGANIZATIONAL SCREEN

ORGANIZATIONAL DEVELOPMENT ORGANIZATIONAL STRUCTURE
- Geocentric
- Use of third-country nationals
- Flat
- Organic
- Multicultrual

INTERNATIONAL HUMAN-RESOURCE MANAGEMENT
- Career-pathing
- Re-entry management
- Selection criteria assessment
- Succession planning
- Communications

Figure 13.1 Factors contributing to the development of a global leader

spheres of influence on the development of the global leader. The strongest influences on both leadership qualities and the ability to adapt culturally stem from childhood background and psychological development. However, these attributes can be further enhanced by early leadership responsibilities, international work, and educational experiences. Finally, the organizational structure provides a framework focusing the global leadership qualities that already exist and encouraging their further development.

Looking further at the framework in Figure 13.1, we can also see that in the development of a global leader, ideally it helps to have a childhood background characterized by cultural diversity—one aspect being early international experience. Such a combination can enhance language skills and an attitude of cultural empathy. At the base of it all, however, is how one's sense of self is experienced, which is determined by the nature and quality of the person's narcissistic development.

Within the organization, early exposure to leadership experiences (meaning some kind of measurable project responsibility) is important as these will hone an individual's capacity to cope with difficult leadership challenges later in his or her career. These early experiences also need to be combined with a talent management system and an organizational structure conducive to the management of international careers.

In the personal sphere, the attitude of the spouse is essential—and depends largely on the spouse's own exposure to other cultures and the kind of options she or he will have available. Finally, the match between life cycle and career cycle plays a critical role. We are more mobile at some stages in life than others, because of children or other factors.

CONCLUSIONS

Keeping Figure 13.1 in mind, the following general propositions can be made:

1. Cultural empathy and adaptability are key factors for effective functioning in a global world.
2. Executives are strongly influenced by the degree of cultural diversity that existed within the family and early cultural exposure.
3. Leadership qualities depend on healthy narcissistic development and early career challenges.

4. Global leadership qualities need to be developed through the experience of challenging foreign assignments early and onwards in an executive's career trajectory.
5. A multicultural organizational ambience creates a learning environment for global leadership.
6. The cultural openness of spouse and children, and their successful adaptation to global lifestyles, will influence the development of additional global leadership qualities.

Apart from any predisposition to become a global leader, the evolution of a global leader at a later stage in life is, ironically, very much determined by the experience of being a global leader. The earlier the experience in an individual's career, the greater the ability to adapt to and empathize with new cultures and the more prepared that person will be for global leadership. If early assignments are followed later in the career trajectory with the successful completion of a very difficult task (such as a turn-around problem, a merger and acquisition challenge, or a new business venture) the likelihood is greater that the individual will be ready to take on a top executive position in the organization.

Globalization can be the answer to many of the world's conundrums. Globalization is changing companies. Moreover, globalization no longer applies to a company's selling and sourcing activities but very much has to do with attracting and retaining the world's most talented people. And whether we like it or not, globalization is here to stay. As the former Secretary General of the United Nations, Kofi Annan, once said, 'arguing against globalization is like arguing against the laws of gravity.'

ENDNOTE

Text in this chapter has appeared elsewhere in print under the same title and co-authored with Christine Mead as a chapter in V. Pucik, N.M. Tichy, and C.K. Barnett (eds), *Globalizing Management: Creating and Leading the Competitive Organization*, New York: John Wiley & Sons, Inc. (1992).

CHAPTER 14

IN SEARCH OF THE NEW EUROPEAN BUSINESS LEADER[1]

High culture is nothing but a child of that European perversion called history, the obsession we have with going forward, with considering the sequence of generations a relay race in which everyone surpasses his predecessor, only to be surpassed by his successor. Without this relay race called history there would be no European art and what characterizes it: a longing for originality, a longing for change. Robespierre, Napoleon, Beethoven, Stalin, Picasso, they're all runners in the relay race, they all belong to the same stadium.

—Milan Kundera

INTRODUCTION

The founding fathers of the European Union, Robert Schuman and Jean Monnet, dreamed of creating a community of nations that would become more directionally convergent as the years went by. The result of their vision is the EU, the most far-reaching plan for economic integration ever to be attempted among a group of sovereign countries. Its founding covenant, the Treaty of Rome (1957), aimed at the establishment of a common market, progressively bringing the economic policies of its members into alignment, in order:

> to promote the harmonious growth of economic activity in the Community as a whole, regular and balanced expansion, augmented stability, a more rapidly rising standard of living, and closer relations between the participating states.

Today, with a membership of twenty-seven states, and a combined gross domestic product (GDP) that accounts for approximately 30% of the world's economic output, the sense of community and relative simplicity of management in the original EU has been lost. Its growth has brought baffling complexity. There are more candidates for membership waiting in the wings, several post-communist nations, and Turkey, a culturally, historically, and religiously very different country. The manageability and viability of the European Union is an issue debated by many political analysts. Business organizations wanting to navigate through this complex network of relationships require extremely talented leadership.

To illustrate the complexity of navigating in the entity called Europe, take the incident at the Perrier bottling plant, at a source near Vergèze, in France which occurred a number of years ago. It demonstrated some of these complexities—the kinds of paradoxes executives have to deal with. Returning to our example, Perrier bubbled away profitably from 1898 through the roaring 1980s, when Perrier was the 'it' drink for the scions of Wall Street and their transatlantic peers. Profits were shared with Perrier workers, who had regular pay raises and generous holiday leave, and were referred to as 'co-managers' of the plant. Then in 1990, traces of benzene were found in a bottle bound for the USA, and by 1992 Perrier's US market had dried up.

The company was saved from bankruptcy by Nestlé, a Swiss organization with the global experience and clout to pull Perrier out of its slump and reposition the iconic green bottle in the world's classiest watering holes. And yet, Nestlé has not made much of a profit on the Perrier brand. The *Conféderation Générale du Travail* (CGT), a staunchly left-wing French union supported by nearly all of Perrier's workers, dug firmly into its entrenched position, determined to protect employees' perks. By late 2004, Nestlé was thinking seriously about selling the company. In response, the CGT decided to begin the process of classifying Perrier as an AOC (*Appellation d'Origine Controlée*); if awarded, this classification would mean that the Perrier brand name could only be used for water bottled in Vergèze—in other words, it would remain 100% French. Nestlé executives believe that if the CGT would back down, Perrier could be transformed into a robust global brand, bottled at several international locations. This stalemate almost led to an outcome that would be dismal for all concerned, with Nestlé dumping Perrier, and the workers in Vergèze left with nothing but their pride. It appeared difficult to adapt Perrier's 'time-warped proletarians' (as one journalist labeled them) to twenty-first-century market forces.

This pattern of distrust and passive aggression can arise in many contexts. For example, near-mutiny occurred after the $25 billion merger of Swiss Bank Corp and the British investment bank Warburg in 1995. The merger became a clash of titans, pitching button-down British merchant bankers against the deal-oriented Swiss who had acquired their organization. Miscommunication and cultural differences led to a climate of fear and loathing, and before long prime assets were, as one observer put it, 'going down in the elevator in the evening, and not coming back in the morning.'

These are only two examples among many. Nearly every CEO can recount similar experiences. But these particular examples are archetypal, in that they illustrate what I see as the underlying cause for the failure of many European cross-border alliances: a fundamental and often subconscious fear and loathing on the part of followers, and a preconceived notion on the part of many business leaders that workers in countries other than their own tend to be 'time-warped proletarians.' If these preconceptions and attitudes are ignored, the developments of successful pan-European business organizations will be nothing more than an illusion.

However, there is hope. I have observed European business leaders who are able to calm the fears of the people in their organizations and build a truly European organization in which their followers can gradually build on, and go beyond, traditions tied to their individual cultural identities and create an organization based on trust. Effective leaders are able to foster a sense of purpose, affiliation, and community in their organizations that unifies their employees, wherever they may be in the world.

But what are the major challenges faced by the leaders of the new EU and what does it mean to be a European business leader?

THE CHALLENGE OF DIVERSITY

It is important to first take a clear-eyed look at the primal 'soup' from which European business organizations are beginning to emerge.

The new configuration of the EU has brought great expectations and considerable anxiety for organizations and their members. On the one hand, it can be seen as an opportunity to develop a powerful economic entity with a strong cultural heritage, similar values, and enough diversity to foster creativity and innovation. On the other, it brings the fear of diluting national identities, clashing cultural norms, religious strife, and incompatibility of leadership styles and work practices.

Xenophobia within organizational systems is usually more benign than xenophobia in society at large, but it can still be detrimental if left unexplored. Organizational systems arise from implicit cultural assumptions, and as long as people are unaware of these assumptions, they risk underestimating the validity and tenacity of the correlated systems.

While almost all organizations—not just European ones—face the diversity challenge, Europe presents a much more complex situation. Diversity issues, according to any human resources management or organizational behavior textbook, traditionally include local minorities, gender, disability, sexual orientation, and the like. Obviously, Europe faces all of these, but if we see Europe as a single economic entity, unlike other economies, it also faces diversity issues in several additional dimensions.

To start with, there are significant differences in national culture across a wide spectrum of issues, including perspectives on time, individualism versus collectivism, power distance, performance orientation, tolerance of uncertainty, ascription versus achievement orientation, emotional expressiveness, and general role differentiation—to name but a few. People and organizations cannot help being influenced by these differences between nations.

There are also important religious differences within Europe, which impact on the way people work in organizations and affect values, beliefs, attitudes, and behavior. These also have an influence on legal matters, marriage law being one among many. Different levels of penetration of religious values and practices in society mean differences in the spiritual needs of organizational members. For example, when the draft of the European constitution was being written, Poland insisted on the inclusion of the notion of Christianity. Europe already has a significant proportion of non-Christians among its citizens; if Turkey is admitted, it will have a member-state that is predominantly Muslim.

Europe is also multilingual, and there is still no common language that can be used with equal ease in its different parts. Even the official bodies of the European Union have considerable difficulty finding sufficient qualified translators and interpreters for all the languages used by the member-states. The costs of keeping up with translation have grown exponentially. Any reduction in the number of languages used has been met with howls of protest, reflecting sensitivities and pride of each country's standing.

Then there are the different educational systems within the different European countries, which frequently have incompatible curricula and requirements. The Bologna Process has tried to deal with the situation by means of a voluntary agreement of 40 countries, signed in 1999, with the aim of introducing a transparent, uniform system of higher education degrees across Europe. Although the Bologna Process was geared toward the unification of degree-granting rules and procedures, so that levels of educational attainment will be similar, there is still quite a way to go.

There is also the issue of the perceived value attached to degrees. In some European countries a university degree in management is much less prestigious than a degree in engineering or law. This sort of perception will affect the attitude employees have toward their leader and the credibility and trustworthiness of the latter in the business community.

Furthermore, Europe is characterized by a variety of political systems (parliamentary monarchies, presidential republics, and parliamentary republics) that influence individual attitudes to power and authority. The system of government at state level can be reflected in internal power and authority issues within organizations.

European nations also differ in the extent to which their populations rely on the government in their daily lives. There are welfare states where citizens can expect to benefit from the redistribution of wealth, and there are countries where citizens are expected to take care of their own well-being. There are other countries that used to operate a form of forced redistribution of wealth and whose citizens are now craving opportunities for personal enrichment.

With the recent expansion of Europe to the East, we must also take into account the ways in which its members experience different socio-economic systems. A substantial part of the population of almost all of the new members of the EU has lived under communism. While many may not have liked the system, quite a few grew used to it or learned to adapt to it and survive, and these people carry their previous experiences into their new European organizational life.

There is also the question of graft and corruption. Different countries have different standards of what is permissible concerning the interface of political and business leaders. The developments in countries like Romania and Bulgaria are good cases in point.

Individual European countries have their own particular relationships with neighboring nations and other parts of the world. The recent war in Iraq demonstrated dramatically contrasting views on US policy within Europe. Similarly there are differences in different countries' relationships with Russia, a country on which many European countries rely for their natural resources. Different points of view have also been expressed vis-à-vis the Georgia–Russia 'adventure.'

Furthermore, European history is one of tension as well as co-operation. The jokes that the British and French tell about each other's working style and social habits are an obvious example. A much more serious issue is how other nations have worked through their response to Germany's Nazi past. The wounds of twentieth-century wars and even remoter conflicts have not healed, and can still hurt on both conscious and unconscious levels.

All of these many differences mean that Europeans have vastly diverse organizational experiences, starting in the very first form of organization we all experience—the family—through school, military training, university, entering employment, etc. These different experiences mean that people develop different kinds of behavior—and they bring these into their organizations. Early family experiences and influences also create dissimilar organizational leaders and followers, and different expectations about them. A successful leader in, say, the Netherlands would not be guaranteed the same level of success in Portugal, Hungary, or Europe at large.

(Of course, even within the same national culture we witness considerable differences in perceptions of leadership—influenced by every individual's experience of parental authority or their relationship with a primary caregiver.)

Obviously diversity, when managed properly, enables major breakthroughs in creativity, competitiveness, and flexibility. However, tolerating and valuing diversity does not come naturally to human beings. The unknown always causes discomfort. Not understanding what signifiers signify is associated with a great deal of anxiety. People have to overcome this anxiety, learn to accept differences in relationship patterns, learn to value them, and learn to work with different styles. New European leaders have a responsibility to help their people cope with this process: they have to encourage their employees to use diversity to its maximum potential.

INTERNAL AND EXTERNAL COMPETITION

'Time-warped proletariat' is clearly not a complimentary phrase, but it does raise an interesting point. Many European workers, when faced with the need to accept diversity, do not fully understand why they should bother with it. Nearly everyone is aware that, as an economy, Europe faces strong pressures from global competitors. The US or Asian economies are probably the first to come to mind when we talk about Europe's competitors. However, a development less visible to non-Europeans, but nevertheless an extremely hot issue for the workforce inside Europe, is the internal competition from organizations in other European member-states or from their domestic economies at large.

Blue-collar jobs, call centers, and some white-collar activities such as back-office support, financial data-processing, programming, and even research jobs have been drifting from Europe to Asia for some time—but a similar phenomenon is occurring within Europe. Activities that might have moved to Asia previously are now moving instead to Eastern Europe, where there is a well-educated workforce that speaks multiple European languages, but still costs considerably less to employ than workers in the home country.

Krakow in Poland, for example, has been chosen by the German airline Lufthansa as the site for its European accounting center, because this university city offers a relatively low-cost, well-educated workforce capable of speaking many European languages. Diageo, a British drink company boasting such brands as Johnnie Walker and Guinness, has established its European back-office support in Budapest, Hungary, for similar reasons. State-of-the-art new industrial facilities create employment opportunities in the new member-states of Eastern Europe, forcing workers in 'older' Europe to tighten their belts in order to keep their jobs. Thus, Volkswagen and DaimlerChrysler have recently struck deals with the initially reluctant trade unions that would slash labor costs in exchange for not moving jobs to the East. Similarly, Siemens introduced longer working hours without extra pay to let its people keep their jobs at home.

With external competition, the situation is more or less clear—competitors are well-known, and the threats are easily understood. But intra-European competition presents a much bigger challenge for both leaders and followers. People in Europe have to overcome a serious case of cognitive dissonance: on the one hand, an enlarged, unified Europe will help Europeans, as it opens new opportunities and makes the totality stronger and more successful. On the other hand, the direct consequence of the enlargement of the European Community for a particular employee in the older EU countries is a threat of job loss, or a perceived deterioration in working conditions (increase in working hours, lower pensions, etc.). Two such incompatible cognitions will be difficult to reconcile. All of a sudden, organizational leaders are deprived of an external threat or enemy: a lever that has been used for centuries to motivate, unite, and energize subordinates. With increased competition from within, as well as without, this lever requires much more delicate handling.

IS A SINGLE MODEL POSSIBLE?

All these differences between and within European countries and their organizations, combined with the challenge of external and internal competition, raise the questions of whether Europe can and should be treated as a uniform entity, and whether a single model of European leadership is real or illusory. The answer to the first question is quite likely to be 'no.' The second question would be better phrased as: 'Can European organizations afford *not* to have some form of European leadership?' Can an organization remain Belgian, or Polish, or Italian and *not* include a toolset of European capabilities?

While a US company with US leadership can, in principle, remain American and still succeed, this is not an option for European companies. The free movement of goods and human capital, and the many policy synchronization processes taking place at the European level, mean that most medium-sized and large companies will simply not have the option of remaining purely national. If they do, they will lose out in the European and global marketplaces. Their leaders have no choice but to become more European and to acquire some common elements in their styles that will allow them to face the new challenges.

This brief exploration of differences in Europe and European organizations should have made it obvious that with so much diversity, and the pressures of both external *and* internal competition, it will be difficult to apply a standard set of universal approaches to leaders and leadership in European organizations. But a parochial, single-nation-based approach would not work either. We have to look for another way.

A MIDDLE PATH

Humans have a basic need to feel at home in a crowd, yet simultaneously to stand out from it. All of us are engaged in this delicate balancing act, wanting to belong to something bigger than ourselves while retaining our individuality—the characteristics that make us unique. The 'something bigger' is our social identity; retaining our individuality is about keeping and valuing our personal identity. Globalization can thus be challenging and overwhelming for each of us because, subjectively, it leaves less room for individual differences and idiosyncrasies. Complete individuality, however, may also be unrealistic; as social animals we are made isolated and highly vulnerable by singularity.

Globalization

Europe as an economic entity may be in a very promising position to deal with this paradox. Being a member of a European entity can strengthen our social identity: we are more than a representative of a particular nation or an employee of a specific organization. At the same time, each of us will be trying to maintain our more individual national identity (e.g. French, Estonian, or Swedish). A European company could be seen as a kind of developmental learning center, teaching the European how to survive, as well as to maintain his or her sense of self, in a global world.

So how can we help this optimally distinctive European develop? It means finding a way to combine the characteristics of the common European identity with those of the national, regional, individualized, organizational, or personal identity. Finding this road is infinitely preferable to the bubble or chameleon approaches adopted by too many European leaders.

The bubble is blown up to protect an organization and its systems, opportunities, core competencies, and identity from any form of contagion from the outside world. In bubble organizations, leaders obstinately stick to what they know, ignoring the context in which they are operating.

Chameleon leaders, by contrast, opt for total immersion in the national flavor-of-the-month, and are too ready to give up the organization's basic cultural identity—to let go of the characteristics that made for its original success—to follow the latest trend.

I suggest a middle way, a 'glocal' route to Europeanization, which will help combine elements of the core (an organization's unique competencies and opportunities) with the capacity to adapt to other cultures.

To be effective, European companies or global organizations operating in Europe have to ask themselves: what kinds of functions need to be centralized at the European level, or even globally? What has to remain at the national level? In Diageo, for example, decisions about information technology, corporate communication, and accounting can be made at a centralized level. However, human resources, industrial relations, and specific sales-management decisions are frequently made at local level.

DEALING WITH CHANGE

The unlearning of habitual patterns that is necessary in becoming European can provoke a great deal of anxiety. Under stress, people are inclined to regress to habitual patterns of behavior, illogical as these may appear to others, and they cannot seem to change their perspective on the world without expending a great deal of effort. The challenge for European leaders, then, is to find ways to trigger a willingness to experiment and try out new things. And this is true whether we are talking about personal change or organizational change. Both processes have to happen one individual at a time. Many organizational psychologists (basing their theories on the findings of developmental and clinical psychology) consider that organizational change and transformation has to be embedded in the process of individual change.

An important task for new European leaders is therefore to mobilize their followers' resources and help them avoid the paralysis that sometimes greets the new and unknown. We have already noted some of the diversities that exist within Europe. Here are some of the associated worries that preoccupy Europeans:

- Job security.
- Surviving in the world of competition (both external and internal).
- Maintaining a European identity versus a national identity, both for people and companies, goods, and services (optimal distinctiveness).
- Managing relationships with large and unpredictable neighbors (e.g. Russia) and large economic and political powers in other parts of the world (e.g. USA, China, India, Brazil).
- Surviving with a diverse workforce (different languages, religions, work ethics, work practices, etc.).
- Dealing with the loss of certain benefits or social achievements because of increased competitiveness.
- Withstanding the global threat of terrorism, which, in addition to an overall psychological toll on the feeling of safety and security, has direct economic consequences on businesses.

These anxieties are accompanied by the huge expectations held by European nations and the rest of the world regarding this unprecedented experiment in building a super-economy. Together, they can give rise to a set of psychological defenses within an organization's workforce and culture, and this is the root cause of the kind of resistance to change manifested by the Perrier workers, for example, and helps to explain why they sought to take control of their destiny by creating an AOC for the company.

The Leader and 'Good-Enough' Care

It is the role of leaders to help their employees overcome such anxieties and assume greater control of their lives. In many ways, the challenge for new European organizational leaders is analogous to that of being a 'good-enough' caregiver in a child-rearing situation. Leaders need to provide what psychoanalyst Donald Winnicott referred to as 'transitional space' (Winnicott, 1975) (see p. 232).

So, how can organizational leaders create such an environment? Some suggestions are:

- increasing tolerance for cultural diversity in organizations and societies;
- being prepared to give up the not-invented-here approach;
- adopting new and progressive industrial relations;
- preparing for constant learning, unlearning, and relearning; and
- developing a tolerance for ambiguity.

Some degree of confusion when operating in a new environment is inevitable and, in fact, is fine, as long as confusion time (think of it as play time) is spent constructively and creatively.

Organizational leaders who make room for the creation of confusion time will be at a great advantage because their employees will be better prepared to survive in a world of global competition, have the ability to deal with a high level of diversity, and be ready for future challenges. Not all European leaders, however, will be able to create and maintain such space in their organizations. Those who want to be effective in this new world of work will have to make sure that the right conditions exist for playfulness and creativity, as well as the provision of safety for doing new and unusual things.

Claiming a European identity for an organization, its goods and services, its leadership style and practices, and disseminating this identity to the outside world is a challenging task and cannot be accomplished in one step. Time is needed to experiment and play with the development of a European identity and its presentation to the outside world, and leaders need to be helped to play their parenting role.

I will now briefly consider how leaders who will do this can be created.

THE MAKING OF THE EUROPEAN LEADER

It goes without saying that a leader's job will be made much easier if he or she speaks more than one European language, comes from a mixed-culture family, or has spent significant time living outside his or her country of origin. However, there are other things a leader can do whether or not these factors are present. The individual needs first to examine what makes him or her an effective leader. One of the first challenges for a European leader is 'Know thyself,' that is, understand his or her own personal developmental paths. This awareness is important for a leader in any context, but particularly so for someone aspiring to lead in such a diverse environment as the new EU.

One popular and effective way for executives to explore their early developmental history is to participate in one of the leadership development programs that are becoming more common in Europe. For example, the educational methodology of the programs at the INSEAD Global Leadership Center allows mixed-culture groups of senior executives to undertake a personal journey of self-exploration in a highly diverse executive context (European and beyond) with the help of faculty members, leadership coaches, and peers participating in the programs (Kets de Vries *et al.*, 2007). Through personal storytelling, portraiture, and multi-part feedback instrumentation, a transitional space is created (facilitated by the faculty) during which participants acquire a deeper understanding of themselves as well as how others perceive them. This process is an opportunity to obtain a better understanding of their own developmental journey and the journeys of others. They also acquire a deeper understanding of organizational and national cultures.

As this process takes place in a group setting, the other leaders in the group will make their own contributions to the learning process, while vicariously experiencing the exploratory journey of each member. This particular educational methodology not only helps people understand their developmental challenges; they also learn and understand how to:

- become more effective in cross-cultural and virtual teams;
- give feedback in a culture-sensitive way;
- make coaching part of their leadership style;
- make knowledge management a reality.

Although this methodology is beneficial in a mono-cultural context, leaders who run European organizations face a special challenge in taking this journey. In fact, their role goes beyond ensuring the success of a particular organization: it extends to proving the success of Europe as a united economy to the world.

In my work with executives, I have also discovered that leadership perceptions and expectations are very different in various parts of Europe because perceptions of what leaders are, or should be, are influenced by the diverse cultural and family backgrounds found in the member-states. During my consulting, coaching, and executive education work with thousands of European executives in various parts of Europe I found that different aspects of leadership behavior are more or less important. However, there are some universal elements that make for highly effective leadership. They include:

- taking time to listen to your subordinates and making their opinions count;
- caring about the people who work for you and being ready to help them when they have personal problems or doubts;
- setting a good example of what is expected of the people in the organization by 'walking the talk';
- creating stretch opportunities for staff and supporting their personal growth and development;
- encouraging employees by giving them praise and recognition when warranted;
- keeping people informed by creating transparent organizations;
- setting clear expectations by providing regular feedback;
- promoting a culture that helps your people obtain a feeling of collective identity, encouraging people to move from 'I' to 'we';
- making work meaningful for employees.

LEADERSHIP IN EUROPE AND BEYOND

Interestingly, a number of global companies have discovered that the time spent in Europe by their senior international executives often serves as the best possible preparation for taking on a global role. In a significant way, Europe represents challenges that are typical for global businesses at large. Mastering leadership in Europe, therefore, can be see as a nursery for any leader aspiring to global leadership responsibility.

Leaders fulfill many different roles in their employees' imaginations. They are catalysts of change, symbols, objects of identification, and scapegoats when things go wrong. The most effective leaders are those who know how to balance action with reflection by using self-insight as a restraining force when the sirens of power are calling. Leaders who keep their curiosity about other ways of doing things will be the best equipped to retain their sanity in what can seem insane places, the European Union being one of them.

After the rise and fall of so many empires in Europe—of which the Roman Empire is one of the more memorable—the business community has been given a great opportunity to unite Europe. And business leaders have gone a long way toward making this challenge come true. Henry Kissinger's famous question, 'Who do I call when I want to call Europe?' is losing its poignancy. The US president, George Washington, may have been more visionary when he said, 'Some day, following the example of the United States of America, there will be a United States of Europe.'

ENDNOTE

1. Material in this chapter has appeared elsewhere in print in Kets de Vries, M.F.R. and Korotov, K. (2005). '"The future of an illusion": In search of the new European business leader,' *Organizational Dynamics*, **34** (3): 218–230. The author would like to thank Konstantin Korotov for his contribution to this chapter.

CHAPTER 15

LESSONS FROM THE 'WILD EAST': RUSSIAN CHARACTER AND LEADERSHIP

> Russia on its path has oftentimes discussed and overdiscussed what had happened earlier, instead of moving forward. The result is always the same: It is very difficult to move forward when you're looking backward.
> —Mikhail Khodorkovsky

THE RUSSIAN CHARACTER

Romancing the Past

In the 1930s, film-makers Grigori Kozintsev and Leonid Trautberg directed a trilogy about the life of the Russian writer Maxim Gorky. Through the medium of film, the viewer is given an unusual picture of the Russian mindset as the directors portray some of the forces that make the Russians who they are. The first part of this classic depicts the Bolshevik legend of Gorky's youth.

The fairy-tale quality of the film facilitates audience identification with what Russians are likely to view as essential characteristics of their native country and their own childhood. However, we should probably assume (given the era when the film was made) that the images represent a compromise between artistic insight and political correctness.

The film begins with a view of the empty plains and the Volga (to the accompaniment of balalaika music); the cameras then shifts to a *mir*, one of the myriad communal villages that are scattered across Russia, giving an intimate portrait of the behavior of the inhabitants. The film paints a stark contrast between the conduct of the men and the women. Women are portrayed as warm, caring, strong, generous, and reliable (*babushka* types), but also as fatalistic and long-suffering. Men, on the other hand, are presented as having a self-destructive streak manifested through episodes of sudden violence and bouts of alcoholism.

The compelling *babushka* imagery reflects a mindset that is typically Russian. The picture of the generous, beneficent grandmother lingers on, serving as the mother-image of adulthood as well as childhood. For someone ruled by this kind of mental imagery, adult reality is likely to be disappointing as they probably experience a lifelong yearning for 'Paradise lost,' an undefined sense of pre-Oedipal, regressive nostalgia—a romantic sentimentality that is part of being Russian (Chasseguet-Smirgel, 1975).

Suffering and Violence

But this nostalgic yearning is not the only pattern explored in Kozintsev and Trautberg's film. Viewers are subjected to sudden, unexpected eruptions—violent beating scenes fill the screen periodically, and sadistic and masochistic behavior patterns intertwine. Accurately reflecting Russian life, the film identifies suffering in various forms as another prevailing theme: suffering is needed to attain salvation for whatever 'crimes'—imagined or real—a person has committed. Sin, remorse, and punishment have always been important themes in Russian history. The Russian Orthodox Church, with its imagery of torment, agony, and martyrdom, its view of suffering as the means by which to seek and find God's grace and mercy, has played an important role in the formation of this aspect of the Russian psyche.

It can be argued that a sadomasochistic identification with authority—whether the authority figure is the tsar, a nobleman, a landowner, Lenin, Stalin, or a Communist Party commissar—has also characterized the Russian people over the centuries (Murray, 1995). This attitude toward authority figures implies not only a readiness to be abused but also a willingness to assume the position of sadistic authority over others.

In the seminal book *Childhood and Society* (1963) by psychoanalyst and human-development scholar Erik Erikson, we find a chapter entitled 'The Legend of Maxim Gorky's Youth.' Erikson uses Kozintsev and Trautberg's film about Gorky to explore what he saw as timeless, salient patterns in the Russian character; in particular, the sadomasochistic orientation. And he is in good company in emphasizing such patterns, because they permeate Russian literature. The idea that suffering is a virtue is a recurring theme. Many of that tradition's most respected writers have painted shattering pictures of poverty and slavery, emphasizing distortions of the psyche caused by many centuries of serfdom (a practice that ended in 1861 but left a deep imprint on superior–subordinate relationships).

These stories from history and fiction portray the Russians as people prone to dramatic mood swings, expressing extreme anger one moment and reverting to masochistic behavior the next. This swinging of the emotional pendulum was well exemplified by Tsar Ivan the Terrible, who, after the murder of his son, was consumed by remorse and repentance.

The Capacity to Endure

In spite of (or perhaps because of) the harsh circumstances under which they live or have lived—predominantly on vast, empty plains or on the Siberian tundra—Russians are a people of enormous endurance and stamina. I observed this incredible courage, endurance, and putative love of suffering firsthand in 1993, when I was a member of an expedition in the Pamir mountains in Tadjikistan, one of the former republics of the old USSR on the Russian-Chinese border. The purpose of the trip was to observe the rut of the mythical Marco Polo sheep, the largest wild sheep in the world. Unfortunately, we were not lucky with the weather. Not only did we have to deal with extreme temperatures (more than −30°C, without even factoring in the wind chill) and dramatic heights (over 5500 m), we also faced unusually deep and challenging snow conditions. Our lack of equipment for dealing with the deep snow, in combination with the oxygen-scarce air of extreme altitude, made climbing exceptionally difficult. To my inexperienced eye, it looked as if it would be impossible to get close to the sheep. Other people would have given up—but not the Russians. They decided to press on, and to do so when the sheep could not see us so as to avoid scaring them away.

So I found myself, in the dark, at 2 a.m. one December morning, trudging through the snow and trying to minimize the extreme exertion by stepping in the footsteps of my guides—who, it should be noted, carried all my gear (tent, sleeping bag, cooking utensils, food, and so on) on their backs. I have been in many difficult situations, but this was the most grueling. Later my Russian friends named this night walk 'the battle of Pamirgrad,' in reference to the most terrible Russian battle of

World War II. While I almost died of frostbite in the process, they manifested few signs of discomfort.

Character in Transition

Years have passed since the making of Kozintsev and Trautberg's film about Gorky's youth and the writing of Erikson's article, and many dramatic changes have occurred in Russia. The USSR has imploded into the Russian Federation; many of the countries that belonged to the old Soviet Socialist Republic have become independent; the *glasnost* and *perestroika* introduced by Mikhail Gorbachev and the reforms attempted and implemented by Boris Yeltsin and his senior advisors, and afterwards by Vladimir Putin and Dmitry Medvedev, have resulted in a dramatic transformation of Russian society. The consequences of many of these changes have been mixed: although certain segments of society have profited from the new situation, the chaotic transitional stage of the Russian economy has left much of the population feeling alienated and disenfranchised.

The fact that Russia is still in the middle of a radical transformation makes any attempt to decipher the Russian personality a challenging task. The great geographical diversity of Russia, which has long been a melting pot of different races, religions, languages, regions, and cultures, and whose territories stretch from Eastern Europe through Siberia to the Far East, makes the task even more difficult. Nonetheless there is a certain stability to the essential nature of Russian character—there are certain distinctive characteristics that have retained their significance regardless of place, time, or regime.

CONTEXTUAL FACTORS IN THE FORMATION OF THE RUSSIAN CHARACTER

The Impact of Nature

Given the extremes of weather in Russia—a country half given over to permafrost—Russians know what it means to be subject to environmental whims, a fact that may help explain their patience, submission, and caution. They do not experience the sense of control that characterizes people in many cultures not exposed to such extreme climate conditions. As they alternate bursts of activity with periods of weather-determined passivity, Russians oscillate between feeling that they are in control and feeling that they are being controlled.

The harsh climate has given rise to the bear metaphor associated with Russia—symbolic of low energy levels in the winter and an elevated mood state in the summer, when food is abundant. Like bears, Russians can 'hibernate' for long periods of time, awaking to remarkable spurts of activity. In Russia, given the short planting and harvesting seasons, farmers can work only for a limited amount of time, but they show their capacity for hard work and endurance during those short seasons. While the bear metaphor primarily illustrates the duality between passivity and activity among Russians, it can also be used to address the duality between order and disorder—a theme I develop later.

The Legacy of the *Mir*

Despite Russia's heavy industrialization, the country is still highly agricultural. In previous centuries, the vastness of the land was broken only by the occasional agricultural village commune, or *mir*. While the *mir* was largely succeeded by the communal farm (run by a Soviet, or community council) and in some regions supplanted by urbanization, the philosophy behind this self-contained community lives on. It affects, for example, the Russians' outlook toward what we in the West tend to call personal space—the extent to which one's immediate environment is private as opposed to public. Because of the closeness of living conditions in the *mir* (and in overcrowded communal apartments), Russians tend to be intrusive; they do not respect other people's private space as much as people in other cultures do.

The *mir* mentality has also had an influence on the way the Russians view relationships. In all realms of human endeavor, they favor the collectivist orientation at the heart of the *mir*, an orientation that subordinates individual interests to those of the group. The collective will is more important than the will of any individual.

The legacy of the *mir* is also revealed in Russia's atmosphere of mutual dependence, in which the group provides emotional support and moral guidance for its individual members. Russians display a great need for affiliation. They like to belong, to be attached to a group, and they feel extremely uncomfortable when excluded. Many of their activities, social or otherwise, are conducted in a group setting.

The *mir* legacy also makes for a clannish loyalty that expresses itself in chauvinism and passionate patriotism: the love for the motherland. A corollary to the *mir* mentality is an emphasis on the role of self-sacrifice out of a sense of duty. Russians are prepared, when the situation warrants it, to make extraordinary sacrifices for the sake of the community or the nation. Russia has seen incidents of mass heroism seldom paralleled in history.

The *mir* mentality has also contributed to the Russians' preoccupation with egalitarianism. Leveling has always been a popular pastime, and envy an important controlling device for reminding people of their proper place. A well-known Russian proverb states that 'The tallest blade of grass will be the first to be cut,' and illustrates the degree to which individualism and personal achievement are frowned upon in Russia. While in certain other cultures it is a sin to be a loser, in Russia—until the dissolution of the communist regime—it was a sin to be a winner. The expression of individual desires was associated with selfishness. Anyone wanting to stand out was looked at with suspicion. As a consequence, Russians are still very low-key about their individual accomplishments, boasting is frowned upon, and people are careful not to be ostentatious in their habits. Succumbing to these perceived faults is a sure invitation to envy, pity, and vindictiveness.

Under communism, this spirit of egalitarianism and collectivism became perverted. Over time, ideological, even romantic, communist fervor turned into stark disbelief for many and disillusionment with the system and alienation from it set in. These factors led to a rise in materialism and opportunism, an increase in corruption and insidious moral decay. The privileges of the *nomenklatura* (the secret roster of people in positions of party leadership or in jobs within the party apparatus), with their reserved shops and special hospitals, became all too common. Ironically, this oscillation between egalitarianism and privilege has continued, as demonstrated in the behavior of the new rich, and their status consciousness in the new Russia.

Character Formation in Childhood and Youth

Swaddling in Infancy

In his article on Gorky's childhood, Erikson (1963) hypothesizes that the ancient Russian custom of swaddling babies is significant to the development of the Russian personality. Swaddling is a practice whereby newborn infants are bound from neck to toe in *pelenka* (a wrapping similar to that used in mummification) for the greater part of the day and night for three to five months—or, less typically, for as long as a year and a half (Kluckhohn, 1961). This approach—making what they call a 'log' out of their babies—is rarely practiced today, mainly in rural areas. Swaddled infants experience long periods of serious restraint alternating with short periods of freedom. They can only experience the joy of locomotor liberation, along with the ability to discharge emotion physically (the only emotional outlet other than crying that newborn infants know) in temporary bursts. The freedom of movement that babies in other societies enjoy is not permitted.

Given the influence of other significant factors throughout the life cycle, oversimplified cause-and-effect inferences based on early childcare practices are always open to question. Nevertheless, I would agree that Erikson had a point in assigning some significance to swaddling. It may have a conditioning effect, influencing character formation and leaving a legacy in terms of the child's management of emotion and action. Although swaddling may have passed into history, patterns of extreme emotional management linger on.

Schooling and Moral Upbringing

Whereas the influence of swaddling may still be open to debate, there is no question that throughout their lives, Russians are subjected to a kind of psychological swaddling that begins in early childhood. Because of their great rigidity, the school years prolong the sense of externality that Russian youngsters develop, 'externality' meaning that they perceive having very little control over their lives. Discipline and regimentation are the order of the day in the Russian classroom. Authoritarian methods prevail; a uniform and tightly controlled curriculum dominates; rote learning and unquestioning acceptance of authority are generally the rule (Bronfenbrenner, 1970; Pearson, 1990; Eklof and Dneprov, 1993).

Public shaming for misbehavior or poor performance is the usual method of behavior modification at school (a method that also colors superior–subordinate relationships in the adult world). As a result, Russians tend to be very sensitive to public humiliation. Pride plays an important role in their *Weltanschauung*. Russian teachers engage in what we might call 'intrusive guidance': they are involved in every detail of a child's upbringing and are not respectful of a child's private space. From nursery school onward, teachers are extremely active in socializing each child in the 'right' way of doing things. Few deviations from the rules are permitted.

In the Soviet past, 'moral upbringing,' implying training in patriotism, atheism, collectivism, and other state-supported activities, was an important function of Russian schools (Ispa, 1994). The role of teachers was to bring children up in the spirit of communist morality. In accordance with the centrality of collectivism, the well-being of the group superseded individual considerations; all conduct had to be aligned with the wishes and actions of the group.

In this educational atmosphere, children learned early (and repeatedly) the futility of arguing with authority figures. And parents supported that model, toeing the line drawn by teachers. Under the communist regime that line had authority: teachers often informed parents' supervisors of problems with specific children. In contrast to child-rearing practices in most Western societies, decision-making about the proper education for any given child was one-directional: educators were all-knowing givers, while parents were passive receivers. Suggestions about alternative ways of doing things were almost unheard of (and certainly unwelcome).

Such an educational approach cultivated the belief that, in public situations, one could think what one wanted but not say it. While free thinking was not constrained by this approach, neither was it fostered. And just as the posing of imaginative, probing questions was not encouraged, neither was creativity or innovation.

In this setting, children learned early the importance of conforming and blending in. Conformity offered the least painful passage through their school career, and indeed through life. The cost of non-compliance was simply too high for most people. Bad enough in the classroom, that cost became increasingly unpleasant as life progressed, involving public denouncements at the local Party headquarters, workplace demotion, and the loss of privileges or even position.

The practice of institutionalized tattling, a popular pastime under the communist regime, strengthened the urge to conform. A head boy or girl was responsible for reporting to the teacher on the conduct of the children under his or her supervision. In addition, each child was taught, at an early age, to look over his or her shoulder and observe others. Children who deviated from the prescribed code of conduct were publicly criticized, shamed, and humiliated. This educational pattern is still prevalent with all its consequences.

As already described, a significant common thread running throughout Russia's history is violent oscillation between order and chaos. Time and time again we have seen 'orderly' Russians create pandemonium when freed from control. They seem to share a hidden (and sometimes not so hidden) desire for totally unrestrained behavior.

In my visits to a number of Russian organizations, this oscillation between order and chaos was quite noticeable, though more so in 'brown fields' (existing organizations) than in 'green fields' (new start-ups). Time after time, senior management told stories of violent eruptions in the workforce. Strikes, destruction of equipment, and violent behavior vis-à-vis senior management were listed as some of the manifestations. Closer analysis showed that these eruptions were often the result of a systematic pattern of injustice within the organizations finally coming to a head. Those employees who resorted to verbal or physical violence often expressed the feeling of victimization, frequently noting specific wrongs that had been done them. In some instances, alcohol abuse played a major role in initiating emotional explosiveness, rendering the brakes of propriety ineffective. To cope with such incidents, a number of senior executives I spoke with had instituted a policy of instant dismissal for consumption of alcohol on the job.

Internal Conflict

While great discipline was stressed at school and in other public organizations (for example, in communist youth organizations such as the Young Pioneers and later the Komsomol), in the communist era, permissiveness ruled the home. Family life revolved around the children, as it does now. Always the centre of attention, children were pampered, spoiled, and protected. To be sure, the cramped living conditions of communal apartments (with the expected intrusions into private space) sometimes sparked emotional and explosive disciplining. Yet children had a counterweight to such explosions: the conviction that they were loved by their parents. And because many parents had experienced serious hardships during their lives, they made a strong effort to create a better life for their children.

Integrating two such different worlds—one of harsh discipline, the other of warmth and carefree abandon—was a great challenge to young Russian people, as it would be to any individual. A certain amount of confusion is inevitable in such circumstances, however. The 'true self' evolves through the kind of care that supports the child's continuity of being—of spontaneity or self-expression. But when people's developmental processes are governed by compliance—especially when they are subjected to unempathic authority figures—they are in danger of being seduced into a 'false life' (Winnicott, 1975), of presenting a 'false self' to the outside world. Such a state of affairs contributes to a sense of futility, makes for pseudo-maturity, and does not foster anybody's creative sides.

Although a certain split between the public self and the private self is inevitable, in Russia—at least until *glasnost*—the conflict of the presentation of self made a major contribution to the experience of a 'false self.' The warmth and permissiveness that children experienced at home simply did not fit with the conformity-for-conformity's-sake that they experienced at school. Furthermore, the lack of sincerity and consistency in the public sphere during the communist regime—idealism having increasingly deteriorated into cynical opportunism—would not have escaped their notice (since children always hear more than their parents tell them).

In the best of all worlds, children internalize an inner compass that is aligned to true north by their parents, establishing a direction that is later reinforced by other important authority figures giving similar signals. Such development makes for a sense of consistent direction and inner stability. The Russians have not had the luxury of consistent direction. How could parents—or teachers, for that matter—teach clear standards of right and wrong when they were unclear about those standards themselves?

The existence of the KGB did not teach people about the distinction between right and wrong but about the need for sensitive attunement to external, often contradictory, signals of approval and disapproval. Rather than listening to their conscience in deciding the morality of an issue, people listened for the early-morning knock that would send them to a *gulag* for some fabricated transgression.

With *glasnost*, this incongruous situation changed. The older generation still has to work through the after-effects of their moral upbringing, but they are adapting to greater freedom of thought and action. The country, however, has not dealt with the atrocities of its past. There has been a remarkable lack of soul-searching about the terrible things that happened under Lenin and Stalin—the endless number of slave labor camps, and the mass killings. School books have not sufficiently dealt with this subject, creating a society that hasn't mourned its past.

The younger generation has come to their freedom without the baggage of the previous generation. The words 'freedom,' 'liberation,' 'independent problem-solving', and 'creativity enhancement' can now be heard in the context of child-rearing. However, there is still considerable tension, especially in schools, between old and new approaches to dealing with children (Ispa, 1994). The question Russia faces, in the classroom and elsewhere, is how to balance this increased freedom with obedience and structure. How these changes in attitude will affect the newer generations is only just beginning to be seen. Preliminary hints suggest that the effects will be for the better.

The Supremacy of Friendship

Because of this legacy of fear, Russians sometimes come across as cold and harsh in their dealings with outsiders, but when a person has been accepted into their private sphere, they are capable of great warmth. Russians make deep personal friendships. In fact, the Russian language has a variety of words for 'friend,' depending on the closeness of the relationship (Dabars and Vokhmina, 1995). Russians value close friend-ships highly, setting great store by those they honor as *druzya*—the closest of friends. Such relationships are a compensation for the cold impersonality and unpredictability of public life. They are a kind of social insurance, serving as part of a mutual-support system and offering an outlet for frustrations. The intense nature of their friendships means that Russians will go to extraordinary lengths to help their friends, making great sacrifices for those in their trusted circle.

The importance of friendship also affects Russian business dealings. While American and northern European executives are more task- than relationship-oriented, Russians feel a need to develop relationships in order to accomplish tasks successfully. For them, it is not the enterprise that counts, but the people in the enterprise. Whatever Russians do, friends come first. Since they see business and friendship as closely inter-twined, they like to create networks of friends in their business dealings. Not surprisingly, then, new business is most often the result of references given by friends and acquaintances. Furthermore, Russians believe in bending the rules to help a friend: social obligations take priority over everything else. They take a contingency approach to rules, in other words, how they apply rules depends on the situation. Personal loyalty is much more important than fair play.

Emotional Expression

As noted earlier, Russians are characterized by great emotional expres-siveness. They can be extremely cold, controlled, and even rude in a public setting, but can exude great warmth among friends. They can be melancholic and apathetic at certain times, while exuding tremendous vitality at others. They can shift abruptly from serious introspection, self-doubt, and self-torment to total exuberance, abolishing all bounds and limitations. In unguarded moments, Russian emotions are displayed flagrantly. There is a cyclothymic quality to their management of emotions, a continuous oscillation between unbridled optimism and crushing pessimism (Whybrow, 1997; Kets de Vries, 1999).

Russia is a nation of stoics, as we saw earlier, but Russians are also romantics and often extremely sentimental. In their best moments, Russians are the warmest, most cheerful, most generous people one could hope to encounter. At those moments, there is a spiritual immoderation to their behavior. Their body language is very telling: they like to touch, to embrace. There is an intensity of physical contact, of closeness, that is foreign to many Western cultures.

Russians can have great moments of illumination, but they often give in to impulsiveness, even when it leads to self-destruction. Furthermore, they can be extremely emotionally self-indulgent. Not great believers in moderation or frugality, they live for the moment. Although they can be extremely stoic when necessary, they an also be very hedonistic, devoting themselves to pleasures such as eating, drinking, and bathing. Writers such as Ivan Goncharov, Nikolay Gogol, and Mikhail Saltykov wrote unsurpassed satirical portraits of idleness, uselessness, and drunkenness. In particular, the novelist Goncharov, in his famous novel *Oblomov*, painted a devastating pattern of passivity and futility.

Oblomovism

Oblomov, written and set in the mid-nineteenth century, emanates doom and futility. Its eponymous hero, Oblomov, is unable to understand the realities of life. In this tale of passivity and apathy—a tale that epitomizes the backwardness, inertia, and futility of nineteenth-century Russian society—daydreaming, fantasy, and escapism are substitutes for action. From the story of Oblomov is derived the Russian word *oblomovshchina*, a term encompassing behavior patterns such as inertia and laziness.

Although this novel caricatures a bygone epoch, it does speak to contemporary Russia as well. Even today, an element of phlegmatic fatalism, a sense of impotence regarding the powers that be, colors the behavior of many Russians. Many take a reactive stand toward life, giving a low priority to personal drive, ambition, and achievement. Years of serfdom and communism did little to transform the Oblomovian outlook. Nor did Russia's history of great suffering, some self-inflicted, some imposed—its terrible losses in war, its grievous struggles with nature, its incredible suffering in the *gulags*. The consequence of the lingering Oblomovian outlook is the absence of a national work ethic ('We pretend to work; they pretend to pay us').

In a number of the companies I visited, the Oblomovian outlook still prevailed. For the most part, the negativity of that outlook was grounded in reality: these companies were doing very poorly; in some, the workers had not been paid for long stretches of time, getting by on the barter system. However, some people at a number of these companies were making a heroic effort to sweep lingering Oblomovism aside, taking a more proactive attitude in an effort to create a meaningful work environment. In general it was easier to co-opt the younger people into taking a more proactive stand. Many of the older workers found it difficult to overcome their disbelief in a better future.

'Bureau Pathology'

Russian bureaucracy, often corrupt and ineffective, was first consolidated around 1700 under the rule of Peter the Great and reached a summit in the last phase of communism. The vast and venal bureaucracy was like a foreign invading force strangling the population. The State Planning Committee—an army of bureaucrats known by the acronym GOSPLAN—drafted plans in Moscow for every economic unit in the country, micro-managing behavior without a full realization of the various constraints placed on these economic units.

The excess of meaningless rules and regulations found under the Communist Party (and still largely in effect today) can be interpreted as 'social defenses'—a way of dealing with persecutory and depressing anxiety (Jaques, 1955; Menzies, 1960).[1] In other words, the Russian people furthered an already excessive bureaucracy in an attempt to deal with the angst and unpredictability of life under the communist regime, and with the glaring contradictions between espoused theory and theory in practice (particularly when Stalin was in power). Every new rule or regulation, every additional protocol (a written record of a transaction, meeting or statement of intent) created the illusion of certainty. Although at a subliminal level Russians were aware of the meaninglessness of the whole exercise, the dysfunctional bureaucracy served a purpose: bureaucratic routines and pseudo-rational behavior obscured personal and organizational realities, allowing people to detach from their inner experiences, thereby reducing anxiety.

These social defenses are still very much present, albeit not as strong today as they were at the height of communism. This 'bureau pathological' element in Russian society contributes to the Russian perception that people are subjected to forces over which they have very little or no control. Ironically, however, the same bureaucratic routines that offer comfort make it hard to get anything done. Managing an organization 'by rules' is well-nigh impossible once the rules take on a life of their own. As a consequence, when rules proliferate, so do loopholes. During the Soviet regime, Russians became expert at finding subtle ways to beat the system. Knowing that a frontal attack on authority was dangerous, they had no ambition to reform the system. They preferred instead to step back, endure, go around, and find another solution.

As we saw earlier, Russians have long combined outward civility with inward disobedience (Hamilton *et al.*, 1995). They rebel against regimentation, however, whenever they can get away with it. Therein lies one of the great paradoxes of Russia: the Russian people developed rigid programming of activities as an expression of great discomfort with uncertainty (their preference being for predictability and stability); but now, with the process reversed, they have a strong desire to overturn that programming.

Unfortunately, there are still many organizations (particularly in the public sector) where petty bureaucrats—people who can make life extremely difficult for others—seem to be in control. This problem needs to be dealt with if Russians hope to be players in the global market economy.

Paranoia: Legacy of the Tsars

Russia has had more than its share of tyrannical rulers and the Tsar legacy created a preference for strong leaders long before Lenin or Stalin came along. The tyranny of Lenin and Stalin was foreshadowed by the terrifying rule of Ivan the Terrible in the sixteenth century, the authoritarian controllers instituted by Peter the Great in the seventeenth and eighteenth centuries (and further refined by Catherine the Great), and the autocratic role of Nicholas I in the nineteenth century. The communists only strengthened a centralized authoritarian system that started centuries ago.

Most tsars saw any form of criticism against their rule as *lèse-majesté*, a challenge to their sovereignty, and responded with banishment or even death. This coercive process created in Russians a perception of humankind as basically evil. Even today Russians tend to assume that people will exploit others for personal gain and view the social environment beyond their immediate circle of family members and close friends as dangerous. Vladimir Putin's outlook is not much different.

Because of this outlook—especially in conjunction with what we know about Russian child-rearing—Russians have always sustained a deep ambivalence toward authority. Anarchists have always found a place among them. Even under the tsars there was an enormous amount of revolutionary activity, with very bloody results (Figes, 1998). The central role of informers in Russian life has contributed to this deep ambivalence toward authority. The various governments of Russia, from the tsars' repressive regimes through communism, have used informers to control the population, backing their authority with terrifying institutions—the *Oprichnina* under Ivan the Terrible, the *Cheka* under Lenin, the KGB under Stalin, and now the Federal Security System under Vladimir Putin.

This paranoid *Weltanschauung* has been reinforced by the collectivist nature of Russian society. Collectivist cultures tend to be more distrustful than others of outsiders (Triandis, 1972; Triandis *et al.*, 1988), distinguishing clearly between in-groups and out-groups (and regarding the latter with suspicion). The sense of being besieged by external forces has been a recurring theme throughout Russian history and has, indeed, a basis in reality. Russia has always been surrounded by adversaries; in addition, it has been infiltrated by informers and other native opponents. For much of its history, Russia has been simultaneously waging war externally and struggling to maintain order internally.

This mistrust of foreigners has been reinforced by institutions such as the Russian Orthodox Church and the Communist Party, both deeply suspicious of the outside world, and sometimes hostile to it. Under the banner of communist internationalism, the world was kept at bay until the coming of *glasnost* and *perestroika* in the late 1980s.

Unfortunately, given the nature of the business environment in Russia, someone with a paranoid outlook can always find a reality that meets expectations (and certainly the pervasiveness of the Russian mafia and the Federal Security Service keeps this climate of conspiracy alive).

Culture and Organization

Avoidance of Reality

Russians have difficulty facing facts that are perceived as unpleasant. When the truth is evaded too often, however, reality and fantasy become blurred.

This avoidance of reality reached incredible heights under the State Planning Committee (GOSPLAN). Because decision-making was imposed from above, people charged with the day-to-day operation of the enterprise—whether company or government agency—were relieved of the task of setting realistic plans and targets. This led to an abdication of personal responsibility for the work that needed to be done.

This decision-making process made for extremely unrealistic production targets. What developed was a finely tuned, deeply rooted practice of deceiving higher authority. Many executives spent all their energy trying to reduce often excessive targets set from above and to shift responsibility to others. They colluded with managers and local Party officials to cook the books and deceive the higher-ups about the real levels of output in the factory or on the farm. 'In principle it can be done,' was a manager's favored response to authority. But that attitude led to what by Western standards were irrational, cost-ineffective behaviors, such as maintaining extremely high inventories of finished goods, hoarding materials and labor, and accepting unconnected goods that could be bartered for badly needed supplies.

During GOSPLAN days, 'storming'—working in a mad frenzy to fulfill certain agreed-upon quotas—was part of the routine. Crash programs became a national pastime. This fire-fighting mode of 'storming' is still typical of many organizations in Russia. Setting goals for the future is not a high priority. Long-term planning and strategic thinking are often taken with a pinch of salt. In most organizations, short-term survival is what counts (Michailova, 1997).

The Fluidity of Time

Russians do not see time as a finite resource, structured in a sequential and linear fashion (Hall and Hall, 1990). Rather, they see it as a loose entity or even non-existent. This perspective is a legacy of their agricultural heritage: on the farm, time is multi-focused, expanding as necessary to accommodate a variety of activities. Thus Russians plan activities concurrently, causing considerable fragmentation. In Russian business dealings, constant interruption is the norm, punctuality is often disregarded, deadlines are seen as mere suggestions, and scheduling is difficult.

This polychromic view of time reflects the fact that Russia is a 'being', not a 'doing', culture (Hall, 1966, 1973; Laurent, 1983). Russians tend to be contemplative rather than action- or task-oriented. As mentioned earlier, their activities are relationship-centered. Experience counts more than goal accomplishment or achievement. The harsh climate of Russia has certainly contributed to this 'being' orientation: when people feel that they have little control over nature, they are not as inclined to take action.

Moreover, Russians demonstrate a greater preoccupation with the past than is the case in other cultures. In contrast to Americans, for example, they are more concerned with seeing things in a historical context—Russians place a high value on the continuation of tradition. They readily acknowledge—in spite of the attempts during the time of communism to reconstruct history—that their present and future are influenced by their past. This orientation affects their attitude toward change. Change is perceived with apprehension because it threatens long-established traditions. The result is an 'if it ain't broke, don't fix it' mentality.

RUSSIA'S TRANSITION: FROM COOPERATIVES TO CAPITALISM

In 1987 Mikhail Gorbachev, then General Secretary of the Communist Party, dealt a mortal blow to the communist system and the centrally planned economy, when the Soviet Parliament approved the so-called Law on Co-operative Movement, authorizing the creation of co-operatives. The co-operatives were to be private enterprises, owned by at least three people. That law unleashed the pent-up entrepreneurial energy of the Russian people, and led to a dramatic transformation in Russia in the years that followed. The early cooperatives were hothouses for young Russians fascinated by the idea of a free-market economy. Some of them were to become future billionaires—among them, Mikhail Khodorkovsky (now in a prison cell at the Chinese border) and Mikhail Friedman—and hundreds of thousands were to become millionaires. Millions of Russians became entrepreneurs. The co-operatives also fostered the creation of industries new to Russia, such as investment banking and cellular telephony. By 2003, only 15 years after the Law on Co-operative Movement went into effect, the private sector represented 70% of the Russian economy (*Handbook of Russian Statistics*, 2003).

One can hardly overestimate the importance of private entrepreneurs' contribution to the recent history of Russia. Today, however, as their businesses grow and mature, these entrepreneurs face new challenges in transforming loosely structured start-ups into large-scale, efficient organizations (Kets de Vries, 2000; Puffer and McCarthy, 2001; Kets de Vries, Korotov, and Shekshnia, 2008). These challenges are to some extent similar to those of entrepreneurial ventures elsewhere in the world, and therefore the experience of business leaders from developed countries can and should serve as worthwhile case material for their Russian peers. However, Russia has a long history of according itself special status in the world, and one result of this is the common assumption in Russia that 'foreign things do not work in this country.' A fascination with Western management practices of the late 1980s and early 1990s was followed by disillusionment for many when those practices failed to produce quick results, reinforcing the traditionally negative attitude of Russian entrepreneurs and business executives (Puffer and McCarthy, 2001). Some of them then embarked on the process of creating a specific Russian business model to restore Russian pride.

The suspicion was often mutual. Business and political leaders outside Russia also have a tendency to put Russian entrepreneurs in a special category, but a far less complimentary one. The entrepreneurs were often called 'new robber barons' or, more simply, 'robbers.' Their success was chalked up either to the dubious support of a Russian mafia or to less violent but equally pervasive government corruption. The term 'new Russian' was almost universally considered derogatory, denoting wealth built on the backs of exploited and befuddled Russian workers tricked out of their heritage during the time of mass privatization of state-owned property in the early 1990s.

Since 1998, I have been studying the new Russian business élite and I have identified the emergence of a group of business leaders whose success has been built on their own efforts and drive rather than on political connections. They have created organizational systems and structures that draw on Western (or Asian) best practices, and yet remain uniquely Russian.

NEW LEADERS AND NEW FOLLOWERS

There are two kinds of leaders at the top of successful companies:

1. 'Russian' Russians, who retained a faintly xenophobic attitude toward Western organizations. These Russians were convinced that they should move into relationships with Western partners only with great caution. They sought to build 100% Russian organizations. Many of the businessmen with a KGB background fall under this category.
2. 'Global Russians,' who have gained respect within the Russian business community and internationally. Many trade actively with

foreign partners, acting as both vendors and buyers of goods and services. Some of the organizations led by new-generation executives are actively pursuing foreign investment, attracting shareholders globally. Some of them remain quite idealistic (perhaps too idealistic), believing that Western management practices are the answer to all ills—and they are very disappointed when this idea proves wrong, as it inevitably does.

Older Leaders: the Process of Unlearning

For the 'Russian' Russians the main challenge is unlearning. These people are mainly the administrators and bureaucrats who used to supervise the 120 000 factories, farms, and other industrial units of the former USSR, who will need to replace their authoritarian mentality with a dramatically different mindset. This group is not homogeneous, however; there are two distinct subgroups.

One belongs to Russia's present business élite. With deep roots in communism and a sturdy foundation of wealth and power, many of them were well-enough connected to retain their privileged positions through the post-*glasnost* period. These people have used the new openness as an opportunity to unleash their previously constrained entrepreneurial potential. In setting up new enterprises, they are making a valuable contribution to the market economy.

The other subgroup among the older generation, having retained the Soviet mentality, focused on self-preservation. These people derived their power from their political skills in the old Soviet bureaucracy and from knowing both how to play the system and how to manipulate and control their employees. Many of these are the political elite, heirs to the old Soviet *nomenklatura* who saw how the wind was blowing and took advantage of privatization programs, acquiring precious state companies at well below their value. Aware that in today's shifting Russian society they could lose their privileges, they make whatever superficial adjustments are needed to maintain their status. Despite giving lip service to the new economy, they run their private monopolies in the same way they ran the state monopoly. They apparently subscribe to the 'Russian doll' school of management: after the doll (or economic system) is taken apart, a similar doll is found inside. Reluctant to make the kind of dramatic adjustments needed to be truly effective in the new global economy, and uncommitted to the new values that underlie such adjustments, this group may not be able to master the skills needed to run an enterprise without state protection.

The New 'Global Russian': Open to New Opportunities

New global Russians are nascent entrepreneurs—young, enthusiastic, talented people—who recognize the opportunities the new open society presents. This group also includes former black marketers turning to legitimate business and children of the *nomenklatura* whose original career path via the Komsomol (communist youth league) no longer exists, but who have been able to adapt to the new circumstances. What these individuals have in common is that they see the creation of business as an opportunity. They know how to deal with the 'Wild East' environment. Thriving under chaos, they are able to deal both with long-term, discontinuous problems and with short-term, routine problems. More achievement-oriented and focused on the success of their enterprise, this new generation will have the drive, the energy, and the motivation to move Russia ahead. They will be less inclined to pass the buck—more willing to take responsibility for their actions.

The Changing Workforce

As Russian business practices have matured, so has the Russian labor force. There are more and more individuals with Western business education and experience, and even those with no international experience have been exposed to Western business ideas and concepts, now included in educational curricula at universities in Russia. As the challenges of organizations become more complex, this growing corps of talented young managers may become both a blessing and a curse for top executives.

New ways of doing business are necessitating new ways of managing talent. The leaders of the organizations that I have studied embody a wide range of approaches to managing their human resources. Some treat their workers as disposable commodities, while others see their people as their most important capital and treat them accordingly, investing heavily in their training and development, both in financial and emotional terms. The very concept of human resource management is itself new to Russia (Jukova and Korotov, 1998).

Managing Human Resources

Human resource efforts in the new Russia need to respond to people's motivational systems in an effort to encourage creativity and innovation. Better selection processes can help ambitious companies identify people who are able to function in a market economy. Additionally, companies need to address the need for performance appraisal systems, cross-cultural training, and management development (see below).

Under the communist system, people were selected for their positions because of their ties to the Communist Party or the military. Administrators moved from the Komsomol to a trade union position, and then to a party position (and then another and another). Compensation—often supplemented with perks such as cars, special housing, *dachas*, or medical services—was linked to job hierarchy rather than performance. Complete job security was the norm and there were no incentives for working hard, or harder. The Communist Party controlled management appointments in the business world, and those appointments carried little prestige. Most people saw them as transitional steps and aspired to move past them into high-level Party work. *Perestroika* ended all that. Jobs are less secure these days, and individual contributions to the success of an organization are increasingly important factors in assessment. Variable financial reward systems such as profit sharing and bonuses are becoming more common. New, radically different career paths are on the horizon.

Performance and accountability Singling out individuals for special financial reward because of their extraordinary contributions, however, violates the basic Russian urge to equalize. This element of the Russian character is a serious impediment to new business creation. Successful business people are quickly labeled profiteers—a label reinforced by the behavior of the new oligarchs. But gradually, as the new generation of executives becomes more influential, that perception is likely to change.

They advocate that accountability needs to be driven deep down into organizations by creating profit or responsibility centers. The new Russian leaders realize that specific responsibility and authority over organizational sub-units need to be delegated to executives (at all levels).

If the Russians who attempt to reinvent a new human resource management agenda are to succeed, they must build on the Russian cultural heritage, however. Business leaders must work with existing values and reshape them in a way that Russians will accept and internalize. In this process, a reinvented concept of leadership will be essential.

Management Development

Russian organizations are most likely to achieve a productive corporate renewal process if change management is initiated at senior levels. Many executives who have the will to change lack the skill to do so. There is no real tradition of management education in Russia, and executive training, if any, is directed toward running a centrally planned economy. Russian executives need to be given the tools to learn other ways of doing things. Even something as basic as the language of business needs attention. Many Russian executives, new to the concepts of free enterprise, lack the vocabulary to communicate effectively about productivity, free pricing, competition, markets, customer satisfaction, new forms of corporate governance, and profits. Most Russian executives are also unfamiliar with fundamental psychological concepts. They frequently treat their employees like robots and have little respect for them. Because the technocratic imperative has ruled for so long, the human factor is rarely included in the productivity equation.

The learning process can be accelerated via the exchange of 'best practices,' in other words, via benchmarking with successful companies. Although there is no tradition of benchmarking in Russia—given the communist era's legacy of secrecy and information-hoarding, and the fact that lateral relationships between economic units were uncommon—it is a process that holds great promise.

EIGHT LEADERSHIP LESSONS

Lesson 1: Be Flexible with Self and Environment

Many of the more effective leaders in present-day Russia have an internal 'locus of control'; they feel able to control their environment and have a strong sense of self-efficacy (Rotter, 1966; Bandura, 1989). In addition, they are motivated by a desire to continually develop their potential. They have a capacity to reinvent themselves, and reorient their organizations, with a rapidity rarely seen at the top of modern corporations outside Russia.

Lesson 2: Create Leadership Networks

In a collectivist culture such as Russia, relationships are far more important than rules. Global Russian business leaders are exceptionally good at creating and maintaining networks of all kinds, in which they position themselves as the essential hub. This is one reason why some have been very effective in forming successful partnerships with foreign partners.

Lesson 3: Strive to be a Catalyst of Change

The new Russian business leaders proactively shape the environment, establishing the rules of the game for business organizations, rather than waiting for the government to do it for them. In the early days of capitalism a handful of entrepreneurs pushed hard for accelerated privatization. They ended up with extremely valuable assets for themselves, but arguably also gave a great boost to private economy development in Russia.

Lesson 4: Develop Tenacity

Once they had decided on a course of action, all the leaders I have studied were persistent and resilient. Persistence and resilience go hand in hand with an ability to frame events in a positive way and to regard failures as opportunities.

Lesson 5: Cultivate Emotional Intelligence

Russian business leaders are good at reading the emotional state of their counterparts and using it to their own personal advantage. This application of emotional intelligence skills by Russian business leaders may be manipulative when done consciously, but nonetheless works extremely well.

Lesson 6: Use a Council of Boyars

Behind most successful global leaders of any nationality, there is a well-balanced executive team. But there is a uniquely Russian twist to the concept of executive role constellations: Russian leaders often work with a handful of trusted collaborators who operate quietly, out of the limelight, to support the leader's position. (This inner circle is sometimes called *Boyarskaya Duma*, or the Council of Boyars, after the influential advisory body to the tsar, later dissolved by Peter the Great.) Within the shadowy protection of the Council of Boyars, leaders can discuss their ideas, concerns, and doubts in private, preserving their highly self-confident public image. This Russian inner circle often works according to the model of 'democratic centralism': everybody has a say in the discussion, the leader makes the final decision, and that decision becomes a law for all.

Lesson 7: Foster a Charismatic Leadership Style

Whatever a Russian leader's competencies and management style, he or she has an enormous amount of power within the organization, simply by virtue of their position. The Russian people have an archaic cultural need for powerful charismatic leaders, assuming that their leaders are superior beings who have unique rights and, by definition, deserve compliance. This attitude on the part of Russian workers gives Russian business leaders far greater room for maneuvering than their Western counterparts have.

Lesson 8: Manage Meaning

Despite the difference in the scope and complexity of businesses headed by the leaders mentioned so far all the men and women have one thing in common: they actively employ the concept of a mission—an overarching goal—in mobilizing the efforts of their people.

CHALLENGES FOR GLOBAL RUSSIAN BUSINESS LEADERS

The collective wisdom generated through these eight leadership lessons has enabled many Russian business leaders to make unprecedented advances, and enormous profits, in the newly opened market economy in Russia. However, there are still many demands on Russian leaders, as they and their organizations mature—challenges that they should prepare themselves to face in the near future.

Challenge 1: Identify and Develop Successors

Leadership succession represents the single largest challenge for global Russian leaders. Russian business leaders can learn something from the rest of the world about effective succession planning. None of the entrepreneurs I met was planning to hand their organizations over to their own children, nor had they shown much interest in preparing younger employees to take over as business executives (possibly because they are quite young themselves). However, time marches on, and professional management succession is becoming a more urgent challenge for all these leaders. Whatever form that succession takes, it will be successful only if the leader takes the issue seriously and regards it as the number one priority, personally as well as professionally.

Challenge 2: Build Trust

The general lack of trust in today's Russian organizations is the second largest threat to Russian organizations. Russian leaders have to learn to instill a climate of trust in order to foster creativity. Too many of them have created a 'Darwinian soup,' meaning the survival of the fittest—not a very appropriate way to deal with human capital. In addition, Russian organizations must become more open to the outside world. Rather than thinking of themselves as fortresses besieged by enemy armies, they need to develop open systems that benefit from give-and-take within an ever-changing environment. To foster this, continuous learning and development should be part of the organizational architecture.

Challenge 3: Protect Assets and Manage Government Relations

Vladimir Putin and his entourage from the secret services consolidated unprecedented power in Russia. As a result, the owners of large businesses are seriously concerned about the protection of their assets, and smaller entrepreneurs fear power abuse at the regional and local levels. New power dynamics have created important challenges for individual entrepreneurs, but this issue tests the stability and maturity of Russian industries and markets within the whole business community in Russia.

Challenge 4: Build 21st century Organizations

The leaders we studied are, in many ways, the frontrunners in the process of business development in Russia: transforming the prevalent organizational model from the old 'command and control' paradigm to a new 3I organizational structure in which information, innovation, and involvement—the three Is—are key values (Kets de Vries, 2000). This work is not yet complete, but the trend is impressive and encouraging for others. The experiences of these leaders can be distilled into some key objectives for future development:

- To be competitive, businesses should be designed for long-term value creation. If, in the past, most Russians saw every business as a cash-producing black box, the new global Russians have learned to create organizations that see transparent relationships with stakeholders and respect for the social and physical environment as prerequisites for steady growth.
- To compete in the global world, Russian businesses should also develop the organizational competencies mastered by their international rivals—speed and flexibility, customer-orientation and productive innovation, information-sharing, and continuous learning.
- Russian business leaders need to practice empowerment and delegation. Employers must learn to no longer rely on hundreds of rigid procedures to regulate all aspects of internal life. Networks, virtual or otherwise, should replace hierarchy.
- Information has always been regarded as a sacred source of power in Russian organizations. It has been secretly collected, stored, classified, and traded for very high stakes, including human lives. These practices have resurfaced in many new Russian companies, creating enormous barriers to the information flow. The real challenge is to create information systems that support the sharing of data and best practices, and that strengthen corporate values. Cross-functional projects, job rotation, and geographical moves should encourage communication and co-operation at all levels.

Adapting a new organizational model will require abandoning some of the current well-established practices and behaviors of executives, middle managers, and employees. This fundamental transformation will require strong leadership from the top and effective change agents at all organizational levels. Successful entrepreneurs turned corporate executives are likely to provide high-level leadership. They should look for support to Western executives and professionals with experience in Russian organizations; to so-called hybrids—that is, Russian managers with Western experience returning home; and to Russian graduates of Western business schools. Eventually, Russians should establish their own well-functioning system of management education.

THE END OF THE BEGINNING

Previous generations of Russian leaders largely failed to provide their people with positive direction and a productive organizational environment. They led them into bloody wars and revolutions, devastating political and economic experiments, intellectual oppression and physical destruction. Now, as the center of gravity in Russian society moves from politics toward economics, new business leaders are emerging as a principal force shaping the society and its future. Are these people, who built their wealth and influence on the ruins of the Soviet Empire, capable of leading their nation to prosperity, civil society, personal freedom, and openness?

The signals are mixed so far, as traditional behavior and attitudes still act as a strong undertow. Russia has not fully mourned its devastating past, and influential forces in the society still push it toward chauvinism and federalism. However, one thing is clear: young Russians who decide to take control of their destiny and to embark on an entrepreneurial career will no longer have to do the hard labor of path-breaking. There is now an impressive diversity of successful Russian role models for them to follow. Global Russians have collectively created a hybrid leadership model, flexible enough to reflect the requirements of different types of organizations that will serve not only a new generation of Russian entrepreneurs, but also other business professionals engaged in creating organizations that will provide sustainable returns in global markets.

ENDNOTES

Much of the material in this chapter is taken from the following three articles already printed elsewhere:

- Kets de Vries, M.F.R. (2000). 'A journey into the "Wild East": Leadership style and organisational practices in Russia,' *Organisational Dynamics*, **28** (4): 67–81.
- Kets de Vries, M.F.R. (2001). 'The anarchist within: Clinical reflections on Russian character and leadership style,' *Human Relations*, **54** (5): 585–627.

- Kets de Vries, M.F.R., Shekshnia, S., Korotov, K., and Florent-Treacy, E. (2004). 'The new global Russian business leaders: Lessons from a decade of transition,' *European Management Journal*, **22** (6): 637–648.

1. Social defenses are systems of relationships, reflected in the social structure, constructed to help people control and contain feelings of anxiety in difficult situations. They function like individual defenses, but they are sewn into the very fabric of a society.

CONCLUSION: CREATING HIGH-COMMITMENT ORGANIZATIONS

I long to accomplish a great and noble task, but it is my chief duty to accomplish humble tasks as though they were great and noble. The world is moved along, not only by the mighty shoves of its heroes, but also by the aggregate of the tiny pushes of each honest worker.

—Helen Keller

THE FUTURE OF ORGANIZATIONS

A father had a family of sons who quarreled among themselves perpetually. When he failed to put an end to their disputes by his exhortations, he decided to give them a practical illustration of the evils of disharmony. One day, he told them to bring him a bundle of sticks. He put the bundle of sticks into the hands of each of them in succession and ordered them to break it into pieces. They tried with all their might but could not do so. He then undid the bundle of sticks, took them one by one, and put them into his sons' hands. They broke them easily. He then addressed them in these word: 'My sons, if you are of one mind, and unite to help each other, you will be like this bundle of sticks, uninjured by all your enemies' attacks; but if you are divided among yourselves, you will be broken as easily as these sticks.'

This fable of the ancient story teller Aesop is a very good illustration of the power of teamwork, an essential quality of high performance organizations. The fable also illustrates the kind of leadership that will be required to make organizations effective.

But what are the implications of the inevitable march of globalization on the nature of leadership? What does excellence mean in the global organization and by what criteria should it be judged? I have tried to unearth some answers to these questions by looking at the results of a large number of consultations and research projects that I have conducted in global organizations.

Although many structural dimensions of the global corporation have been identified, very few researchers have touched on the underlying drivers of the most successful among such corporations. I concluded from my discussions with top executives from global corporations that only when leaders establish a state of complementarity with the universal motivational need system of their followers (whatever their national culture may be) will global organizations (like any organization) blossom. To be a successful global corporation, vision, mission, and cultural and strategic factors in an organization have to be aligned with the motivational need systems of employees. Without such alignment, no organization can be truly effective on a global scale. Although there is no easy solution to the development of leaders in a global age, companies, however, that carefully select and strategically develop people with leadership qualities that are adapted to the new requirements, and use them at all levels in the organization, will have a competitive edge. To be more specific, organizations that are best places to work pay attention to the values that are really important to their employees. Unfortunately, many organizations—and this includes the global ones—are anything but best places to work.

META-VALUES FOR GREAT COMPANIES

Although CEOs worldwide are fascinated by global organizations, their employees do not always share their enthusiasm. I have observed a great deal of dissatisfaction among the people who work in such corporations. As a matter of fact, the global corporation has increasingly come under attack, as local communities have had to deal with the consequences of decisions made completely outside their sphere of influence. Leaders of a car manufacturer may strive for optimum use of the company's resources, whatever the locale may be, but it's the little person who has to bear the brunt of a plant closure in his or her hometown.

Psychological consequences can be every bit as tough to take as plant closures, and yet global managers often ignore what might be called the cultural repercussions of their actions. A hire-and-fire mentality that is acceptable in one country may be totally unacceptable for people in a culture where job security is a major life anchor—and yet a global manager lacking a geocentric orientation would apply that mentality universally. For example, one Spanish entrepreneur I worked with was delighted that high-potential employees were voluntarily leaving the local subsidiary of a large global corporation in droves, because many of them were coming to work for her. They joined the Spanish entrepreneur after being, in their words, 'burned out and used up' by the constant rounds of restructuring in the large global organization. Incidents of employee dissatisfaction like this clearly illustrate the significant difficulties faced by global organizations in their attempts to implement a geocentric orientation and a culture in which all employees feel part of the global 'family.'

Unfortunately, feelings of mistrust and anxiety are frequently common among employees in global organizations. Too often, the 'FUD factor' dominates the organizational culture, meaning Fear, Uncertainty, and Doubt poisons the atmosphere. And the presence of these negative attitudes is ominous since it is important that all employees, down to the shop floor, feel part of the global team. But achieving a strong sense of teamwork makes considerable demands on organizational leaders. How can the loyalty of the thousands or hundreds of thousands of employees in a global organization be generated?

Almost all the global leaders I interviewed said (often without knowing exactly how to do it) that one of their main priorities was to establish and maintain a corporate culture that transcends cultural differences and to establish 'beacons': values and attitudes that are comprehensible and compelling for employees with diverse backgrounds and cultural differences. So how does a leader create that kind of corporate culture? What can be done to diffuse employee anxiety and foster loyalty, trust, and teamwork among widely diverse groups?

MOTIVATIONAL NEED SYSTEMS

The conclusion that I reached after completing the interviews was surprisingly consistent across the companies involved. The leaders in the organization have to provide focus, are seen as decisive, need to be viewed as possessing integrity and honesty—all conditions favorable to high performance—but the most effective leaders also connect with a universal layer of human functioning that prompts people to make a greater-than-usual effort. Such leaders recognize (consciously or unconsciously) the existence of the basic motivational need systems present in all human beings. When they pay attention to these needs, their employees make an extraordinary effort.

Some human motivational need systems are designed to ensure our basic survival. One regulates our physiological needs for food, water, sleep, and breathing, for example. Another handles the need for sensual enjoyment and, later, sexual excitement. A third deals with the need to respond to situations perceived as threatening, through either antagonism or withdrawal. Although these three motivational need systems have a determining effect on the way people work, there are two additional systems that more directly impact the way people behave in organizations: attachment/affiliation and exploration/assertion:

- The need for *attachment/affiliation* can be expressed simply as a need for human connectedness. This need is met in organizations through a perception of community, of belonging, and through the creation of a group identity.
- Our *exploratory/assertive* needs are closely associated with learning and personal growth. This need system lays the foundation for creativity and strategic innovation. It is also addressed through having fun, experiencing pleasure, and knowing enjoyment.

Best places to work make an effort to respond to these needs. In particular, they pay attention to three meta-values: community, pleasure, and meaning.

- **Community** The leaders of successful global organizations nurture good-citizenship behavior. The prevailing attitude within such organizations is one of mutual support, respect, and collaboration. Teamwork is a mantra in these organizations: workers subordinate their individual agendas to the well-being of the group.
- **Pleasure** In successful global organizations, having fun by doing new things—which results in continuous learning, creativity, and innovation—is an essential part of the organization culture. Predictably, this makes people more productive.
- **Meaning** As one CEO said, 'People will work for money but die for a cause.' Meaning constitutes a very powerful motivational force for many people. People come to realize that there's not so much to be gained from being the richest person in the graveyard. It is extremely motivating for employees to feel that as individuals they are contributing something to society through their efforts, and this sense of meaning motivates people toward higher commitment.

World-class leaders in successful global corporations go to great lengths to create congruence between these personal needs and the fundamental purpose of the organization. Let's look at each of these meta-values in more detail.

Community

Knowing that true teamwork is extremely difficult to achieve without trust, excellent leaders put a high priority on establishing trust in their organizations. Toward that end, such leaders are very accessible and don't misuse the power of their position. Nor do they practice mushroom treatment (keeping people in the dark); on the contrary, they keep their people fully informed. They run very transparent organizations. Because they are interested in creating a cohesive community, they also strive to make the entry of new people into the organization a good experience.

In one of my interviews, John Stewart, the former group CEO of the National Australian Bank, talked about how important a cross-border blend of trust and learning is in a global organization. It is worth noting here that many of the more effective leaders possess a 'teddy bear' quality; they have a special knack for containing employees' anxieties during periods of change. It is rare to find someone as people-oriented as John Stewart, who knows how to get the best out of people. Such exemplary executives genuinely care about their people; they take the time to listen to them and help them find solutions when they have personal problems. In this way and many others, such leaders set a good example of what leadership is all about: they are encouraging, they give constructive feedback directly (when such feedback is needed), and they create a safe, positive environment for change. These people have a great ability to motivate others.

Pleasure

In the more effective companies, employees seem to enjoy themselves. Some organizations have found that an atmosphere not just of enjoyment but of controlled exuberance can be highly motivating. Richard Branson tries hard to lead by example in this: he strives to take his people on an exciting journey peppered with fun, thereby gratifying their need for exploration and assertion. He said in one interview with me:

If your staff is happy and smiling and enjoying their work, they will perform well. Consequently, the customers will enjoy their experience with your company. If your staff is sad and miserable and does not have a good time, the customers will be equally miserable. So it is a critical thing ... We've done things differently, and that's made life more fun and enjoyable than if we'd taken the more traditional approach that business schools teach. I've been determined to have a good time.

I have also observed that an emphasis on pleasure is particularly important in large organizations in order to encourage the spirit of innovation. Sir David Simon affirmed this point when asked, during his time as chairman of BP, how he kept this huge company, once considered as sprightly as a supertanker, at the forefront of new developments. When asked what he looked for when picking key executives, Simon replied:

Integrity, enthusiasm, and humor. I think humor is about putting things into perspective. It's about which mirrors you are shining on life, and how you view things ... If people don't have perspective when they get to a level where they have big responsibility, they are potentially dangerous. I like people who are able to defray the pressure of decisions and the pressure of conclusion by taking perspective. Humor is a good indicator of that capacity ... Having fun, the buzz, the humor is, in my view, what makes the difference between the organization being machine-like or a real part of life ... [We ask ourselves] how do we create a buzz—meaning the attitude thing, the fun—so that we are not just another oil company?

Meaning

When people see their jobs as transcending their own personal needs (by improving the quality of life for others, for example, or contributing to society) the impact can be extremely powerful. We all struggle with the temporary nature of things, so we look for ways to leave a legacy, ways to master existential anxiety. Because good experiences are temporary islands in a sea of meaninglessness, finding happiness in any form is a perpetual goal of mankind. We all look for reasons to feel good about what we do. Granted, these reasons are sometimes public-relations–oriented, but CEOs and employees are often driven to engage in something meaningful by genuinely altruistic motives. And the employees know the difference. Successful leaders of global organizations make it clear that they want their people to feel proud of their organizations and to experience a sense of meaning in their daily activities.

To illustrate, companies operating in certain industries have a competitive advantage in this regard—the pharmaceutical industry, for example. Being part of a group of people that is striving to preserve and improve human life through the development of new medicines helps sustain the meta-value of meaning in these organizations. Merck & Co Inc. produces a drug that combats river blindness, a disease common in Africa, Latin America, and Yemen. Since the people in areas most affected by the disease are often unable to pay for treatment, Merck decided to give the drug free of charge, for as long as necessary.

Similarly, the top executives of Novo Nordisk, the world's major insulin producer, have encouraged their employees to collaborate with the international Diabetes Federation in starting projects in developing countries to improve diabetes treatment. The company hands out its products to many people in need, an act that creates a deep sense of meaning for employees. This pervasive commitment to helping people, as observed at close hand by one of my co-authors, is what makes Novo Nordisk such a special company.

Nokia also believes in extending a healing hand as well. In the business of connecting people—not surprisingly for a company that originated in Finland, a country of vast distance—Nokia is a major player in China, taking millions of people from no phones (and no land-line infrastructure) to mobile phones, significantly changing lives in the process. It all amounts to profit with purpose.

Other companies in more traditional heavy industries are also working hard to change their image for employees and the world. Social responsibility is increasingly their rallying cry. In a study of why companies 'go green,' interviewees from ecologically responsible firms were asked why they had undertaken particular ecological responses. They claimed to derive feel-good factors—not just window-dressing—from this type of initiative, resulting in employee satisfaction and high morale. Altruistic satisfaction can be a powerful driver (Kets de Vries, 2009).

LEADERS AND META-VALUE CREATION

Putting these meta-values in place takes careful thought and hard work, but it's an essential investment for organizations in this global age that want to be successful and a best place to work (even mom-and-pop corner stores and local manufacturers reap rewards from their attention to key values). Whether such an investment is made—and made successfully—very much depends on the leadership capabilities of the person or people at the helm. The top executive team need to have the foresight to recognize their own needs for community, pleasure, and meaning, and to externalize and position those needs on a public stage. In addition to that strong foundation of excellent leadership, global leadership also requires openness to diverse cultural experiences—including gender diversity.

Earlier I suggested that the most effective leaders take on two roles, and handle each one well: a *charismatic* role (envisioning a compelling future, empowering followers, and energizing the staff) and an *architectural* role (designing the organization, setting up structures, and formulating control and reward systems). I have also emphasized that these two roles need to be aligned. For example, it is not good enough to preach the value of teamwork but then reward employees individually. From an architectural point of view, effective leaders know that a sense of community will be enhanced when they design their organizations as a set of interconnected small units.

Thus to be a truly effective leader in the global economy means paying attention to the meta-values that drive the employees. It also means alignment between the charismatic and architectural dimensions of leadership. In addition, it requires a cosmopolitan mindset. These leaders must rise above the particularities of many regions and national cultures, while at the same time meeting the expectations of followers in those different cultures. As I discussed in Chapter 13, an outlook of cultural relativity, excellent relational skills, curiosity, and emotional intelligence distinguish successful global leaders. Such leaders also have a strong sense of adventure and are prepared to leave their comfort zone and take risks when needed. Finally, many of them possess a well-developed sense of humor.

CONCLUDING COMMENTS

In this book, we have looked at some of the stock figures in the cast of organizational theatrics—the maverick entrepreneurs who can't find a place where they feel comfortable until they make their own; the dead fish, fakes, and neurotic impostors who are conditioned to suspect their own abilities and successes; and the heroes and villains we all seem to need. Among the great and the good are Alexander of Macedon and the transformational leaders of multinational corporations; the bad and the ugly include Shaka Zulu and a selection of corporate executives, whom I have mercifully allowed to hide behind pseudonyms. The organizational troupe is now taking its productions to a world stage—and the challenge of dealing with individuals and their needs, systems and their impositions, stakeholders and their expectations and demands is now extended across cross-cultural boundaries, as well as time zones.

The good news is that the leaders these organizations need are out there and their numbers are growing. Leaders with a multicultural background, years of cross-cultural work experience, and exceptional global leadership qualities transmit a contagious excitement that puts a company into overdrive. As change-agents, cheerleaders, coaches, teachers, mentors, process consultants, and integrators, these leaders are changing the way their people work by helping them to reframe their attitudes toward work. They are generating in their employees a pride that goes beyond the numbers game and overcomes cultural biases. Their global emotional intelligence should sieve out the Shakas, and encourage the Alexanders, in an environment where everyone feels the confidence to remain true to themselves. And if those leaders need a reminder of what they are striving for, they could do worse than keep close to their hearts Mahatma Gandhi's image of the best place to live and work: 'I do not want my house to be walled in on all sides and my windows to be stuffed. I want the cultures of all lands to be blown about my house as freely as possible. But I refuse to be blown off my feet by any.'

ENDNOTE

Some of this material has been published elsewhere as:

Kets de Vries, M.F.R. and Florent-Treacy, E. (2002). 'Global leadership from A to Z: Creating high-commitment organisations,' *Organisational Dynamics*, **30** (4): 295–309.

REFERENCES

Aarons, Z.A. (1959). 'A study of a perversion and an attendant character disorder,' *Psychoanalytic Quarterly*, **XXVIII** (4), 481–492.

Abagnale, F.W. and Redding, S. *Catch Me if You Can: The Amazing True Story of the Youngest and Most Daring Con Man in the History of Fun and Profit*. New York: First Broadway.

Abraham, K. (1955). 'The history of an impostor in the light of psychoanalytical knowledge,' in *Clinical Papers on Psychoanalysis*. New York: Brunner/Mazel.

Adler, N.J. (1991). *International Dimensions of Organizational Behaviour* (2nd edn). Boston: PWS-Kent.

Adorno, T., Frenkel-Brunswik, E. *et al.* (1950). *The Authoritarian Personality*. New York: Harper.

Ahrens, S. and Deffner, G. (1986). 'Empirical study of alexithymia: methodology and results,' *American Journal of Psychiatry*, **40** (3): 430–477.

American Psychiatric Association (2000). *Diagnostic and Statistical Manual of the Mental Disorder, DSM-IV-TR* (4th edn). Washington, DC: American Psychiatric Association.

Arendt, H. (1969). *On Violence*. New York: Harcourt, Brace & World.

Arendt, H. (1973). *The Origins of Totalitarianism*. New York: Harcourt Brace Jovanovitch.

Arrian (1971). *The Campaigns of Alexander*. Harmondsworth: Penguin Books.

Ashley, J.R. (1997). *The Macedonian Empire: The Era of Warfare under Philip II and Alexander the Great, 359–323 B.C.* New York: McFarland & Co.

Asprey, R.B. (1986). *Frederick the Great: The Magnificent Enigma*. New York: Ticknor & Fields.

Athens, L.H. (1992). *The Creation of Dangerous Violent Criminals*. Urbana: University of Illinois Press.

Auletta, K. (1984). *The Art of Corporate Success: The Story of Schlumberger*. New York: Putnam.

Bandura, A. (1989). 'Perceived self-efficacy in the exercise of personal agency,' *The Psychologist: Bulletin of the British Psychological Society*, **10**: 411–442.

Baumol, W.J. (1968). 'Entrepreneurship in economic theory,' *American Economic Review*, **58** (2).

Baynham, E. (1998). *Alexander the Great: The Unique History of Quintus Curtius*. Ann Arbor: University of Michigan Press.

Bennis, W. and Nanus, B. (1985). *Leaders: Strategies for Taking Charge*. New York: Harper & Row.

Bergler, E. (1937). 'A clinical contribution to the psychogenesis of humor,' *Psychoanalytic Review*, **24**: 34–53.

Bergson, H. (1928). *Laughter: An Essay on the Meaning of the Comic* (transl. C. Brereton and F. Rothwell). New York: Macmillan.

Berlyne, D.E. (1964). 'Laughter, humor, and play,' in Lindzey, G. and Aronson, E. (eds), *Handbook of Social Psychology* (Vol. 3). Reading, Massachusetts: Addison-Wesley.

Bertelsen, A., Harvald, B. and Hauge, M. (1977). 'A Danish twin study of manic-depressive disorders,' *British Journal of Psychiatry*, **130**: 330–351.

Bion, W.R. (1961). *Experiences in Groups*. London: Tavistock.

Birch, P. (2000). *Imagination Engineering: A Toolkit for Business Creativity* (rev. edn). London: Financial Times Prentice Hall.

Blanchard, E.B., Arena, J.G., and Pallmeyer, T.P. (1981). 'Psychosomatic properties of a scale to measure alexithymia,' *Psychotherapy and Psychosomatics*, **35**: 64–71.

Block, S. (1987). 'Humor in group therapy,' in Frye, W.F. and Salameh, W.A. (eds), *Handbook of Humor and Psychotherapy*. Sarasota: Professional Resources Exchange.

Blum, H.P. (1983). 'The psychoanalytic process and analytic influence: A clinical study of a lie and loss,' *International Journal of Psychoanalysis*, **64**: 17–33.

Boesche, R. (1996). *Theories of Tyranny: From Plato to Arendt*. University Park, Penn: Pennsylvania State University Press.

Bosworth, A.B. (1988). *Conquest and Empire: The Reign of Alexander the Great*. Cambridge: Cambridge University Press.

Bowlby, J. (1969) *Attachment and Loss* (Vol. I), *Attachment*. New York: Basic Books.

Breuer, J. and Freud, S. (1893–1895). 'Studies on hysteria,' in Strachey, J. (ed.), *The Standard Edition of the Complete Psychological Works of Sigmund Freud*, Vol 2. London: Hogarth Press/Institute of Psychoanalysis.

Brockhaus, R.H. (1980). 'Risk taking propensity of entrepreneurs,' *Academy of Management Journal*, **23** (3): 509–520.

Brockhaus, R.H. and Horovitz, P.S. (1986). 'The psychology of the entrepreneur,' in Sexton, D.L. (ed.), *The Art and Science of Entrepreneurship*. Cambridge, MA: Ballinger Publishing.

Bronfenbrenner, U. (1970). *Two Worlds of Childhood: US and USSR*. New York: Sage.

Bullock, A. (1962). *Hitler: A Study in Tyranny*. London: Penguin.

Bunzel, R.L. (1932). 'Zuni Katcinas,' *Bureau of American Ethnology Annual Report, 1920–1930*, **47**. Washington, DC: Bureau of American Ethnology.

Bursten, B. (1973). *The Manipulator: A Psychoanalytic View*. New Haven and London: Yale University Press.

Byrd, J. and Brown, P.L. (2003). *The Innovation Equation: Building Creativity and Risk Taking in Your Organization*. San Francisco: Jossey-Bass.

Campbell, J.D. (1953). *Manic-Depressive Disease: Clinical and Psychiatric Significance*. Philadelphia: J.B. Lippincott.

Carlson, S. (1951). *Executive Behavior: A Study of the Workload and the Working Methods of Managing Directors*. Stockholm: Strömberg.

Cawkwell, G. (1981). *Philip of Macedon*. London: Heinemann.

Charles, L.H. (1945). 'The clown's function,' *Journal of American Folklore*, **58**: 25–34.

Chasseguet-Smirgel, J. (1975). *L'Idéal du moi*. Paris: Claude Tchou.

Chirot, D. (1994). *Modern Tyrants*. Princeton, NJ: Princeton University Press.

Clance, P.R. (1985). *The Impostor Phenomenon*. New York: Peachtree Publishing.

Clance, P.R. and Imes, S.A. (1978). 'The impostor phenomenon in high achieving women: Dynamics and therapeutic intervention,' *Psychotherapy: Theory, Research and Practice*, **15** (3): 241–247.

Dabars, Z. and Vokhmina, L. (1995). *The Russian Way*. Lincolnwood, IL: Passport Books.

DeGraff, J. and Lawrence, K.A. (2002). *Creativity at Work: Developing the Right Practices to Make Innovation Happen*. San Francisco: Jossey-Bass.

Des Pres, T. (1976). *The Survivor: An Anatomy of Life in the Death Camps*. New York, Oxford University Press.

Deutsch, H. (1942). 'Some forms of emotional disturbance and their relationship to schizophrenia,' in *Neurosis and Character Types: Clinical Psychoanalytic Studies*. New York: International Universities Press 1965.

Deutsch, H. (1965). *Neuroses and Character Types*. New York: International Universities Press.

Dowling, C. (1981). *The Cinderella Complex*. New York: Summit Books.

Dupont, R.L. (1970). 'The impostor and his mother,' *Journal of Nervous and Mental Disease*, **150** (6): 444–448.

Dupuy, T.N. (1969). *Military Life of Alexander the Great of Macedon*. New York: Watt, Franklin.

Edelson, M. (1993). 'Telling and enacting stories in psychoanalysis,' in Barron, J., Eagle, M. and Wolitzky, D. (eds.), *Interface of Psychoanalysis and Psychology*. Washington, DC: American Psychological Association.

Eklof, B. and Dneprov, E. (eds) (1993). *Democracy in the Russian School: The Reform Movement in Education since 1984*. Boulder, CO: Westview Press.

Erasmus (1971). In Levine, A.H.T. (ed.), *Praise of Folly* (transl. B. Radice). Harmondsworth: Penguin.

Erikson, E. (1975). *Life History and the Historical Moment*. New York: W.W. Norton.

Erikson, E.H. (1958). *Young Man Luther*. New York: W.W. Norton & Co.

Erikson, E.H. (1959). 'Identity and the life cycle,' *Psychological Issues*, **1** (1).

Erikson, E.H. (1963). *Childhood and Society* (2nd edn). New York: W.W. Norton.

Erikson, E.H. (1969) *Gandhi's Truth: On the Origins of Militant Non-violence*. New York: W.W. Norton & Co.

Fenichel, O. (1954). *The Collected Papers of Otto Fenichel* (2nd series). New York: International Universities Press.

Figes, O. (1998). *A People's Tragedy: The Russian Revolution 1891–1924*. New York: Penguin.

Fildes, A. and Fletcher, J. (2001). *Alexander the Great: Son of the Gods*. London: Duncan Baird.

Finkelstein, L. (1974). 'The impostor: Aspects of his development,' *Psychoanalytic Quarterly*, **XLIII** (1): 85–114.

Fisher, S. and Fisher, R.L. (1981). *Pretend the World is Funny and Forever: A Psychological Analysis of Comedians, Clowns, and Actors*. Hillsdale, NJ: Lawrence Erlbaum Associates.

Freud, A. (1966). *The Ego and the Mechanisms of Defense*. Madison, Conn: International Universities Press.

Freud, S. (1900). *The Interpretation of Dreams: The Standard Edition of the Complete Psychological Works of Sigmund Freud*, Vol. 5. London: Hogarth Press/ Institute of Psychoanalysis.

Freud, S. (1905). 'Jokes and their relation to the unconscious,' in Strachey, J. (ed.), *The Standard Edition of the Complete Psychological Works of Sigmund Freud*, Vol 3. London: Hogarth Press/Institute of Psychoanalysis.

Freud, S. (1910). '"Wild" psycho-analysis,' in Strachey, J. (ed.), *The Standard Edition of the Complete Psychological Works of Sigmund Freud*, Vol 11. London: Hogarth Press/Institute of Psychoanalysis.

Freud, S. (1916). 'Some character types met within psychoanalytic work,' in Strachey, J. (ed.), *The Standard Edition of the Complete Psychological Works of Sigmund Freud*, Vol 14. London: Hogarth Press/Institute of Psychoanalysis.

Freud, S. (1921). 'Group psychology and the analysis of the ego,' in Strachey, J. (ed.), *The Standard Edition of the Complete Psychological Works of Sigmund Freud*, Vol. 18. London: Hogarth Press/Institute of Psychoanalysis.

Freud, S. (1927). 'Humor,' in Strachey, J. (ed.), *The Standard Edition of the Complete Psychological Works of Sigmund Freud*, Vol 11. London: Hogarth Press/Institute of Psychoanalysis.

Freud, S. (1933). *New Introductory Lectures: The Standard Edition of the Complete Psychological Works of Sigmund Freud*, (Strachey, J. (ed.)), Vol. 22. London: Hogarth Press/Institute of Psychoanalysis.

Freud, S. (1939). *Moses and Monotheism: The Standard Edition of the Complete Psychological Works of Sigmund Freud*, (Strachey, J. (ed.)), Vol. 23. London: Hogarth Press/Institute of Psychoanalysis.

Friedrich, C. (1954). *Totalitarianism*. Cambridge, Mass: Harvard University Press.

Friedrich, C. and Brezezinsky, Z. (1965). *Totalitarian Dictatorship and Autocracy.* Cambridge: Harvard University Press.

Fromm, E. (1973). *The Anatomy of Human Destructiveness.* New York: Holt, Rinehart & Winston.

Fry, W. and Allen, M. (1975). *Make 'em laugh.* Palo Alto: Science and Behavior Books.

Fuller, J.F.C. (1989). *The Generalship of Alexander the Great.* New York: Da Capo Press.

Fuller Torrey, E. and Knable, M.B. (2002). *Surviving Manic Depression: A Manual on Bipolar Disorder for Patients, Families, and Providers.* New York: Basic Books.

Fynn, H.F. (1950). *The Diary of Henry Francis Fynn.* Pietermaritzburg: Shuter & Shooter.

Gardner, H. (1993). *Creating Minds: An Anatomy of Creativity Seen through the Lives of Freud, Einstein, Picasso, Stravinsky, Eliot, Graham, and Gandhi.* New York: Basic Books.

Gartner, W.B. (1989). 'Some suggestions for research on entrepreneurial traits and characteristics,' *Entrepreneurship Theory and Practice,* **14** (1): 27–38.

Gediman, H.K. (1985). 'Imposture, inauthenticity and feeling fraudulent,' *Journal of the American Psychoanalytic Association,* **33** (4), 911–935.

Geertz, C. (1973). *The Interpretation of Culture.* New York: Basic Books.

Geertz, C. (1983). *Local Knowledge.* New York: Basic Books.

Glass, J.M. (1995). *Psychosis and Power: Threats to Democracy in the Self and the Group.* Ithaca: Cornell University Press.

Goffman, E. (1967). *Interaction Ritual.* Garden City: Anchor Books.

Goffman, I. (1971). *Relations in Public.* New York: Harper Colophon Books.

Goldenberg, J. and Mazursky, D. (2002). *Creativity in Product Innovation.* Cambridge, New York: Cambridge University Press.

Gottdiener, A. (1982). 'The impostor,' *Contemporary Psychoanalysis,* **18** (3): 438–454.

Grand, H.G. (1973). 'The masochistic defense of the "double mask": Its relationship to imposture,' *International Journal of Psychoanalysis,* **54**: 445–454.

Green, P. (1991). *Alexander of Macedon.* Berkeley: University of California Press.

Greenacre, P. (1958). *Emotional Growth, Psychoanalytic Studies of the Gifted and a Great Variety of Other Individuals.* New York: International Universities Press.

Greenson, R.R. (1967). *The Technique and Practice of Psychoanalysis,* Vol. I. New York: International Universities Press.

Grossman, D. (1996). *On Killing: The Psychological Cost of Learning to Kill in War and Society.* Boston: Little, Brown.

Grossman, W.I. (1986). 'Notes on masochism: A discussion of the history and development of a psychoanalytic concept,' *Psychoanalytic Quarterly,* **LV** (3): 379–413.

Hagen, E. (1962). *On the Theory of Social Change.* Homewood, IL: Dorsey Press.

Hall, E.T. (1966). *The Hidden Dimension*. Garden City, NY: Doubleday.

Hall, E.T. (1973). *The Silent Language*. Garden City, NY: Anchor Press.

Hall, E.T. and Hall, M.R. (1990). *Understanding Cultural Differences*. Yarmouth, ME: Intercultural Press.

Hamilton, V.L., Sanders, J., and McKearney, S.J. (1995). 'Orientations toward authority in an authoritarian state: Moscow in 1990,' *Personality and Social Psychology Bulletin*, **21** (4): 356–365.

Hammond, N.G.L. (1993). *Sources for Alexander the Great*. Cambridge: Cambridge University Press.

Handbook of Russian Statistics (Rossiysky Statistichesky Sbornik) (2003). Moscow: Goskomstat.

Harlow, H.F. and Harlow, M.K. (1965). 'The affectional systems,' in Schrier, A.M., Harlow, H.F., and Stollnitz, F. (eds), *Behavior of Nonhuman Primates*. New York and London: Academic Press.

Hartocollis, P. and Graham, I.D. (eds) (1991). *The Personal Myth in Psychoanalytic Theory*. New York: International Universities Press.

Harvey, M.G. (1985). 'The executive family: An overlooked variable in international assignments,' *Columbia Journal of World Business*, **20** (1): 84–92.

Hasek, J. (1972). *The Good Soldier Svejk* (transl. C. Parrott). New York: Thomas Y. Crowell.

Hedlund, G. and Adne Kverneland, A. (1985). 'Are strategies for foreign markets changing? The case of Swedish investment in Japan,' *International Studies of Management and Organisation*, **15** (2): 41–59.

Herschman, J. and Lieb, J. (1994). *Brotherhood of Tyrants: Manic Depression and Absolute Power*. Amherst, NY: Prometheus Books.

Hershman, D. and Lieb, J.(1998). *Manic Depression and Creativity*. Amherst, NY: Prometheus Books.

Hesselbein, F. and Johnston, R. (2002). *On Creativity, Innovation, and Renewal: A Leader to Leader Guide*. San Francisco, CA: Jossey-Bass.

Hirschmeier, J. (1964). *The Origin of Entrepreneurship in Meiji Japan*. Cambridge, MA: Harvard University Press.

Hodgson, R., Levinson, D.J. and Zaleznik, A. (1965). *The Executive Role Constellation*. Boston: Division Research, Harvard Business School.

Hogarth, D.G. (1977). *Philip and Alexander of Macedon*. New York: Ayer Co. Publishing.

Horney, K. (1945). *Our Inner Conflicts*. New York: Norton.

International Herald Tribune (1989). 'From rags to riches to penitentiary.' July 20.

Isaacs, N. (1836). *Travels and Adventures in Eastern Africa*. Capetown: C. Struik.

Ispa, J. (1994). *Child Care in Russia*. Westport, CT: Bergin & Garvey.

Jamison, K.R. (1993). *Touched with Fire: Manic-Depressive Illness and the Artistic Temperament*. New York: Free Press.

Jaques, E. (1955). 'Social systems as a defense against persecutory and depressive anxiety,' in M. Klein, P. Heimann and R.E. Money-Kyrle (eds), *New Directions in Psychoanalysis*. London: Tavistock.

Jardim, A. (1970). *The First Henry Ford: A Study in Personality and Business Leadership*. Cambridge, MA: MIT Press.

Johnson, A.M. and Szurek, S.A. (1952). 'The genesis of antisocial acting out in children and adults,' *Psychoanalytic Quarterly*, **XXI**, 323–343.

Jukova, M. and Korotov, K. (1998). 'From a personnel department in the Soviet Union to a human resource department in Russia,' *Tchelovek, Trud*, **8**, 88–91.

Jung, C.G. (1969). 'On the psychology of the trickster-figure,' in *The Collected Works of C.G. Jung*, Vol. 9, Part 1. Bollinger Series, Princeton: Princeton University Press.

Kaplan, L.J. (1974). 'The concept of the family romance,' *Psychoanalytic Review*, **61** (2), 169–202.

Kelley, T. and Littman, J. (2000). *The Art of Innovation: Lessons in Creativity from IDEO, America's Leading Design Firm*. New York: Currency/Doubleday.

Kernberg, O. (1975). *Borderline Conditions and Pathological Narcissism*. New York: Jason Aronson.

Kernberg, O. (1978). 'Leadership and organizational functioning,' *International Journal of Group Psychotherapy*, **28**: 3–25.

Kernberg, O. (1985). *Internal World and External Reality*. New York: Jason Aronson.

Kernberg, O. (1992). *Aggression in Personality Disorders and Perversions*. New Haven: Yale University Press.

Kets de Vries, M.F.R. (1970). *The Entrepreneur as Catalyst of Economic and Cultural Change*. Unpublished doctoral dissertation, Harvard University, Graduate School of Business Administration.

Kets de Vries, M.F.R. (1977). The Dionysian Quality of Charismatic Leadership. INSEAD working paper.

Kets de Vries, M.F.R. (1977). 'The entrepreneurial personality: A person at the crossroads,' *Journal of Management Studies*, **14**: 34–58.

Kets de Vries, M.F.R. (1980). *Organizational Paradoxes: Clinical Approaches to Management*. London: Tavistock.

Kets de Vries, M.F.R. (1985). 'The dark side of entrepreneurship,' *Harvard Business Review*. November–December, 160–168.

Kets de Vries, M.F.R. (1988). 'Prisoners of leadership,' *Human Relations*, **41** (3): 261–280.

Kets de Vries, M.F.R. (1989). *Prisoners of Leadership*. New York: John Wiley & Sons, Inc.

Kets de Vries, M.F.R. (1990). 'The impostor syndrome: Developmental and societal issues,' *Human Relations*, **43** (7): 667–686.

Kets de Vries, M.F.R. (1990). 'The organizational fool: Balancing a leader's hubris,' *Human Relations*, **43** (8): 751–770.

Kets de Vries, M.F.R. (1993). *Leaders, Fools, and Impostors*. San Francisco: Jossey-Bass.

Kets de Vries, M.F.R. (1995). *Life and Death in the Executive Fast Lane*. San Francisco: Jossey-Bass.

Kets de Vries, M.F.R. (1996). 'The anatomy of the entrepreneur, clinical observations,' *Human Relations*, **49**: 7.

Kets de Vries, M.F.R. (1996). 'Leaders who make a difference,' *European Management Journal*, **14** (5): 486–493.

Kets de Vries, M.F.R. (1999). 'Managing puzzling personalities: Navigating between "live volcanoes" and "dead fish",' *European Management Journal*, **17**, 8–19.

Kets de Vries, M.F.R. (2000). 'A journey into the Wild East: Leadership style and organisational practices in Russia,' *Organisational Dynamics*, **28** (4): 67–81.

Kets de Vries, M.F.R. (2001). *Struggling with the Demon: Perspectives on Individual and Organisational Irrationality.* Garden City, NY: Psychosocial Press.

Kets de Vries, M.F.R. (2001). 'The anarchist within: Clinical reflections on Russian character and leadership style,' *Human Relations*, **54** (5): 585–627.

Kets de Vries, M.F.R. (2001). *The Leadership Mystique.* London: Financial Times/Prentice Hall.

Kets de Vries, M.F.R., Shekshnia, S., Korotov, K., and Florent-Treacy, E. (2004). 'The new global Russian business leaders: Lessons from a decade of transition,' *European Management Journal*, **22** (6): 637–648.

Kets de Vries, M.F.R. (2004). *Lessons on Leadership by Terror: Finding Shaka Zulu in the Attic.* Cheltenham, UK: Edward Elgar.

Kets de Vries, M.F.R. (2004). 'The spirit of despotism: Understanding the tyrant within,' *INSEAD Working Paper Series*, 2004/17/Ent.

Kets de Vries, M.F.R. (2005). 'The Dangers of Feeling like a Fake,' *Harvard Business Review*, **83** (9): 108–116.

Kets de Vries, M.F.R. (2006). 'The Eight Roles Executives Play,' *Organizational Dynamics*, **36** (1): 28–44.

Kets de Vries, M.F.R. (2006). *The Leader on the Couch: A Clinical Approach to Changing People and Organizations.* New York: John Wiley & Sons, Inc.

Kets de Vries, M.F.R. (2009). *Sex, Money, Happiness and Death: Musings from the Underground.* London: Palgrave.

Kets de Vries, M.F.R. and Engellau, E. (2004). *Are Leaders Born or are They Made? The Case of Alexander the Great.* London: Karnac.

Kets de Vries, M.F.R. with Florent-Treacy, E. (1999). *The New Global Leaders, Percy Barnevik, Richard Branson, and David Simon and the Making of the International Corporation.* San Francisco: Jossey-Bass.

Kets de Vries, M.F.R. and Florent-Treacy, E. (2002). 'Global leadership from A to Z: Creating high-commitment organisations,' *Organisational Dynamics*, **30** (4): 295–309.

Kets de Vries, M.F.R. and Miller, D. (1984a). *The Neurotic Organization: Diagnosing and Changing Counterproductive Styles of Management.* San Francisco: Jossey-Bass.

Kets de Vries, M.F.R. and Miller, D. (1984b). 'Group fantasies and organizational functioning,' *Human Relations*, **37**: 111-134.

Kets de Vries, M.F.R. and Miller, D. (1985). 'Narcissism and leadership: An object relations perspective,' *Human Relations*, **38** (6): 583–601.

Kets de Vries, M.F.R. and Miller, D. (1987). 'Interpreting organizational texts,' *Journal of Management Studies*, **24** (3): 233–247.

Kets de Vries, M.F.R. and Perzow, S. (1991). *Handbook of Character Studies*. New York: International Universities Press.

Kets de Vries, M.F.R., Carlock, R. and Florent-Treacy, E. (2007). *The Family Business on the Couch*. Chichester: John Wiley & Sons, Ltd.

Kets de Vries, M.F.R., Korotov, K. and Florent-Treacy, E. (2007). *Coach and Couch: The Psychology of Making Better Leaders*. New York: Palgrave/Macmillan.

Kets de Vries, M.F.R., Korotov, K., and Shekshnia, S. (2008). 'Special Issue on Russian Leadership,' *Organizational Dynamics*, **37** (3): 211–299.

Kets de Vries, M.F.R., Zevadi, D., Noel, A., and Tombak, M. (1989). 'Locus of control and entrepreneurship: A three-country comparative study,' *INSEAD Working Paper*, No. 89/59.

Klapp, O.E. (1972). *Heroes, Villains, and Fools*. San Diego: Aegis Publishing.

Klein, E.B. (1977). 'Transference in groups,' *Journal of Personality and Social Systems*, **1**, 53–63.

Klein, M. (1948). *Contributions to Psychoanalysis: 1921–1945*. London: Hogarth Press.

Klein, M. (1988). *Love, Guilt and Reparation and Other Works: 1921–1945*. London: Virago.

Kluckhohn, C. (1961). 'Studies of Russian national character,' in A. Inkeles and R.A. Bauer (eds), *Soviet Society: A Book for Readings*. Boston, MA: Houghton-Mifflin, pp. 607–618.

Knight, F.H. (1940). *Risk, Uncertainty and Profit*. Boston: Houghton-Mifflin.

Kobasa, S.C. (1979). 'Stressful life events, personality and health: An inquiry into hardiness,' *Journal of Personality and Social Psychology*, **42**, 168–177.

Koestler, A. (1964). *The Act of Creation*. New York: Macmillan.

Kohut, H. (1971). *The Analysis of the Self*. New York: International Universities Press.

Kohut, H. (1985). *Self Psychology and the Humanities*. New York: W.W. Norton.

Kohut, H. and Wolf, E.S. (1978). 'The disorders of the self and their treatment: An outline,' *International Journal of Psychoanalysis*, **59**: 413–426.

Koser, R. (1900). *Koenig Friedrich der Grosse*, Vols. 1 and 2. Leipzig: J. Hirzel.

Kotter, J.P. (1982). *The General Managers*. New York: The Free Press.

Kotter, J.P. (1988). *The Leadership Factor*. New York: The Free Press.

Kozintsev, G. and Trautberg, L. (1934). *Maxim's Youth*, part 1, music by D. Shostakovitch. Moscow: Mosfilm (film).

Kraepelin, E. (1913). *Psychiatry: Ein Lehrbuch*, Vol. 3 (8th edn). Leipzig: Barth.

Kris, E. (1938). 'Ego development and the comic,' *International Journal of Psychoanalysis*, **19**, 77–90.

Kris, E. (1975). 'The personal myth: A problem in psychoanalytic technique,' in *Selected Papers of Ernst Kris*. New Haven: Yale University Press, pp. 272–300.

Krystal, H. (1979). 'Alexithymia and psychotherapy,' *American Journal of Psychotherapy*, **33**: 17–31.

Lane Fox, R. (1994). *Alexander the Great*. New York: Viking Pinguin.

Langer, S.K. (1953). *Feeling and Form*. London: Routledge & Kegan Paul.

Langs, R. (1976). *The Therapeutic Interaction*. New York: Jason Aronson.

Lasswell, H.D. (1960). *Psychopathology and Politics* (rev. edn). New York: The Viking Press.

Laurent, A. (1983). 'The cultural diversity of Western conceptions of management,' *International Studies of Management and Organisation*, **13** (1–2): 75–96.

Lefcourt, H.M. (1976). *Locus of Control*. New York: John Wiley & Sons, Inc.

Lehmann, H.E. (1975). 'Unusual psychiatric disorders and atypical psychoses,' in Freedman, A.M., Kaplan, H.I. and Sadock, B.J. (eds), *Comprehensive Textbook of Psychiatry*, Vol 2 (2nd edn). Baltimore: Williams & Wilkins.

Leites, N. (2007). *Operational Code of the Politburo*. Santa Monica: Rand Corporation.

Lesser, I.M. and Lesser, B.Z. (1983). 'Alexithymia: Examining the development of a psychological concept,' *American Journal of Psychiatry*, **140** (10), 1305–1308.

Lever, M. (1983). *Le sceptre et la marotte*. Paris: Fayard.

Levine, J. (1961). 'Regression in primitive clowning,' *Psychoanalytic Quarterly*, **30**: 72–83.

Levinson, H. (1971). 'Conflicts that plague family business,' *Harvard Business Review*, **49** (2), March–April, 90–98.

Lewy, E. (1967). 'The transformation of Frederick the Great,' *The Psychoanalytic Study of Society*, **4**: 257–311.

Lifton, R.J. (1961). *Thought Reform and the Psychology of Totalism*. New York: W.W. Norton.

Lorenz, K. (1966). *On Aggression*. London: Methuen.

Lucas, R.W. (2003). *The Creative Training Idea Book: Inspired Tips and Techniques for Engaging and Effective Learning*. New York: AMACOM.

MacGregor Burns, J. (1977). *Leadership*. New York: HarperCollins.

Machiavelli, N. (1977). *The Prince* (transl. R.M. Adams). New York: Norton.

Mahler, M.S., Pine, F. and Bergman, A. (1975). *The Psychological Birth of the Human Infant*. New York: Basic Books.

Makarius, L. (1969). 'Le myth du "trickster",' *Révue de l'histoire des religions*, **175**: 17–46.

Makarius, L. (1970). 'Clowns, rituels, et comportements symboliques,' *Diogènes*, **69**: 47–74.

Makarius, L. (1973). 'The crime of Manabozo,' *American Anthropologist*, **75**: 663–675.

Malone, P.B. (1980). 'Humor: A double-edged tool for today's managers,' *Academy of Management Review*, **5** (3): 357–360.

Mann, T. (1969). *Confessions of Felix Krull, Confidence Man*. New York: Vintage Books.

Martin, J. (1988). *Who am I This Time: Uncovering the Fictive Personality.* New York: Norton.

Mauzy, J. and Harriman, R.A. (2003). *Creativity, Inc: Building an Inventive Organization.* Boston, Mass: Harvard Business School Press.

McClelland, D.C. (1961). *The Achieving Society.* New York: Irvington.

McClelland, D.C. (1975). *Power: The Inner Experience.* New York: Irvington.

McClelland, D.C. (1987). 'Characteristics of successful entrepreneurs,' *Journal of Creative Behavior,* **21**: 219–233.

McDougall, J. (1974). 'The psychosoma and the psychoanalytic process,' *International Review of Psychoanalysis,* **1**: 437–459

McDougall, J. (1980). 'A child is being eaten,' *Contemporary Psychoanalysis,* **16**: 417–459.

McDougall, J. (1982a). 'Alexithymia: A psychoanalytic viewpoint,' *Psychotherapy and Psychosomatics,* **38**: 81–90.

McDougall, J. (1982b). 'Alexithymia, psychosomatics, and psychosis,' *International Journal of Psychoanalytic Psychotherapy,* **9**: 379–388.

McDougall, J. (1989). *Theaters of the Body (19).* New York: W.W. Norton.

McDougall, J. (1991). *Theaters of the Mind: Illusion and Truth on the Psychoanalytic Stage.* London: Routledge.

McLean, B. and Elkind, P. (2003). *Smartest Guys in the Room: The Amazing Rise and Scandalous Fall of Enron.* New York: Simon & Schuster.

Meissner, W.W. (1978). *The Paranoid Process.* New York: Jason Aronson.

Melville, H. (1954). *The Confidence Man.* New York: New American Library.

Mendenhall, M.E., 'The elusive yet critical challenge of developing global leaders,' *European Management Journal,* **24** (6): 422–429.

Mendenhall, M.E., Dunbar, E. and Oddou, G.R. (1987). 'Expatriate selection, training and career-pathing: A review and critique,' *Human Resource Management,* **26** (3): 331–345.

Menzies, I. (1960). 'A case-study in the functioning of social systems as a defense against anxiety: A report on a study of the nursing service of a general hospital,' *Human Relations,* **13**: 95–121.

Michailova, S. (1997). 'Interface between Western and Russian management attitudes: Implications for organisational change,' *CEES Working Paper Series, 8.* Copenhagen: Center for East European Studies, Copenhagen Business School.

Milgram, S. (1975). *Obedience to Authority.* New York: Harper & Row.

Miller, A. (1979). 'Depression and grandiosity as related forms of narcissistic disturbances,' *International Review of Psychoanalysis,* **61**: 61–77.

Miller, D., Kets de Vries, M.F.R. and Toulouse, J.-M. (1982). 'Top executive locus of control and its relationship to strategy making, structure, and its environment,' *Academy of Management Journal,* **25**: 237–253.

Miller, N.G. (1965). *The Great Salad Oil Swindle.* Baltimore: Penguin Books.

Miller, W.C. (1998). *Flash of Brilliance: Inspiring Creativity Where You Work.* Reading, Mass: Perseus.

Millon, T. (1986). 'A theoretical derivation of pathological personalities,' in T. Millon and G.L. Klerman (eds), *Contemporary Directions in Psychopathology: Toward the DSM-IV.* New York: Guilford Press, pp. 639–669.

Millon, T. (1996). *Disorders of Personality: DSM IV and Beyond.* New York: John Wiley & Sons, Inc.

Mintzberg, H. (1973). *The Nature of Managerial Work.* New York: Harper & Row.

Monahan, T. (2002). *Do-it-yourself Lobotomy: Open Your Mind to Greater Creative Thinking.* New York: John Wiley & Sons, Inc.

Murray, D. (1995). *A Democracy of Despots.* Boulder, CO: Westview Press.

Neill, J.R. and Sandifer, M.G. (1982). 'The clinical approach to alexithymia: A review,' *Psychosomatics,* **23**: 1223–1231.

Nemiah, J.C. (1977). 'Alexithymia: Theoretical considerations,' *Psychotherapy and Psychosomatics,* **28**: 199–206.

Nemiah, J.C. (1978). 'Alexithymia and psychosomatic illness,' *Journal of Continuing Education in Psychiatry,* **39**: 25–27.

Nemiah, J.C. and Sifneos, P.E. (1970). 'Affect and fantasy in patients with psychosomatic disorders,' in Hill, O. (ed.), *Modern Trends in Psychosomatic Medicine.* London: Butterworths.

Noel, A. (1984). Un Mois dans la Vie de Trois Présidents: Préoccupations et Occupations Stratégiques. Unpublished doctoral dissertation, McGill University, Faculty of Management.

Noel, A. (1991). 'Magnificent obsession: The impact of unconscious processes on strategy formation,' in Kets de Vries, M.F.R. (ed.), *Organizations on the Couch.* San Francisco: Jossey-Bass.

Olinick, S.L. (1988). 'Book review of "The Family Romance of the Impostor—Poet Thomas Chatterton" by Louis G. Kaplan,' *Psychoanalytic Quarterly,* **58** (4): 672–676.

Oppenheimer, P. (1972). *A Pleasant Vintage of Till Eulenspiegel.* Middletown, Connecticut: Wesleyan University Press.

Parsons, T. (1951). *The Social System.* New York: The Free Press.

Paykel, E.S. (ed.) (1982). *Handbook of Affective Disorders.* New York: Guildford Press.

Pearson, L. (1990). *Children of Glasnost: Growing up Soviet.* Seattle: University of Washington Press.

Perlmutter, H.V. (1969). 'The tortuous evolution of the multinational corporation,' *Columbia Journal of World Business,* **4** (1): 9–18.

Phares, J.E. (1976). *Locus of Control in Personality.* Morristown, NJ: General Learning Press.

Plato (1955). *The Republic.* Harmondsworth: Penguin.

Plutarch (1973). *The Age of Alexander: Nine Greek Lives.* Harmondsworth: Penguin.

Pollio, H.R. and Edgerly, J.W. (1976). 'Comedians and comic style,' in Chapman, A.J. and Frost, H.C. (eds), *Humor and Laughter: Theory, Research and Applications.* London: John Wiley & Sons, Ltd.

Taylor, G.J.R., Bagby, M., Parker, J.D.A., and Grotstein, J. (1999). *Disorders of Affect Regulation: Alexithymia in Medical and Psychiatric Illness*. Cambridge: Cambridge University Press.

Tichy, N.M. and Devanna, M.A. (1986). *The Transformational Leader*. New York: John Wiley & Sons, Inc.

Tinbergen, N. (1968). 'Of war and peace in animals and men,' *Science*, **160**: 1411–1418.

Triandis, H.C. (1972). *The Analysis of Subjective Cultures*. New York: John Wiley & Sons, Inc.

Triandis, H.C., Bontempo, R., Villareal, M.J., Asai, M. and Lucca, N. (1988). 'Individualism and collectivism: Cross-cultural perspectives on self-in group relationships,' *Journal of Personality and Social Psychology*, **54** (2): 323–338.

Tung, R.L. (1984). 'Strategic management of human resources in the multinational enterprise,' *Human Resource Management*, **23** (2): 129–143.

Tung, R.L. (1988a). *The New Expatriates: Managing Human Resources Abroad*. Cambridge, Mass.: Ballinger Publisher.

Tung, R.L. (1988b). 'A contingency framework of selection and training of expatriates revisited,' *Human Resource Management Review*, **8** (1): 23–27.

Tung, R.L. (ed). (2001). *Learning from World Class Companies*. London, UK: Thomson Learning.

Vaillant, G. E. (1977). *Adaptation to Life*. Boston: Little Brown.

Volcan, V. (1988). *The Need to Have Enemies and Allies*. Northvale, NJ: Jason Aronson.

Von Krogh, G. (2000). *Enabling Knowledge Creation: How to Unlock the Mystery of Tacit Knowledge and Release the Power of Innovation*. New York: Oxford University Press.

Von Lang, J. and Sibyll, C. (eds) (1983). *Eichman Interrogated*. New York: Farrar, Straus & Giroux.

Von Rad, M. (1984). 'Alexithymia and symptom formation,' *Psychotherapy and Psychosomatics*, **42**: 80–89.

Walter, E.V. (1969). *Terror and Resistance: A Study of Political Violence*. New York: Oxford University Press.

Weber, M. (1947). *The Theory of Social and Economic Organizations* (transl. A.M. Henderson and Talcott Parsons). New York: Oxford University Press.

Weber, M. (1958). *The Protestant Ethic and the Spirit of Capitalism* (transl. T. Parsons). New York: Charles Scribners & Sons.

Weinshel, E.M. (1979). 'Some observations on not telling the truth,' *Journal of the American Psychoanalytic Association*, **27** (3): 503–532.

Welch, J. and Byrne, J.A. (2001). *Jack: Straight from the Gut*. New York: Warner Business Books.

Welch, J. and Welch, S. (2005). *Winning*. New York: HarperCollins.

Welsford, E. (1935). *The Fool*. London: Faber & Faber.

Whybrow, P.C. (1997). *A Mood Apart*. New York: Basic Books.

Wijsenbeek, H. and Nitzan, I. (1968). 'The case of Peter, an impostor.' *Psychiatria, Neurologia, Neurochirurgia*, 1968, **71**: 193–202

Willeford, W. (1969). *The fool and his sceptre*. Chicago: Northwestern University Press.

Willner, A. R. and Willner, D. (1965). 'The rise and role of charismatic leaders,' *Annals of the American Academy of Political and Social Science*, **358**: 77–88.

Winnicott, D.W. (1975). *Through Paediatrics to Psychoanalysis*. New York: Basic Books.

Winokur, G., Clayton, P. and Woodruff, R.A. (1969). *Manic-Depressive Illness*. St Louis: Mosby.

Wittebort, S. (1987). 'Behind the great Swedish scandal,' *Institutional Investor*, August, 93–104.

Zaleznik, A. (1989). *The Managerial Mystique: Restoring Leadership in Business*. New York: Beard Books.

Zaleznik, A. and Kets de Vries, M.F.R. (1976). 'What makes entrepreneurs entrepreneurial?' *Business and Society Review*, Spring, **17**.

Zaleznik, A., Kets de Vries, M.F.R. *et al.* (1977). 'Stress Reactions in Organizations: Syndromes, Causes and Consequences,' *Behavioral Science*, **22**: 151–162.

Zeira, B. and Banai, M. (1985). 'Selection of expatriate managers in MNCs: the host-environment point of view,' *International Studies of Management and Organization*, **15** (1): 33–51.

Zeira, Y. and Banai, M. (1981). 'Attitudes of host-country organizations towards MNCs staffing policies: A cross-country and cross-industry analysis,' *Management International Review*, **21** (2): 38–47.

INDEX

Abagnale, Frank 81–2
ABB 196, 211, 212, 213, 217–19, 221,
    251
Abraham, Karl 82–3
absenteeism 108
accountability 314
achievement orientation 268
admiration, need for 27–8
Aeschylus 106
Aesop 307
aggression 142–3, 171
al-Assad, Hafez 163
Al-Bashir, Omar Hassan 166
alcohol 49–50
Alexander the Great 195, 198–210,
    241, 315
  aspiring to greatness 200–1
  conquests 202–3
  discontent with 204
  education and training 199–200
  legacy 205–6
  lessons in leadership from 206–10
  life 199–205

personality 204–5
as strategist 203–4
succession 201
alexithymia 3, 44
  as communication disorder
    64–6
  coping 75–7
  degrees of 68–9
  identification 63–4
  management of 73–4, 76–7
  origins 66–8
  primary 68, 75, 76–7
  secondary 68–9, 76–7
  warning signs 74–5
  in the workplace 69–70
alexithymic CEO 70–2
  detached CEO 70
  social sensor 71–2
  systems person 70–1
alexithymic executive 62–78
alexithymic manager, working
    with 72–3
alienation 216

all-or-nothing attitude 23
Al-Qaeda 165
ambiguity, dealing with 256
American Express Company 81
Amin, Idi 146, 182
Andersen, Hans Christian 94
anger 11
animists 157–8
anthropological approaches 9
Antipater 207
antisocial behavior, malevolent
    171–2
anxiety 11, 53, 234, 309
apathy 43
applause, desire for 14–15
Archimedes 231
architectural role 194, 211, 214–23,
    314
  all change 221
  bureaucracy 218
  creating good corporate
    citizens 221–3
  creativity, nurturing 219–20
  flat structures, not tall
    hierarchies 214–15
  know thyself 223
  new idea for new times 215–16
  role of IT 218
  small is beautiful 216–17
  structuring for success 217–18
  swifter than light 220–1
  valuing customers 220
Arendt, Hannah 153
Aristotle 199
Armenian holocaust 163
'as if' qualities 259
ascription 268
ASEA 213, 217
associative thinking 230
Astra 93
attachment affiliation 310
attribute listing 230
authoritarianism 148–9
authority 11, 29, 44, 45
  conflicts 35
  search for 136–9

autocratic leadership 240, 244
autogenic training 77

Bach, Johann Sebastian 235
Bach, Richard 98
Bacon, Francis 227
Bailey, Thomas 146
Barnevik, Percy 196, 211–19, 221–6
basic assumptions tendency 140
Beckett, Samuel: Waiting for Godot 61
Beethoven, Ludwig van 265
benchmarking 300
Benz, Karl 18
Bergman, Ingmar 235–6
Berlin Wall, fall of 164
bi-sociative thinking 231
Bierce, Ambrose 106
Bin Laden, Osama 151
biofeedback 77
Bion, Wilfred 139, 140
bipolar disorder 44, 46
  characterization 50–1, 53
  genetic basis 56
Black, Conrad 132
Bologna Process 268
Bonaparte, Napoleon 265
Bosnian war 164
brainstorming 230
Branson, Richard 195, 196, 211–26,
    237, 311
Brewer, Marilynn 272
British Airways 225
British Petroleum 251, 267
Brown Boveri 213, 217
brutalization 185
bubble organizations 273
buffoon 114
builder role 213
Bullock, Alan 86
Bureau Pathology 291–2
business process re-engineering 213,
    215, 217

Caligula 128, 132, 146, 176
capriciousness 182–3
Carnegie, Andrew 18

Castro, Fidel 146
catalyst of change 301
Catch Me If You Can 81
Catherine the Great 292
Ceausescu, Elena 162
Ceausescu, Nicolae 146, 162, 163
centralized leadership 244
Cervantes: *Don Quixote* 80–1
'Challenge of Leadership' seminar 104
chameleon leaders 273
change, dealing with 273–5
charisma 7, 43, 44–5
charismatic attribution 46
charismatic leadership 44–6, 194, 211, 223–5, 302, 314
charm 43
Chatterton, Thomas 85–6
Cheka 293
Chesterton, G.K. 97
childhood experience 17–18, 234, 258–60
    character formation in Russian 284–9
Chirico, Giorgio de 234, 235
Christensen, Roland xvii
Churchill, Winston 159–60
Cinderella complex 103
Clance, Pauline 100, 101
Clark, Robert 131, 142
clowns 114–15
cognitive dissonance 271
Cold War 164
Coleridge, Samuel Taylor: 'Kubla Khan' 230
collectivism 268, 293
colluding mind 179–83
Colton, Charles Caleb 79
command-and-control style of management 215, 303
Communist Party 293
community 310–11
company culture 245
competition 28–9
competitive advantage 207
competitive analysis 207
compulsive organization 69

Conféderation Générale du Travail (CGT) 266
confidence, lack of 18
conflict, inner, externalizing 135–6
consensual leadership 244
consolidation of gains 209
conspiracy, culture of 177–9
contagion effect 105
control 26–7
    cruelty as 173–5
    need for 11–13
    thought-control 179–80
control-and-reward system 314
convergent thinking 230
coping
    alexithymia 75–7
    with distance and aggression 143
    hypomania 59–60
    with terror 188–90
corporate downsizing 215
Council of Boyars 301–2
court jester 114, 115
creative destructor 11
creative management 236–40
    difficulties 240–1
    leadership factors 240
    organizational cultural factors 239
    organizational factors 238–9
creative strategy 206–7
creativity 53, 196
    characteristics 228–30
    constructive 233–4
    enhancement 288
    genetic factors 231–3
    management 227–41
    reactive 234–6
    stimulating 230–1
crimes against humanity 163
cruelty as control device 173–5
cultural adaptability 256–8
cultural relativity 245
cyclothymia 50, 204, 290

DaimlerChrysler 271
Danone 311
Darius III, King of Persia 202

De Angelis, Anthony 81
dead fish syndrome 62–3, 77
decentralization 215, 236
decision-making 36, 159, 210
defense mechanisms 139
definition of entrepreneur 8
dehumanization 187–8
delusions
    of grandeur 143, 177
    of persecution 143
democracy, need for 159–60
democratic centralism 301
democratic leadership 240, 244
denial 58
dependency 33, 140
dependency orientation 176
depersonalization 216
depression 20, 23, 28, 47, 57, 234
depressive organization 69
desensitization 185
despair, fleeing into 189–90
despotism 129, 146–66, 171–9
    judicial remedy 163–5
    maintenance of regimes 152–3
    need to fight 161–2
    toolbox 153–8
Deterding, Henry 18
Deutsch, Helen 83
Diageo 271, 273
*Diagnostic and Statistical Manual of the
    Mental Disorders
    (DSM-IV-TR)* 50–1
Dingiswayo, King 169, 178
Diogenes 241
Dionysian quality 44–6
Dirty War, Argentina 163
Disraeli, Benjamin 264
dissociation 43, 189
distance 142–3
distrust, sense of 13–14
divergent thinking 230
diversity, challenge of 267–70
divide-and-conquer leadership
    180–1
divine-animal 114
Dongier, Maurice xviii

Dupont 225
dysfunctional developments 35–6

Ebony 18
economic perspective 9–10
economies of scale 216
edifice complex 15
educational attainment 269
ego ideal 136
Eisner, Michael 132
elation 43, 50–3
Ellison, Larry 15
El-Sayed, Refaat 92–5
emotional expressiveness 268
emotional intelligence (EQ) 194, 257,
    301
emotional reactivity 229
empathy
    among alexithymics 64,68
    lack of 172
employee-turnover rates 108
empowerment 255
encouragement of followers 208
energy 225, 228
Enron 120
enterprise, decline in 36–7
entrepreneurial life cycle 33–9
entrepreneurial personality: case
    study 18–33
    background 21–2
    competition and self-defeating
        behavior 28–9
    control 26–7
    falling into extremes 22–4
    grandiosity and depression 28
    la vie en rose 23–4
    major issues 22
    meaning of work 26–8
    medusa women 24–5
    need for admiration 27–8
    presenting picture 20–1
    process of change 31–3
    psychoanalytic process 18–20
    symbolic nature of enterprise
        29–31
environmental dynamism 36

envisioning 254–5
envy 106, 132
Erasmus 115
  Praise of Folly 113
Erikson, Erik 280
ethnocentrism 249
Eulenspiegel, Till 80
euphoria 49, 136
European leader, making of
  275–7
executive role constellation
  198, 207
expatriation 252–3
experiential training 261–2
exploratory/assertive needs 310
external competition 270–1

failure 11
  fear of 110
fake connection 137
false self 99, 287–8
family dynamics, effects of 17–18,
  37–8
family reaction 258
family therapy 77
fear 11
  of failure 110
  as reality 105–7
  of success 102–3
Fermenta 92–4, 95–6
Field, W.C. 91
fight–flight orientation 140–1, 176
Fleming, Alexander 231, 240
flight into action 17, 204
flight into health xix
flight into reality 22
fool, characteristics 117
Ford, Edsel 38
Ford, Henry 38
fraudulence 106
Frederick the Great 132–5, 137
freedom, fighting for 190
Freud, Sigmund xvi, 102, 116, 118,
  136–7, 139
Friedman, Mikhail 295
FUD factor 309

gain sharing 219
gamesmanship 7
Gandhi, Mahatma 135, 166, 316
General Electric 196, 211, 212, 213,
  217, 218, 219, 220, 221, 223, 224,
  225
general leadership qualities
  254–6
General Motors 214
general role differentiation 268
geocentrism 249–50, 251, 309
Gestapo 155
glasnost 288, 293
global leaders
  framework for analyzing
    development of 262–3
  qualities 253–62
global organizations
  career-path management 252–3
  case study 248–9
  facilitating return 253
  forms of 249–53
globalism, concepts of 249–52
globalization 245, 247–64,
  272–3, 307–8
glocalization 273
Gogal, Nikolay 290
Goldman Sachs 313
Goncharov, Ivan 290
good-enough care 274–5
Gorbachev, Mikhail 282, 295
Gordon, Ralph 108
Gorky, Maxim 279, 280
GOSPLAN 291, 294
Goya, Francisco 235
grandeur, delusions of 143, 177
grandiosity 28, 175
Greenacre, Phyllis 83–4
Gresham's Law of Creativity 236
group
  primitive, formation 176–7
  regressive behavior 139–42
group identification 208
group mind 86–7
group therapy 77
groupthink 187

guided imagery 77
Guinness 271

hardiness 256
Hasek, Jaroslov: *Good Soldier Svejk,
The* 118–19
helplessness, sense of 33, 34, 127, 140
Hephaiston 204
heterogeneity 36
Himmler, Heinrich 167
historical truth 19
Hitler, Adolf 45, 86–8, 128, 132,
    146, 151, 153, 155, 176, 185
Hitlerjugend 154
Hollinger International 132
Homer 200
homo economicus xv
homo politicus 135
hostility 36–7
Howell, Ted 141–2
hubris 112–23, 204
Hughes, Howard 132
human resource management 298–9
humor, benefits of 115–16
Hussein, Saddam 45, 128, 146,
    156, 165, 176, 182
Huxley, Aldous: *Doors of Perception,
The* 230
hyperactivity 34
hypnosis 77
hypomania 43–61
    case study 46–50
    coping strategies 59–60
    elation 50–3
    interventions 56–8
    management 53–5
    plus side for organizations 60–1
    self-help measures 58–9
    warning signs 55–6
    in workplace 55–6

IBM 250, 252, 253
ideal-hungry followers 189
idealization 45, 46
idealizing transference 138, 140, 187
identification with the aggressor 139,
    188–9

identity crisis 90
identity, sense of 19
ideology 153–5
illumination phase 231
illusion 139
imaginativeness 39
Imes, Suzanne 100, 101
impostors 3–4
    in business world 81–2
    causes 82–5
    character sketch 89–97
    creative artist 85–6
    as entrepreneur 92–5
    in literature 80–1
    kinds of 82
    as national leader 86–9
    neurotic 98–111
impostor syndrome 79–97
imposturous feelings, creation
    of 99–103
impulsivity 33–4
incubation phase 231
individualism 6, 268
Industrivärden 95
inferiority, feelings of 34
innovation 8, 207–8
insecurity 18
insomnia 21
integrator role 214
internal competition 270–1
internal locus of control 10, 300
internal–external scale 10, 42
internalization 45
    case study 248–9
International Criminal Court
    (ICC) 165–6
International Criminal
    Tribunal 164
International Diabetes
    Federation 313
introspection 233, 289
intrusive guidance 285
irritation 53
Ivan the Terrible 146, 176, 293

Jefferson, Thomas 128
Jesuits 257

Jet 18
job loyalty 217
job rotation 238
job tenure and security 217
Joffé, Jacques 311
Johnnie Walker 271
Johnson, John 18
Johnson Publishing Company 18
Jones, Ernest xvi

Kafka, Franz
  Letter to his Father 235
  'Metamorphosis, The' 235
Kahlo, Frieda 234, 235
Kambanda, Jean 164
Karadzic 185
Keats, John 86
Kekule 231
Keller, Helen 307
Keynes, John Maynard xv
KGB 288, 293
Khmer Rouge 154, 155–6
Khodorkovsky, Mikhail 295
Kim Il-Sung 163, 176
Kim Jong Il 146
Klein, David 47–50, 56, 57, 58–9
komosomols 154
koyemci 114
Kozintsev, Grigori 279, 280
Kraepelin, Emil 50
Krystal, Henry 64
kulaks 157
Kundera, Milan 265

language, illusion and 91
Larix Corporation 141
Larson, Mike 107
Lasswell, Harold 135
lateral thinking 230
Law of Creativity (Gresham) 236
Law on Co-operative Movement
  (Soviet Union) 295
Lay, Kenneth 120
left-brain capabilities 227, 261
Lenin, Vladimir 280, 288, 292, 293
Leonidas 199
leveraged buyouts 215

Levinson, Harry xx
Lifton, Robert Jay 153
Lincoln, Abraham 130
lithium, hypomania and 56, 57
Lorsch, Jay xviii
Louis XIV 210
loyalty 309
Lufthansa 271
Luther, Martin 135
Lysimachus 200

Machiavelli, Niccoló 152
  Prince, The 113
Mahler, Gustav: *Songs on the Death of
  Children* 235
malevolent antisocial behavior 171–2
manic defense 22
Mann, Thomas: *Confessions of Felix
  Knoll, Confidence Man* 81
Mao Zedong 146, 153, 155, 182, 185
masochistic behavior 92
mature markets 69
McDougall, Joyce xvii, 67, 68
meaning 310, 312–13
meaning-management actions 198,
  208, 302
media, despotism and 156
Medvedev, Dmitry 282
megalomania 87
Melville, Herman: *Confidence Man,
  The* 81
Mengistu Haile Mariam 159
mental imagery 280
Mercedes-Benz Corporation 18
Merck & Co. Inc. 313
merger and acquisition 215
meta-values 308–9
  creation 313–15
MicroChem 93
Milgram experiment 186, 187
Milosevic, Slobodan 164
Milton, John: *Paradise Lost* 234
mimicry 90
Minzberg, Henry xviii
mirror transference 138, 140
mirror-hungry leader 189
mirroring 204

mistrust 309
mnemonic mode 91
Mobutu, Joseph Désiré 159
model excellence 207
Monnet, Jean 265
mood disorders, creativity
    and 229
morosophe 4, 115, 118
motivational need systems 309–13
Mugabe, Robert 45, 128, 132, 146,
    149, 159, 176
Munch, Edvard 234–5
Münchausen, Baron 82
Münchausen syndrome 82
Mussolini, Benito 45
mutual identification 178
myth-making 135–6
mythological heroes 10, 14, 33

Nandi 168
narcissism 90, 127, 171, 191, 209
narcissistic development 259–60
narrative 19
national culture 245
nature–nurture controversy 232
Nazi Germany 155,157
Nero 146
Nestlé 266
neurotic impostor 4, 98–111
    CEO as 111
    fear 105–8
    finding solutions 109–11
    impact on businesses 108–9
    in the workplace 103–5
neurotic overachievers 98
Nicholas I 292
nightmares 21
Nokia 313
not-invented-here culture 240, 245
Novo Nordisk 313
Novorex 47, 50
Nuremberg International Military
    Tribunal 163
obfuscation 91
Oblomovism 290–1
Oedipal concerns 27–30, 84, 90, 102

Oedipal memory 24
Oedipus complex 42
Olympias, Princess of Epirus 199
on-the-job training 260
open-mindedness 256
Oprichnina 293
optimal distinctiveness 272
Oracle 15
organizations
    leaders' behavior in,, management
        of 143–4
    leaders, effects on 212
    significance of 35
organizational fool 4–5, 112–23
    as cultural hero 114–15
    value of 123
organizational governance 209–10
organizational inertia 144
organizational networks 255
orgasm, fake 102
Orwell, Lynn 108–9
out-of-awareness behaviour xxi

pairing 140
paranoia 138, 143, 144, 161, 171, 175,
    178, 191, 205, 239
paranoid grandiosity 175
paranoid *Weltanschauung* 175–6
Parmenion 207
parochialism 240
participative leadership 240
passivity 33
Pasteur, Louis 231
Patagonia 313
patriarchal leadership 244
pattern recognition 255–6
Patton, General George S. 211, 222
perceived kindness 174–5
perestroika 293, 299
perfectionism 105, 110
performance orientation 268
Perrier 266, 274
persecution 177
persecutory paranoia 175
persecutory transference 138–9
Peter the Great 292, 301

Philip I, King of Macedonia 199,
    200, 201
Philips 250, 252
Picasso, Pablo 265
Pierce, Robert 106
Pinochet, Augusto 164
Pioneers 154
Plato 146, 150
playfulness 228
pleasure 310, 311–12
Poe, Edgar Allan 235
Pol Pot 146, 151, 155–6, 157, 164,
    176, 182
political leadership 244
polycentrism 249
Porus, King 202–3
post-traumatic states 64
power
    abuse of 210
    dangers of 160–1
    see also despotism and under names
power distance 268
power-sharing 224–5
praise-singing 198
preparation phase 230–1
primitive group formation 176–7
prisoners of leadership 130–45
procrastination 110
Proctor & Gamble 250
product life cycles 220
propaganda 158
protective reaction 161
Protestant ethic 9
pseudologica phantastica 90
psychological perspective 10
psychology of elation 46
Putin, Vladimir 282, 292, 293, 303

Qaddafi, Muammar 146
quackery, language of 91

rage 29
reactive model 34–5
real impostor 4
reality-testing 4, 90, 132, 161, 205
rebelliousness 11

Red Guards 154
regressive group processes 139–42
rejection 33
relaxation training 77
resistance to change 39
reward systems 238
Rhone-Poulenc 250
Riboud, Jean 248, 249
right-brain capabilities 196, 227–8,
    261
rigidity 39
risk-taking 8, 39
Robespierre 265
Route 128 10
Roxanne 203
Royal Dutch Shell 18
Rückert, Friedrich 235
Russian character and
    leadership 279–306
    21st-century organizations 303–5
    asset protection 303
    avoidance of reality 293–4
    Bureau Pathology 291–2
    capacity to endure 281–2
    challenges for leaders 302–5
    character formation in childhood
        and youth 284–9
    character in transition 282
    cooperatives to capitalism, transition
        from 295–6
    culture and organization 293–5
    emotional expression 289–90
    fluidity of time 294–5
    friendship 289
    Global Russians 296–7, 298
    government relations
        management 303
    human resource management 298–9
    impact of nature 282–3
    internal conflict 287–9
    leadership lessons 300–2
    leadership networks 300
    legacy of the mir 283–4
    management development 299–300
    new leaders and new
        followers 296–300

nomenklatura 284
Oblomovism 290–1
paranoia, Tsars and 292–3
performance and accountability 299
process of unlearning 297
Russian Russians 296
schooling and moral
upbringing 285–7
successors 302–3
suffering and violence 280–1
swaddling in infancy 284–5
tenacity 301
Russian doll school of
management 297
Russian Orthodox Church 293
Rwandan genocide 164

sadism 171, 174–5
sadomasochism 29
sage–fool 118–19, 120, 123
Saltykov, Mikhail 290
Saul, King 132
scapegoating 16–17, 139, 157–8
Schiele, Egon 234, 235
Schlumberger 248–9
Schuman, Robert 265
Schumpeter, Josef 11
Scott, Clifford xx
Security Council 164
seductiveness 7
self-blame 106
self-confidence 256
self-contempt 173
self-deception 183–6
self-defeating behavior 28–9
self-deprecation 106
self-doubt 289
self-efficacy 104, 111, 300
self-employment 9
self-esteem 18, 28, 31, 45, 52, 127,
232
self-flagellation 110
self-symbols 136
self-torment 289
self-worth, lack of 127
Senzangakhona 168
separation–individuation 30, 90, 99

September 11th, 2001 165
Shaka Zulu, King 128, 129, 146,
167–92, 195, 315
legacy 190–1
life and death 168–71
Shakespeare, William
As You Like It 115
Henry V 212
King Lear 115
share ownership 220
Shaw, George Bernard 123
Shell 250, 252
Siemens 225, 271
Sifneos, Peter 63
Silicon Valley 10
Simon, Sir David 312
single model of European
leadership 271–2
Skinner, Wickham xviii
Sloan, Alfred 214
sociological approaches 9
sociopaths 172
Solan Corporation 131
solidarity, illusion of 156–7
Sony 252
Sophia Antipolis 10
Soviet Union totalitarian regime 154
Speer, Albert 88–9
splitting 15–16, 22, 25, 293
Stalin, Joseph 45, 146, 149, 151, 155,
176, 182, 185, 265, 280, 288, 291,
292, 293
state within the state 155–6
Stewart, John 311
Stoddard, John 110
storming 294
strategic innovation 198, 207–8
submission 33
substance abuse 49–50, 53
success, fear of 110
succession 37–9
succession planning 198, 209
suicidal risk 57
suicidality 53
superego 28
support of followers 208
Svenska Handelbanken 95

swaddling of infants 284–5
Swiss Bank Corp 266
sycophancy 102
synectics 230

talent management 208–9, 238–9
Taliban 165
Tamerlane 146, 176
Tapie, Bernard 121
task interdependency 238
teamwork 260–2
technocratic leadership 244
teddy bear factor 195, 311
'Teddy, The Great' 84–5
tension 11
terror 150
thematic analysis 2
thought-control 179–80
three 'B's of creativity 231
time-warped proletariat 270
tolerance of uncertainty 268
totalitarianism 147–8, 156, 158–9
training and development 198,
    208–9, 260–2
transfer 260–2
transference 45, 46, 137
    idealizing 138, 140, 187
    mirror 138, 140
    persecutory 138–9
transformer role 213–14
transitional object 30
transitional space 232, 275, 276
Trautberg, Leonid 279, 280
travel 260–2
Treaty of Rome 265
tricksters 114
trust 239
    building 303
    culture of 194–5
    mutual 40, 41
tyranny 128
    economic costs 158–9
    means used by tyrants 153–8
    motivation 150
    operation 150–1
    scene setting 149–50
    see also despotism; power

Unilever 252
United Nations 164
upbringing 258–60
    see also childhood experience

Vaillant, George 116
Van Gogh, Vincent 235
verification process 231
vindictive gratification 172–3
Virgin 211–13, 215–22, 237, 239
Virgin Atlantic 225, 237
vision 198, 206, 223–4
Vlad the Impaler 146
Volkswagen 271
Voltaire 62
Volvo 94, 95

war crimes 163
Warburg 266–7
Watkins, Sharon 120
Weber, Max 9, 44, 45
Welch, Jack 195–6, 211–26
Weltanschauung 246, 257, 285, 293
    paranoid 175–6
Westinghouse 225
whistle-blowing 119–20
willpower 228
Winnicott, Donald 150, 232, 275
wise fool see morosophe
women, imposturous feelings
    of 100–2
Wordsworth, William 86
work/life balance 105
workaholism 106, 110
working effectively with
    entrepreneurs 39–42
worthlessness, sense of 30
xenophobia 267

Xerxes, King 201, 206

Yeltsin, Boris 282
Young, Alex 47–8

Zaleznik, Abraham xvi, xvii, xviii, xx
Zuni Indian tribal clowns 114
Zwide, King 169